BOUNDARYLESS HR:
Human Capital Management
in the Global Economy

Edited By Karen V. Beaman

International
Association for
Human Resource
Information Management

Boundaryless HR: *Human Capital Management in the Global Economy*

An IHRIM Press Book
Published by Rector Duncan & Associates, Inc.
314 Highland Mall Boulevard, Suite 510
Austin, Texas 78752 USA

ISBN 0-9679239-4-8 US$39/CAN$52

Table of Contents

Preface

The benefits of globalization are so well known that most businesses would take full advantage of them immediately, if only it were easier to do. Making globalization work demands new types of expertise that traditional organizations often lack. While technology has eliminated many barriers to globalization (most notably those involving time and space), many significant barriers still remain, particularly those involving people and the organizations we build around them. The purpose of this book is to provide some insight to help HR professionals on how to overcome these barriers.

Some of the barriers to globalization are *external* to the organization and have already been embraced by the HR profession. Global corporations are more vulnerable than local ones to the effects of political disruptions, such as those created by terrorism and cyber-terrorism. Maintaining the security of data and of personnel, as well as the integrity of the supply chain, is a far greater challenge to global corporations than to local ones.

But of special concern to HR are the *internal* barriers to effective globalization. As Christopher Bartlett explains in the foreword to this book, the heritage of the industrial age prevents many organizations from creating the organizational structures, operational infrastructures, HR policies, and company cultures required to effectively function in the global economy. Bartlett maintains "most companies are trying to pursue third-generation strategies, using second-generation organizations, staffed with first-generation human resources." As HR professionals, responsible for leading change in our organizations, it's sad to think we are that far off the mark.

So if we are to globalize our company, our business unit, our HR department, how might we do this? Bartlett refers to a concept incorporated into our title, "boundarylessness," a term popularized by former GE chairman Jack Welch. Boundarylessness is both a major benefit of globalization and an essential technique for making it work. It is the ability to take expertise from anywhere in the world and leverage it rapidly anywhere throughout the organization — transcending the traditional boundaries of business units, organization-chart hierarchies, and even internal and external origins. But, as Bartlett explains, to become truly boundaryless, organizations must change — and change radically.

Finding the right approach to such change is never easy. Even ignoring the problem of industrial-era legacies, globalization has properties that make it challenging. One is that it requires us to manage the paradox — the simultaneous coexistence of opposing forces — even more so than ordinary business does. While the paradox of globalization comes in many forms, an overarching example is the need be both global and local at the same time. The advantages provided by global reach include access to a vastly increased marketplace and to a far larger pool of employee expertise; likewise, the rewards associated with being small and local include responsiveness and sensitivity to national country needs and diverse cultures. We must figure out how to customize our products and services — likewise our administrative policies, structures, and HR systems — to each locale, while at the same time take full advantage of the benefits of scale, scope and shared expertise that a global centralized system offers. As you will discover in this book, Bartlett's concept of the transnational organization affords us this opportunity.

The purpose of this book is to present important recent thinking on overcoming the obstacles to successful globalization of HR. We hope the book will help HR professionals in their ongoing quest to manage the paradox and overcome the internal and external barriers that still burden most organizations.

This book's nineteen chapters are organized into seven sections, as follows:

▶ **Part One, "The Global Organization:"** For the opening chapter, I had the good fortune to be able to interview Chris Bartlett. The groundbreaking work on the transnational organization that he and Sumantra Ghoshal have published over the last two decades provides a framework for understanding the types of change required of organizations today.

In the second chapter, Al Walker and I investigate the transnational business model developed by Bartlett and Ghoshal, applying it to the field of human resources. In our pilot study, we found that while certain functions and operations are more effectively dealt with globally, others (most notably those involving "face time") are generally better handled locally. Determining whether to globalize, regionalize, or localize certain functions in order to produce the best return is the greatest global challenge facing management today. This chapter gives some advice on how to make this determination.

The need for significant restructuring becomes clear when we consider the global marketplace. As Jay Galbraith points out in his chapter, businesses have traditionally been organized around internal business units rather than around the demands of customers. Many businesses are now readdressing this legacy; but organizing around the needs of *global* customers raises challenges beyond those found in purely domestic business. Galbraith discusses some ways for us to meet these demands.

▶ **Part Two, "Global Strategy and Planning:"** Moving HR forward into the "boundaryless" era requires mastering various strategy, planning, and deployment approaches that suit the global stage. This section applies that principle to both the HR organization and to the human resource management system (HRMS).

Ian Ruddle and Jeff Alderton point out in their chapter that most HR organizations still use a "decentralized administration" structure (one that was prominent in the 1980s), rather than a shared services model that is more appropriate for effective global operations. These authors discuss how to develop the necessary vision and strategy to meet the demands of virtual global HR.

In the next chapter, Peter Weinberg gives a step-by-step approach to developing an effective global HRMS strategy. And since deploying a global HR system is as challenging as developing one, Scott Bolman provides a strategy for global deployment.

> **Part Three, "Cultural Dimensions:"** One of the most familiar external challenges of globalization for HR is the diversity of cultures that a global organization encompasses. In her chapter, Row Henson analyzes and categorizes the cultural differences that affect business in different parts of the world and suggests how to plan for them systematically. In the following chapter, Don Tosti discusses how to foster "global fluency" — a kind of *lingua franca* of international business culture that is becoming essential for all global organizations.

Jackie Penticost explains that while both global HR and global HRMS are "emerging disciplines," we can't wait for them to mature. The consequences of delaying our response to the challenge of creating effective global HR are extreme. Of course, so are the consequences of missteps. Penticost discusses the challenges to implementing global HR and provides a helpful checklist for practitioners.

> **Part Four, "The Global HR Function:"** Globalization can change the role of HR significantly. Dan Sullivan argues that in managing human capital assets, global corporate HR needs to pay attention not only to such traditional concerns as managerial experience, training, and skills but, in addition, to varying managerial mindsets. He identifies several such "multi-centric" mindsets, discusses how they can apply more or less effectively to different global business situations, and makes recommendations on how HR professionals can use this knowledge to increase their organizational effectiveness.

Jim Spoor reminds us of the importance of thinking about yet another parameter: organizational size. Spoor notes that while the same general strategic principles underlie all globalization decisions, the issues facing a midsize organization as it globalizes differ in many ways from those facing large companies.

In the final chapter of this section on the global HR function, Don Harris notes that we must address the diversity not only of cultures and languages, but also of laws, standards and regulations. He points out that the European Union's Data Privacy Directive has made the careful handling of employee information a sudden priority for U.S. corporations doing business overseas. U.S. corporations had previously considered the issue insignificant. The example is no doubt the first of many similar ones to come.

➤ **Part Five, "Global Human Capital Systems:"** One internal legacy that often impedes globalization is the human capital management system (HCMS) itself, the most common of which are the various enterprise resource planning (ERP) systems available on the market. Such systems often straitjacket businesses, forcing them to maintain industrial-era, command-and-control-like procedures and structures. To develop a new kind of system suitable for a global HR organization is, however, a daunting task fraught with the possibility of failure. In their chapter, Jenni Lehman and Synco Jonkeron analyze the benefits, risks, strategies and methods needed to develop and implement a successful global HCMS.

In implementing a global human resource information system, John Johnston distinguishes between "best practices" — which can be problematic when applied outside their original organizational context — and "leading practices," which tend to be more generic and hence more applicable across a broad spectrum. He discusses several "leading practices" to be considered when in the process of a global implementation. In our final chapter on global human capital management systems, Catherine Veinbachs gives us detailed guidance on how to select a global HR systems vendor.

➤ **Part Six, "The Virtual Connected World:"** If boundarylessness is the essence of success today, the question arises of how to make it happen. We need to have the tools and capabilities to leverage the business' worldwide pool of knowledge. Research has shown, Wayne Baker notes, that "as much as 70 percent of organizational learning takes place via informal networks and social interaction." Baker examines how businesses can build what he calls social capital, thereby creating, not only trust, cooperation, and goodwill, but also promoting access to information, opportunities, and many other business advantages.

Valdis Krebs discusses a number of elements of working in the global connected world — including not only the benefits brought about by organizational connectedness but also the risks that inevitably emerge. Controlling the risks while reaping the benefits is a particularly striking example of the need to manage the paradox in the global age.

➤ **Part Seven, "Our Global Future:"** The final section of this book, "Our Global Future," contains two chapters about the future of human capital management in the global economy. Both Bob Stambaugh and John Sullivan explore the paradoxes that exist and describe the often-unfortunate record of past attempts. In "Global Networks, Local Systems," Stambaugh expresses concern over excessive globalizing of systems. In "Globalize or Perish," Sullivan argues that it is essential that each and every business function within the enterprise also become globalized. Their standpoints and conclusions are quite different, giving us ample food for thought in our globalization efforts.

That experts should disagree on topics as fraught with contradiction as this one is both understandable and fruitful. The ability to manage the paradox and reconcile differences is the essential skill that globalization demands of HR professionals — indeed, of all business leaders. We hope this book will give you some of the tools you need for resolving and mastering the paradoxes in your life and for responding to the demands being made of all of us in the boundaryless era.

Karen V. Beaman
Portland, Oregon

Foreword

By Christopher Bartlett, Ph.D.

The most important corporate transformation in 75 years is taking place right now. It will radically change human resource management and its role in the organization. And those who understand it will guide their organizations far more effectively than those who don't.

Behind this transformation are numerous forces, such as privatization, deregulation, the information revolution, and above all, globalization. But at its root is a deeper change. Global business has always had to focus on gaining access to one resource of particular scarcity, and thus of special strategic importance. Which resource fills this role has changed over the centuries, and when it does change — as is occurring today — the implications are enormous.

In the past century, global business was most concerned with procuring scarce *raw materials*: bauxite or rubber or timber. Then, in the early 20th century, the global corporation's critical scarce resource became *capital*. Today, however, corporations often have more capital than ideas about how to use it. (They have, as a result, sometimes turned to dubious mergers and acquisitions and have built excess capacity.) The critical scarce resource for global business, then, is no longer financial capital — it's *human capital*. As we evolve into an information-based, knowledge-intensive service economy, the critical resource is now *expertise* and *knowledge*.

Just as the critical scarce resource has changed, so must the organizational design that maximizes access to it. Consider the organizational form that most of us take for granted — today's hierarchical divisionalized model. This model arose in response to the increased importance of financial capital as a scarce resource. Its development in the 1920s allowed major corporations to diversify both their product lines and their geographic operations; it thus created economies of scope and scale and helped management allocate its scarce capital resources by letting it review each division's strategic plans and budgets.

But the traditional corporate organizational model is ill suited to the new scarce resource of knowledge and expertise — human capital. If you want to foster, link, and leverage knowledge across a whole organization, you need the opposite of strict departmental compartmentalization. That is because knowledge grows through human interaction. The larger the network of minds interacting on a problem, the deeper the insight it will yield, and the faster the resulting knowledge will develop and spread. Top-down and divisionalized structures restrict the growth of knowledge because they discourage important forms of interaction and exchange — notably those that come from the bottom up, but also those that occur laterally between divisions.

In addition, the formality of business systems is often poorly suited to the nature of knowledge. Knowledge is impossible to budget and allocate through a formalized system. The linking and leveraging of organizational knowledge often occurs not in formal systems, but in informal exchanges.

For all these reasons, the bureaucratic, command-and-control hierarchies of the former industrialized world have become increasingly counterproductive. Recognition of this problem has led to such reactions as de-layering, empowerment and organizational learning efforts. But to maximize access to knowledge and expertise, organizations must go much further. If our central task has now become to develop and leverage scarce knowledge, we need a new model for the organization.

Leading-edge companies are creating this model today. They are realizing that the new model must center not on structures but on core *processes*. Rather than reinforcing lines of command, these processes counter the top-down orientation of the old approach. Rather than defending the company's current business strategies, these processes foster the continual re-invention of the company.

As the new model takes hold, human resource management will play an increasingly crucial strategic role in the corporation. HR is uniquely positioned to foster the global linking of knowledge and expertise, the core purpose of the new model. In addition, HR's ability to attract, motivate, and retain skilled employees is increasingly differentiating successful companies from unsuccessful ones. The transformation of a company — a long process, as successful transnational companies have shown — requires tremendous skill in change management, a traditional concern of HR.

In the age when financial capital was the main scarce resource, the executive who sat at the right hand of the CEO was the chief financial officer. In leading-edge corporations today, however, the people who sit at the CEO's right hand are human resources experts. This trend will grow stronger as the HR title loses the stigma it still holds in traditional corporations — a legacy of the era in which employees were looked upon as mere factors of production, just as is machinery or other capital assets.

As this book shows, leading-edge companies no longer think of their employees in that old paradigm. The subject of the present volume is by no means just a special topic in human resource management. Rather, it will be the most important strategic concern that corporations have to face in the next century. It will define the organizational model that will soon dominate business.

Few HR professionals have yet grappled with all its implications, and fewer

HR organizations are fully prepared to address its needs. I realize that the formal structure, systems, and processes of an organization are important and still absorb a great deal of corporate time and attention. But the leading companies I work with no longer even conceive of their organization in that traditional manner. As they demonstrate, to avoid being locked into the bureaucracy that remains with us from the divisional model, we need to stop thinking about an organization as a formalized hierarchy of tasks.

If we try to manage our new scarce resource with the static organizational structures that worked in the divisional model, we are bound to fail. The nature of our new scarce resource is different. We need to create organizations that — like working knowledge and relationships — are flexible, dynamic and multidimensional. Our organizations must be far more networked and organic than the old model allowed. HR professionals will help their organizations attain this goal to the extent that they can think strategically in a new organizational world. This book's goal will be met if it can help HR professionals contribute the maximum to evolving the new organization.

Christopher Bartlett
Cambridge, Massachusetts USA

Acknowledgements

The articles collected in this volume are the results of many years of toil by countless HR professionals and thought leaders who are breaking new ground in the previous non-existent field of global human resource systems. While it is certainly not possible to acknowledge everyone I have crossed paths with and have been influential in the publication of this book, there are certainly a few people who deserve special recognition.

Many of the articles in this book come from the IHRIM Journal. I'd like to extend my sincerest thanks to all those who have contributed to the Journal since its inception and who have played a part in making the Journal a success. Special thanks also goes to all the sponsors of the Journal who have kept the publication financially alive even through these difficult, recessionary times. Without the IHRIM Journal, this book simply would not have been possible.

I am also deeply appreciative of the work of two leading academics, Christopher Bartlett from the Harvard Business School and Jay Galbraith from the Marshall School of Business at the University of Southern California, for their contributions to this book in extending their general global business management concepts to the field of human resources.

I would also like to thank my employer, ADP and AG Consulting, for affording me the opportunity to work in a global environment and for supporting my work for IHRIM, the IHRIM Journal and this book. Special thanks to John Barfitt, Gary Butler, Bill Campbell, and Regina Lee for their encouragement and collaboration of my global efforts and for their trust and confidence in me as a person and a business leader.

I would like to thank my many IHRIM colleagues — in particular, Row Henson, Bob Stambaugh, Jay Stright, John Sullivan and Al Walker who have all been true sources of inspiration to me over the last 15 years. These individuals provide practical illustration of one of the basic philosophies of Dee Hock, the founder and Chairman Emeritus of VISA Corporation: that to understand and influence events you must see things not only "as they were, as they are, as they might become, [but also] as they *ought* to be."

I'd also like to extend a special word of thanks to Barney Sherman, my editor, for his patience and responsiveness and for reacting quickly, effectively, and with a digital smile to my every request.

And finally, special thanks go to Tom Faulkner, IHRIM's publisher, for his understanding and flexibility in working around the crazy schedule of a globetrotter. Without Tom's undying belief and inexorable support of IHRIM, neither the IHRIM Journal nor this book would exist today.

Part One:
The Global
Organization

"*If one is to properly understand events and to influence the future, it is essential to master four ways of looking at things: as they were, as they are, as they might become, and as they ought to be.*

— Dee Hock

• • • • • • • •

As markets and economies change, so do organizations. A century ago, the move from an agrarian economy to an industrial one gave rise to the type of organization — as well as to the nature of the human resources field — that we've come to take for granted. Today, the move from an industrial to a knowledge economy is transforming organizations just as profoundly.

Such changes will press on regardless of what you or I do as individual professionals. But those of us who can understand, anticipate and even guide the changes will be far more effective than those who are pushed onward by forces they don't comprehend. The first section of this book aims to give insight into the trends that are revolutionizing business and HR today, and of the new organizations that are emerging as a result.

An Interview with Christopher Bartlett

By Karen V. Beaman

Managing across Borders: the Transnational Solution, *by Christopher A. Bartlett and Sumantra Ghoshal, has been called one of the 50 most influential business books of the 20th century. The 1989 book, recently reissued in an updated edition, has shaped the way many HR professionals think about global management. Of course, Bartlett's work ranges further. When I interviewed him in December 2000, he had a good deal to say, for example, about the implications of his work for human resource management.*

Dr. Bartlett is the Daewoo Professor of Business Administration and Chair of the Program for Global Leadership at Harvard Business School, whose faculty he joined in 1979. He holds masters and doctoral degrees from Harvard. Previously, he was a marketing manager with Alcoa in his native Australia, a management consultant for McKinsey and Company in London, and a general manager at a Baxter Laboratory subsidiary in France. He has written or co-written eight books, the most recent being The Individualized Corporation *(co-authored with Sumantra Ghoshal, published in 1997).*

I interviewed Bartlett by telephone in December 2000 to find out how his thinking about global organizations had evolved and, in particular, how it applies to the human resources professional.

KB: *You and Sumantra Ghoshal introduced the model of the transnational organization in 1989. How has the concept developed since then?*
CB: Our first book was based on research done in the 1980s. While the companies in our sample were clearly heading in the transnational direction, none of them had yet achieved the transnational model that we described in its idealized form. But now many companies have. For example, at Asea Brown Boveri (ABB), which Percy Barnevik was creating after the merger of two firms, he

talked about being both big and small, both centralized and de-centralized, both with responsibilities at the periphery and control at the center. He was, in short, creating a classic transnational organization.

As we discussed in our book, a transnational organization is based neither on centralized nor on decentralized operations. Today's transnational companies are indeed creating organizations that are interdependent, rather than relying on dependent or interdependent operations. Another key point that is being confirmed is that they use worldwide operations not only for market access but also —even more importantly — for the ability to tap knowledge and expertise, and to link and leverage it around the world. This is enormously significant, and raises important issues for HR, which often has yet to address them.

KB: *My experience is that HR tends to be localized and very top-down, focusing more on legal and cultural issues within their own country than leveraging resources and knowledge from other countries.*
CB: Yes, HR has traditionally been a centralized and top-down function. I think that most companies today are still that way, as they remain caught in their administrative heritage.

This administrative heritage dates from the 1920s when leading corporations developed a model that compartmentalized organizations into divisions. From this came the "professional management model" that has driven companies through enormous growth and expansion over the past 75 years. In this model of "strategy-structured systems," top management sets strategy by allocating scarce capital resources, after reviewing the strategic plans and the capital budgets for each division.

It was an appropriate model in its time, because during much of the 20th century, capital was the critical scarce resource for global management. But in today's leading-edge companies you're starting to see enormous changes. The fundamental reason is that capital is no longer their constraining scarce resource. Instead, as we move into an information-based, knowledge-intensive service economy, the critical scarce resources are information, knowledge and expertise. These scarce resources reside in the heads of individuals. They also exist in the relationships between people who are at the front lines of the organization, closest to the customers, competitors and technology.

Everything that the standard corporate model was designed for — to allocate, measure and control scarce capital resources — is becoming less and less central to business success. Today, the key task of management is to develop, leverage, diffuse and apply scarce knowledge. This flips the whole organizational form.

KB: *What sort of form does this suggest?*
CB: The traditional divisional model sees the organization as a hierarchy of *tasks*. The new model sees it as a portfolio of core *macro-processes*. In our new

book, we identify three especially important ones. The first core macro-process is the *entrepreneurial* process: entrepreneurial initiative that drives from the bottom up and that counters the strong top-down direction that we are left with from the old organizational form. The second is a *horizontal learning* process, which links and leverages across the compartmentalized structures of divisions and departments. It runs counter to the vertical capital-allocating process that we inherit from the older model. The third is a *continuous renewal* process. This is not just continuous refinement, or getting better and better at what we've done. Continuous renewal is about companies constantly reinventing themselves to avoid self-obsolescing. Instead of just driving down the learning curve, it's jumping the curves.

Within the macro processes are various micro-processes; but it's around the core macro-processes that global organizations need to build. We can no longer compartmentalize ourselves into functions. And the leading edge companies are a country mile ahead of the followers in this respect.

KB: *A lot of companies are still locked in the command and control structure. Could you give some examples of companies that demonstrate the new model?*
CB: Jack Welch, during his years at GE, led one of the most widely followed transformations — and it has embodied all three of these core macro-processes. First, he developed a process called "getting a workout." This would begin with gathering front-line people into groups together with their boss. The boss left and the front-line people, with a facilitator, could say, "Here's what's wrong with this business. Here's where we could do things better. Here's what could really help us." After a couple of days, the boss came back and the front-line people presented their notions of what should change, what should go, and what should be added.

That process developed a different relationship between the front line and the managers: bosses would listen to front-line people. The front line was given authority, encouragement and reward for taking the initiative and pushing ideas up. In short, the workout was creating *entrepreneurial initiative*, this bottom-up kick-start core macro-process. It took place in the late 1980s and early 1990s — you can't hurry these transformations, and if you try to they fail.

GE's second stage of the transformation, after workout, was called "boundarylessness." It asks, what are the best practices in our class in the world? And then once we capture them, how do we leverage them rapidly across the organization? This is about creating the "horizontal" macro-process, the second one on our list — the linking and leveraging of knowledge.

For example, Canadian GE noticed that an appliance manufacturer in the tiny market of New Zealand was running its business incredibly efficiently and with highly innovative products. So Canadian GE flew some people over to find out what on earth this tiny company was doing. They brought back the ideas they learned, and realized huge increases in efficiency. Then people from GE's Appliance Park in North Carolina came up to Canada to find out what was going on. They brought the ideas back to Appliance Park, started re-engineering their processes, and got more inventory out and reduced their time to market. Then other divisions came to them to learn what they could.

The conventional wisdom is that GE is a conglomerate and should just spin off its businesses. Well no, it shouldn't, because Welch has learned to make full use of its human assets. He released the entrepreneurial spirit that had been held hostage in the old corporate hierarchy and let it drive bottom-up initiative. And he linked and leveraged expertise around the organization. He embodied the principle that the biggest advantage of globalization is to increase corporate access to the main scarce resource of our time — knowledge.

He also embodied our third macro-process, "continuous self-renewal." Welch asked his people, "Who says we have to be just an industrial product company? Why don't we define ourselves as an industrial products and services business?" As a result, they are radically transforming their business from product only to products and services. For example, the medical products business that was in x-rays and CAT scans started putting sensors in all of their equipment, and monitoring them centrally so that they could see when they needed service.

All of these approaches demonstrate *processes* of change, not structures. They have loosened the grip of the old divisionalized heritage and have contributed enormously to GE's success.

KB: *It's an impressive example, because the divisionalized approach is ingrained in so many companies. Yet you're saying that the approach is becoming counterproductive.*
CB: Well, HR is a perfect example of why the compartmentalizing of the divisional model is outmoded. The role of HR is to help line managers manage the human resources of the organization. HR has to help line managers attract, develop and motivate people because it's the key competitive advantage today, not just because it's a nice thing to do. But it has to be done in a very different way than we've done it in the past. How does HR help line managers? By being rolled into line management. HR isn't to be compartmentalized off into some corporate staff function that's managed at the headquarters or at the region.

As it becomes more integrated, HR also plays a more prominent role in the corporation. Welch spends 80 percent of his time on people issues, and at his right hand are his HR specialists, who help him manage that. By contrast, in the traditional organization, with its focus on capital resources, the CEO keeps the chief financial officer at his right hand.

KB: *Could you say more about what the new model implies for HR?*
CB: The implications for HR go deeper, of course. The traditional organization sees its employees as factors of production. Henry Ford said that when all he

wanted was a good pair of hands, unfortunately a person came attached to them. Harold Geneen, the CEO of International Telephone and Telegraph in the 1960s, said that he wanted to make people as predictable and controllable as the capital assets for which they were responsible. The implication was that capital assets were at the center, while people were at the margins.

We may scoff at this sort of attitude, but a bit of it carried over even when we started talking about human resources as our most critical asset. Our treatment of the human resource still is often focused on deployment — on moving people as if they were machines that we try to put into the most efficient application.

We need a very different model of how to think about them. The new organization is learning to see people as *volunteer investors* in their organizations — people who invest their scarce knowledge and expertise into the organization, just as traditional shareholders bring monetary capital to invest. This is a radical change of attitude towards employees. Perhaps the biggest challenge it raises is learning how to access the scarce resource of people's knowledge on a global basis.

KB: *Why do you think it has been such a challenge for companies to share and leverage their people's knowledge globally?*
CB: In the old model, the purpose of corporate staff was to provide top management with increasingly sophisticated information-planning control systems — whose information flowed *up* the organization. What most companies keep doing today, without questioning that old "strategy-structured systems" corporate model, is merely to haul more and more *sophisticated* information up to the top of the organization. But this misses the point. Most companies are drowning in information — managers throughout the organization are up to their eyeballs in it.

What they are starved for is real knowledge. Knowledge is very different from information. Although knowledge is built on an infrastructure of information, it's ultimately based on a social network. Knowledge is people. If you're going to build a plant, you don't just ship over the blueprints. You also ship over the engineers who understand it. The knowledge that you're really transferring is imbedded and implicit, built into these engineers' heads and relationships. The blueprints or the description are not sufficient; they are just information.

The principle applies to any kind of knowledge we create. So building social networks within an organization is what allows you to take the resource from one country, link it to the expertise in a third, apply it to an asset in a fourth, and leverage the product you produce around the world. That's the real challenge of global knowledge management: the diffusion of innovation around the globe. Here we're describing the second of the three macro-processes that we spoke about — the horizontal learning process, which links and leverages knowledge across divisions internationally.

KB: *We've published a lot in the IHRIM Journal about building social networks for knowledge transfer. The traditional approach of putting all your knowledge into a database so others can search it has proven not to work. Could you speak more about how one can build social networks?*
CB: A key is to realize that formalized and centralized processes are probably not relevant to these networks. Of course, you probably still will use formalized processes to manage the flow of *goods and products* around the organization; and you'll use centralized processes to manage the flow of resources. But for the flows of *information, knowledge and expertise* around the organization, what you need is the less formal process of socialization. That means career paths that engage people in moving among different businesses, functions and geographies.

In developing these, you're building a matrix in managers' *minds*, as opposed to installing a matrix structure in the organization. A lot of people talk about a matrix structure as if you formalize it and wire everyone in to report to multiple people. But what you need is a more dynamic, fluid matrix in which you build mini-matrices. Those are teams and task forces that overlay the ongoing operations and line responsibilities of managers.

In one example in our first book, a corporation had its marketing and technology managers from different countries work together on developing their first euro-brand. In such mechanisms and processes companies start building informal contacts and relationships. These bring understanding, communication and respect across barriers of distance, language, time and culture. After you've been moving people through careers and have been assigning them into these teams, task forces and projects, an informal network eventually starts to build up in the organization.

It's expensive to move people around, of course — but once the connection is established you don't have to physically meet in Brussels or wherever. Enough of a relationship is established that people can pick up the phone or send an e-mail. You've already built trust — which is the critical element to creating a knowledge network. I trust that if I deliver on my part, you're going to do the same. We have no formal relationship that's going to force us to. But we have come to trust that we'll each contribute to the shared effort.

KB: *You spoke about barriers of distance, language and so forth. Overcoming these linguistic, legal, and cultural barriers has been a challenge for global organizations.*
CB: It can be done, however. Again, the key is in the informal rather than the formalized structure. A company can be said to have a "psychology," in addition to its more formal structures. The "psychology" is the corporation's culture, the values and the way people think and act. When people join your organization, your goal is that they engage in and become part of this entity.

In other words, they should be made to feel that they don't just work for the company — they belong to an institution whose values, beliefs and purpose they identify with. Fostering this identification is at the heart of international management. And if management isn't making those values clear, finding the kinds of people who align with that "psychology," and bringing that to bear across the organization, then it's failing in its job.

That doesn't mean that we don't respect national or cultural differences and try to understand them. Global managers are managing a corporate culture, but also national cultures. There will always be a tension between the global and the national and local. On the one hand, you want the efficiency of across-the-border integration and coordination; on the other you want local responsiveness to each country's consumers, infrastructure, host governments, culture and values. At the heart of the global organization is managing that tension, asking people to nudge a bit this way and move a bit that way. To facilitate that, the corporate culture must be integrating a powerful coordinating mechanism.

KB: *This seems to relate to the question of decentralization, centralization, and the interdependence that characterizes the transnational model.*
CB: It does. National responsiveness — delegating, responding and adapting to the local market — is not about centralization versus decentralization. Companies have to learn how to do both. And they have to figure out, business-by-business, function-by-function and task-by-task, which issues need to be managed in a more coordinated and integrated fashion and which ones need to be managed in a more differentiated fashion. You'll manage your global research in a very different way than your sales and service. You'll manage your telecommunications business very differently than your brand and package-goods industry business.

That's a fundamental task for management, sorting out the roles and responsibilities and relationships, business-by-business, function-by-function, task-by-task. It's not a matter of looking for the simplistic solution. Saying we're centralized or de-centralized is lazy management. The world isn't that simple. The world is complex, diverse and dynamic.

In *Managing Across Borders* — which focused on the link between global strategic requirements and organizational capabilities — we spoke about an integrated network as a corporate model. But our newest book, *The Individualized Corporation*, proposes a more flexible and dynamic network-based organization. That dynamism and flexibility reflects the nature of human knowledge and its increased strategic importance. These qualities are increasingly essential to global organizations.

KB: *What role do HR systems have to play in the transformation you've discussed? The ERP systems like SAP, PeopleSoft and Oracle often impose top-down uniformity on the organization, and in some ways inhibit us from doing a lot of the things that you talk about. I'm wondering about how we can use these systems to enable the human resource function.*
CB: As you imply, there is nothing wrong with systems *per se*, whether they're in budgeting or strategic planning or HR. The problem is in how they're used. We

talked about the old strategy/structure systems model. Underneath it lay the assumption that top management has the knowledge, expertise and wisdom, and thus will set strategy and the budgets. But this top-down assumption — that the people at the top of the organization are smarter than everyone else — was part of the problem. It is largely why the powerful systems that are hauling all this information to the top can become pathological. It's pathological, for example, when the budgets create a sort of cops-and-robbers war between corporate staffs and line management because they're seen as opposite sides of a game. The front line is hiding performance in their hip pockets, and the corporate staffs are chasing around and playing "gotcha."

That's why I think that more critical than such systems are these more dynamic core processes, which I think will transform the organization. Once you transform it, you can build structures to provide the backdrop for what you've built, and the systems to support it. But at the heart of what we've got to create are these core processes. And that requires a very different approach than going back to the old strategy/structure and systems model.

KB: *Still, it seems that many organizations are inhibited from making the necessary changes partly because they're locked into ERP systems. They've made huge investments in these monolithic systems, and the costs for modifying them would be enormous.*

CB: As you say, it doesn't help to create powerful systems to drive information through the organization rather than standing back and saying, "Wait a minute, at the core of our task is to build a very different corporate model." You need to stand back and be strategic and corporate and top-management minded and take a long-term view in this instead of an operational and tool-oriented one.

I don't pretend to be an HR specialist; I'm a guy from strategy who wandered in and feels as if he's not in Kansas anymore (like Dorothy in the Wizard of Oz). But this issue you raise is at the core of the research that Sumantra and I are doing. The next piece we're looking at is the strategic role of human resource management — in fact I don't even want to call it human resource management; let's call it "how companies can manage people for competitive advantage." We're coming at these issues not through a human resource view, but through a strategic one. I think that is what's necessary today.

Globalizing HRIS:
The New
Transnational Model

By Karen V. Beaman and Alfred J. Walker

"It is not the strongest of the species that survive, nor the most intelligent, but the one most responsive to change."

— *Charles Darwin*

• • • • • • • •

■ *Introduction*

The term "global HRIS" (human resource information system) has been used to denote many different types of organizations, systems and environments. Indeed, the word "global" has become one of the hottest buzzwords of recent years. With the accelerating pace of change brought about by the Internet and by high-speed communications and transportation, distances are shrinking and borders are breaking down. Every organization is now running into so-called global issues. A direct outcome of the Digital Age, there are two major trends that are having a profound effect on the way we do business:

➤ Increasing globalization and accelerating change in the international business environment is drawing more and more companies beyond their national borders. Studies show that 50 percent of all major corporations now have at least some international operations.

➤ The complexity of inter-organizational relationships between companies and their stakeholders (e.g., employees, outside service providers, regulatory authorities) is growing, as corporate boundaries become permeable and, in some cases, even disappear. Increasing competition due to the ease of doing business across borders is putting pressure on companies to be more competitive. Hence, organizations are looking for strategies to contain costs in order to increase productivity and effectiveness. In addition, the continuous quest for best practices has companies looking beyond their borders for solutions to increasingly complex problems.

Yet local and regional differences, even with the accelerating rate of globalization, remain strong. Cultural and national identities still play a prominent role in the international business world. While the new international business environment is clearly pushing us closer together, it is opposed by a strong counterforce attracting us to our own local customs and traditions.[1] Balancing needs on the international front with local and/or national agendas is far from a simple task.

... only organizations who are able to escape from traditional thinking will survive.

This new *Sturm und Drang*[2] is bringing about momentous change. Trends are barely recognized before they become *passé* in the "blur" of new approaches to age-old problems.[3] The connected economy has catapulted us into a period of unprecedented change and we are being forced to develop new, creative approaches if we want to stay competitive. Indeed, only organizations who are able to escape from traditional thinking will survive.

Likewise in HR and HRIS, our traditional models are no longer adequate. The world has changed and so must our thinking about how we organize and manage ourselves, our companies, and our systems. In this article we define a new model for global HRIS that encompasses a new organizational structure, alternative system architectures, and distributed methods of HR service delivery. Drawing on the work of Christopher Bartlett and Sumantra Ghoshal, as well as on our own previous work in this area, we attempt to elucidate and evaluate the myriad models and architectures that have appeared over the past decade and to craft a new model for Global HRIS.

We also wanted to test our model by using a small sample of large global corporations to determine the real-world fit between what organizations are actually doing and what we, as consultants and theorists, are saying. Thus, we present the results of a small survey we conducted with 35 global companies and discuss the implications of our new model on corporations today and in the future.

■ Four Types of HRIS Organizational Models

In *Managing Across Borders: The Transnational Solution*, Christopher Bartlett and Sumantra Ghoshal[4] categorize worldwide organizational models into the following four types:

➤ Multinational,

➤ Global,

➤ International, and

➤ Transnational.

Each of these models differs according to its degree of centralization, its level of responsiveness to local issues, and its ability to leverage and share innovation and learning worldwide. We will discuss the applicability of each of these models to HRIS.[5]

➤ **Multinational HRIS.** The first of these models — the "Multinational HRIS" — comprises a portfolio of separate, distinct organizations that are delineated

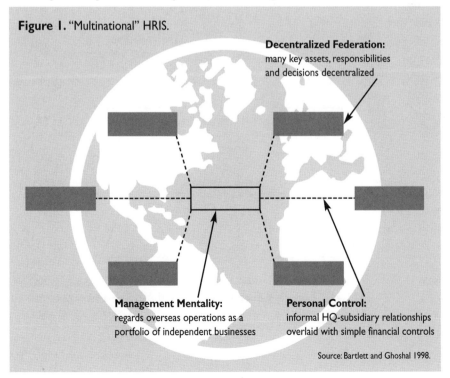

Figure 1. "Multinational" HRIS.

Decentralized Federation: many key assets, responsibilities and decisions decentralized

Management Mentality: regards overseas operations as a portfolio of independent businesses

Personal Control: informal HQ-subsidiary relationships overlaid with simple financial controls

Source: Bartlett and Ghoshal 1998.

by national boundaries (see Figure 1). Within each independent organization, many key assets, responsibilities, and decision-making are localized (decentralized with respect to the core), giving local business units considerable freedom, autonomy, and control over their own operations. This type of HRIS is particularly adept at addressing and responding to local needs and is thus most sensitive to individual cultural and national differences.

The Multinational HRIS is less focused on centralized corporate direction. Central management's role is informal and consists of little more than consolidated financial reporting. The disadvantage of such extreme decentralization is that such organizations can turn into multi-headed monsters, where "anything goes," and whose various heads don't communicate or coordinate with one another, causing needless re-invention.

On the other hand, this type of organizational model can be quite suitable for large conglomerates in which there is little benefit to be gained from centralized processing or decision-making (such as, certain types of retailers or service organizations). Likewise, organizations with strong autonomous cultures can benefit from the Multinational HRIS because responsiveness and sensitivity to local business unit needs play a paramount role.

➤ **Global HRIS.** At the opposite extreme is the highly centralized organization, what Bartlett and Ghoshal call the "Global Organization" (see Figure 2).

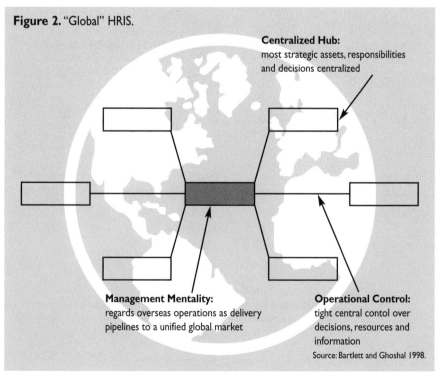

Figure 2. "Global" HRIS.

Centralized Hub: most strategic assets, responsibilities and decisions centralized

Management Mentality: regards overseas operations as delivery pipelines to a unified global market

Operational Control: tight central contol over decisions, resources and information

Source: Bartlett and Ghoshal 1998.

The Global Organization views overseas operations merely as delivery pipelines from the parent company to an undifferentiated worldwide market. Most strategic assets, resources, responsibilities, and decision-making are centralized. The driving force behind the Global HRIS is a focus on maximizing efficiency and on building a single standardized organization within a uniform operating environment.

Naturally, this approach minimizes the needs of local, national, and regional business units. One single, sanitary solution is developed — "one size fits all" — or is supposed to. The disadvantage to this model is the tendency to force diverse operating units into such rigid structures that they rebel, causing renegade or covert behaviors to develop outside the established standards.

The Global HRIS organizational model is appropriate for organizations with a need to deliver a single standardized product (e.g., software providers) or service (e.g., telecommunications providers) to a worldwide market. The focus on efficiency and standards provides for greater volume, promotes ease of integration, and reduces overall costs. In addition, organizations with strong homogeneous cultures benefit from such a model.

➤ **International HRIS.** Between these two extremes lies the third model — the "International Organization" (see Figure 3). While allowing for local control over

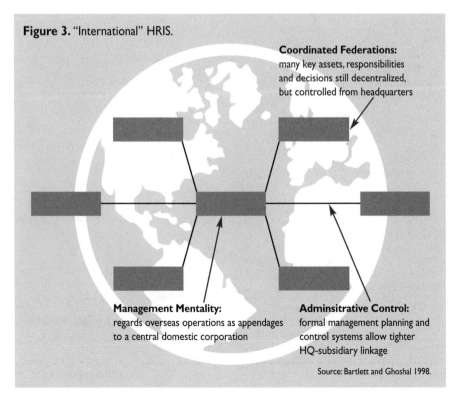

Figure 3. "International" HRIS.

Coordinated Federations: many key assets, responsibilities and decisions still decentralized, but controlled from headquarters

Management Mentality: regards overseas operations as appendages to a central domestic corporation

Adminsitrative Control: formal management planning and control systems allow tighter HQ-subsidiary linkage

Source: Bartlett and Ghoshal 1998.

many decisions, responsibilities, and assets, this type of organization views overseas units as appendages that exist only to carry out the goals of the central organization. The International HRIS strikes a balance between local autonomy and central oversight.

The great advantage of the International model is its focus on sharing cross-border learning and innovation. This model facilitates the transfer and adaptation of knowledge to other business units from any country that develops it. The whole organization benefits when advances made in one country are shared immediately across all the others. Thus, this model retains many of the advantages of centralized control and process, while at the same time shares best practices across local business units.

This type of HRIS is useful for developing organizations that still have unbalanced skills sets and operations around the world. Resources, knowledge, innovation, etc. can be shifted and shared among operating units such that the whole is greater than the sum of its parts.

▶ **Transnational HRIS.** However, none of these models addresses simultaneously all three sides of the paradox facing us: the need to be sensitive to the requirements of local business units, the desire to obtain efficiencies that result from centralized operations, and the keenness to share and leverage learning

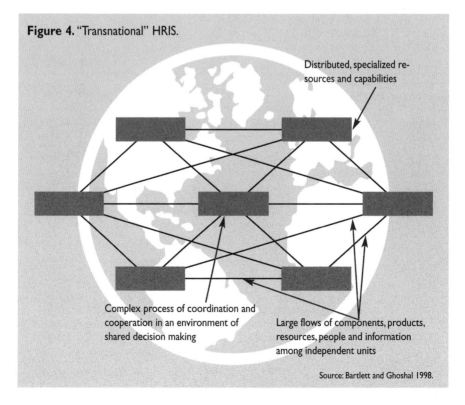

Figure 4. "Transnational" HRIS.

Distributed, specialized resources and capabilities

Complex process of coordination and cooperation in an environment of shared decision making

Large flows of components, products, resources, people and information among independent units

Source: Bartlett and Ghoshal 1998.

and innovation across the worldwide organization. A completely new model — the Transnational HRIS — is centered on resolving this paradox (see Figure 4).

With the Transnational HRIS, regional business units are treated as distributed resources. Each one contributes to the rest of the organization based on its particular area of strength. Corporate HR consists of a complex set of processes for the coordination and facilitation of sharing among the different operational units. Although corporate headquarters still lies at the center of this model, local units are genuinely interdependent. No one unit has more control than any other. This model is particularly useful for large, multinational conglomerates with heterogeneous cultures, under significant competitive pressures due to the increasing globalization and fast-paced change brought about by the Internet.

For example, if one regional unit has developed a particularly effective solution to the challenge of recruiting, it can easily and quickly share its solution with other units around the world. HR is the advocate, and HRIS is the tool for facilitating a high degree of inter-unit information flow and coordination. Clearly, the advantage to the Transnational HRIS model is its ability to respond effectively and swiftly to the demands brought about by the *Sturm und Drang* of the Digital Age.

▶ **The Developmental Curve.** Our experience suggests that these four models represent a development curve as shown in Figure 5.[6] The 1980s were dominated

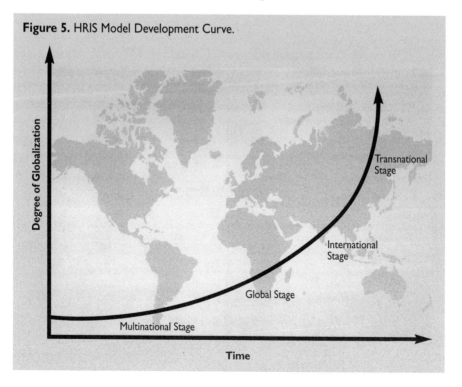

Figure 5. HRIS Model Development Curve.

by HRIS in the first stage — the Multinational stage. Many organizations just starting their overseas operations knew little about local business practices and constraints and thus let regional companies pretty much run themselves.

In the 1990s, however, large organizations came up against issues of cost control and containment. Such concerns swung the pendulum in the direction of totally centralized control, and the Global model began to dominate the HRIS landscape. With this approach, centralized organizations began to force corporate standards onto their regional and local operating units.

However, this forcing of corporate standards and practices onto local operations was not always perceived positively. Thus, the next trend in the evolution of HRIS models was toward balancing local and corporate needs through the International model. However, the limitations with the International model were quickly uncovered as being neither "fish nor foul" — not particularly responsive to local needs and not particularly focused on operational efficiency.

This has led us to the final stage — the Transnational Model — which attempts to resolve the paradox by finding the right balance between local responsiveness and centralized control, while at the same time promoting learning, sharing and innovation across the organization.

Each of these models differs systematically in such attributes as capabilities, operations, management, knowledge and control (see Figure 6). Consider knowledge as an example. In the Multinational model, knowledge is developed and retained in the local units, whereas in the Global model, it is developed

Figure 6. Moving to the Transnational HRIS.

MULTINATIONAL	GLOBAL	INTERNATIONAL	TRANSNATIONAL
CAPABILITIES:			
Decentralized and self-sufficient	Centralized and globally scaled	Only sources of core competencies centralized	Dispersed, interdependent and specialized
OPERATIONS:			
Seeking and exploiting local opportunities	Implementing parent company strategies	Leveraging parent company competencies	Differing contributions by national units
MANAGEMENT:			
Subsidiaries comprise a portfolio of independent businesses	Subsidiaries are delivery pipelines to global market	Subsidiaries are appendages to domestic corporation	Coordination; cooperation and shared decision-making
KNOWLEDGE:			
Knowledge developed and retained within each unit	Knowledge developed and retained at the center	Knowledge developed at center and transferred overseas	Knowledge developed jointly; shared worldwide
CONTROL:			
Personal and informal; simple financial controls	Operational and strict; tight control over everything	Administrative and formal; tight linkage with headquarters	Large flows among individual business units

Source: Bartlett and Ghoshal 1998.

and retained in central headquarters. In the International model, knowledge is developed at central headquarters and then distributed to the international subsidiaries. In the Transnational model, knowledge is developed in any unit that has the skills and resources and is then shared with all other units throughout the organization.

■ Three Types of System Architectures and the Four HRIS Models

One defining difference with the four HRIS models is the technological architecture of the systems they use. Although there is considerable variation we can identify, broadly speaking, three basic systems architectures commonly found in HRIS[7]:

➤ Standalone System Model,

➤ Data Warehouse Model, and

➤ Single Integrated System Model.

➤ **Standalone System Model.** The most basic of models is the Standalone System Model, in which each operating unit runs its own independent system, with no worldwide standards in place and no integration (see Figure 7). In fact, there may be no systems at all in some areas. Consolidated reporting, perhaps done through a global data warehouse, is often quite basic, even primitive, being built off of extracts of reported data. Business units may send in updates via fax, telephone, mail, or in person. These communications may necessitate extensive translation and heavy data entry.

The Standalone System Model makes it difficult to do data analysis. Even the most basic headcount reporting becomes laborious. This type of architecture clearly identifies a company as a Multinational HRIS model — the "many-headed monster" approach. This model is quite common in large, diversified multinational organizations, particularly those that have grown through acquisition.

➤ **Data Warehouse Model.** Another common but more advanced architectural model is the Data Warehouse Model. In this model, all operating units use the same software system (e.g., Oracle, PeopleSoft, or SAP) (see Figure 8), albeit with separate database instances set up for each region or country. In the

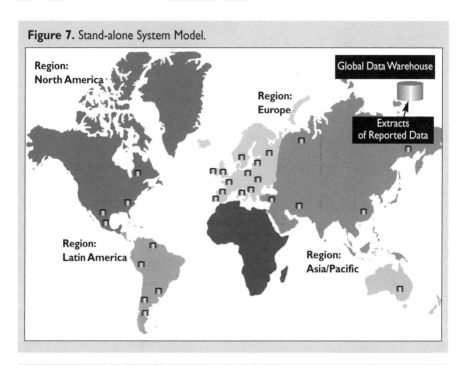

Figure 7. Stand-alone System Model.

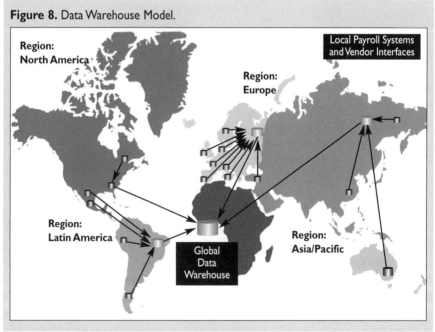

Figure 8. Data Warehouse Model.

best of these models, all units run the same version of the software, maximizing resources and saving costs through commonality, shared applications, and enterprise advantages in dealing with the vendor.

This type of system is completely centered on the data mart; however, as opposed to the Standalone System model, the data come from all operating units automatically and in a standardized format. Such standardized data require little or no translation and are available to all operating units as soon as updated (within the rules of data privacy and protection, of course). All users know how the data were generated and what each data element means. The limitation to this type of architecture, however, is that not everyone uses the same database. We typically see this type of architecture in an International HRIS model.

➤ **Single Integrated System Model.** This third type of system architecture — Single Integrated System Model — is the most advanced (see Figure 9). There is only one instance of the database, generally located at corporate headquarters (a worldwide Brazilian-based company in Figure 9).. Updating a name anywhere in the system automatically updates it throughout the organization. There is no need for a separate reporting database, although some organizations do opt for one in order to separate transaction processing from analytical reporting. The single-system HRIS also uses the same screens worldwide, with appropriate changes for different languages in different countries.

Single integrated systems are quite common in some fields — airlines typically use them for flight operations — but they are still rare in the HR world. Global and Transnational HRIS models will most commonly have a single integrated HRIS.

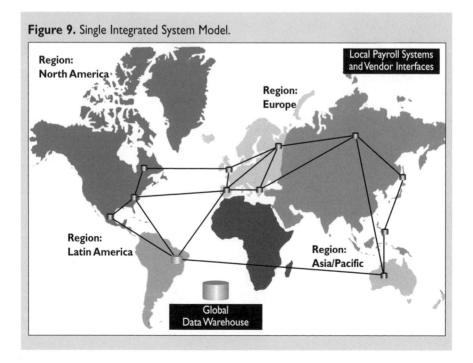

Figure 9. Single Integrated System Model.

In summary, the most advanced HRIS architectural model strikes a balance between the two extremes of being locally diverse and centrally controlled. As that balancing act suggests, the most enlightened approach to worldwide HRIS management is not necessarily to globalize all HRIS functions. Some functions are better handled locally, some internationally, and some in between. Part of the evolution of the worldwide HRIS involves finding the right balance.

■ The HR Service Delivery Model

As has been said, all international organizations exist on four broad levels: local (Frankfurt), national (Germany), regional (Europe), and global (headquarters). Within local sites further subdivisions might include employees and managers (for use in establishing self-service) and lines of business (by product or industry). In the design of a global HRIS, it is important to decide which HR service activities should be performed on which levels — which should be global, which should be regional, and which should be done locally. What is most important is to find the right balance. Figure 10 depicts this stratification between global, regional, and local activities. Using such a hierarchy, activities to be performed globally are assigned to the uppermost level — headquarters. Activities to be carried out regionally are assigned to the regional business units. And, activities to be done locally are assigned to the individual country business units.

➤ **HR Activities that are Typically Performed Globally.** Some HR activities clearly work best when managed at the global level. One example is executive

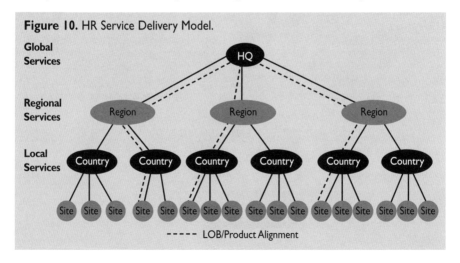

Figure 10. HR Service Delivery Model.

management — the management of the top 50 to 100 people in the organization, including succession planning and compensation management. Obviously, an organization has only one group of such people. Another example of data best administered globally is stock allocation (both purchases and grants), since a company generally has only one set of stock, controlled by the governing body. Global management is also suitable for expatriate strategy and administration, since some expatriate employees prefer (for tax reasons) to be compensated in the local currency of whichever country they are working in.

➤ **HR Activities that are Typically Performed Regionally.** Other functions, however, are harder to manage on a purely global basis and so may be best distributed regionally. Among these are leadership development, management development training, workforce communication, incentive compensation, and records management. Another possibility is policy definition and administration: it is difficult to develop a useful global policy on anything, except for very general principles such as fair labor treatment. Some compensation activities should also be handled regionally, if there is a need to maintain parity between workforces in related countries, as is becoming more and more the case in the European Union. Regional handling might also be effective for recruiting and for some compliance activities, if the same laws apply across the region.

➤ **HR Activities that are Typically Performed Locally.** Local handling is essential for activities that involve "face time" — activities that need to done in the presence of the employee or manager. If an employee has a personal problem — perhaps a conflict with a supervisor or a death in the family — handling by unknown parties at headquarters thousands of miles away is inappropriate. In addition to performance management, other activities best handled locally include hiring, staffing, team building, employee relations, works councils, labor relations, employee development, and local compliance activities. Local administration is also required for health and welfare benefits, since countries vary greatly in terms of which benefits are provided by the company and which by the government. Headcount is also often better suited to local management, partly due to the rise in contract and part-time workers, rehired pensioners, temporary workers, and so forth. The challenge is to define what an employee is, even within one country.

Thus, some functions inherently suit one level of management better than another. Nonetheless, in deciding the right level for managing the functions in your own company, a good deal of choice and judgment is required. There is a lot of variety, even within one organization, depending on the culture, management style, and priorities of the company. In designing the global HR organization, input should be sought from all levels, and, in many cases, the ultimate decision should be left to local discretion.

➤ **Alignment to the Business Model.** One critical factor in deciding what type of HRIS model to adopt is the nature of the overall business model that the company already has in place. For example, certain types of businesses offer a highly standardized product, e.g., Coca-Cola, and are clearly candidates for the Global HRIS (while the amount of sugar and carbonation in Coke may be adapted from country to country, the basic product remains the same). In contrast, other companies seek to differentiate their products depending on the customs and tastes in the markets in which they operate (e.g., Mars Candy), and thus may be better to suited to the Multinational HRIS (Mars offers different candies under different brand names to suit local preferences). You cannot force a company into a model that is inherently opposed to its overall philosophy and culture. The ideal is to fit the HR system into the day-to-day operations of the company.

➤ **Alignment to the Enterprise.** Another ideal is that enterprise business issues should drive HR, and HR in turn should drive the HRIS. If HR is fully aligned with the needs of the business, the HRIS applications and data will automatically serve both HR and the enterprise. And for many organizations they do. In practice, however, sometimes conflicts arise. In such cases, we suggest that the HRIS must at least serve the needs of the HR function, especially in compliance and plan administration areas. The HRIS is delivering services to the employees, their agencies, line managers, and HR, whether they utilize service centers, databases, or anything else. Therefore, how HR runs itself should be a primary determinant of how the HRIS is run. After satisfying the implicit mandate to support HR plan delivery, then alignment with the business priorities can be addressed. In doing so, HRIS management can then build the applications that are more focused on business priorities, such as recruiting, performance management, succession planning and others.

■ The Survey: Testing the Four-Stage Model Empirically

➤ **The Hypotheses.** Intuitively convincing though we found the above models, we wanted to test our assumptions empirically to find out if current so-called global companies were like the models. Thus, we formulated several hypotheses (see sidebar) and developed a survey to test them (see Figure 11).

➤ **The Survey.** Our survey uses a self-report questionnaire sent by email to the IHRIM Global Special Interest Group Listserv, which is made up of global American and European companies. We had 50 responses, but had to eliminate 15 because the companies weren't truly international in operations or because their surveys weren't completely filled out. We recognize the limitations of self-report data and small sample sizes, but we felt it important to begin the research, and we believe that our preliminary results are sufficiently interesting to justify reporting the results.

The Hypotheses

■ In HRIS architecture, we would expect:
➤ Global companies to be using the same system
➤ Multinational companies to be using different systems
➤ Transnationals and Internationals to be balanced between the two

■ In sharing of best practices, we would expect:
➤ Global companies to be "enforcing" standards and low cost
➤ Multinationals to have little or no control over practices
➤ Transnationals and Internationals to be balanced between the two

■ In HR operations, we would expect:
➤ Global companies to be controlled by the home office
➤ Multinationals to be skewed toward local control
➤ Transnationals and Internationals to be balanced between the two

Following is some background on the demographics of the companies surveyed (see Figure 12):

• Of the 35 companies in the final survey, over half (18) were large corporations, i.e., companies with more than 29,000 employees. About a quarter (9) were medium-sized, and another quarter (8) were small — fewer than 10,000 employees.

• For 63 percent of the respondents, all business units in the company conducted the same kind of business. About 23 percent of the respondents were conglomerates of different businesses, and 14 percent were holding companies for different businesses.

➤ **Categorizing the Respondents.** To test our hypotheses we began by categorizing each organization according to the four-stage model. To classify a company, we developed a flow chart based on the questions in the survey (see Figure 13). The first questions dealt with whether the company ran their worldwide operations on a single system, with one instance of the database. If not, and if the organization didn't leverage learning, sharing best practices worldwide, our model classified the company as being at our first stage — "Multinational."

If the company lacked a single system but did share best practices and leverage learnings, we classified it as "International" — the third model in our typology. If the company had a single integrated system with one instance of the database, and if it did not share and leverage learnings, we classified it as "Global."

If, however, the organization did have ways to share best practices and leverage learning, we asked another set of questions concerned with whether they had a global web site and allowed local variations on that site. If the answer

Figure 11. The Survey Questionnaire.

ABOUT YOUR COMPANY:

1. What type of Company do you consider yourself to be?
   - ❑ Holding company with many independent and separate lines of business
   - ❑ Conglomerate with some synergies among businesses under common leadership
   - ❑ Similar business with good interaction among business units

2. Where is your Company's worldwide headquarters based?

3. How many countries do you have a presence in (more than a sales office)?

4. List the major ones.

5. How many total employees are there in your Company (approximately)?

6. How many in the Home Country (approximately)?

7. How many ex-patriots and/or third country nationals do you have (approximately)?

ABOUT YOUR HR SYSTEMS ENVIRONMENT:

8. How would you characterize your HR/Payroll systems environment?
(Select only one)
   - ❑ Multinational — focused on "flexibility" — highly decentralized, with muliple, independent locations, united primarily through financial reporting to Corporate
   - ❑ Global — focused on "efficiency" — highly centralized/standarized, with major decisions made at Corporate and then rolled out to local operations
   - ❑ International — focused on "learning" — moderately centralized, leveraging competencies and sharing learning from both Corporate and local operations
   - ❑ Transnational — focused on "the paradox" — a combination of all of the above, leveraging efficiencies, maintaining flexibilities, and sharing learnings and innovations worldwide.

9. Where are the following HR Plans primarily administered and controlled (Although more than one answer may be valid, please check only one for each function. Check the one where the work is predominately done).

		Home Country/HQ	Regionally	Locally
a.	Base Salary/Compensation	❑	❑	❑
b.	Incentives/Bonus	❑	❑	❑
c.	Stock	❑	❑	❑
d.	Pension Plans	❑	❑	❑
e.	Succession Planning	❑	❑	❑
f.	Executive Hiring	❑	❑	❑
g.	Management Development	❑	❑	❑
h.	Technical/Professional Recruiting	❑	❑	❑
i.	Technical/Professional Training	❑	❑	❑
j.	Payroll	❑	❑	❑

10. Do you use the same, common HR system throughout your Company, i.e. do all countries and subsidiaries use SAP or PeopleSoft or some other global HR system?

was "no," we classified the company as "International." But if they did have a global, localizable web site, as well as met all the criteria above (a single system, one instance of the database, etc.), then our model classified the company in the fourth category — the "Transnational." The Transnational model satisfies

Figure 11. The Survey Questionnaire. (*continued*)

11. If so, is there one instance of the HR database?

12. Do you use the same HR database for administration, reporting and analysis?

13. If not, do you have a single data mart/data warehouse that all countries supply HR data to, and report into, with a set of standard data elements?

14. If so, how many data elements are reported by the regions to headquarters?

15. On what frequency?

16. If you have no common HR system, or data mart, how do you administer and/or report on global HR populations and HR plans?

17. Do you have a global HR web site?

18. If so, are there local web pages maintained separately by the individual local entities?

19. Are you supplying HR services through your web site to all employees on a worldwide basis?

20. If so, which ones?

21. If not, do you plan to in the future? If not, why not?

ABOUT YOUR HR ORGANIZATION:

22. Do you provide an international clearinghouse and/or help referral service to your international HR staff on matters such as new technologies and innovative solutions?

23. Do you incorporate best practices from your regional/local operations into the company's overall policies and processes? I.e., Is it likely that an innovation created in São Paulo, Brazil would be embraced by the Corporate Headquarters and implemented throughout the organization worldwide?

24. Do you have regular, face-to-face meetings of your international HR/HRIS staff?

25. If so, how many people attend (from the Home Country and internationally)?

26. How often are such meetings held?

27. Where are they held?

28. What topics are generally presented/discussed?

29. Do you regularly use cross-functional, cross-national teams to work on special projects?

30. If so, how are team members picked and managed?

31. What methods/processes exist to support the team's ability to work together across large geographic distances?

32. What types of projects do they work on?

33. Do all team members have the same compensation plan and objectives?

34. Are the teams members specifically compensated on the results of their teamwork? E.g., a team bonus.

all three imperatives of local responsiveness, global efficiency, and leverage of worldwide learnings.

We wanted to compare this classification of the companies in our sample to their own categorization of themselves to see if the results were similar or dif-

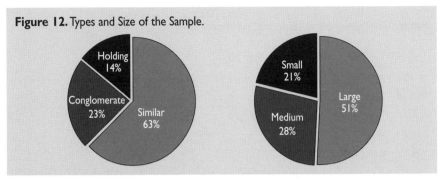

Figure 12. Types and Size of the Sample.

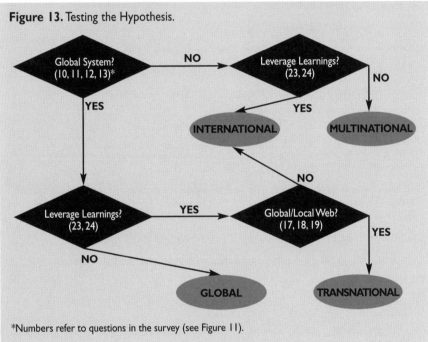

Figure 13. Testing the Hypothesis.

*Numbers refer to questions in the survey (see Figure 11).

ferent. The differences turned out to be systematic. Interestingly, companies tended to classify themselves as being at a more advanced stage than our model suggested (see Figure 14). About 40 percent of the companies classified themselves as Transnational, while our model put only 17 percent in this category. Our model put the majority of the self-described Transnationals into the International category. Undoubtedly, some of this bias towards transnationalism was influenced by the actual wording of the question in the survey, which clearly showed the superiority of the transnational approach.

We want to emphasize that the use of one model or another appears to have no relationship with the profitability or management quality of the company. There are many strong companies in all stages. Our conclusion has to do not with business results, but with self-perceptions: companies tend to perceive themselves as

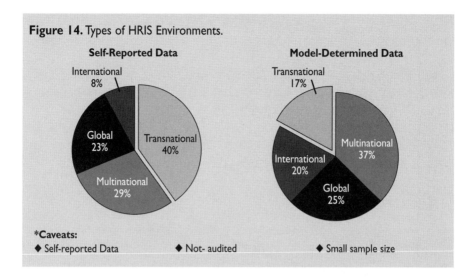

Figure 14. Types of HRIS Environments.

Self-Reported Data

International 8%

Global 23%

Transnational 40%

Multinational 29%

Model-Determined Data

Transnational 17%

International 20%

Multinational 37%

Global 25%

***Caveats:**
◆ Self-reported Data   ◆ Not- audited   ◆ Small sample size

more "advanced" in globalizing HRIS than objective measures based on actual practices suggest. Figure 15 plots the number and percent of companies from our sample on the development curve from Multinational to Transnational. As the figure shows, 37 percent of the companies in our sample are in the Multinational stage, followed next by 25 percent in the Global stage. We found the remaining companies to be split between the International and Transnational HRIS models.

➤ **The Findings**. By definition, the companies our model classified as Global and Transnational all use the same HR system worldwide (see Figure 16). As expected, only 20 percent of the companies we classified as Multinational did. Interestingly, however, International companies were more likely than not to use the same system worldwide.

The majority of companies across all four categories had a global HR web site. Once again, as expected, this trend was much more pronounced among the Transnational and Global companies.

By definition, all the Transnational and International companies focus on sharing best practices (see Figure 18). Less predictably, a third of the Multinationals did. More predictably, only 20 percent of the Global companies did. As the model states, a Global company is less concerned about what its units are doing locally; efficiency is what matters in these centralized organizations.

The same findings emerge with respect to regular global HR meetings (see Figure 19). Global organizations rarely bother to hold them. Such meetings allow headquarters to listen to the needs and concerns of local staff, but such responsiveness is not a concern for Global companies.

➤ **Global versus Local Handling of HR Functions.** Our next area of inquiry considered the question of whether certain HR functions are inherently better

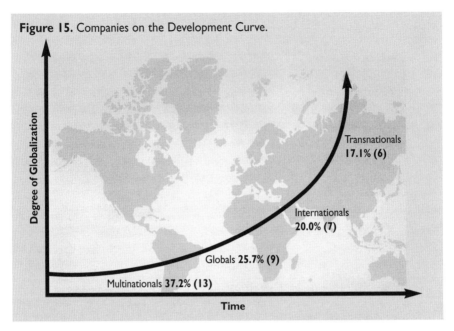

Figure 15. Companies on the Development Curve.

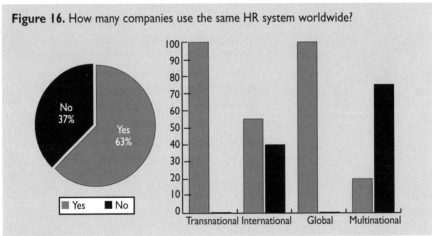

Figure 16. How many companies use the same HR system worldwide?

handled globally or locally. We asked organizations about ten common areas of HR. Our model suggested that certain functions would best be handled locally and others centrally. At the same time, however, the hypotheses predicted that most Global company functions would be controlled by the home office, most Multinationals would be skewed toward local operations, and Transnationals and Internationals would be balanced.

The results fit our hypotheses only partially (see Figure 20). Although our model led us to expect that Multinationals would handle most functions locally, our expectations were only partially verified. These organizations turn out to be "bi-polar" (see Figure 21). They handle more functions in the central office than we expected,

Figure 17. How many companies have a global website for HR?

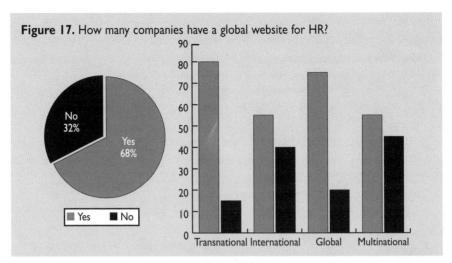

Figure 18. How many companies share and implement global HR best practices?

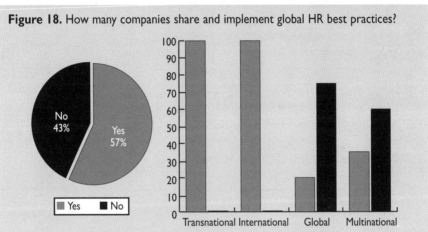

Figure 19. How many companies have regular global HR meetings?

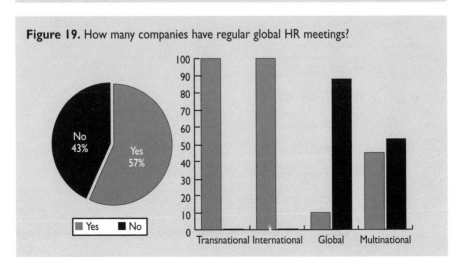

Figure 20. Analysis of HR Service Areas in Surveyed Corporations.

Base Salary	Home	Region	Local
Multinational	23%	23%	54%
International	14%	43%	43%
Global	11%	33%	56%
Transnational	17%	33%	50%

Bonus	Home	Region	Local
Multinational	47%	38%	15%
International	72%	14%	14%
Global	11%	78%	11%
Transnational	66%	17%	17%

Stock	Home	Region	Local
Multinational	77%	15%	8%
International	100%	0%	0%
Global	100%	0%	0%
Transnational	83%	17%	0%

Pension	Home	Region	Local
Multinational	31%	23%	46%
International	43%	14%	43%
Global	78%	22%	0%
Transnational	17%	17%	66%

Succession Planning	Home	Region	Local
Multinational	70%	15%	15%
International	86%	14%	0%
Global	56%	22%	22%
Transnational	50%	17%	33%

no doubt because those functions — stock options, executive hiring, succession planning — are best done centrally by almost any company, regardless of category.

Our model also predicted a strong home-office bias among Globals; however, the survey suggests that they are only slightly biased in that direction. Globals do handle five of the ten functions we examined from the home office, but tend to leave four of them to local or regional units (base salary, payroll, and technical/professional hiring were likely handled by local units, and bonuses by the regions). Again, stock options, succession planning, executive hiring, management development, and pensions are all handled centrally — but that is equally true of the less centralized Multinational companies.

... companies are not as far along the development curve as we had thought they would be or as they themselves imagined.

Figure 20. Analysis of HR Service Areas in Surveyed Corporations. (*continued*)

Executive Hiring	Home	Region	Local
Multinational	62%	38%	0%
International	72%	14%	14%
Global	78%	22%	0%
Transnational	66%	34%	0%

Mgmt Development	Home	Region	Local
Multinational	46%	39%	15%
International	0%	57%	43%
Global	44%	22%	34%
Transnational	66%	34%	0%

Tech/Prof Hiring	Home	Region	Local
Multinational	0%	39%	61%
International	0%	43%	57%
Global	34%	11%	55%
Transnational	0%	50%	50%

Tech/Prof Training	Home	Region	Local
Multinational	8%	39%	53%
International	33%	33%	44%
Global	11%	0%	89%
Transnational	0%	83%	17%

Payroll	Home	Region	Local
Multinational	0%	15%	85%
International	14%	14%	72%
Global	22%	0%	78%
Transnational	0%	34%	66%

■ *Implications and Conclusions*

The basic conclusion from our research is that companies are not as far along the development curve as we had thought they would be or as they themselves imagined. This is not necessarily negative: presumably companies are using a model that best fits their business needs.

Another finding was that most functions are performed on the level that suits them best. For example, succession planning and executive hiring are done by the home office; hiring, training, and payroll are performed locally; "face- to- face HR" and "HR as the business partner" functions are being done locally. We believe that these "high touch" activities should be close to the client. The companies we surveyed agree.

Because certain functions inherently call for local or international handling, the four organizational models were not as differentiated as we expected in

Figure 21. Comparison of HR Service Areas in Surveyed Corporations.

HR Service Area	Multinational (majority)	Global (majority)	International (majority)	Transnational (majority)	Overall Percentages
Base Salary	Local	Local	Local	Local	Local 54%
Bonus	Home office	Regional	Home office	Home office	
Stock	Home office	Home office	Home office	Home office	Home 89%
Pension	Local	Home office	Local	Local	
Succession Planning	Home office	Home office	Home office	Home office	Home 65%
Executive Hiring	Home office	Home office	Home office	Home office	Home 57%
Management Development	Home office	Home office	Regional	Home office	
Technical/Prof Hiring	Local	Local	Local	Local	Local 60%
Technical/Prof Training	Local	Local	Local	Regional	Local 51%
Payroll	Local	Local	Local	Local	Local 77%
SUMMARY	5 home, 5 local	5 home, 4 local, 1 regional	4 home, 4 local, 2 regional	5 home, 4 local, 1 regional	
	Bi-polar	**Slightly skewed Home**	**Balanced**	**Slightly skewed Home**	

their apportionment of local and international control. Future work should focus on more detailed questioning in this area to ascertain the differences.

▶ **Areas for Future Growth.** One surprise for us was that very few functions are performed regionally. Regional control may represent an area for future growth, as greater efficiencies and increased responsiveness may be made possible by regional control of some functions. A lack of sufficient regional staff may be one reason why companies have not taken advantage of what regional control might offer.

Current levels of technological sophistication may also be holding back the globalization of some functions. For example, few global payroll products are yet available on the market. Perhaps new versions of PeopleSoft, SAP and other products will allow more functions to be handled on regional or global levels.

With the increase in globalization, we believe that more and more companies will adopt the Transnational model. This new model strikes an effective balance between the conflicting demands facing worldwide organizations, such as the complexity of inter-organizational relationships, the dissolving of corporate boundaries, and the growth in the use of the Internet. For addressing these trends, the Transnational model, with its balance between central and local control, is especially effective.

■ Keys for Success

So how do you go about globalizing your HRIS? We recommend that you consider the following points:

➤ Decide function-by-function and task-by-task where each activity should be performed. Activities should be distributed across all three levels: global, regional, and local. This is not an all-or-nothing activity.

➤ Push those functions toward global implementation that demand efficiencies and not face-time. When a function demands face-to-face responsiveness, push it toward local implementation. And when neither approach is clear, look to knowledge sharing and seek out best practices.

➤ Put yourself in the shoes of those on the other side — those receiving instructions about the HRIS. If you ask front-line staff whether HR adds value to their activity, the local HR person receives strong support, the regional office minimal value, and home headquarters none whatsoever. Data on such reports hasn't changed in 25 years. In trying to win local support, then, bear in mind that units are unlikely to view corporate HR as a friend. Winning buy-in is always crucial.

➤ Make decision-making part of the mainstream of the organization and obtain buy-in by getting input and involvement from those who will be implementing the decisions. Instead of making all decisions at headquarters, involve people from across the organization by setting up annual strategic conferences, quarterly theme meetings, ad hoc development committees, Internet chat rooms, etc.

➤ Make sure that your technology is first-rate and not holding you back. Most of the companies we surveyed would agree that technology is a restraining factor today. Technology is not a be-all and end-all: it is an enabler, and we need to make sure it is not getting in our way or pursued for its own sake.

➤ Preserve cultural differences and value diversity. International diversity is one of the main values brought by globalization. Letting such diversity flourish produces the best results for the entire organization.

➤ Develop global thinking and relationships. Get out of the office and travel. You won't really be able to appreciate best practices and bring them into the organization unless you experience them directly. Even a short international assignment can be an eye-opener.

➤ Get and stay connected to the business, as well as to the HR and IT functions — at multiple levels in the organization. We recommend that you establish "three-by-three relationships" in your organization: that is, develop at least three relationships horizontally across the organization (in, say, HR, Payroll, and Finance) and also three relationships vertically, from analysts to managers to executive management. Unless you have a broad cross-section of support, your focus will be too narrow and your influence on the organization will be limited.

➤ Develop standards and consistency. Given the communication barriers that exist between national cultures, the potential for miscommunication is enormous. You need to define terms so that they mean the same thing to everyone in your organization.

➤ Remember: "one size does not fit all"! There's never just one solution to a problem. To find the best solution for your situation, you have to look at where you are on the development curve and what type of systems your people are willing to accept. You can't force change on people.[8]

➤ Finally, provide the connectivity and be the "glue" in your organization. As HR professionals, we must assume the leadership role.

Karen V. Beaman is division vice president and general manager for ADP Professional Services (also known as AGConsulting), a global HR/Payroll consultancy focused on providing strategic planning, best practice innovation, and system implementation services to Global Fortune 500 corporations. Previously based in Paris, France, she was responsible for building and leading ADP's professional services business in Europe and for launching the company's professional services in Latin America. Beaman has more than 20 years of experience with information systems and human resource management specifically in the development, integration, and management of enterprise-wide HR systems. She has been responsible for all aspects of the business, including strategic planning, international business development, sales and marketing, product and services development, client delivery and customer satisfaction, administration, recruiting, hiring, training, and staffing. Beaman has degrees from Old Dominion and Georgetown Universities and was promoted to Ph.D. candidate in Sociolinguistics and Historical and Computational Linguistics. She is an internationally recognized speaker and has published works in the fields of both Linguistics and HRIS. She is currently the editor-in-chief of the IHRIM Journal, past-chair of the IHRIM.link magazine Editorial Committee, and a former member of the IHRIM Board of Directors. She can be reached at **Karen_Beaman@adp.com**.

Alfred J. Walker, Senior Fellow at Towers Perrin, is the author of the best-selling book, Handbook of Human Resource Information Systems, *and renowned lecturer in the human resources field. Walker is an adjunct university professor, founder and board member of IHRIM and the Human Resources Planning Society. He is the global thought leader and leading technologist of the Technology Solutions practice at Towers Perrin, which includes optimizing the performance of the HR function. His newest book* Web-Based HR, *has just been published by McGraw-Hill. He also was a recipient of the* IHRIM Summit *Award in 1994. Walker can be reached at* **walkeaj@towers.com**.

■ Endnotes

1   See Karen Beaman, "'Europeanisation' and the New European Business Environment." *IHRIM Journal*, September 1999, Volume III, Number 3, pp. 44-50.

2   *Sturm und Drang* [or storm and stress] refers to a late 18th century German romantic literary movement whose members depicted in their work highly emotional individuals struggling against conventional society and generally accepted standards.

3   Stan Davis and Christopher Meyer, *Blur: The Speed of Change in the Connected Economy*, Little Brown and Company: 1999.

4   Christopher Bartlett and Sumantra Ghoshal, *Managing Across Borders: The Transnational Solution*, Second Edition, Harvard Business School Press: 1998.

5   See Karen Beaman, "On Globalizing HRIS: Moving to a Transnational Solution," *IHRIM.link*, December/January 2000, pp. 32-36.

6   See Alfred J. Walker, "The Future of the Human Resource Function," *IHRIM.link*, December 1999/January 2000, pp.14-19.

7   See Alfred J. Walker, "Transforming the Global Human Resources Function: A Technology Driven Model," *IHRIM Journal*, Volume 2, Issue 2, June 1998, pp. 11-17, and Alfred J. Walker, *Handbook of Human Resource*

Information Systems: Reshaping the Human Resource Function With Technology. McGraw-Hill: 1992.

8   Obviously, these trends will require a good deal of change management. The traditional change model starts with the formal structure and responsibilities of the organization. The interpersonal processes and relationships in the organizational are supposed to change as an inevitable result. These changes, in turn, are supposed to lead to change in the individual attitudes in the organization. But we think that a better approach to change models is the reverse. First, you change individual attitudes and mentalities in the organization. When these change, the interpersonal processes and relationships change as a result. On that basis, it becomes easier to change the formal structures and responsibilities. Why do we prefer this approach? Because if you install a new formal structure when the culture isn't ready you will encounter a lot of resistance and little acceptance. Also, it's very important when you look at implementing any kind of change that you ask what the need is. If the need — the pain — isn't there, then you won't have the support to go forward. Is the capacity there? Do people have the resources and cycles they need to change? And then, do they have the knowledge and tools they need to adapt? Addressing all these questions will lead to more effective change management.

Organizing Around the Global Customer

BY JAY GALBRAITH

Over the past decade companies have seen an increase in the strategic priority assigned to the customer dimension of the business. As a result, many companies are organizing around the customer in general, and the global customer in particular. Creating these customer-facing organizational units is a challenge because these companies still have structures based on business units, countries and functions. This article addresses the challenge of creating and adding a global customer dimension to the organization. The first section deals with the question of "Why is the customer dimension increasing in importance?" Then, "What capabilities will the company need to respond to the global customer priority?" And finally, "How do we build these new capabilities and integrate them with our existing capabilities?"

■ The Rise of the Customer Dimension

The trend in most industries is toward the increasing importance of the customer. The factors causing this increase vary with the industry, but either individually or collectively, all businesses are experiencing them. These factors are:

1. The globalization of the customer,

2. The preference of the customers for partnerships or relationships,

3. The customer's desire for solutions,

4. The rise of electronic commerce, and

5. The steady increase in the power of the buyer.

1. Globalization

Since 1985, the process of globalization has been driven by increasing amounts of foreign direct investment (FDI). The result is that more companies, and therefore more customers, have a direct presence in more countries. Often these global customers, who are a preferred customer in existing countries, object to receiving marginal treatment from a supplier's subsidiary upon entering a new country. These customers want a consistent and consistently high level of service in all countries where they buy from a supplier. Indeed, one supplier had a customer point out that the supplier had 37 sales forces calling on the customer with 37 different standards of service, which was unacceptable. So the global customer is creating pressure on suppliers to coordinate across countries and businesses to better serve this customer. This desire for cross-unit coordination can also be an advantage for the supplier. ABB was an early mover into many countries and Eastern Europe in particular. It now uses its extensive presence to host and provide services to its customers as they enter new countries where ABB is already present.

2. Customer Relationships

The pressure for coordination across existing structures is even greater when the customers want partnerships or relationships with their suppliers. Professional services firms are finding that clients want one or two global advertising agencies, auditors, cash management banking suppliers and outsourcers for information technology. In most industries, customers prefer fewer suppliers and establish closer, longer-term relationships with them. For suppliers, these global partnerships mean that they must coordinate all countries in which the customer desires integrated services.

3. Solutions

Many customers prefer solutions or systems instead of stand-alone products. To be sure, customers still order truckloads of desktops from computer manufacturers. However, they also are ordering trading rooms or call centers. At IBM, these solutions require the integration of multiple business units in multiple countries with multiple outside suppliers for the benefit of the customer. These solutions are not simply multiple stand-alone products that are bundled together and offered at a 10 percent discount. The customer-preferred solutions create value for the customers by packaging products and services in ways that the customers cannot easily do for themselves.

Solutions, therefore, require an in-depth knowledge of the customer and an ability to integrate product lines. In-depth customer knowledge is needed to identify the solutions that will be seen as valuable by the customer. Then the supplier will need the ability to coordinate multiple profit centers from both inside and outside of the company to create the

> *Solutions . . .*
> *require an in-depth knowledge*
> *of the customer and*
> *an ability to integrate*
> *product lines.*

value. Neither of these capabilities comes easily. Real estate agencies and banks have been searching for years for a mortgage solution for time-short homebuyers. Such a solution would combine the home loan, appraisal, title, title insurance, home insurance, etc., into a single, sign-once package. Most of us are still waiting.

In addition to creating a solution, suppliers are also trying to customize them. Many companies are becoming sophisticated at identifying the most profitable customers. But when everyone pursues the most profitable customers, they compete away the profits. One approach to holding on to valuable customers is to customize the solutions that the customer wants. Customization requires yet more in-depth knowledge of the customer and additional capability to integrate products and services into unique solutions.

4. Electronic Commerce

Another integrating force to focus on the customer is electronic commerce. When a company with a single brand uses its web site as its store front, it presents a single face to the customer. The web site should be designed around the customers' needs and not around the suppliers' product capabilities. The site should be designed to do business the way the customer wants to do business. In order to appear as a single company to the customer, the company needs to integrate its businesses, subsidiaries and functions and act like a single company.

Yet another integrating force is the management of interactivity with customers. Electronic connections with customers allow the company to recognize and remember each customer, to interact with them and remember more about them, and then to customize the company's offerings based on the knowledge of the customer. Most companies, however, have not mastered integrated customer interactions. Interactivity requires the management of dialogues and content across all media with which the company interacts with the customer — web site, e-mail, call center, salespersons, service representatives, and so on. The dialogue needs to be managed over time. The last contact with the customer needs to be remembered along with the last issue concerned and how it was resolved. The resolution needs to be recorded and then the next dialogue starts from there. All contacts and issues are to be remembered. The idea of interactivity is to collect and integrate all data across all functions, subsidiaries, and product lines in order to get a complete picture of each customer's value and needs. Only then can the company react as a single company and be seen by the customer as a single company.

5. Buyer Power

One of the main reasons that the factors mentioned above are taken seriously is that the power in the buyer-seller interaction has been moving to the buyer. In many industries, global competition and industry overcapacity has given buyers more choices and they are learning how to use them. Electronic commerce and information transparency have reduced seller knowledge advantages. So the competitive game has shifted to one of pleasing an increasingly more global, knowledgeable and powerful customer.

One of the ways that companies have responded is to increasingly organize around the customer. Whether it is global accounts, global customer teams or customer business units, the trend is to grow a customer dimension of the organization. The customer focus is a challenge because most companies are organized around product lines (called business units), countries and functions. The next section describes the capabilities needed to create a global customer dimension and the last section describes how a company actually added and then grew such a global customer dimension into customer profit centers.

■ Deliver the Company to the Customer

In order to manage the evolving global customer dimension, most companies are organizing around the customer. This organization requires three capabilities. These capabilities are intended to deliver the company to the customer. To be effective in organizing around the customer the company must:

1. Create a customer-centric capability,

2. Perfect a lateral coordination capability, and

3. Create a leadership mindset that says, "You compete with your organization."

■ Customer-Centric Capability

In order to create and customize solutions and appear as one company on a customer friendly web site, the company needs a customer-centric capability. This capability is often presented as a contrast to the product-centric capability. Figure 1 shows the management mindset, culture, and organizational features of a product-centric company.

A product-centric company is one that tries to find as many uses and customers as possible for its product. Sony and its Walkman are typical of such a company and product. Until recently business units at Sony were even called "Product Companies." As shown in the figure, the profit centers, processes, measures and human resource policies are all focused on creating great products. Taken together, these policies create a culture of product excellence. Many good companies have thrived under this business model like Hewlett Packard, Procter & Gamble, and Chase Manhattan Consumer Bank. There is nothing wrong with this model when customers want to choose the best product and integrate it themselves. But when customers want solutions and a customer-friendly web site, a customer-centric capability is needed in addition. A customer-centric capability is shown in Figure 2.

A customer-centric company tries to find as many products as possible for its customer. It is based on economies of scope and on turning scope into solutions valuable to the customer. The customer-centric company becomes an expert in the customer's business. It helps the customer become more effective or more competitive. And perhaps the most telling feature of a customer-centric company is that it is on the side of the buyer in the buyer-seller exchange. In or-

Figure 1. The Product-Centric Company.
1. Best Product for Customer
2. Value Through Cutting-Edge Products, Useful Features, New Applications
3. Divergent Thinking
    ➤ How Many Possible Uses of Product?
4. Manage Through Product Profit Centers, Product Reviews, Product Teams
5. Most Important Process: New Product Development
6. Measures
    ➤ Number of New Products
    ➤ Percent Revenue from Products less than two years old
    ➤ Market Share
7. New Product Culture — Open to New Ideas, Experimentation
8. Most Important Customer is Advanced Customer
9. Priority Setting Around Portfolio of Products
10. Highest Reward is Working on Next Most Challenging Product
11. Manage Creative People Through Challenges With a Deadline
12. Power to People Who Develop Products
13. On the Side of the Seller in a Transaction
14. Price to Market

Figure 2. The Customer-Centric Company.
1. Best Solution for Customer
2. Creates Value Through Customizing for Best Total Solution
3. Convergent Thinking
   ➤ What combination of products are best for this customer?
4. Organized by Customer Segments, Customer Teams, Customer P&Ls
5. Most Important process: Customer Relationships Management
6. Measures
   ➤ Customer Share of Most Valuable Customers
   ➤ Customer Satisfaction
   ➤ Lifetime Value of a Customer
   ➤ Customer Retention
7. Most Important Customer is Most Profitable, Loyal Customer
8. Priority Setting Around Portfolio of Customers — Customer Profitability
9. Power to People with In-Depth Knowledge of Customer's Business
10. Personalized Packages of Service, Support, Education, Consulting
11. On the Side of the Buyer in a Transaction
12. Price to Value and Risk Share

der to stay on the customer's side Amazon.com does not accept advertising from sellers. On its new e-Services web site, the United Bank of Switzerland will offer competitive products, even those of Credit Suisse. Thus, a customer-centric company will recommend the best product for a customer, even a competitor's product, in order to earn the trust of the customer. The customer-centric company then sees these customer relationships as assets to be managed. The business model of Amazon.com and AOL has evolved to the point where they are now selling access to their customer base. In order to appear on Amazon's or AOL's web site, a vendor must qualify, then pay a fee and/or give Amazon some of its equity in order to access Amazon's 29 million proven Internet shoppers.

The argument above has painted the extremes of product and customer centricity. Not every company will need the extreme version of customer centricity. The main point is that in most businesses today, the forces of the business are requiring a more customer-centric orientation. This orientation is achieved by creating organizational units for global customers or customer segments and the leadership mindsets to support them. In the next section, a variety of these global customer organizations are described.

■ *Lateral Networking Capability*

In order to create multi-product solutions for global customers, a company must work through lateral networks. A simple company with a few local customers selling a single product can work through a functional hierarchy. But a company with multiple product lines in multiple countries using multiple functions must work less through hierarchy and manage more through networks. Indeed, a company needs a network for each strategically-important dimension. Some companies like General Electric have organized around global product lines called Business Units. They have created country and functional networks to coordinate across product lines. Other companies like Nestlé have organized around country and regional profit centers. They have created product (called Strategic Business Units) and functional networks to coordinate across the geographical structure. With the rise in importance of the customer dimension, there is now a need for a global customer network across the product lines, countries and functions.

The organization design decision is to match the right kind of network with the strategic importance of the customer dimension. That is, there are different kinds of networks. Some are informal while others are formal with varying degrees of strength. These formal networks vary in their power and their cost to coordinate across the other dimensions. A list of these networks is shown below. The list is ordered so that the simplest, cheapest, and easiest to use are listed first. The farther down the list a company goes, the more powerful are the networks, and the more costly and difficult it is to employ them. The implication is that the designers should start at the top of the list and proceed down the list until a network is found that matches the coordination requirements of the customer dimension for their business.

➤ **List of Networks:**

1. Informal or Voluntary Networks

2. Formal Teams

3. Coordinator for the Network

4. Matrix Across the Other Dimensions

5. Separate Customer Line Organization

1. Informal or Voluntary Networks

Informal or voluntary networks form naturally in all organizations. Management, however, can initiate them and then let them proceed under their own energy. Nestlé is an example of such informal networks that have formed around global customers. Unlike P&G, Nestlé has not strategically focused on the cross-border customers like Carrefour or Wal-Mart. However, country managers and country account managers for Wal-Mart routinely exchange information and ideas about Wal-Mart on an informal basis. This informal exchange was judged to be sufficient until the Internet allowed more formal communication. Now the country manager in the country of the headquarters of the global customer maintains a database about that customer and issues e-mails and updates about the customer. Anyone dealing with the customer can add information and ideas. But while the communication has formalized, the coordination is still informal. Each country treats the information as an input and then acts in the best interest of its product lines and country P&L.

The formal communication among all people interacting with customers is the approach taken by companies wanting to show one face to the customer. Each contact is recorded and entered into a database. Others can see this running record when they deal with the customer. Each person then deals with the customer according to their function but records all information to be used across functions.

2. Formal Teams

Formal teams are the next level of strength that can be applied to a customer network. Usually this step is taken when a customer desires more than informal coordination. For example, global or key account teams are formed by appointing all the sales and account representatives serving a customer to an account team for that customer. These representatives from all product lines and all countries exchange information like the Nestlé informal networks. But they also meet regularly, prepare an account plan, and agree upon customer specific goals. ABB started with teams for a few accounts and expanded them to over 50 within a few years for those customers who wanted this coordinated service. The account manager in the customer's home country usually leads the team, which consists of a few core members and a larger extended team to encompass the sales people from all of the customer's locations.

The customer teams can be strengthened and assume more activities when customers want partnerships along the supply chain. Wal-Mart and P&G are an example. P&G initially formed a team of its sales people representing all products that P&G provided to Wal-Mart. The team was expanded to include manufacturing, distribution, marketing, information technology and finance. This team of about 80 people from various functions from all product lines worked to synchronize the product and order flow from P&G factories to Wal-Mart warehouses to minimize inventories and cut cycle times. Today, as Wal-Mart expands globally, this team consists of 450 people from different functions, product lines and countries.

Degussa Automotive Catalysts takes the team one step further and includes R&D participation. The Degussa sales people coordinate across borders to serve Daimler Chrysler like ABB serves its customers. It also partners along the supply chain to synchronize their production with the Daimler-Chrysler assembly lines like P&G and Wal-Mart. But its engineers also determine Daimler Chrysler's new product needs and coordinate with them on creating new catalysts for new automotive platforms. Degussa creates customer-specific, platform-specific catalysts for exhaust emissions.

The next step to escalate the global customer dimension to a more powerful position is to create a coordinator for key accounts.

So these formal customer networks can vary from a few key account teams for sales people, to supply chain partnership teams of sales, logistics and other functional people to new product development teams that include all functions including the various engineering functions. For some companies like Degussa, this customer team organization is sufficient to meet the needs of its most important customer. Other companies like Citibank chose to take a further step of creating a full-time coordinator to manage all customer team activities.

3. Network Coordinator

The next step to escalate the global customer dimension to a more powerful position is to create a coordinator for key accounts. When companies like ABB create 50 or more teams and customers want still more coordination from a supplier, the Key Account or Global Account coordinator role is a useful addition to the informal networks and formal customer teams. The coordinator provides two new factors.

First, the coordinator becomes a voice for the global customer on the management team. These teams usually consist of managers of product lines, geographies and functions. The coordinator gets the leadership thinking in terms of a portfolio of customers, customer priorities and customer-centricity. Customer teams can also appeal to the coordinator in resolving conflicts.

The second task of the coordinator is to build and manage the infrastructure to support customer teams. The formal communications were mentioned earlier. The coordinator would assume the role of managing customer information systems and communications across customer teams. They usually create training programs for management and team members on the role and operation of key accounts. Many coordinators create a common planning system for customer plans. If 50 customer teams are creating plans, they are likely to create 50 planning formats. The coordinator agrees on a single common format.

Another key addition to the infrastructure is a global customer accounting system leading to customer P&Ls. Customer profitability is a key measure in setting customer priorities. In addition, asymmetries in costs and revenues always occur across geographies. That is, the customer account manager and team in the customer's home country put in extra efforts to make a sale to their customer. Often the initiative is successful but the customer's first purchases are for its subsidiaries in other countries. Thus, the costs are incurred in the home country and revenues are booked in other countries. A global accounting system for customers can identify these asymmetries and management can correct for them.

All of these infrastructure additions can be combined in the planning process. The countries and product lines can then set customer specific goals for key accounts. Then customer teams, countries and product lines will pursue an aligned set of goals.

4. Matrix Organization

The next step to enhance the power base of the global customer dimension is to form customer or customer segment dedicated units within countries and product lines and report them to the customer coordinator. The assumption is that the customer dimension has attained a strategic importance equal to the countries and/or business units. This importance is expressed by making the customer organization an equal partner in the decision-making process. In countries where the company may not control 100 percent of the equity, joint ventures to serve multi-national clients are often created between the parent company and the local subsidiary.

5. Separate Customer Organization

A final step is to create a separate customer-facing structure by gathering all dedicated customer-specific resources from the product lines, countries and functions. Companies serving the automotive customer, like Johnson Controls, have formed Customer Business Units. Companies like IBM formed customer segment profit centers by gathering all relationship managers into industry groups. These global industry groups call on product profit centers for additional staffing as the opportunities require. These separate customer-facing units are the most powerful form and most customer-centric form of organizing around the customer.

In summary, there are five major steps from which an organization designer can choose in implementing a customer-centric orientation. A step-by-step approach is probably best at implementing and building the customer-centric capability. The designer may stop on any of the steps when sufficient customer centricity has been built to match the strength of the five customer forces described in the first section of this article.

■ Organization as Competitive Advantage

The third factor needed to successfully deliver the company to the customer is a mindset among the leadership that they are competing with their organization. That is, the company's ability to deliver value to global customers desiring solutions depends on the company's organization to assemble and implement a customer-centric dimension across the existing business unit, country and functional organizations. Delivering value to today's customer means managing the four dimensions of organization.

The creation of a four-dimensional organization runs counter to most current mindsets. Today the preference is to "keep it simple" and create simple, autonomous business units that control their resources and are accountable for their performance.

We also believe in keeping it simple, but with the twist that we want to "keep it simple for the customer." Organizations should be designed to do business the way that the customer wants to do business. And how do the customers want to do business? They want seamless integration across functions. They want solutions that are seamlessly integrated across the products of multiple business units and countries. This integration is difficult. Thus, keeping it simple for the customer makes it difficult for management. But overcoming this difficulty is a real source of competitive advantage. Most companies cannot easily integrate their profit centers in the service of the customer. And since many customers see value in this integration, competitive advantage comes from creating this value that others cannot match. Mastering the management of four dimensions is just such an advantage.

When most people say, "keep it simple," they mean keep it simple for management. That kind of simplicity then means making it difficult for the customer. It is then up to the customer or a third party to do the integrating and capture the value of serving the customer. Keeping it simple for management leaves money on the table for more complex organizations to capture.

The management of Degussa Auto Catalysts recognized that their organization was their secret weapon. They partnered with their customers on developing new engines and new catalysts. They formed global customer teams across functions and countries. They created global customer profit and loss measurement systems. The members of the Executive Committee sat on the teams. Issues were quickly escalated and resolved since one level separated the teams and the leadership. They recognized that the link between R&D (research and development) and manufacturing was critical. They created an Applied Technology Group, organized by customer, to bridge the gap. They exchanged people across the manufacturing/R&D interface. They co-located the two units. They sponsored workshops to improve the process of working together. These workshops always had an overnight feature that allowed people to get to know one another and build interpersonal networks. Management rewarded those people who were effective in this environment and removed those who fought it. In short, Degussa management knew that they were competing with their organization as well as their technology.

In summary, it takes a customer-centric capability, a lateral networking capability, and a leadership that sees and builds its organization as a source of advantage in order to deliver the company to the global customer. But how does one build these capabilities if the company does not possess them today? In short, the capabilities are built by moving down the list of lateral coordination mechanisms. The next section traces the steps of Citibank's Global Relationship Bank.

■ Building a Customer Dimension

In 1984, Citibank's commercial banking business was examining its ability to serve its multinational clients. The informal contacts between relationship managers in different countries were insufficient to deliver service to these customers. After some debate they resurrected the World Corporation Group (WCG) to serve as a coordinating role and created a few global account teams for a few interested customers.

After a couple of years, the teams expanded from a few to a few hundred. For each team, there was a leader, a Principal Account Manager (PAM), from the customer's home country. In other countries where the customer wanted service, there was a Subsidiary Account Manager (SAM). The WCG trained all of these teams. So in several years thousands of people were trained in customer relationships. The Nestlé team alone was 60 people. The WCG also started recruiting and training the PAMs. These account managers usually stayed in the WCG.

The WCG trained top management in managing a portfolio of customers. They also developed a customer focused planning system and measures of customer profitability and share of the customer's financial spending. They developed customer P&Ls. Then in 1995, they led a strategy review. In that review, Citibank articulated its customer first strategy. Before, the priorities were country first, product second and customer third. After 1995, the priorities were customer first, product second and country third (in the developed world). The strategy recognized that Citi was a bank (took deposits and made loans in local currencies) in over 100 countries. Their nearest competitor was a bank in only 43 countries. Citi had an unmatchable advantage of global presence from which to serve the global customer. All it had to do was to get 100 country managers to work together.

So in 1995, Citibank created a global customer profit center organization. It eliminated country P&Ls in the developed world and grouped 1,300 customers into industry segments. It focused on delivering global products, foreign exchange and cash management, to the global customer. It stopped serving domestic-only customers.

Today, this Global Relationship Bank serves over 1,700 customers. It is delivering the product-centric capabilities of Salomon, Schroeders, Smith Barney to its global customers through its customer-centric Global Relationship Bank. The Financial Times (July 20, 2000, p. 18) suggests that the synergies of the investment banking products with the global customer relationships have earned a place for Citigroup among the bulge bracket firms of Goldman Sachs, Morgan Stanley and Merrill Lynch. Citi's profits are higher and it is trading at an earnings multiple of 19 versus 13 to 17 for the others. So, from a base of informal contacts in 1985, Citi built a customer-centric and lateral capability to deliver the bank to the customer anywhere in the world.

An internationally recognized expert on organization design, Jay Galbraith helps major global corporations create capability for competing in the next century. His work focuses on the areas of organizational design, change, and development; strategy and organization at the corporate business unit and international levels; and international partnering arrangements including joint ventures and network-type organizations. He is currently examining organizational units that are rapidly re-configurable to suit quickly changing demands of customers and markets across multinational boundaries. His most recent book, Designing the Global Corporation, *describes how leading multinational corporations deal with the demands of their increasingly global customers to provide solutions, not just products. Galbraith is Professor Emeritus at the International Institute for Management Development (IMD) in Lausanne, Switzerland. He is also a Senior Research Scientist at the Center for Effective Organizations at the University of Southern California. He can be reached at* **SashaGAL@aol.com**.

■ References

This article is based on the author's most recent book, *Designing the Global Corporation*, San Francisco: Jossey-Bass, 2000.

Reprinted from the *IHRIM Journal*, Volume V, Number 4, November 2001, pp. 12-17.

Part Two:
Global Strategy and Planning

"*Most companies are trying to pursue third-generation strategies, using second-generation organizations, staffed with first-generation human resources.*"

—Christopher Bartlett

••••••••

Anyone who picks up this book recognizes that 21st-century business is moving towards increasing globalization. The trend is clear enough, but recognizing it brings up some difficult questions — and the never-ending challenge on how to globalize one's own organization most effectively.

Nowhere is this challenge more daunting than in HR. Most corporate systems and policies — not to mention our own orientation/mindset — have become, in the boundaryless era, irrelevant or even counterproductive to the effective management of people. This industrial-era legacy is deeply ingrained. Its inertial mass can handicap HR.

Fortunately, the new approaches that HR needs to meet the challenge of change have begun to emerge. The following chapters concern themselves with developing a successful strategy for global HR and HR systems, and particularly with the crucial first step of planning.

Visions
of the Future —
Virtual Global HR
Organization

BY IAN RUDDLE AND JEFF ALDERTON

Managing the Human Resource (HR) function is more complicated today than it has been in the past. Global expansion, mergers and acquisitions, and changing regulatory requirements, all engender a situation where both enormous opportunity and monetary risk abound. As a result, a company's human resources should be managed as aggressively as its other enterprise assets and carefully positioned to take advantage of changing economic conditions.

All too often, however, global HR professionals find their existing people, processes, and technology cannot meet the increased demand for workforce management, operational effectiveness, or business performance criteria measurement. Most organizations do not know who their best revenue generation staff are, which senior employees are the best overall performers, or whether their current workforce strategies are effective in response to predicted market conditions.

The world-class company in the next millennium will be the best manager of its main assets — the people. The company will know where their employees are located, who are their best performers, where the best skill matches are for key positions, who has the highest and lowest retention rates, who has the best balanced health and welfare programs, and where are the best places to work — making it easy and effective for managers to manage their people on a global basis.

Most global HR technology solutions do not keep a global view of skills and competencies, and less than 20 percent of corporations have actively invested in true performance management programs to address the anticipated skilled labor shortage over the next five years. Many corporate human resource organizational structures are still based on the decentralized administration model of the 1980s. Fewer than five percent of corporations have invested in the recommended shared services model with the re-engineered HR organization emphasizing a "customer service" approach — referred to as the "2000" model, and currently recognized as the best practice human resource organization model.

Some of the challenges seen today:

➤ **Merger or acquisition is affecting 40 percent of U.S. firms business in some way**
• Either the company, its major supplier or customer is under a merger or being acquired.
• Any disruption in business flow has an effect on the human assets.
• HR services, support infrastructure and systems must be nimble.

➤ **Workforce demographics are shifting**
• Labor demand will outpace labor supply by eight percent through 2005, increasing competition for skilled workers.
• Targeted workforce (16-34 year olds) will become a shrinking percentage of the total population.
• Workforce diversity will continue to increase.

➤ **The process of recruiting and selecting candidates has moved to the Internet**
The Internet is becoming a much more cost-effective and convenient alternative for recruiting.
• Seventy-nine percent of companies now use the Internet to recruit new hires, 50 percent of companies employ workers recruited via the Internet, and 45 percent of Fortune Global 500 companies recruit on the Internet.
• There will be 25,000 job-posting sites available and 16 million résumés on the Web by 2002.
• US$1.7 billion will be spent on online recruitment by 2003, 20 percent of the print classified ad budgets for recruitment will be spent online in 2003.
• Twenty days average reduction in hiring cycle.

➤ **Demand for knowledge management increasing**
Traditional classroom training is rapidly becoming archaic. Online learning will become standard in the next few years:
• Distance learning ranked as a key business priority in a survey of 300 IT executives.
• Global instruction can be delivered around the clock, without travel costs. Employers will have to deliver an intellectually stimulating e-learning environment to retain the best employees.

- Companies are also developing self-service e-learning initiatives aimed at customers and the public.
- International Data Corporation says that the U.S. market for web-based training will exceed US$6 billion by 2002.

➤ Compensation plans must be nimble with clear ties to performance

Compensation plans must be even more nimble. The dot-com syndrome has forced compensation to be viewed with much wider parameters:

- A total comp viewpoint is essential for effective staff management.
- Tying comp clearly to performance increases buy-in from all levels of staff.
- The key players in the organization should be reviewed from a global aspect.

With the overall skill level of the labor force dropping, companies with a high/low income workforce need to manage their retention and benefits programs far more aggressively.

The global HR function must demonstrate that it is strategic in thought, knowledgeable in intellectual business understanding and nimble in support structure. It must demonstrate sensitivity to local cultures while striving to provide the most effective level of service — just as for any business function.

■ *Developing the Virtual HR Vision and Strategy*

Developing and maintaining a vision for the company is one of the primary functions of the corporate human resource professional — fewer than five percent of companies have a published vision for their human resource group. The human resources vision and strategy is built in alignment with business strategy and operational infrastructure. The primary outcomes of a human resources strategy are:

➤ Identification of HR strategic services to be provided to the organization,

➤ Identification of HR administrative services that must be provided to the organization,

➤ Design and implementation of the HR service delivery model through which human resources services are provided to the organization, and

➤ Design and implementation of enablement technology infrastructure.

The HR service delivery model is developed with an understanding of HR strategic services and HR administrative services. Figure 1 identifies the typical components of vision and strategy model. It is important to note that the model may be used to develop a local or global strategy. Consulting firms will typically recommend between four to 10 weeks be spent on developing a combined vision and strategy assessment that would be used to base business development investments. It is typical that a shorter period of time will only give a thumbnail sketch of the general goals and will contain basic statistics related to administrative needs. If more time is spent, the analysis may be going too deep for the purpose of setting vision and strategy.

One of the most confusing issues at this stage is how much information is needed to develop a business case to support transformation investment. Generally, the vision and strategy analysis will generate directional information supporting the value of the HR business plan and its corresponding support infrastructure. The value case will highlight areas of direct, opportunity and strategic value cost savings along with a broad estimate of time, resources and infrastructure. The main focus is to outline the business reasoning with the strategic and opportunity items supporting growth, lost market share and risk issues. For many companies this will be sufficient to support the business investment. Further detailed analysis would need to be done to develop return on investment (ROI) calculations.

Measuring or justifying the value of the HR organization, its people, and its support technology has traditionally been a difficult exercise for a number of reasons. Any service-related business has few value measurements, except for customer satisfaction and price acceptance. Using these attributes to define the "right level" of HR service is a new concept and is still in the process of being generally accepted in the marketplace. Changing an enterprise information HR system requires a major effort, generally involving a multi-million dollar investment — in software, hardware, and in project resources to deliver the solution. Building a business case for this investment is a challenge. The presence of a value case to support a major business or technology transformation is critical in gaining approval for the investment.

One of the most confusing issues at this stage is how much information is needed to develop a business case to support transformation investment.

Even in today's market, it is estimated that over 45 percent of the firms undertaking a global HR transformation initiative gain board approval for their initiative with the starting details from a value case rather than a formal ROI. The primary driver is the accepted need for the transformation to meet prevailing market and environmental conditions.

Figure 1. Sample Vision and Strategy Model.

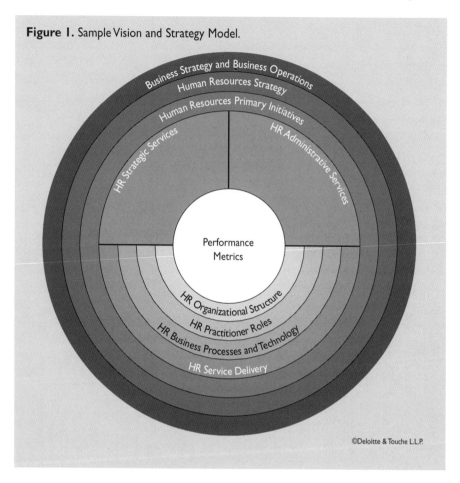

©Deloitte & Touche L.L.P.

■ Developing the Virtual HR Model

A world class global HR organization should provide consultation to the employees on human resource issues. It should be operated as a business unto itself, incorporating goals, cost management and strategy among its roles and responsibilities.

HR is responsible for providing effective and efficient people-based programs, processes and technology to the organization. The most effective HR organization would exhibit the following "modus operandi:"

➤ **Key business leaders and employees share accountability for HR transformation** — Strategic HR does not exist in a functional silo isolated from the rest of the organization.

➤ **HR measurably tracks the organization's progress** — The organization's people-based programs, processes and technology are strategically integrated to maximize business results.

➤ **The HR administrative and compliance requirements are conducted at minimal cost** — HR designs and delivers programs to minimize cost and maximize potential value. Administration and compliance generally require the most effort for the least value while business service centers provide the most effective customer service support.

➤ **Strategic Outsourcing of non-core tasks will reduce administration complexity and (sometimes) save costs** — Several administrative functions of HR are regular candidates for outsourcing to reduce costs and/or to perform tasks where internal skills do not exist.

In order to effectively develop the HR vision and strategy, the proposed services need to be carefully defined from a functional aspect. They must also be defined in relation to one another for the purposes of determining the most effective organization staffing structure.

Over the past decade the role of services included in the HR portfolio has expanded to include such items as expense reimbursement, payroll administration, sales compensation administration, expatriate administration and attendance tracking. To effectively analyze these new and traditional functions, a generic model of the major service groupings is needed.Figure 2 shows a sample Virtual Service Delivery Model that has been effectively used at several

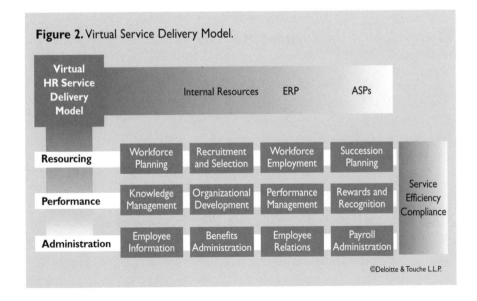

Figure 2. Virtual Service Delivery Model.

©Deloitte & Touche L.L.P.

global organizations to prioritize their global HR services. This model can be used to achieve several objectives:

➤ Facilitate HR service strategy sessions,
➤ Determine service priorities to business alignment,
➤ Determine non-strategic services for consideration of outsourcing, and
➤ Facilitate organizational structure development around service linkages.

The model reflects the latest thinking in the focus on resourcing and performance management as opposed to administration activities. One of the general complaints of the business organizations of the typical HR services is that much of their time (and budget) is spent on administrivia. The model above has been used with several organizations to drive value case discussions on the costs/benefits of making strategic changes to the focus and support for the resourcing and performance groupings.

So, what about strategic outsourcing? Once the model has been used to analyze and determine the priority functions, the discussion extends into the criticality of the function to the core business and the risks associated with having a professional third party undertake the administration of the function. It should be noted that the ultimate management and accountability of the function cannot be outsourced — this must remain within the organization — a fact that many organizations forget.

Figure 3, the Virtual Service Delivery Model with Strategic Outsource Opportunities, shows where strategic outsourcing has played a role for some global organizations. There are some minor components of workforce planning and

Figure 3. Virtual Service Delivery Model — Strategic Outsource Opportunities.

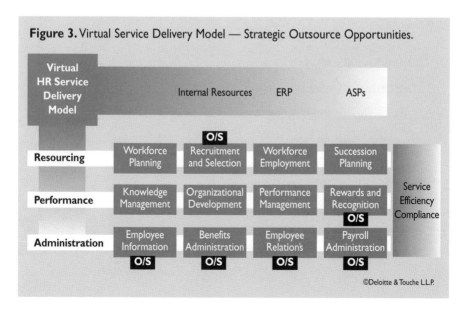

©Deloitte & Touche L.L.P.

deployment that can be outsourced, but these are typically handled in house. In addition, the business services organization and IT infrastructure are also popular candidates for consideration for outsourcing.

■ Business Services Model

One of the key strategies employed in a virtual global HR organization is the appropriate use of a business services concept, sometimes referred to as a shared-services model. The concept builds on the following assumptions:

➤ The value of the human resource organization is to help attract and retain talent not administer it;

➤ The primary function of the HR generalist is to be a consultant to their line business partner. There is a need for experts in human resource policy and procedures, but not in every position;

➤ The business of HR administration is similar to a customer service business. Trained administrative staff or web-based information systems may handle the majority of questions from employees; and

➤ The technology support investment should be appropriate for an integrated, global system.

The technology support investment should be appropriate for an integrated, global system.

Global organizations will consider several regional business service centers to accommodate language and time zone differences; the typical locations would be U.S. (for Americas — North and South), Brussels or London (for Europe) and Singapore (ASPAC).

The typical HR Services model incorporates the three primary organizations with a fourth grouping if outsourcing is implemented:

➤ **Centers of Excellence (COEs):** By organizing around a defined set of delivery platforms, relative to areas of deep expertise, the COEs are in a position to provide more focused HR expertise to strategic business partners and the organization as a whole. They are generally part of the strategic HR organization.

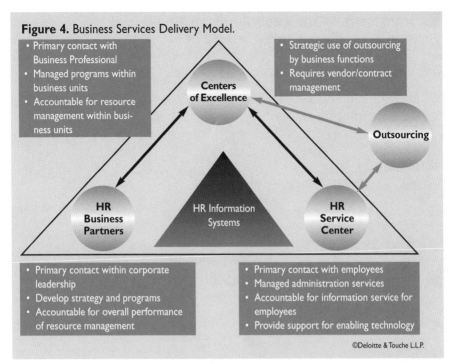

Figure 4. Business Services Delivery Model.

- Primary contact with Business Professional
- Managed programs within business units
- Accountable for resource management within business units

Centers of Excellence

- Strategic use of outsourcing by business functions
- Requires vendor/contract management

Outsourcing

HR Business Partners

HR Information Systems

HR Service Center

- Primary contact within corporate leadership
- Develop strategy and programs
- Accountable for overall performance of resource management

- Primary contact with employees
- Managed administration services
- Accountable for information service for employees
- Provide support for enabling technology

©Deloitte & Touche L.L.P.

➤ **Business Partners:** By organizing around a defined set of delivery platforms, strategic business partners are in a position to provide more strategic HR expertise within the context of the specific line of business' needs, working in partnership with the line management. These are the traditional HR Generalists now acting more in a consulting capacity.

➤ **HR Service Center:** The HR Service Center must satisfactorily respond to employee inquiries and process HR transactions in order to significantly reduce strategic business partner and COE involvement in administratively based employee inquiries (e.g., benefits, payroll, data maintenance). These are a combination of the HR administrators, payroll/time administrators, and customer service/help- desk operators blended into one organizational hierarchy.

➤ **Outsourcing:** The strategic outsourcing of non-core competency functions and/ or those that are more efficiently delivered by the third party allows the HR function to improve HR service delivery, while reallocating resources to more value-added activities. Maybe one, or more likely, a combination of several organizations.

■ Transforming the Global HR Strategy to Operational Stability

Once the global HR strategy has been identified, the next step is to develop the implementation plan. The goal is to reach operational stability where the costs of supporting the HR services and organization have been optimized.

Figure 5 shows a business transformation model that provides a very effective structure to implement an HR strategy within the global organization. It has been tried and tested on several global organizations who have sucessfully transformed their global HR organizations and support operations.

■ What do Successful Global firms have in Common?

➤ **A Visionary HR Leader** — The leader of the HR function needs to be a visionary for people development with a focus on the competencies required to meet market needs — and above all, a business professional.

➤ **Understanding of Customer Service Principles** — The HR function is in the customer-service business but with several very different and self-centered

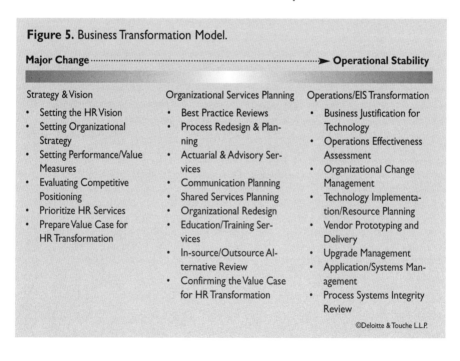

Figure 5. Business Transformation Model.

Major Change ⋯⋯⋯⋯⋯⋯⋯⋯⋯⋯⋯⋯⋯⋯⋯⋯⋯⋯⋯⋯➤ **Operational Stability**

Strategy & Vision	Organizational Services Planning	Operations/EIS Transformation
• Setting the HR Vision	• Best Practice Reviews	• Business Justification for Technology
• Setting Organizational Strategy	• Process Redesign & Planning	• Operations Effectiveness Assessment
• Setting Performance/Value Measures	• Actuarial & Advisory Services	• Organizational Change Management
• Evaluating Competitive Positioning	• Communication Planning	• Technology Implementation/Resource Planning
• Prioritize HR Services	• Shared Services Planning	• Vendor Prototyping and Delivery
• Prepare Value Case for HR Transformation	• Organizational Redesign	• Upgrade Management
	• Education/Training Services	• Application/Systems Management
	• In-source/Outsource Alternative Review	• Process Systems Integrity Review
	• Confirming the Value Case for HR Transformation	

©Deloitte & Touche L.L.P.

audiences: executives, business management and employees. They need to be organized on a global basis to fully leverage process and technology.

➤ **A Grasp of Strategic Outsourcing Concepts** — All or nothing doesn't work in this day and age.

➤ **An HR Vision and Strategy** — One that's built on the projected business needs. Sounds simple — does your organization have one?

Ian Ruddle is a Principal with Deloitte Consulting, New York, Technology Competency group where he is the deputy leader of the Human Resource Dynamics technology competency group in the U.S.A., and holds direct management responsibility for the U.S. East region practice. For more than 30 years he has provided consulting services in the information technology arena, primarily focused on global enterprise systems solutions with full service coverage from strategic technology advisory services, benchmarking, re-engineering through to business strategy development, systems planning and delivery. He has an extensive track record of Enterprise IT systems delivery in the global marketplace including the U.S., Europe and Asia. He has more than 11 years experience with client/server based ERP application suites and has been responsible for more than 15 enterprise implementations using PeopleSoft, Oracle and SAP packages. His multi-year experience with information systems and networking architecture in the corporate environment has allowed him to provide a substantial contribution to all IT-related design issues and practices. He holds a U.S. patent for an Internet firewall security system. He has acted as advisor and engagement partner for several global HRMS initiatives and is a recognized speaker on the topic of the global vision for e-HR strategy, organization and services. He can be reached at **iruddle@dc.com**.

Jeff Alderton is a Principal with Deloitte & Touche, New Jersey, Human Capital Advisory Services group where he is the market leader for Human Resources Transformation Services, the East Coast Practice Leader of Deloitte & Touche Human Resources Strategies, and the Global Director of the e-HR Transformation services initiative. For more than 20 years, he has provided consulting services in the human resource strategy, ERP solutions, and shared-service application areas. He specializes in human resource delivery models, workforce transition planning and organizational design. Alderton has a wide range of industry experience in providing perspective relating to the development of global human resources vision, workforce transition strategies and retention programs, performance competency plans, productivity assessments and management efficiency programs. He has acted as advisor and engagement partner for several global HRMS Business Transformation initiatives and is a recognized speaker on the topic of the global vision for the Virtual HR organization. He can be reached at **jalderton@ dc.com**.

Reprinted from the *IHRIM Journal*, Volume V, Number 3, September 2001, pp. 24-28.

Global Planning —
Don't Leave Home Without It!

By Peter Weinberg

So your company's senior management has finally relented and agreed to sponsor a global human resources information system (HRIS). Now, it's up to you to implement it and make it work, but the only guidance you've had to date sounds like, "Well, we're a global company, so make HR global." Ring a bell?

With the rapid increase in global expansion and web-enabled technology, the desire to standardize and globalize administrative processes is obviously an appealing priority. It's your job to see that many of the fundamentals like return on investment, strategic planning, and global preparedness aren't sacrificed on the altar of rapid deployment. Resist the temptation to start the pilot site implementation next Monday, and let's contemplate what you can do to get the job done and make it look easy.

■ So What Does "Global" Mean Anyway?

Ask any group of 10 executives from different parts of your company what they think a global HRIS should look like, and you'll get 10 different views. That is the first clue to guiding you along the correct path — let's find out just what it is that your company needs and wants. Senior executives can be starry-eyed about wanting lots of global processes and consistency and uniformity and other good things, because first they have no clue how to go about it, and second, that's what they hired you for. So make your first foray into the process the effort to crystallize and bring into crisp focus the *visioning* behind the project. What is it that your company really wants to achieve with this global HRIS, and what do you want the end product to look like? The critical factor here is consensus. People may have differing views, but it is your duty to ensure that the rules of the game are clearly defined and signed off on before the first pitch is thrown. And you are never going to make everyone happy. The best you can hope for is to make sure that everyone is prepared to sing along, whether or not they like the tune.

So how do you achieve this? Not easily. But with a few well thought out steps, we can ensure that we cover the bases.

1. Ringfence the Technology

Because technology is changing at an alarmingly rapid pace, it is becoming more and more difficult to predict what will be available in the near and middle term. So don't try to second-guess progress. Define the vision within the limits of existing or at least imminent technology. And make sure those who contribute to the visioning are fully aware of the technological limitations. I once heard a CIO say that he didn't care whether the technology existed yet; he was basing his solution on what he thought it was going to look like by the time the project ended. He is currently looking for a new job, and the company is looking down the barrel of a failed, yet expensive project. So use technology, but don't abuse it. You want to be leading edge, not bleeding edge!

2. Ringfence the Processes

One of the best ways of getting senior management to agree to a global HRIS is to glamorize the extent to which the system will provide global processes to the organization. Get a reality check! The system will not *provide* global processes; it will *facilitate* the execution of these processes once you have designed them. So don't rely on the system to provide the answers. You need to address the feasibility and desirability of global processes *within the context of your business structure and ecosystem*. Recognize that some processes simply don't lend themselves to being global. Some processes are too intricately interwoven in the cultural fabric of the countries in which you operate to try and standardize or globalize them. The most obvious example of this is compensation structure. Domestic tax laws are so diverse throughout the world that it would be lunacy to try and create a global salary structure. It may be acceptable to develop a global process of determining compensation levels, but leave the structuring of the remuneration packages to local executives who know and understand local needs.

So don't try and shoehorn processes that don't lend themselves to commonality and uniformity just for the sake of delivering an increased array of global processes. And do make sure that the various stakeholders are briefed on the limitations surrounding global processes as they contemplate the global vision.

3. Poll all the Stakeholders

If you want to get consensus, you must be prepared to sleep with the enemy. It is no use basing the vision on the views of a group of like-minded people — that is a complete waste of time. Remember that there is a whole world out there, not just geographically, but functionally, divisionally, and hierarchically. Different people will want the system to provide different answers and perform different functions. Be sure you know what these are before you put pen to paper. So assemble the stakeholders in a room, present the various options/wants/desires/fears/regrets and then let them carve out the middle ground into a global vision acceptable to all, one with which they can all live in the end. This methodology will ensure that you have provided a forum in which all stakeholders are given the opportunity to present their views. The last thing you need midway through the project is for someone to confront you with: "Well, you never asked me!"

4. Get Senior Executive Sign-off

They say that doctors' failures are buried, lawyers' failures are imprisoned, and engineers' failures are left standing for all to see. It is a bit similar in the case of systems project executives. If things go wrong, they're the ones that fall from favor. Projects like a global HRIS should have collective responsibility emanating from the very top. So before you start the project, get senior executive sign-off on the things that really count — what the end product should look like, how much you can spend, what internal resources you can count on, and how long you have to complete it. And be sure to get a definition of victory right up front. Otherwise you'll never know if you won!

■ And What Do We Want to Get from our HRIS?

There's no getting away from it — a HRIS is expensive — expensive to buy, more expensive to implement, and still more to maintain. Justifying the expenditure is one of the more challenging tasks facing those who ask senior management for these systems. I have seen a wonderful spectrum of approaches to this issue, ranging from "cost replacement" to "value added" to "process empowering." None is incorrect, but all suffer from the same basic flaw — no one ever follows it up! And often the reason for this is because, by the time the system has been implemented, we've lost sight of the original vision. So perhaps we need a different approach, and to direct our global planning to incorporate this approach from the very start and ensure that it percolates through all the life of the system. I am talking about the "business decision tool" justification for HRIS.

An HRIS is far more than a large transaction-processing engine designed to minimize administrative effort, and so assist HR to shift its focus from "administrivia" to planning and strategy. This argument was in vogue at the end of the 1990s and is easily understood in Figure 1.

An HRIS facilitates the transition from the bottom-heavy, transaction-based HR role to the diamond on the right, with the time freed up to concentrate on planning and strategy. This is all well and good, but does it go far enough in the current milieu? There is a more important and far-reaching reason for implementing an HRIS, and that involves winning the war for talent. The new millennium will move more and more towards web-based business ecosystems, with the mobility of employees increasing in geometric proportion. Companies can no longer rely on the physical immobility of much of their labor force to ensure that employees stay in their jobs. The companies that are going to be successful in the brave new world are going to be the ones who can *Recruit, Reward and Retain the best and most talented employees: the new 'Three R's' of the 21st century.* This should be the new focus of an HRIS — putting the company in a position to win the business race by winning the recruiting, rewarding and retaining battle.

So what does this have to do with the subject of global planning? Quite simply, any project leader of an HRIS project needs to ensure that the system that is implemented is one that provides the company with the *business toolkit* necessary to win the war for talent. The emphasis of configuration decisions should be aimed at the creation of a business management tool, not a system only for managing HR functions. It is not what we put into the system that is most critical — it is what we can get out. And it must be in a form that enables managers to make informed choices. Remember that all areas and aspects of business

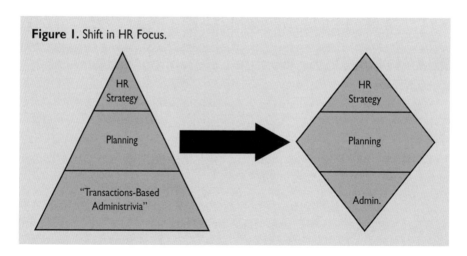

Figure 1. Shift in HR Focus.

are dependent on the quality of its people — the need for talent permeates every level of the company, and the managers in these areas must be given the best toolkit available to improve the quality of their staff.

■ So What Do We Do First?

The battlefield of global HRIS implementations is strewn with the bodies of the "Cookie-Cutter Brigade!" This is the group of project sponsors who approach a global project as if it were a series of domestic implementations that will somehow magically become unified and standardized by some kind of arcane equivalent of Vulcan mind-transfer. "Let's implement it first in the home country," they say. "Then we can take this model and roll it out to the rest of the world." Wrong! You can't! There is something very important you need to do first. And that is to IDENTIFY AND DETERMINE THE GLOBAL ELEMENTS OF THE SYSTEM before you take another step.

Figure 2 shows a comparison of the methodology used by the Cookie-Cutter crew and compares it with that of the Smart and Thoughtful.

■ Now Can I Get Started?

Well, almost. But there is one more philosophical tenet we need to explore: the "bottom-uppers" versus the "top-downers." The first group focuses their initial attention on the collection and collation of the various data elements, and derives the reporting capabilities from the data that has been collected and collated. The second group does it the other way around — it identifies the reporting strategy first and uses that strategy to derive the data requirements.

Which is correct? It depends on the results you are trying to achieve. If your intention is to create a large processing engine capable of reducing administrative tasks, but do not really care about the kind of management information you can eventually get out, or how you can analyze it, then you are a "bottom-upper." If, on the other hand, you want to create a system capable of providing management with the means to succeed in the war for talent, then you must consider what information management needs to make informed choices, and how it should be sliced and diced. This can only be achieved using a top-down

Figure 2. Comparison of Cookie-Cutter View and Smart and Thoughtful View.

A "smart and thoughtful" company would ...	A "cookie-cutter" company would ...
establish a global vision for information systems and try to ensure that the current implementation is in line with the global vision.	probably not have such a global vision. Rather, they would develop a vision for their home country and impose that vision on the subsidiaries in other countries.
be aware of the importance of global business metrics, i.e. the ability to extract metrics on a consistent basis throughout the world.	focus on the requirements of the home country and hope that the other sites can produce the same metrics.
focus on the need to "slice nd dice" information consistently across all subsidiaries in all countries.	focus on the slice and dice requirements of the home country and try to "shoehorn" the other sites into its matrix.
precede an implementation with a global strategic planning session which would tease out the requirements of all countries before reaching any reporting, data or configuration decisions.	only focus on the reporting, data and configuration of the home country in the belief that "most countries will be able to use what we use at corporate."
involve as many of the representatives of overseas subsidiaries in the strategic decision-making to ensure buy-in and facilitate the rollout to those countries when the time comes.	limit decision-making to the home country project team, then expect the overseas subsidiaries to comply because "head office demands it."
create a global baseline or blueprint of configuration decisions before any implementation takes place, so that every subsidiary is "singing from the same songsheet."	create a blueprint for the home country in the belief that "the requirements of the other countries can't be that different."
in most cases, not require any retrofitting or reverse engineering when rolling out to overseas subsidiaries because the baseline will take account of the overseas requirements.	almost always need to go back and rethink and refit configuration decisions because, believe it or not, they have different requirements in different countries!

approach. Figure 3 demonstrates this concept in a graphic that I call "The Global Diamond."

The Global Diamond describes the issues we need to take to progress from a global vision to a global or enterprise data strategy. Once we have finalized the vision, we need to look at three main areas:

1. Enterprise Structure

Most modern global companies exhibit a combination of global, multinational and international attributes. These are optimistically described as "matrixed organizations," in which the direct reporting organization chart sits on top of a wonderfully filigreed and variegated set of "dotted line" relationships that connect the

Figure 3. The Global Diamond.

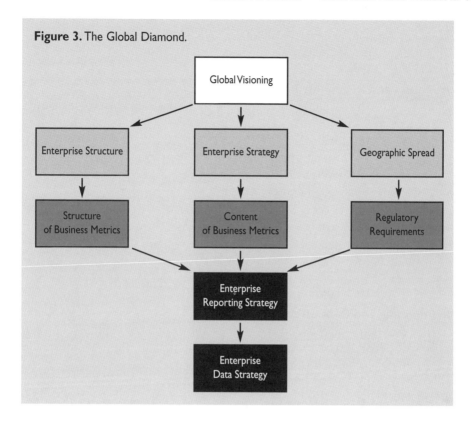

mother ship to its far-ranging fleet. This is not necessarily a bad thing; in some cases, it is the only way in which an organization can operate. But what is important from an HRIS planning point of view is to understand the enterprise structure so that you know how information needs to be sliced, diced and rolled up.

2. Enterprise Strategy

Remember that the HRIS does not only have HR as its customer. All the rest of the enterprise can benefit from the kind of management information produced by the HRIS. It is important, then, to make sure that the HRIS strategy is in sympathy with the operational strategy of the business — where are the expansion/contraction areas, what is the product line/marketing strategy, etc. Only by knowing this can you create the correct microclimate for your HRIS. A client of mine was expanding its operations very rapidly in southeast Asia, opening a new factory every six months. The recruitment module was clearly a very high priority in this region.

3. Geographic Spread

You probably know where your existing offices are and have factored this into your planning. But do you know in which areas there are going to be new operations, and are some operations possibly closing down? The geographic landscape both present and future will have a significant impact on your reporting strategy (especially in matters like language and statutory requirements!)

➤ Metrics and Regulatory Reporting

We need to know what to measure, how to measure it, when to measure it and how people want to see it. Call them by whatever name you will (KPI — key performance indicators — seems to be currently in vogue), these metrics are the lifeblood of the management decision-making process of your business. And you'd better be pretty sure up front what they are before writing a whole slew of reports that miss the target!

And don't forget to cover the reporting requirements dictated by the regulatory authorities in the countries in which you operate. These are as many and varied as the countries themselves, so take a practical approach. If a complicated report is only needed once a year on a pre-printed government form, it may be easier just to complete the form by hand than to try and get your HRIS to do it.

➤ Reporting and Data Strategy

Now that you've assembled the metrics and regulatory requirements, you can translate and embellish them into a reporting strategy. This strategy should answer the following questions:

- What does the report contain?
- Who needs it?
- How often?
- When?
- Where?
- In what level of detail or summary?
- How sliced and diced?

It is simple to see how the data elements needed for these reports can percolate out of the reporting strategy. So now you know the type and nature of the data you need to capture.

■ So How Do I Structure this Global Planning?

There are many different methodologies, and they are all acceptable provided they have the following characteristics:

➤ They involve most of the major stakeholders — nobody can "global plan" on his own;

➤ They are geared towards defining the distinction between "global" elements (those used commonly and uniformly throughout the enterprise — whether they be processes, reports or data) and "country-specific" elements, which may be unique; and

➤ They evaluate levels of preparedness or readiness throughout the organization. It is no use trying to sell socks to a country where they don't wear shoes!

The methodology that I'm going to describe in the rest of this chapter contains all these elements, and can be used as a roadmap for producing a global plan. I have identified four main steps:

➤ Strategic planning,
➤ Tactical planning,
➤ Readiness assessment, and
➤ Global blueprint creation.

Without trying to assign relative importance to each step, I believe that the first three are precursors to the creation of the global blueprint, which is really the crucial deliverable from the global planning phase of the HRIS project.

1. Strategic Planning

Strategic planning is the stage at which we nail down all the things we have talked about earlier:

➤ Global visioning,
➤ Enterprise type and structure,
➤ Operational strategy,
➤ End product vision,
➤ Business metrics,
➤ Enterprise-wide common processes,
➤ Enterprise-wide reporting requirements, and
➤ Global architecture.

The way in which you assemble this information is going to depend on the nature of your business, the corporate culture, the geographic spread of your operations and the time people can devote. The methods include workshops, one-on-one interviews, questionnaires, report-back sessions and so on. The important thing is not how we do it, but what we cover, and whom we cover it with. Remember the principle of involving all the major stakeholders!

2. Tactical Planning

The tactical planning stage determines the way in which the project will be run, and identifies the key participants, the logistics and the methodology. Be sure to include:

➤ Project team composition
• Create a suitable mix of participants with the correct skill sets at both global and local level.
• Ensure they are committed to the project and, more importantly, that their bosses are committed to making them available for the project.

➤ Project team training
• Make sure that this is done in a timely manner. There is nothing like trying to get people to make decisions in the dark!
• Don't just train direct team members. Sometimes it makes sense to provide some limited training or overview to senior management that is going to be asked to make strategic decisions.

➤ Decision-making structure
• This is probably the most important thing to finalize up front.
• Know the limits of each level of decision-making, and create an escalation path that is known and manageable. It is no use escalating decisions to some-one who doesn't have the time or the knowledge to make them.
• Set a decision-making timeframe, limiting the time a decision can flounder before it gets escalated.

➤ Communications structure
• Second most important! Everyone must know where and when communications will flow.
• Over communicate. People who communicate in a project on a "need to know" basis end up on the "about to fail" track.

➤ Budget considerations
• Make sure you prepare a detailed budget before you start.
• And make sure senior management signs off!

3. Readiness Assessment

This is the part most often forgotten, but it can be very dangerous to ignore. Never assume things in other countries and other offices are the same as your own. Get out there and look for yourself. And it's no use asking someone in another country if there are any "curve balls" — they live in the environment, it all seems perfectly normal to them! One of my clients had an operation in an area with a questionable electricity supply. When we arrived to start the implementation (carefully planned, timings all calculated), we were greeted with the unhappy news that electricity was only available between 9 am and 3 pm!

Readiness assessment is aimed at establishing early in the project the status of the systems, infrastructure and personnel at the various rollout sites. It includes an evaluation of:

➤ Existing systems, people and infrastructure; and
➤ Ease of implementation.

Some of the things you should look out for include:

➤ Status of local record keeping techniques and processes,
➤ Accuracy and completeness of local records,
➤ Number and complexity of external interfaces,
➤ Number and training of local personnel,
➤ Level of computer literacy of local personnel,
➤ Status of local infrastructure,
➤ Assessment of local "needs and wants,"
➤ Complexity of local language issues, and
➤ Data privacy and protection implications.

Try to make site visits to at least the most important areas of implementation. You can probably get away with using some kind of questionnaire in smaller sites, but do remember that it is often the smaller countries that present most of the challenges. There is nothing like kicking the tires yourself to make sure that you know what is out there.

4. Global Blueprint Creation

Now we turn to the most critical phase in the planning cycle, one that I believe is the cornerstone of any successful global HRIS. Teasing out the global issues in advance of the implementation and documenting them in a detailed set of global design decisions will not only provide you with a road map going forward, but it will form your most important frame of reference during the project and provide you with checkpoints to make sure you are still heading in the right direction. Remember that the project sponsors will have a pretty decent idea of what the end product should look like — after all, you spent the time helping them to create the global vision. So don't meander off course and end up delivering something unexpected.

This part of the process is the first real attempt to move from the theoretical to the practical. It brings the rather lofty and sometimes fuzzy concepts of the vision into sharp focus, and forces people to delineate in a more finite sense exactly what they mean by such statements as "empowering the employees through self-service methodologies."

So how do we achieve this? The most useful is to hold a workshop or series of workshops to which the major stakeholders are invited, and to use this to extract from them a set of guiding principles to power the project. This is not always practical because it is often quite difficult to get all the players available to take the field together. And then of course there's the cost! How can you justify hauling senior executives from all over the world to a workshop on HRIS? Quite simply: how can you face the cost of not doing it?

The cornerstone of the global strategy is the creation of a global blueprint or baseline, which identifies the global issues involved in the implementations, and creates a set of decisions on global parameters to act as guidelines for the regional and local implementations. I call this set of decisions the *Global Baseline*.

The Global Baseline defines the functionality and processes that will be used consistently throughout all business units, irrespective of location. It contains the high-level blueprint for the rollout strategy and also determines which control table values will be consistently applied throughout the implementation. The Global Baseline concentrates on areas of commonality within an enterprise's processes and data requirements.

So how do we get to this Global Baseline? Clearly, there are wide areas we need to address with a wide spectrum of people from different parts of the organization, functional, operational and geographical. I feel the best way is a global conference in which the relevant stakeholders are assembled in one place and presented with the issues at hand. Only by a careful selection of participants will you get the necessary bandwidth and buy-in. Invite who you think should attend — but give a reason why you believe it is necessary for each person to be there. And give them the necessary training and background reading before they arrive, so that they can feel properly briefed, and won't require lengthy introductions to the matters at hand.

These are the kind of things you might want to include in the conference:

➤ Global vision
➤ Operational strategy
➤ Global, regional and local priorities
➤ Organization structure
➤ Business metrics
➤ Global reporting
➤ Global processes

➤ Data normalization
➤ Data Privacy
➤ Global architecture
➤ Delivery methods
➤ Hardware
➤ Software
• System overview
• Modules to be implemented
➤ Versions
➤ Databases
➤ Multi-language, multi-currency and multi-character sets
➤ Decision-making toolkit
➤ Delivery methodologies
➤ Data conversion and history
➤ Security
➤ Training
➤ Support and maintenance
➤ Support/maintenance
➤ Timing
➤ Resources
➤ Global rollout strategy

The deliverables you should expect from the conference include:

➤ Global Configuration Strategy
• Global processes
• Modules to be implemented
• Global control tables/translate tables
• Global data fields
• Global field formatting
➤ Reporting and data strategy
➤ Technical/architecture strategy
➤ Security strategy
➤ Delivery strategy
➤ Training strategy
➤ High-level rollout plan

The *Global Configuration Strategy* will act as a backdrop or blueprint for all subsequent design workshops to ensure adherence to an overall global strategy, and ensure consistency and standardization within the parameters determined. The degree of potential standardization will vary by organization, and will be a function of the complexity and geographic spread of the organization.

The *High-level Rollout Plan*, detailing the proposed rollout timetable by region, will include the following areas:

➤ Regional design workshops,
➤ Functional implementation,
➤ Technical implementation, and
➤ Training program.

The *Global Reporting/Data Strategy* will include:

➤ Global reporting requirements,
➤ Global reporting methodology,
➤ Global data strategy: global data fields, and
➤ Data warehousing and OLAP tools requirements.

The *Global Technical/Architecture Strategy* delineates the hardware, software and communications configurations and standards to be applied during the project.

The *Security Strategy* delineates the various operator classes required to give effect to the data access requirements of multi-country and multi-functional implementations.

The *Delivery Strategy* delineates the use of employee and manager level self-service, as well as the use of web-enabled technology for data entry/inquiry.

The *Training Strategy* will include:

➤ Client project team training,
➤ Technical training,
➤ End user training,
➤ Train-the-trainer,
➤ Training locations,
➤ Language considerations,
➤ Timing, and
➤ Continuing education.

Collectively these deliverables will constitute the global blueprint you need before embarking on the project proper. Ignore it at your peril — the ERP implementation world is littered with the bodies of project executives who ignored the need for a global blueprint.

■ *And Finally....*

So now that you have cancelled the pilot site, reinvented your project plan, rescheduled your implementation sequence, and revised your project team requirements, what do you do now? Congratulate yourself on having approached the project in the correct and logical sequence — starting with global planning!

Peter Weinberg is a senior manager, PeopleSoft Practice, with Rapidigm, Inc. He has over 20 years of high level international financial and project management experience, and has been responsible for financial operations of major divisions of international firms. He has led re-engineering and restructuring activities that have resulted in improved operating efficiency and profitability and has led systems selection and implementation efforts for diverse financial and information management functions. He has lived and worked in South Africa, England, Ireland and the U.S., and has managed businesses in Germany, France, Scandinavia, Holland, Japan, Korea and Hong Kong. He can be reached at **pdweinberg@usa.com**.

Developing a Global HR Systems Strategy

By Scott A. Bolman

Some companies "go global" by opening new facilities in new countries, while others acquire operations abroad. Some organizations have the luxury of thoughtful, long-term planning when moving into the global arena; others are quickly thrust into this mode of operation through merger or acquisition.

Regardless of how the globalization happens, or how quickly it occurs, once you cross geographic borders, it becomes necessary to have a global business strategy and a corresponding global human resources (HR) strategy firmly in place. A key part of the HR strategy is an HR systems strategy to help HR contribute fully to the success of the global enterprise.

Simply put, strategy is about choices, or more clearly, the elimination of choices. The ultimate goal of strategy is to provide direction by focusing on one alternative at the expense of others. This chapter provides some guidelines for developing a practical, global HR systems deployment strategy. There are five basic key steps in developing a global systems strategy (see Table 1).

Although the process may appear to be simple when reviewed here, in practice it is complex and very political in nature, which can lead to problems and pitfalls for managers. To illustrate the process, we will use an example involving a manufacturing and distribution organ-

Table 1. Five Steps to Building a Global HR Systems Strategy.

1. Identify key drivers...*to create alignment.*
2. Identify global processes...*to define the scope.*
3. Identify current systems...*to establish a baseline.*
4. Develop alternatives...*to define the desired future state.*
5. Evaluate alternatives...*to arrive at the best possible decisions.*

ization with 15,000 employees worldwide to highlight some of the more difficult aspects of this type of endeavor.

First, let's discuss the make-up of the project team and the supporting personnel involved in the project from the start. The process outlined here assumes a project team has been established for the effort (four to eight full-time resources), as well as a project task force that serves as the subject matter experts and coordinators for each of the countries or regions involved. The project task force should consist of HR representatives from locations around the world. The size of the task force is primarily dependent on the geographical dispersion of the organization. These part-time resources act as extensions of the project team, coordinating interviews, collecting information, and communicating the ongoing status of the project with their respective business leaders. The project team conducts interviews, consolidates and analyzes information, markets the project throughout the organization, and facilitates the overall development of the strategy.

The project should be sponsored by, and report to, a steering committee that is chaired by the senior HR executive for the organization. Other members of the steering committee are likely to include line, finance, and information technology (IT) executives.

■ Step 1: Identification of Key Drivers (Alignment)

Most organizations that operate in multiple countries have a global strategy and business plan in place that is revised and updated at least annually. The HR strategy, and by extension the HR systems strategy, need to be aligned with the overall organization strategy. For instance, an organization's stated direction could be something to the effect of "become the world leader in our industry by acquiring the leading companies in each country or market throughout the world." A corresponding HR strategy would need to be focused on effectively and efficiently integrating the individuals and knowledge from these acquisitions, while at the same time identifying and leveraging synergies created by the acquisitions. Likewise the HR systems strategy would be to identify and deploy technology to convert the knowledge (data) and capture new information as quickly as possible. This type of alignment with the organization's strategy is paramount to the successful adoption of the HR systems strategy.

Example: In our 15,000-employee manufacturing company, their overall strategy was characterized by continued growth in current lines of business through exceptional marketing and continued innovation, as well as further acquisitions of complementary businesses throughout the world. The company had acquired several organizations over the last 12 years, with mixed results. The company had operations in over 30 countries, with a presence in Europe, Asia, and South America, as well as the United States and Canada.

One of the first key steps in establishing alignment is to understand the types of drivers inherent in developing a systems strategy. There are four categories that are normally used in this type of effort, namely business drivers, HR drivers, IT drivers, and external drivers. The business drivers usually are gleaned from interviews with senior management and business unit heads, as well as a review of the current vision and strategy information already available in print and/or online. This represents the customer point of view, in that senior management and the business heads are customers of the HR function. The HR drivers and IT drivers are captured from HR and IT management in much the same way, although stated vision and strategy are less likely to be available. External drivers relate to the competition, workforce demographics/trends, and technology advances that are relevant to the development of HR systems. Some of this data may be available already in the organization; however an in-depth understanding of what the competition is doing may require some research. Ultimately, these drivers shape the decision-making criteria that are needed to evaluate alternative strategies. (The decision-making criteria are developed in Step 5.)

Example: In our manufacturing company, key executives from around the globe were interviewed, as well as the CFO and Controller. The key driver from their point of view was the globalization of the enterprise, e.g., moving from an international group of entrepreneurial oriented business units to a single, united global organization. From an HR perspective, the key drivers included the identification of potential candidates for key jobs and the ability to plan for the growth and development of high-potential employees for future senior management roles. There was some cynicism from the IT organization, which discounted the ability of the HR organization to drive an effort of this magnitude. External to the company, the industry was maturing with stable brands and market share. However, consumers' demand for convenience required rapid innovation and marketing of new products, according to industry analysts. This was seen as a prerequisite to long-term survival of companies within the industry. All of this information was documented and shared with the project team and project task force, as well as the steering committee. With a firm understanding of current drivers, the stage was set for the next step in the process.

■ Step 2: Identification of Global Processes (Scope)

The next step in developing a global strategy is to determine which HR processes need to be managed globally. Ultimately, this step should shape the answers to two questions:
1) What customers need to be served with global HR services?
2) What services does the organization need HR to provide globally?

In some organizations where there is a good deal of decentralization and autonomy, the number of truly global HR processes may be relatively small, while in others that are highly centralized, the number may be large.

It is helpful to first categorize all HR processes at a high level and then, through a process of analysis and elimination, determine which should be considered global versus local. In most organizations, the categories follow the traditional functions of HR (e.g., staffing, compensation, benefits, training and employee relations). It is critical to get input from HR and business unit representatives from around the globe to help in this process. The project task force plays a key role in obtaining this input and discussing the pros and cons of making certain HR functions global. The information acquired through the interviews in Step 1 also provides direction in this process, as well.

Once the high-level categories or functions are identified as global versus non-global, it is important to drive down to the actual processes themselves and make the same distinction (global vs. non-global). For the most part, processes within the categories identified as "global" will be global as well; however, there may be some exceptions, which need to be identified before moving further in the process.

The importance of this step is that it helps narrow the scope of the following steps in the process. However, this step is also one of the most difficult, requiring a great deal of communication, as interpretations of HR functions and processes can vary widely from country to country. The project team plays a key facilitation role, bringing widely disparate views into the open and moving the task force to a set of decisions for moving forward. Ultimately, a presentation to the steering committee will be required, at which point the ultimate decision of scope for the next phases can be determined.

Example: For our global manufacturing company, recruitment, payroll processing, and benefit administration were excluded from a global solution, while reporting, performance management, and succession planning were key categories identified as global. There was lively debate across regions during this process. Some regions were in the process of upgrading their ERP packages to deliver enhanced services, others were in the vendor evaluation stage, and one region had built an HR application from scratch. The advent of the Systems Strategy project caused these other initiatives to be put on hold or delayed substantially, which was not seen favorably by some members of the task force or their customers. At one point the senior vice president of HR stepped in to reiterate the importance of moving the organization to a global enterprise, which would require sacrifice on everyone's part. Once this was stated by the sponsor, agreement followed shortly thereafter.

■ Step 3: Identification of Current Systems (Baseline)

This step involves getting a baseline across the enterprise for any systems currently in place, or being implemented, that will impact the processes that have been classified as global. Most global organizations have a variety of systems in place ranging from Excel spreadsheets to ERP systems to legacy systems. Completing an inventory of systems by process from each of the locations across the enterprise provides you with the necessary information from which to judge the amount of effort required to realize your strategy once it has been developed. This inventory needs to be completed prior to the development of the strategy, as the current systems may provide important information in shaping the final strategy.

Initially, the project team prepares a systems inventory template. Through coordination by the project task force, each location should complete the systems inventory indicating the type of software, hardware, operating system, etc., currently in place to support each process. Any plans for upgrades, replacement, implementation, or other initiatives should be noted, as well. For highly centralized organizations, this already may be available in IT documentation. However, for decentralized organizations, this information will need to be collected from representatives at each location.

The results from all locations should be consolidated into one master inventory and reviewed by the project team and task force prior to developing the strategy statement. A summary of the information should be developed and shared with the steering committee to provide an overall sense of what systems are currently in place around the world to support HR.

Example: Through the task force, the project team collected data from each of four major regions across the world. The systems supporting the organization's HR processes were disparate, ranging from manual processes to homegrown applications to ERP systems. Two different ERP systems were in place: an outdated one serving North America and a tier-one product in Europe. Asia/Pacific was in the RFP process for an HR/payroll system, and South America was rolling out a custom-developed system, which had been built over the last year. The project team consolidated the information in an overall systems inventory for use in later phases. The overall complexity and ownership issues were not lost on the project team or the task force. The steering committee was concerned with the overall cost of maintaining these disparate systems and saw a potential opportunity to reduce overall costs as part of the project.

■ Step 4: Development of Alternatives (Future State)

The development of alternatives is the most creative part of the process. The goal of this step should be to identify a list of potential possibilities and then narrow the list to a manageable number that would then be subject to further analysis in Step 5. To help in this process of creation and subsequent elimination, the team should wrestle with the following questions:

➤ To what extent are local systems needed in a global solution?
➤ Should the direction of data flow be from local to global or from global to local?
➤ Should we support the solution ourselves or look to a service provider?
➤ What reporting/decision support capabilities are needed?
➤ What will be the next likely technology that we need to be ready for?

Following is a more detailed examination of each question.

➤ **Local Systems**
In looking at the question of local systems, the data from the systems inventory becomes very useful. For the processes that are identified as global, what is currently in place? What is still being implemented? What will be the loss (or return) on investment if the system is eliminated? These are a few questions that need to be considered when discussing the fate of local systems. If there are few global processes, then replacing local systems may not make sense. If there are many, the replacement of local systems may be required. If local systems remain, then the solution can be much narrower in functionality and perhaps more cheaply built in-house. Given current technological capabilities, there will be some local systems that cannot or should not be eliminated with a global solution (e.g., payroll).

Example: In our manufacturing organization, their was no global system in place, although some data for senior management was being tracked for stock options and other executive benefits. Local systems were varied and functional, although not as efficient in some areas as in others. There was extensive discussion concerning the comprehensiveness of the data tracked across the world as well as its integrity. We concluded that the local systems probably were not tracking all of the data needed, nor did they have the integrity required for global processing.

➤ Data Flow

The direction of data flow is somewhat dependent on the answer to the local systems question, and again needs to be answered in light of the number and complexity of the global processes that have been identified. A few simple, global processes may lead to a decision to let local systems feed a global system. A larger number of more complex processes may lead to global systems feeding data to the local systems. The complete elimination of all local systems is highly unlikely given the functionality of today's software packages, however, most vendors are looking to build this capacity in the future.

Example: Our manufacturing organization debated this question at length, with a great deal of conversation devoted to data integrity and worldwide access to the data across the network/Internet. Ultimately we decided to analyze variations on both alternatives — one with data flowing from local to global, and the other with data flowing global to local.

➤ Solution Support

Should the solution be supported internally or through an external service provider? This question relates to the IT drivers that were identified early in the process. Most global organizations have made significant investments in technology infrastructure that can be leveraged, and hence, make a good case for supporting the solution internally. However, most IT organizations are taking a hard look at what support costs actually are, and may be moving to outsourcing or Application Service Provider (ASP) approaches for certain types of applications. Total cost of ownership is an important factor in determining the answer to this question, although it should not be the only factor in choosing between these options. As was indicated earlier, the global HR system solution needs to align with other strategies in the organization, including IT. In any event, the answer to this question of internal versus external support can help eliminate some options for the team as it considers alternative solutions.

Example: Our team decided early on to support the solution internally. The immaturity of the ASP marketplace and the quality of the internal IT resources provided the CIO with a comfort level in determining that the application could be supported in-house.

The project team agreed that the IT function was both capable and willing to implement a solution for the organization, given senior management support of the initiative.

➤ Reporting and Decision Support

This is why most global HR systems are considered in the first place. After all, the time and expense to get the information from around the globe is necessary to ensure that executives and managers can use that information to make better decisions. There are a host of other benefits to deploying a global solution; however, the most visible reason is the ability to get the right information to the right people at the right time. So the question here is not whether you need this capability, but to what extent? Is it a full-blown decision support system (DSS)? Or is it a report generator that will help your HRIS analysts quickly respond to the latest report request? This is not a trivial question because of the complexities involved in satisfying the insatiable need for information. In truth, the reporting/decision support issue is always one of the HR processes identified upfront as "global" and is emphasized here because of its potentially large impact on the development of alternatives.

Example: This was a key area for our manufacturing company. Again, the issue of data integrity and availability was discussed at length and the core requirements for reporting were debated. In the end, the company decided the reporting requirements did not justify a decision support system — at least in the short term.

➤ Technological Advances

It's not necessary to become a futurist and try to predict technological advances five to 10 years out, but it is important to consider what some early adopters are doing today that you believe will become mainstream in the next three to five years. Currently, wireless access to the Internet and portal deployment for the enterprise are obvious choices. The idea here is to consider the probable technological advances so that your strategy can incorporate these when they become more mainstream, rather than be pre-empted by them.

The answers to the issues raised in each of the five sub-sections above can help outline a few possibilities that make sense for your enterprise.

Example: A total of five different alternatives were developed and presented to the leadership team. Heated debate concerning pros, cons, costs, timeframes, and philosophies ensued, and two alternatives made it to the next stage. Simply put, one alternative was a global implementation of an ERP HR system with data flowing from global to local, and the other alternative was a custom-built data warehouse with data flowing from existing systems to the data warehouse.

■ Step 5: Evaluating Alternatives (Decision Time)

In this final step, the final strategy is determined through an analysis of the last remaining alternatives. Revisit the initial drivers and global processes and state them as evaluation criteria (one will be ROI, although that may not be considered most important). It is helpful to rank order the criteria and assign weights to them, as this will lead to a weighted evaluation score. Although simple to describe on paper, this process will not be easy and will take some time to complete. However, it is important to do this prior to scoring the alternatives against the criteria.

Once you have the criteria and weights established, evaluate each option on each criterion using a five-point scale. Multiply your scores by the weights assigned to each criterion and total. Which alternative solution results in the highest overall score? Which is next best? Is there a significant difference between the scores? Why or why not? In the end, this process should give you a clear direction for a global systems solution, and provide you with a defensible position when presenting your strategy to senior management.

> **Example:** In our case, the team ultimately decided to pursue a global ERP HR system implementation that would capture HR data worldwide and provide that data back to the local systems for any unique requirements of those areas. The decision was based on the criteria identified and scores assigned; however, a final meeting with all participants was held to review the scoring process and discuss the implementation and change management issues associated with such a large-scale initiative.

■ Implementation

The topic of implementing global systems is beyond the scope of this chapter, however, it would be remiss in not mentioning some key considerations. First, the issue of whether to go with a single language or multiple languages can be a topic of lively debate. There is no clear-cut answer to this question and it needs to be tackled by the implementation team.

Similarly, the implementation team needs to determine the appropriate protocols for storing and presenting salary, bonus, and other financial information. Which currency is to be used for which reports? How is the conversion between currencies handled?

Finally, the cultural issues that surround the implementation need to be explored at length and a plan set forth for dealing with them. These are only a few of the key considerations that need to be dealt with early on in the implementation phase.

■ Conclusion

Ultimately, strategy is about making choices between different paths toward reaching a goal. The five-step process outlined in this article provides guidance for arriving at the best possible choice for your global HR system strategy. The development of an HR systems strategy is really an extension of the overall HR strategy itself, and as technology becomes more and more an integral part of HR, the systems component of overall HR strategy will become only more important to consider.

Scott Bolman is a principal in the HR operations consulting practice of William M. Mercer, Inc. Based in Chicago, he brings over 16 years of human resource and information technology experience to his role. Bolman's areas of expertise include HR strategic planning, portal design and implementation, process analysis, vendor evaluation, decision support systems and enterprise application integration. He has directed numerous strategy, development and implementation projects. His clients have included retail, manufacturing and health care organizations. Bolman has both a bachelor's and a master's degree in industrial/organizational psychology. He is a member of the International Association for Human Resource Information Management (IHRIM) and is a frequent author and speaker on applying emerging technologies to the practice of HR in the workplace. He can be reached at **scott.bolman@us.wmmercer.com***.*

Reprinted from the *IHRIM Journal*, Volume V, Number 4, November 2001, pp. 24-28.

Part Three:
Cultural
Dimensions

"If you treat an individual as he is, he will remain as he is. But if you treat him as if he were what he ought to be and could be, he will become what he ought and could be."

— Johann Wolfgang von Goethe

• • • • • • • •

One of global HR's ongoing tasks is to deal with diverse cultures, particularly those of clients and employees around the world. But those clients and employees must also deal with the opposite problem: they must master the elements of business culture that are, surprisingly perhaps, the same everywhere. These contradictory aspects of culture — the local and the international — are critical to any discussion of global HR.

The range of arenas in which these forces interact can surprise even seasoned professionals. It is one thing to recognize that, say, success in sales depends on sensitivity to local business practices or that primary languages vary. It is more difficult to constantly take into account such wide-ranging issues as international law, cross-cultural differences in "human factors" (ergonomic) parameters, and even varying international fertility rates. Yet successful HR organizations must do all this and more.

The following chapters discuss a number of key issues facing cross-cultural HR in the boundaryless world, and consider both their local and the international aspects.

What's So Special About Global?
HR in the Interactive Age

BY JACKIE PENTICOST

Globalization is one of the common phrases in the HRMS practitioner's handbook, and yet, every system implementer seems to interpret its meaning differently. In order for an implementation to progress quickly, within budget, and to clearly meet stakeholders' needs, it's critical that the HRIS team agrees with their customers upon a clear set of goals to be achieved under the term "globalization."

It may be appropriate for a global business to apply HR processes as standard across all countries. For instance, many businesses need standard training methods. In one business, global may mean managing careers of key people worldwide, but leaving local sites to self-administer local compensation. In another, global may mean supporting operations in many countries, but as isolated entities, simply gathering HR budget data for comparison. Still others might create multi-country processes that need cross-cultural teams to be trained and rewarded as a unit. No description of global is right or wrong, but any one model must be appropriate for the long-term vision of the business.

The volatile nature of global changes in HR practices[1] means that there are few well-trodden paths of best practice that can be used in implementations. Nonetheless, it's essential that the vision is captured at the project's start. Decisions made about architecture, technical infrastructure, interfaces and data, can have a fundamental impact on the nature of the business.

The purpose of this chapter is to provide a checklist of some of the most frequent issues arising from global implementations. There are, of course, many other issues and concerns since there are over 270 countries and territories, countless local, ever-changing laws and statutes and many cultures, but this checklist will act as a road map for discussion. These issues arise as a result of one particular "brand" of global implementation is chosen, and they raise some interesting cross-cultural questions. You might care to use it as discussion prompts with users in order to develop a direction for global HR, as an action checklist after deciding upon a direction or to actively exclude issues as inappropriate for your business.

■ Global HR: Our Discussion Model

To highlight multinational and multicultural issues, this chapter makes a distinction to the effect that global HR has multiple goals which distinguish it from HR practices that support global standardization or manage a pool of international employees. The goals of our model of global HR are:

➤ To support local operations and embrace the local diversities of HR practices worldwide,

➤ To include multiple cultures within an overall corporate culture and vision that transcends geographical and cross-cultural differences,

➤ To support corporate direction, and

➤ To take advantage of new ideas and skill combinations created by cross-border processes.

Do global HR practices differ from single-country HR practices? Any single country has some experience with managing diversity, the U.S. more than most, but globalization differs fundamentally in the scale and depth of diversity of every aspect of its HR practices. As an example, we need only cite the U.S. "Employment at Will" approach versus the (strengthening) European support for employment protection — two 180-degree, diametrically opposed HR practices.

Any global system of HR practices needs to involve common HR goals which can accommodate local practices sanctioned in law or guidelines by economic communities such as the European Union, state or local government, collective bargaining agents, religious groups, or even educational systems. Many of the goals of those local groups are tangential or even directly opposed to organizational goals. In some countries, transitioning from non-free market economies such as Communism or agrarian cultures may even cause you to deal with quasi-legal or military groups.

Furthermore, a global HR practice needs to work with disparate cultural groups whose traditions and views run counter to corporate goals and culture. Local traditions meld views of assertiveness, ethnicity, gender roles, avoidance of uncertainty, need for formality, role of family, directness of communication (to name a few) that may jar with Western styles of doing business.

What's more, the level of interaction between different cultures is higher than it has ever been, facilitated by ease of travel and low-cost communication media. It's now possible to set up and conduct business almost seamlessly (from a technical viewpoint) in almost any country with a suitable infrastructure. Dealing with potential cultural schisms must be part of the role of the global HR practitioner in the "Interactive Age" until we are all familiar with each others' cultural outlook. From the HR practitioners' viewpoint, that means practicing global affirmative action: ensuring that all cultural groups feel included to the same degree and are able to contribute ideas and skills derived from their experience.

Global HR is also concerned with specialist disciplines, unique to cross-border working and may well place a higher emphasis on some aspects of traditional HR. For instance, global implementations have a far more complex way of recognizing legal entities worldwide. There is also more frequent involvement in joint ventures, subcontracting or other legal partnership arrangements as a result of entering new countries or emerging markets using local expertise. Simply tracking your extended family of people and the many and varied legal relationships and career commitments you have to them is a discipline in its own right.

Global HR is also concerned, far more than would a local implementation, with people and their dependents in transition from one country to another and with the complex compensation, taxation, pensions and contractual arrangements that emerge as a result of these transitions. The transfer of expatriates into local sites is a common way of exchanging (or more often, introducing) new skills and cultural viewpoints. Part of the equation of transferring people is to understand that most countries apply immigration restrictions and, for some countries, this is an urgent matter of reducing dependency on imported talent and of forcing the company to train local people.

Lastly, global HR has to stretch traditional HR practices to the limit by requiring "equitable" treatment of individuals. For instance, to encourage people to transfer across the organization, an HR practitioner has to be able to maintain equitable compensation schemes that reflect local market conditions as well as the seniority and marketability of the person. Apply to that different tax regimes, government differences in tax treatment of stock options, pensions and benefits, and maintaining equable systems across borders becomes a specialist discipline.

So, again, what makes global HR special? It seems to me that global HR is a political activity in the sense that it seeks to achieve common goals by accommodating cultural diversity, negotiating legal minefields and reconciling tensions between local pressure groups. Global HR is a volatile activity in that many of these areas are poorly understood as yet, and all of the factors are changing rapidly. Global HR is a leading-edge activity in that it is likely to encounter diverse work practices and be required to absorb them into day-to-day business.

■ *The Global HRIS Challenge*

Just as global HR is an emerging discipline, the development of support systems is an evolving specialist area. As with any evolution, we are at the stage of understanding the "nuts and bolts" by creating an environment that serves many geographically distant users; issues of language, and of cross-border data protection and data transfer are critical.

However, if we don't make immediate strides to work with global HR practitioners to shape worldwide HR practices, we may find that we have indeed created a "one-size-fits-all" HRIS that hinders the global vision by enforcing a single cultural viewpoint on users. The challenge to the HRIS practitioner is best understand by asking these questions:

➤ Can the system change to reflect the changing shape of global HR as laws, cultures and work practices change?

➤ Can the system support specialist practices such as managing joint ventures?

➤ Can the system support the global HR practices needed to maintain the corporate vision, potentially through creating global processes (e.g., corporate intelligence and operational processes) where standardization is required such as training, international compensation, manpower budgeting or skills management?

➤ Conversely, can it support many diverse ways of reaching the same business goal where support for multi-cultural and multi-legislative ways of working is critical?

The need to support rapid change and to create global processes, where appropriate, are challenges of managing technology and of helping people cope with change. Fortunately, these challenges are relatively well understood. The extent of legislative compliance, although complex, is at least, relatively clearly defined. However, it is less well understood that systems can have a major impact on the ways in which groups from different backgrounds work with each other and within a corporate vision. Cross-cultural issues are perhaps the single biggest unknown in a global implementation and the most unquantified in terms of its success or failure.

When a person fills in an employee survey online, reviews personal data, enrolls in a flexible benefits plan using IVR, applies for a job posting on the Web, downloads and participates in online learning, receives a workflow notification to approve a new hire, performs a self appraisal or reads an online message, they form an impression of the company's ability to include them in its corporate culture and respect their individual background.

In this sense, the HRIS, perhaps more than any other system, has reached out to encourage interaction from the most inexperienced IT user, representing the organization to a wider audience than ever before. If people in an organization are to be bound in a common corporate culture that embraces diverse groups, it is primarily HR systems, as much as managerial style, that will embody the corporate face of the organization.

Reaching out to all cultures in an audience has a direct, positive payback.

At best, a well-designed system with which the user feels comfortable can support HR processes which directly impact the bottom line in terms of educating or informing the person, attracting more applicants or helping people to identify skill gaps or opportunities for better deployment. Reaching out to all cultures in an audience has a direct, positive payback.

That doesn't just mean the creation of multilingual systems. It might mean creating systems whose interfaces are sensitive to which data is presented and to the style of presentation, from online help to name formatting to local styles of addresses or bank details. It might mean creating interaction with training systems appropriate to the learning styles of the culture.

Support for diversity also means that users interact with familiar, local procedures where possible. For instance, the norm in one country may be to process recruitment applications *en masse* and therefore, recruitment targets must be planned well ahead. In other countries, ad hoc recruitment is simple. In still others, the authorities must be notified well in advance because they may apply quotas on foreign workers.

It might mean that some cultures are less comfortable with our information-rich HRIS directions than others. In the first issue of the IHRIM *Journal* (November 1997), Bob Stambaugh outlined a vision of an HRIS as a "news center," providing personal, immediate and important information to different stakeholders via an intranet, combining competitor or business news with internal information to deliver real intelligence.[2] It behooves us to understand that we're listening to issues with global ears, not just Western ones. The HR news center in a global HRIS would need to be staffed with people attuned to local economies and to political issues in order to spot things of importance and to relay them in a culturally sensitive way to the appropriate stakeholders.

And so to the checklist of issues that arise from our model of global HR. The questions have been categorized into a number of levels, ranging from the basic entry-level questions to high-impact issues of corporate culture.

■ *Technical Environment Issues*

➤ Is the technical environment geared to support end users even at the most far-flung sites?

➤ Have you supplied sufficient network bandwidth to allow people to access the system quickly?

➤ Have you made decisions about servers based on the ability to create access during the work day of the local sites? Single servers have to be taken down at some point during the day and are distant enough to create access problems for someone, somewhere.

➤ If someone at a local site can't get access to the server, do you provide support outside the work day to assist them? You'll need to think about 24-hour coverage and about the language skills of the various support people.

➤ Have you paid attention to basics, such as ensuring that letters and reports can be printed in the formats used by local printers?

➤ What is your upgrade strategy? Do you have local code or even local systems that feed a global repository? Depending on your strategy, you may need to synchronize local upgrades or you may be able to upgrade at different sites over a period of time.

➤ If you require interaction with the system, does the interface cater to the fact that many cultures will have less exposure to technology than the West? You may need to provide extra training for certain groups of people. It's useful to create profiles of the typical IT experience that you expect a user to have in order to interact with your system and check whether this profile actually exists at different sites.

➤ Can the required technology be introduced into the country at an adequate cost? Are there laws preventing technology being exported to the country? Does it permit the use of software from foreign powers? Does the infrastructure of the country — telephone lines, browser technologies, etc. — allow information transmission?

■ *Global Data Issues*

➤ Do you need to hold multiple currencies? You may need to report on currency conversions, both online and in reports.

➤ Can you represent the person's name format correctly? Can you identify the different concatenations for generating letters and reports appropriately? Different countries build up names in different orders, so that what North Americans think of as a first name is not printed first. This is important for meeting user expectations when lists of people are displayed in reports.

➤ What country-specific structures (e.g., bank details, Social Security identifiers, and address layouts) do you need to use, and what populations of people might they be used for? It may be useful to create case studies of a person who is, for instance, based in the U.S., assigned to work in Germany and who has dependents in France but is living and taxed in Switzerland and who is paid in both the host and home country currency.

➤ Do you need to hold national identifiers (Social Security numbers) for different countries, and what validation or uniqueness checking should you apply, remembering that what's unique in a single country might not be unique across the world? Some countries have multiple identifiers, some have no identifier. You'll probably have to hold different identifiers over time if an individual spends significant time in different countries. National identifiers, depending on culture, may be regarded as private information and therefore, they may not be useful as employee identifiers.

➤ Can you grant viewing, updating or deletion rights or restrictions to specific information for different types of users and employees that comply with the laws of the country? Can you prevent cross-border data transfer if necessary?

Most global systems have to decide whether to hold data that varies both legally and culturally by region or country. The system may also need to prevent or permit certain categories of users from seeing or updating specific data fields about a person employed under certain laws.

A U.S. user may be surprised at some of the EU categories of data described below that are considered sensitive, such as union membership. You'll need to decide what business purpose is served by holding the data at all, whether you will hold current data or history, and if so, what rules you wish to apply to its use. If you do decide to hold sensitive data, you may need to register its use, obtain employee or Works Council (bodies at each company that represent the employees) permission, record comments or refusals and make provision for the employee to regularly see the data and correct or comment on it. Alternatively, you may need to mandate certain processes such as deleting applications after a period of time.

Data protection and privacy laws in Europe exist at both the country level and at the EU level to protect the individual from discrimination. These laws make provision that data should not be held about racial or ethnic origin, political opinions, religious or philosophical beliefs, trade union membership and the processing of data concerning health or sex life, unless for defined purposes or with the person's explicit consent. The laws (in Germany, for instance) make provision for an employee to have access to data about themselves unless the data is in protected categories, to record comments about the data or to have it amended.

The law also provides that people who have automated processing of data that affects credit ratings or performance at work can be challenged. This means that automatic data matching which excludes people from a recruitment process, for instance, may be subject to legal scrutiny. In many EU countries, Works Councils enforce data protection, and data to be held or transferred between countries must be approved by those bodies.

The October 1998 European Data Protection Directive places further restrictions on transferring personal data out of the country unless the receiving country has at least the same level of data protection and privacy enforcement. Some countries insist that data transfer outside the EU must be licensed.

■ *Data Presentation and Interface Issues*

Can information held in the global system be easily accessed and understood by the intended audiences? You may be putting certain groups at a disadvantage by not presenting information in a way that is familiar to them.

Language is a particularly thorny issue, and the pros and cons vary depending on the processes supported. Many organizations use a one-language standard, but many processes are provided that lead to judgments being made about performance. One should take care not to disadvantage groups who do not have the chosen language as their first language. Equally important, care should be taken with "wide access" processes such as job postings, online training, training enrollment or employee surveys so that you do not discourage use by making them available in only one language. Some countries, such as Belgium, mandate that employee communication should be issued in the language of choice for the user or by region, so you may need to set up letters based on language preferences.

Implementers need to decide which categories of data are to be held in one language and which should be multilingual. These categories include data, screen prompts, help text, error messages and warnings. It should be borne in mind that, for some implementations, it may be normal to hold multiple character set versions of data such as the person's name (Japan holds Kanji, Kana and Romaji). Any implementation that holds data in many languages should plan to consolidate data at the global level using extract scripts which map to some common denominator of values.

■ Local and Global Data Ownership

How will you resolve conflicts between local needs and corporate needs for information? Many implementers express anxiety about having to reach worldwide agreement with numerous local sites about enforcing global data to be entered instead of local data. If the implementation is able to decide up front which data is needed for reporting purposes and which is needed for operational purposes, then much of this conflict can be reduced.

A common approach to managing data for global reporting is to create a global data repository or data warehouse and to create batch processes that roll up data at intervals from local operational databases. A lot of data conversion can be done in the extract, so that local sites can still hold local values, languages and data that suits them, while converting to a "common denominator" set of information. This can resolve much potential conflict.

It may be that, on a corporate-wide basis, individuals do not need to be identified at all. At a global level, reporting might only require headcount or compensation costs from a site. Frequently, corporate headquarters only needs to track international employees or a subset of the total population at an individual level. This can ease data protection constraints because local sites can populate summary tables of statistics that can be included in the global analysis.

An approach that has worked in some companies is to supply a "black box" of tables and ask each site to populate these with data on a regular basis. The local site maintains the scripts to populate the black box. Corporate headquarters maintains the tables and extract scripts, and they upgrade the scripts when a new product version is to be used globally.

Standardized operations can be run locally or on a global operational database, but it's important to realize that even processes such as training which are commonly considered to be standardized, may have local reporting needs. For instance, France has complex reporting requirements on training hours and costs in relation to payroll costs.

■ Managing Legal Entities

Identifying organizational boundaries is not as easy as it might seem. Global organizations maintain different types of legal agreements such as joint ventures or subcontracting arrangements with other companies. Can different types of legal entities be identified according to their local definitions and separated for reporting under the laws of different countries? Can you represent a functional view of many organizations that goes across countries and at the same time, group those organizations by country for EEO or ADA reporting in the U.S.? It's essential that human resources can be identified as working within a particular legal entity and reported correctly.

■ Identifying People

In a global implementation, how will people be uniquely identified in a way that does not reveal the Social Security ID (if they have one)? Most companies use a global ID to track employees worldwide. Can every human resource be identified that is related to your business in some way and that needs to be tracked? Unfortunately, it's sometimes easier to lose international employees than one might think.

Tracking might include anyone who contributes work, who has the potential to contribute work now or in the future, or who is related to the person who works. In a global implementation, this could easily include direct hires, contractors, subcontractors, joint venture partners, suppliers, students, partners, dependents or "secondees" to other businesses who expect to return at some time. Each type of human resource needs to be categorized to meet the needs of local and global reporting requirements.

■ Employment Issues

A key role of any implementation is to support the company's duty to comply with the employment laws affecting their employees. In a global implementation, because of the fact that an employee may, both over time and concurrently, be subject to many different legal systems, the fact that these different systems are often at odds with each other must be taken into careful consideration.

The laws under which a person is employed or is taxed can fundamentally affect their healthcare, pension, tax liabilities and ability to sue the company. Therefore, global implementations need to track this information clearly. The issue is more complex than one might think, since the wording, terms and parties involved in a contract can determine which laws apply. Even within the EU, issues such as different country pension provisions, retirement age or the tax treatment of stock options can make a major difference to where an employee wants to be located.

... issues such as different country pension provisions, retirement age or the tax treatment of stock options can make a major difference to where an employee wants to be located.

In many countries or territories that have a history of HR legislation as a result of being governed in the past by European countries, there is a strong emphasis on employment protection and on collective bargaining. In that sense, employee location can affect workers' rights in terms of regulations on termination, minimum wages, work hours, protection of groups such as pregnant women, employee rights when a company changes ownership, maternity, vacation and sick leave, health and safety, worker representation and contractual law.

The notion of employment protection has a number of implications. If you're planning to fill key positions, take care that the person vacating the position isn't on maternity leave or on military service — they have a right to return to an equal job, and that includes working conditions and location as well as pay.

■ Culture Clashes in Managing Standardized Processes

Assuming that a global HRIS needs to support a range of global HR goals in which integrated, operational data is required, it's important to be aware of the legal and cultural influences that can derail the process.

Where processes are deemed to be global and to have wide employee participation such as recruitment, training, skills management or international deployment of key staff, the HRIS practitioner has a duty to make sure that processes can cater to regional differences in HR practices as well as to global needs. The following are just a few examples:

➤ **Balancing global and local recruitment needs** — Processes such as automated job posting and recruitment or international career pathing of key staff may clash with the requirements of the country for employment protection. In many countries, the job has to be posted internally before being advertised externally, and national employment agencies have to be notified. Countries may apply visa quotas and seek to apply rigidly enforced affirmative action programs to local groups. Many countries, such as South Africa, for instance, have programs designed to promote the training of local people to reduce their dependency on skilled people from other countries.

➤ **Recognizing different training and education schemes** — Vocational training and apprenticeships are prized in many countries as a viable alternative to universities, and countries such as the UK have accreditation for "vocational qualifications" gained by on-the-job experience. Can the system reconcile and value different education grades so that managers can make appropriate recruitment and training decisions? Can it recognize the many and varied educational systems of different countries?

➤ **Maintaining equable compensation and reward schemes** — Given the variety of local compensation schemes that are dependent on taxation and local market conditions as well as on the strength of social welfare systems, it's probably not feasible to compensate using a standard system. For instance, the UK places an emphasis on non-cash compensation such as the company car, and they de-emphasize healthcare benefits because of an adequate public health system. That means the base salaries of non-cash countries often look low compared with the U.S.

The system must provide data for compensation specialists to make judgments about equitable compensation schemes that deliver equal total compensation value to the person in each country, enabling them to transfer between countries while maintaining an appropriate cost of living and pension growth. International compensation approaches frequently maintain a nominal "home" rate in a stable currency to provide a benchmark market rate and derive local costs taking into account tax, non-cash compensation and local costs of living.

Can the system distinguish nominal compensation in one currency from actual local compensation in another currency? Can the system make simultaneous payments in different countries under different taxation schemes? For instance, can some portion of payment be made to the home country and some to the host country?

■ Managing Global Skills

Job grading systems are often used globally to enforce a common view of progression and responsibility. You may need to reconcile this with locally agreed-upon systems mandated under national collective bargaining arrangements (such as the job coefficient used in France).

Appraisal schemes are often a source of cultural conflict as companies seek to maintain a global language of skills. Apart from the fact that they can become a vehicle for personal culture clashes between managers and employees across national borders, the organization needs to ask itself whether the skills needed to perform a job can, or indeed should, differ substantially by country.

Hofstede has produced a body of work noting country-specific differences of style in terms of the extent to which people make individual or collective decisions, seek external leadership, seek to compete with each other, value formality, work in an uncertain or ambiguous environment.[3] Many organizations are finding that they can set standards in terms of technical or commercial knowledge and in company vision and values, but that a "Western" style of management is wholly inappropriate in other cultures.

Systems that manage skills, that recruit based on occupational tests, that allow self-testing or self-appraisal or that contain pre-established skills libraries, need to be configured to represent diverse styles of working in different cultures. If a psychometric testing module is used, then the information it uses as a basis for comparison needs to be global or the tests should only be used where the user population is from a similar culture. Many organizations offer different normative data for different populations.

Systems which automate data matching to exclude people who fail to meet certain criteria are likely to come under intense scrutiny as the EU and country data protection laws on the use of automated systems affecting performance are implemented. A global HRIS using specialist systems developed in any one country should determine whether it can meet the laws governing any employee who performs the test over an intranet.

■ Conclusion

As systems become capable of fostering true ownership of data through ease of use and performance, the move from the Information Age to the Interactive Age is inevitable.

The globalization trend must and will continue until all stakeholders in the company have access to information and processes when they need it. We're at the beginning of a long mutual education process in understanding human interaction with complex applications. The proponents of global HRIS have a key role to play in ensuring that such interaction is appropriately tailored to the multitude of worldwide customers.

The stakes are high for global HRIS, which is itself an emerging discipline, as we seek to work within the volatile nature of changing technologies, cultures and legislations. At worst, a poorly designed global HRIS may create informational black holes where people are discouraged from applying for new jobs, where people fail to achieve training standards and where people feel they are alienated from corporate goals. At best, a global system that provides a support infrastructure which transcends cultural and geographic differences may enable the business to create something far more than the sum of its parts from its diverse groups and cultures: a truly global organization. The challenge is there. Failure is not an option.

*Jackie Penticost has spent more than 20 years involved with all aspects of HRMS — as an end user HR professional, as a consultant and most recently as product architect for Oracle HRMS Applications. She is responsible for the functional direction of Oracle's Human Resources applications, including the legislative extensions for many countries. She can be reached at **jpentico@uk.oracle.com**.*

■ Endnotes

1   Tschira, Klaus, "It's Time for a Change", *IHRIM Journal*, Volume I, Number I, November 1997.

2   Stambaugh, Robert H., "The Tectonics of Human Resource Information Systems,"

IHRIM Journal, Volume I, Number I, November 1997.

3   Hofstede, Geert, *Culture's Consequences: International Differences in Work-Related Values*, Beverly Hills, 1985.

Reprinted from the *IHRIM Journal*, Volume II, Number 3, September 1998, pp. 44-49.

Global Fluency

By Donald T. Tosti, Ph.D.

Global Fluency: *Facility with cultural behaviors that help an organization thrive in an ever-changing global business environment.*

■ Introduction

There is growing evidence that the most important source of power in the 21st century will not be government with its military power and regulatory authority.[1] Rather, it will be business, with its economic power and ability to influence behavior through the delivery of products and services. There is already growing recognition of the far-reaching influence of business and economic issues — once largely subservient to government, they can now virtually create or topple governments.

As the global economy increases in complexity and scope, as interdependencies among nations and organizations increase, as more and more companies move into a global business and social environment, people in these companies will need to think and act differently.

Global competition is creating an evolutionary process in which a common "core" of business practices and behaviors will guide the most successful organizations. One key difference between biological evolution and this business evolution is that business leaders can take action *now* to be sure their organizations will be among those that thrive in the global environment we are entering. This chapter examines how we can define global fluency for a given business, and how we can make sure that the people in that organization have that fluency.

Business cultures evolve like organisms in some respects, i.e., they adapt and change in response to environmental pressures. For businesses, the competitive pressure of a global business environment provides the evolutionary force; the fittest and most agile organizations will be the survivors. Protected organizations will not thrive in the coming years; companies that can attract and retain customers while simultaneously changing as market conditions change will be the winners.

■ Business Culture

Culture has been described as "the way we do things around here" (Deal & Kennedy, *Corporate Cultures*, 1982) and as "the customs . . . of a particular group" (*Oxford American Dictionary*, 1980). Culture is not so much *what* people do — the work they perform, but primarily the *way* they do it — how they behave as they perform that work. Culture refers to behavior patterns that people tend to bring to *any* task or decision. Changing culture, then, has the potential for greater long-term, sustained benefits than changing products, services or delivery methods. The work of Kotter and Heskett (1992) suggests that this potential is very real. In a study of more than 200 firms in 22 North American industries, they found strong evidence that an organization's culture is a key factor in its ability to sustain success in a changing environment.

Profiling is Not Enough: Much early literature on organizational culture focused on categorizing cultures and creating profiles. This literature is both interesting and informative; it has taken the understanding of corporate culture far beyond what used to be called "the informal organization." But categorization schemes are of limited value in determining what one can do with or about organizational culture. It is useful to remember that culture is **behavior** — it is the way people in the organization tend to behave as they go about their work. Culture change, then, is behavior change. And technologies of behavior change are not new.

In our efforts to define the culture appropriate for a given business in a global environment, we have found it useful to distinguish two classes of values and practices:

➤ **Leadership values/practices** — the behaviors that people in management/leadership positions must demonstrate to support people in preparing for the future and/or delivering results now; and

➤ **Company values/practices** — the behaviors that everyone in the organization needs to demonstrate if the company is to deliver value to its customers,
its shareholders and its employees.

It is important to note that the values we are concerned with here are not a
matter of personal preference or style. Rather, they are business necessities. Effective business values and practices are as important to success as are effective strategies and goals.

■ *Global Culture*

My colleagues and I have been working in an international business environment for more than 20 years. During that time we have worked with a number of organizations to help them improve their global fluency and modify their
leadership and/or company practices. Though we work with organizations to
define a culture that matches their unique business needs, we have found that
successful global organizations have many practices in common; this is especially true of leadership through providing direction, and company-wide practices related to customer focus. As yet we have seen no evidence that there is
"one right culture" that will work for all organizations and all global business
environments. This is why we consider it critical to conduct an analysis of business needs, strategies, and history to derive the principles and practices
needed for a given organization's success in its environment.

An example: one company we have worked with recently is SITA Global
Telecommunications. SITA is arguably the most global company in the world,
with owners, customers, and employees in more countries than any other organization. SITA is a global telecommunications company set up by the airline industry in the late 1940s to handle all its data transmission needs. It is owned by
most of the airlines in the world, including those of the former Soviet block. In recent years, it has extended its owner base to include virtually every company in
the air transportation field. SITA has offices everywhere that airlines fly; its employees are located all over the world, and a high percentage of them are citizens
of the country in which they work. The company has local representation in 214
countries — more than the number of member nations in the United Nations.

SITA is an excellent example of creating global fluency. Though it is clearly a
global company, it does not have a fluent global culture. It is legally a cooperative that, until recently, had a "captured market" and thus was under no competitive pressure. Recently, increasing demand for cost-effectiveness in the air

transportation business has created opportunities for competitors to move in. Increasing deregulation in the telecom industry has added to the competitive pressure. John Watson, SITA's new chief executive, recognized that the drastic change in the business environment would require a corresponding change in the way the company conducted its business and dealt with its customers. One of his first acts was to commission an organizational change effort in which a key component focused on the organization's business culture.

■ The Change Effort at SITA

This program is illustrative of the process we go through to define an appropriate culture. The change effort addressed three broad questions:

➤ Where does the company want/need to go in the coming years?

➤ What practices are required to take it there from where it is now?

➤ How can people in the organization build those practices into the day-to-day conduct of the business?

The first step was to clarify the organization's strategy and the business drivers that would determine success in the new environment. SITA identified three key drivers:

➤ Increased customer focus,

➤ Streamlining to increase the efficiency and effectiveness of processes, and

➤ Ability to change faster.

The key question at this point is what culture will best contribute to meeting these needs.

The second step was to identify the values and practices — both for the company's leaders and for the company as a whole — that would support the organization's strategy. We began by focusing on company leaders, from the executive team through mid-level managers, to define leadership principles and practices for the organization. Work on defining and implementing company-wide business values and practices began later.

This sequence both built support "at the top" for the change effort, and helped prepare the organization's managers to actively participate in the clarification and implementation of corporate values.

The final step was to put in place programs that would begin to make the written statements of values and behaviors a reality in the day-to-day actions of people throughout the organization.

■ Leadership Values and Practices for Global Fluency

Below are sample leadership values and practices, identified during our analysis of SITA needs. These represent the kinds of behavior that any global organization might expect of anyone in a leadership position — from the top executive to the first-line supervisor to a team leader or project manager. Although they were derived through an analysis of a specific organization, they are virtually identical to those we have found in other international companies.

Vision: *Creating a clear and compelling picture of the future toward which the organization is striving; behaving in a way that encourages people to work toward that future.*

➤ Is willing to make significant change in the way we do things now to meet the challenges of tomorrow;

➤ Challenges and inspires the team around shared values and broad purposes;

➤ Communicates a view of what we can accomplish together that captures the commitment of the team;

➤ Anticipates what the future could hold and how we can make it happen for ourselves;

➤ Communicates a positive view of the company, its customers, and its long-term success; and

➤ Acts as though keeping his/her people informed about the business issues that face us is one of the most important parts of his/her job.

Encouraging Initiative: *Creating an environment that supports and encourages people to take initiative to carry out the organization's mission and vision.*

➤ Gives advice more often than criticism;

➤ Is readily accessible to people seeking advice or guidance;

➤ Creates a challenging environment to encourage individual development;

➤ Encourages people to show initiative and take reasonable personal risks;

➤ Ensures that people feel they have the information, authority, and resources they need to take action;

➤ Works to enhance the confidence and self-esteem of others; and

➤ Links individual and team efforts to the overall success of the organization to help people feel part of a larger effort;

Since the purpose of leadership is to get results through others, one excellent way to get information about what values and practices should be is to ask followers what they need from their leaders to get results, e.g., what do we need to do to be successful in a competitive global environment? Thus, through a process of interviews, surveys and focus groups with organizational "followers," we determine what behavior they need from their leaders to get the job done. The result is a set of values and practices that leaders need to demonstrate to influence people to take purposeful action. Thus, *leadership is targeted to the needs of the business.*

We have found that the practices listed above are common to many global businesses and are selected by people in many cultures when they are asked to identify the behaviors needed to assure success.

■ *Company Values and Practices for Global Fluency*

Using a process similar to that used to identify leadership practices, we identified a number of company-wide values and practices that everyone in the organization might be expected to demonstrate, from the chief executive through front line and clerical staff. These, too, cut across national and regional boundaries.

Create Value: *We look at our work in terms of how it benefits our customers, our company, our people, and all who have a stake in our business success; we continually look for better ways to maximize those benefits.*

➤ We seek opportunities to make frequent incremental improvements in products, systems, services and cost savings;

➤ People are encouraged to take ownership for the tasks they perform and the quality of the products or services they provide;

➤ We are willing to revise our plans if new challenges or opportunities present themselves;

➤ We work to make sure we get it right the first time;

➤ We do what the business needs, not just what the boss wants; and

➤ We take personal responsibility for making wise use of resources.

Work As Partners: *We strive to work constructively and in full cooperation with other groups who contribute to our success; we focus on mutual goals and look for ways to assist other groups and learn from them to deliver the best results.*

➤ People feel free to raise any issues or concerns they may have, and expect a considered reply;

➤ We respond constructively and non-defensively when others disagree with our views;

➤ Our cross-functional working relationships are cooperative and effective;

➤ If something goes wrong, we focus more on trying to find out what happened than on trying to assign blame;

➤ We accept our share of risk and responsibility for problems that arise in our interactions with others; and

➤ We share information and ideas freely across organizational levels and functions.

As with leadership values, these company values and practices were derived by looking at business needs first. It is the force of such global business needs that is driving the creation of a global business culture. By looking at the success factors for a particular organization operating in an international environment through data gathering and analysis, one can identify the values and practices that everyone in the organization should demonstrate. It is important to recognize that the specific practices necessary for success in a global environment now and over the next few years may change as the organization and its environment continue to evolve.

For example, in our early work with British Airways in 1984, we worked with the organization to develop appropriate leadership values and practices. In 1994, we revisited those practices. Approximately 80 percent of the originally selected practices were still critical 10 years later, but a few were dropped, and a number were added. This should be expected with many, if not all, organizations. British Airways in 1994 was quite different from the British Airways of 1984, and was operating in a different competitive global environment. Nevertheless, a substantial core of values and practices remained relevant and important.

Practices tend to be much more susceptible to change over time than do values. For example, in 1987 we conducted a cultural audit for Hewlett Packard to examine the "HP Way." The goal of the study was to determine the extent to which the traditional values of the company were still relevant and still driving the organization's behavior. The study found that HP's fundamental business values were solid and relevant and still driving organizational behavior, but that a number of specific practices — i.e., the way in which people demonstrated those values — had changed over the years in response to changing business conditions and markets. We also found that HP's value of "respect" translated very well across cultures, despite differences in the specific tactics for manifesting respect.

■ Defining Global Values and Practices

The process for working with organizations to define business values and practices begins with clarifying the organization's strategy and business drivers. This typically involves a review of organizational history and existing documents, and interviews with senior executives as well as selected managers across an organization. This information provides a base for working with management to draft value statements that represent a first cut at the principles that will help the organization move successfully into the future.

Given the value statement draft, we can move on to selecting practices that will represent the values in action for a given organization — those that it deems most critical. In SITA we gathered data from more than 300 people, located across the organization, including Montreal, Atlanta, Buenos Aires, Singapore, Tokyo, Seoul, Peking, Cairo, Beirut, Rome, Paris, Geneva, London, Berlin, Madrid, Moscow and Sydney.

We found little difference in the perception of priority and need as a function of geographic location or national culture. Wherever they were in the world, people tended to agree on the validity and importance of a particular practice. Thus, it was possible to define a core set of practices for a global business culture that would deliver the organization's strategy in the competitive environment that they experienced worldwide.

This is not to say that differences do not exist across cultures; they do, of course. But the differences tend to be manifested in the way people exhibit the practices, not in the practices themselves. The practices tend to be both universally understood and observable. For example, these practices were seen as important across all groups:

> We demonstrate a sense of personal urgency, energy, and commitment to achieve quality results; and

> If something goes wrong, we focus more on trying to find out what happened than on trying to assign blame.

While groups everywhere can be evaluated on those practices by others or by themselves, the way in which they manifest it may vary. That is, two people may exhibit the same practice — and be seen as doing so by others — but approach it in very different ways. Thus it becomes possible to create an organization-wide global business culture, even though individual, national, and local differences may exist in the way a particular practice is demonstrated. We think this is evidence of an evolving worldwide business culture — one that is driven by the need to stay competitive in the global marketplace.

The practice selection effort was then used to go back and revise and refine the original value statements to better reflect the behavioral practices chosen. The result was a set of values that both management and people across the company could "buy into." All too often, company values are defined by a relatively small group of senior managers who go off by themselves to devise a set of values that seems "inspirational." Our approach is to strongly link behavioral practices to success in the business environment and then cluster them into value sets that truly reflect the needs of the business. "Inspirational" messages can then be created around these values and become far more meaningful.

■ *Building Fluency in Values and Practices*

Simply publishing the values and practices would have limited impact, and training is not an appropriate intervention for building values and practices into an organization. The practices describe behavior that virtually anyone in an organization knows how to do. Most people have all the necessary *competencies*; the need is for the organization to become *fluent* in them — to demonstrate them consistently and easily or "naturally" in a wide variety of situations.

The process for gaining fluency has been around for many years; it is called feedback and practice. It's the same approach used to become truly proficient in a language or a sport such as tennis or skiing. Becoming a fluent tennis player requires lots of practice and feedback from a good coach. What is lacking in organizations is not so much the opportunity to practice but the feedback. The initial intervention to strengthen leadership principles and practices in SITA was a program called "Leadership for Results." Though it was sometimes called a "training program," it was in fact a management meeting, addressing business issues and revolving heavily around feedback provided to each participant on the extent to which he or she was seen by peers and subordinates as demonstrating the company's leadership practices.

We use peer/subordinate feedback because we wanted to make sure that the participants' feedback came from people who "see them in the game." We deliberately do not include feedback from the boss for two primary reasons. First, this data is usually less valid because the boss seldom sees much of the behavior people exhibit while working with peers or subordinates and acting as a leader of their units. Secondly, feedback from the boss tends to be given great weight by recipients. After all, the boss is the one who makes decisions about such things as promotions, raises and work assignments. The weight given to boss feedback is thus out of proportion to its value for developing fluency. Including it would have created a situation in which the least valid feedback might be given the greatest weight by recipients. In addition, the inclusion of feedback from three sources tends to create "overload."

In SITA the four-day program was designed as a first step in gaining fluency in the practices, with subsequent leadership forums to follow in which participants would have an opportunity to continue to work on business issues, share progress on their action plans, and obtain feedback on the extent to which people had observed changes in their behavior.

■ Summary

Business leaders and professionals need to define the necessary culture for their business success, and incorporating a common core that reflects global business culture will be a matter of survival. No longer will people be "trained" on how to do business in other countries. Instead, everyone will understand the "global language" of business in addition to their national way of working. The "final" global business culture (which will continue to evolve) will not be Asian, European, North American, or driven by any national or ethnic group. It will be, to some extent, a "foreign language" for us all — but one in which we must all learn to be fluent.

Don Tosti has an extensive and varied background in both management and organizational alignment and has been a recognized expert in performance-based approaches to organizational effectiveness for three decades. He is an expert in organization systems and was principle investigator for the multi-media leadership/management course conducted at the U.S. Naval Academy, where he adapted the methods of performance analysis to the study of leadership and management behavior. His subsequent work centered on modifying behavioral norms and cultural values. Since the late 1970s, he has been focused on orga-nizational alignment and the development of performance-based management systems. He has been in-volved in a wide range of organizational change programs for companies in the United States and Eu-rope. Tosti's consulting activities in organizational alignment include work in leadership, management, culture change, internal marketing and strategic alliance. This led him to work with many companies such as British Airways, SITA, BT/Cellmate, Honeywell-Bull, Galileo, IBM, General Motors, Hewlett-Packard, Bank of America, Wells Fargo Bank, Equitable Life Insurance Company, Morgan Guaranty, Commercial Union Insurance, Bank of California, First Interstate, Crocker Bank, Bank of Hibernia and American Express. He is a frequent presenter at conferences and professional society meetings, and has published numerous articles, management development activities, working papers, and invited ad-dresses, book chapters, and books on performance technology and its application in today's business world. In addition, he has held adjunct professorships at University of New Mexico, Coppin State College, Catholic University of America, San Francisco State University, and California School for Professional Psychology. Tosti can be reached at **change111.@aol.com**.

■ Endnotes

1   An Invited Masters Address for the joint conference of the International Soci-ety for Performance Improvement and the International Federation of Training and Development Organization, March 1999.

Culture and the Workforce[1]

By Row Henson

Perhaps the most interesting aspect of the global work environment is the exposure to a variety of people from a wide range of countries, cultures, religions, beliefs and work practices. These differences help identify best practices around the world, grow our businesses, provide our workforces with opportunity and help us as individuals to develop and learn. But understanding and adapting to these "cultural" differences may also be the most difficult process we will need to address in our quest to be "global."

In this chapter I would like to focus on three primary topics:

1. A global demographic view of the workforce itself,
2. Two different looks at cultural differences — from a national or regional perspective and from an organizational one, and
3. A brief look at the global economic differences in the near future.

▪ Global Demographics

Before we take a look at the cultural differences we should expect to experience in the global workplace, I thought it would be of interest to many of you to see what is actually happening around the world with the potential workers we may be exposed to. We are finding today that in countries like the United States where we are dealing with a declining workforce — demand outweighing supply — many organizations are looking outside their home countries to supplement their workforce. This requires a real understanding of cultural differences — even if the workers never leave their home country to work for an organization they may never "see." So we are seeing this situation impact organizations that were never classified as "global" before. They may not be building or delivering product to the global economy, but may have employees or contingent workers throughout the world based on their availability, cost or skill set. Let's take a look at some of the statistics surrounding these phenomena.

If you haven't already noticed, between now and 2050, the population of our planet will slow its growth and begin to decline (see Figure 1). In over 25 percent of all countries (representing 45 percent of the world population), the fertility rate is below replacement levels. Zero population growth (ZPG), long a political rallying cry, has become a reality. During the next generation, we will be learning the managerial skills required to function in an era of permanent global labor shortages.

Because of the decline in births, we are finding that the workforce in general is getting older (see Figure 2). This in provides us with another dimension of cultural diversity — AGE! For the first time (at least in the United States) we are

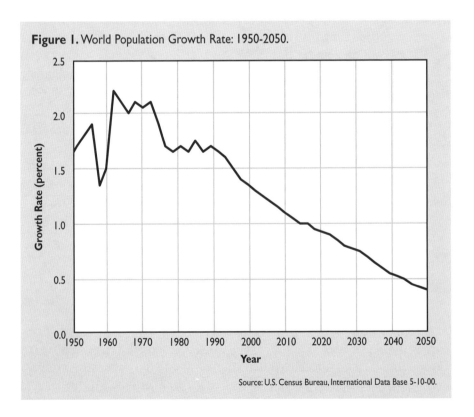

Figure 1. World Population Growth Rate: 1950-2050.

Source: U.S. Census Bureau, International Data Base 5-10-00.

Figure 2. Everyone on the Planet is Getting Older.

	MEDIAN AGE (YEARS)		
	1950	2000	2050
World total	23.5	26.1	37.8
More developed regions	28.6	36.8	45.6
Less developed regions	21.3	23.9	36.7
Africa	18.7	18.3	30.7
Asia	21.9	25.6	39.3
Europe	29.2	37.1	47.4
Latin America and the Caribbean	20.1	23.9	37.8
Northern America	29.8	35.2	42.1
Oceania	27.9	30.7	39.3

Source: United Nations Population Division http://www.popin.org/pop1998/8.htm .

dealing with a workforce that is made up of the mature worker, the "baby boomer," the Generation X and the Generation Y workers. Compound this with regional and organizational cultural differences and we as human capital managers and developers have our work cut out for us over the next decade.

The global average fertility level now stands at 2.7 births per woman; in contrast, in the early 1950s, the average number was five births per woman. Fertility is now declining in all regions of the world. For example, during the last 25 years, the number of children per couple has fallen from 6.6 to 5.1 in Africa, from 5.1 to 2.6 in Asia and from 5.0 to 2.7 in Latin America and the Caribbean. A change of 50 percent over 50 years is nothing short of amazing.

Figure 3 shows labor availability now and in the future in the 61 countries that are operating below replacement fertility levels. In other words, the combination of cost of living, unemployment rate, and labor force size and fertility rate is the basis of considering a particular country or region as a labor source. This table offers a straightforward look at the top level of 60 national economies.

Birth rate (or fertility rate) is the median number of children born to each woman in the economy. A birth rate over 2.11 ensures that the population of a country will remain stable. If it's over 2.11, the population is growing. A birth rate at 2.11 or lower indicates a population in decline. For a population to grow when it has a birth rate of 2.11 or less, other influences — like health care improvements and immigration — must supply the additional people.

Labor force is the number of people in the economy who are available for work. Factors influencing the size of the labor force include the educational attainment of women in the economy and the impact of disability on availability for work.

There is no true standard definition of *unemployment rate*. Each country defines it somewhat differently. In the United Kingdom, for instance, the unemployment rate is a measure of the number of people who have registered for unemployment benefits. The figure is calculated through a combination of sur-

Figure 3. Labor Availability Around the World.

COUNTRY	BIRTH RATE	LABOR FORCE (M)	UNEMPLT RATE	ANNUAL GROWTH	PER CAPITA INCOME
Armenia	1.70	1.60	20.0%	6.0%	$2,700
Australia	1.79	9.20	8.1%	4.5%	$21,200
Austria	1.41	3.70	7.0%	2.9%	$22,700
Azerbaijan	1.99	2.90	20.0%	10.0%	$1,640
Barbados	1.50	0.14	12.0%	3.0%	$11,200
Belarus	1.36	4.30	2.3%	7.0%	$5,200
Belgium	1.55	4.28	12.0%	2.8%	$23,400
Bosnia and Herzegovina	1.35	1.10	0.5%	30.0%	$1,720
Bulgaria	1.23	3.57	12.2%	4.0%	$4,100
Canada	1.55	15.90	7.2%	3.0%	$22,400
China	1.80	696.00	8.0%	7.8%	$3,600
Croatia	1.56	1.63	18.6%	3.0%	$5,100
Cuba	1.55	4.50	6.8%	1.2%	$1,560
Cyprus	2.03	0.30	3.0%	2.3%	$13,000
Czech Republic	1.19	3.66	7.0%	-1.5%	$11,300
Denmark	1.72	2.90	6.5%	2.6%	$23,300
Estonia	1.28	0.72	9.6%	5.5%	$5,500
Finland	1.73	2.53	12.0%	5.1%	$20,100
France	1.71	25.40	11.5%	3.0%	$22,600
Georgia	1.92	3.08	16.0%	4.0%	$2,200
Germany	1.30	38.20	10.6%	2.7%	$22,100
Greece	1.28	4.28	10.0%	3.0%	$13,400
Guadeloupe	1.90	0.13	30.0%	2.0%	$9,900
Hong Kong SAR	1.32	3.21	5.5%	-5.0%	$25,100
Hungary	1.37	4.20	10.8%	5.0%	$7,400
Iceland	2.10	0.13	3.0%	6.1%	$22,400
Ireland	1.90	1.52	7.7%	9.5%	$16,400
Italy	1.20	23.19	12.5%	1.5%	$20,800
Japan	1.43	67.40	4.0%	1.0%	$23,100
Latvia	1.25	1.40	9.2%	3.6%	$4,100
Lithuania	1.42	1.80	6.7%	0.0%	$4,900
Luxembourg	1.67	0.23	3.0%	2.9%	$32,700
Macao	1.40	0.28	3.8%	-0.1%	$16,600
Macedonia	2.06	0.59	30.0%	4.6%	$1,050
Malta	1.89	0.15	5.0%	4.0%	$13,000
Martinique	1.75	0.16	24.0%	2.0%	$10,700
Mauritius	1.91	0.51	2.0%	5.0%	$10,000
Netherlands	1.50	7.00	4.1%	3.7%	$22,100
New Zealand	2.01	1.86	7.6%	-0.2%	$17,000

Figure 3. Labor Availability Around the World. (*continued*)

COUNTRY	BIRTH RATE	LABOR FORCE (M)	UNEMPLT RATE	ANNUAL GROWTH	PER CAPITA INCOME
North Korea	1.65	9.17	5.0%	-5.0%	$1,000
Norway	1.85	2.30	2.6%	2.8%	$24,700
Poland	1.53	17.40	10.0%	5.6%	$6,800
Portugal	1.37	4.74	5.0%	4.2%	$14,600
Republic of Moldova	1.76	1.70	2.0%	-8.6%	$2,200
Reunion	2.10	0.26	35.0%	3.8%	$4,800
Romania	1.17	10.10	9.0%	-7.3%	$4,050
Russian Federation	1.34	66.00	11.5%	-5.0%	$4,000
Singapore	1.68	1.86	5.0%	1.3%	$26,500
Slovakia	1.39	3.32	14.0%	5.0%	$8,300
Slovenia	1.26	0.86	7.1%	3.6%	$10,300
South Korea	2.05	20.00	7.9%	-6.8%	$12,600
Spain	1.15	16.20	20.0%	3.5%	$16,500
Sri Lanka	2.10	6.20	11.0%	3.7%	$2,500
Sweden	1.57	4.55	6.3%	2.9%	$19,700
Switzerland	1.47	3.80	3.6%	2.0%	$26,400
Thailand	1.74	32.60	4.5%	-8.5%	$6,100
Trinidad and Tobago	1.65	0.54	14.0%	4.3%	$8,000
Ukraine	1.38	22.80	3.7%	-1.7%	$2,200
United Kingdom	1.72	28.80	7.5%	2.6%	$21,200
USA	1.99	137.70	4.0%	4.2%	$31,500

veys and factors in the United States. We view the unemployment rate as a rough indicator of a particular economy's ability to absorb growth.

Annual growth is a United Nation's measure of the growth in a particular economy's gross domestic product (GDP). It is a rough measure of the number of jobs created in the economy. These annual growth figures have been modified to account for inflation, so they represent real growth rather than adjustments in living standards.

Finally, *per capita income* is a relative measure of the buying power of an individual in each economy. It is a useful approximation of the cost of living (or the cost of labor) in each country.

Figure 3 shows that, in 60 countries traditionally considered industrialized, population is in a relative decline, economies are growing vibrantly, and the workforce is fully deployed. Although there will be some near term competition for the workers in these countries, the supply of labor is extremely limited. Large growth in the labor supply will have to come from India, South America, and Africa over the next 50 years. At that point, global population will flatten and begin to decline. These statistics underline the most important question facing managers and executives over the next generation: How do you sustain economic growth when population is stable or declining?

I believe it is critical for those of us dealing with a global workforce to understand these demographics and their implications. In the knowledge economy of the 21st century, it is our ability to attract and retain this human capital that keeps us in business and makes us competitive. If we aren't already, in the future we will be looking for talent wherever we can find it. Global or not, it is the global workforce — populated by workers in various phases of a contingent relationship — that will supply this demand. Many critical questions will arise regarding boundary management, privacy and the depth of long-term relationships. Our ability to understand the demographics and the cultural differences associated with where these resources live and how they work will be the differentiating factor between those global organizations that survive and those that fail.

■ Cultural Differences — National/Regional and Organizational

As a global business, you will inevitably deal with diversity on a daily basis. It is important to be flexible and tolerant in your own corporate culture. Things that you take for granted on a day-to-day basis may be challenged in a different office setting. For example, some cultures are greatly hierarchical, others more diplomatic. Different parts of the world also view change in very different lights. Some may value constant change, and others may keep antiquated processes simply because they have always done it the same way.

There are several diverse business values within each company or organization, sometimes even each office. For example, sometimes separating individuals into cubicles provides individuality and some degree of autonomy. However, in some places in the world — especially in the more hierarchical countries — cubicles will not work and only move to isolate workers. In this chapter, I hope to share some research on both cultural challenges.

Windham International provided a model that I've found useful. As you enter or work in a new country, you will find each has its own way of dealing with the following:

➤ **Hierarchy.** Perception of rank in relationship to others.

➤ **Change Tolerance.** Perception of control over one's own destiny.

➤ **Group Dependence.** Importance of individual over the group.

➤ **Diversity Receptivity.** Gender, race, religion, country of origin.

➤ **Status Attainment.** Perceived level of "success."

➤ **Relationships.** Importance for business interactions.

➤ **Communication.** Verbal and non-verbal.

➤ **Time.** Adherence to schedule.

➤ **Space.** Space and privacy needed for personal comfort.

I will present a few quick examples before we look deeper. In Japan, one's overall rank in an organization is as critical as the competence of the individual, while in the United States rank does not tend to rate as high as an individual's contribution. Likewise, in Japan, the sum of the whole or the group is more important than the individual. As I found by living in Tokyo, one of the favorite sayings was "the nail that sticks up is the one that gets hammered." A number of countries including the Scandinavian area embrace change, while many "old world" countries are entrenched in history and find change unacceptable. Using body language as a signal, you may believe that in Asia someone is agreeing with you when they nod their head only to find out later that they are violently opposed, however showing emotion in public would not be acceptable. On the other hand, when an Italian yells at you in a discussion, it doesn't mean he or she disagrees. In the United States where we often find companies operating in a "cubicle" or open environment, this may not work in cultures where privacy and space (and size of office) are deemed critical measures of success. Even in the United Kingdom, many organizations measure the level of employees by the location and size of their office. As for time, in Spain and most of Latin America, adherence to time is not important. It is not unusual for people

Using body language as a signal, you may believe that in Asia someone is agreeing with you when they nod their head only to find out later that they are violently opposed, however showing emotion in public would not be acceptable. On the other hand, when an Italian yells at you in a discussion, it doesn't mean he or she disagrees.

to show up for a meeting hours late and find that perfectly acceptable. But don't try this in very organized, conservative countries such as Germany.

In Fons Trompenaars' book, *Riding the Waves of Culture*, I found his use of charts to be very helpful (see Figures 9, 10 and 11). He uses a survey approach to show from high to low the acceptance of a number of principles across countries, including showing emotions, quality of life — the good of the group versus individual freedom, and what makes a good manager (those who require management or prefer to be left alone). He also uses Lewin's Circles to indicate cultures that are open or closed (see Figure 12). People often find Americans as being "loud" and totally willing to share our every thought with everyone else. People in Germany, France, and Japan will be much more difficult to get to know because they have a much more private persona than the American does. However, once they are accepting of someone, they will tend to be more loyal for longer than their western counterpart.

■ Regional Culture

I will try to describe briefly what took several chapters in Trompenaars' book. The emotional quadrant, first covered in Talcot Parsons' *The Social System* (The

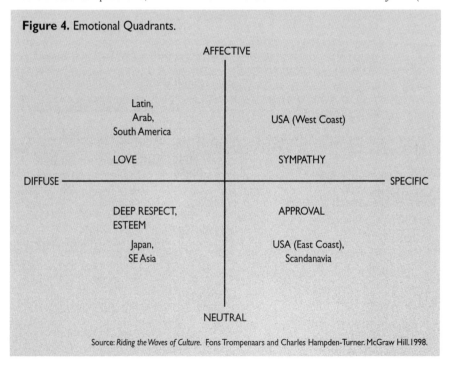

Figure 4. Emotional Quadrants.

Source: *Riding the Waves of Culture.* Fons Trompenaars and Charles Hampden-Turner. McGraw Hill. 1998.

Figure 5. Practical Tips for Doing Business in Different Cultures.

RECOGNIZING THE DIFFERENCES

Specificity	**Diffuseness**
1. Direct to the point, purposeful in relating.	1. Indirect, circuitous, seemingly "aimless" forms of relating.
2. Precise, blunt, definitive, transparent.	2. Evasive, tactful, ambiguous, even opaque.
3. Principles and consistent moral stands independent of the person being addressed	3. Highly situational morality depending upon the person and context encountered.

TIPS FOR DOING BUSINESS WITH

Specific-Oriented (for diffuse individuals)	**Diffuse-Oriented (for specific individuals)**
1. Study the objectives, principles, and numerical targets of the specific organization with which you are dealing.	1. Study the history, background, and future vision of the diffuse organization with which you expect to do business.
2. Be quick, to the point, and efficient.	2. Take time and remember there are many roads to Rome.
3. Structure the meeting with time, intervals, and agendas.	3. Let the meeting flow, occasionally nudging its process.
4. Do not use titles or acknowledge skills that are irrelevant to the issue being discussed.	4. Respect a person's title, age, background, connections, whatever issue is being discussed.

WHEN MANAGING AND BEING MANAGED

Specific-Oriented	**Diffuse-Oriented**
1. Management is the realization of objectives and standards with rewards attached.	1. Management is a continuously improving process by which quality improves.
2. Private and business agendas are kept separate from each other.	2. Private and business issues interpenetrate.
3. Conflicts of interest are frowned upon.	3. Consider an employee's whole situation before you judge him or her.
4. Clear, precise, and detailed instructions are seen as assuring better compliance, or allowing employees to dissent in clear terms.	4. Ambiguous and vague instructions are seen as allowing subtle and responsive interpretations through which employees can exercise personal judgment.
5. Begin reports with an executive summary.	5. End reports with a concluding overview.

Source: *Riding the Waves of Culture.* Fons Trompenaars and Charles Hampden-Turner. McGraw Hill. 1998.

Free Press, New York, 1951) looks at various combinations of levels of emotion or affectivity — high, low, or neutral (see Figure 4).

➤ **Diffuse-affective (DA) interactions** — the expected relational reward is *love*, a strongly expressed pleasure diffusing many life spaces.

➤ **Diffuse-neutral (DN) interactions** — the expected reward is *esteem*, a less strongly expressed admiration also spread over many life spaces.

➤ **Specific-affective (SA) interactions** — the expected reward is *enjoyment*, a strongly expressed pleasure specific to a certain occasion or performance.

➤ **Specific-neutral (SN) interactions** — the expected reward is *approval*, a job task, or occasion-specific expression of positive, yet neutral approbation.

Of course, these four quadrants might also contain negative evaluations: hate (DA), disappointment (DN), rejection (SA) and criticism (SN). It is important to remember that love and responsiveness have their mirrors in hate and rejection, while more neutral cultures do not risk such extreme mood swings.

In Figure 4, Trompenaars has attempted to overlay countries that typically meet the characteristics in the chart. We should all note that even in "theatres" of operation, such as Europe, Asia and the United States, there can be wide cultural differences.

■ *Measuring Cultural Differences in Relation to Time*

Tom Cottle uses a series of circles to depict time as it relates to past, current, and future. His instructions are:

> "Think of the past, present and future as being in the shape of circles. Please draw three circles on the space available, representing past, present, and future. Arrange these circles in any way you want that best shows how you feel about the relationship of the past, present, and future. You may use different size circles. When you have finished, label each circle to show which ones is the past, which one the present, which one the future."[1]

Figure 6 shows how this has been interpreted by a number of countries.

■ *Corporate Cultures*

As difficult as it is sometimes to understand the culture in our own organizations, when we take a company global, we must best determine how to mesh the local or regional culture with that of our company, as we've seen from the wide array of differences in the last section. I will try to demonstrate how our own organization might overlay those characteristics.

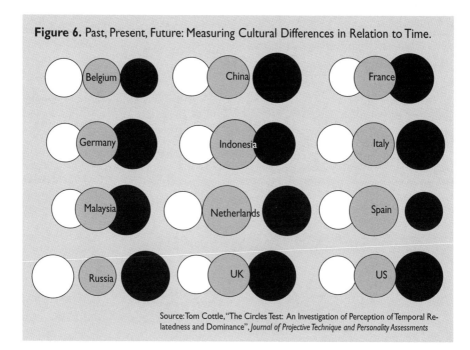

Figure 6. Past, Present, Future: Measuring Cultural Differences in Relation to Time.

Source: Tom Cottle, "The Circles Test: An Investigation of Perception of Temporal Relatedness and Dominance", *Journal of Projective Technique and Personality Assessments*

Trompenaars states:

> "Organizational culture is shaped not only by technologies and markets, but also by the cultural preferences of leaders and employees. Some international companies have European, Asian, American, or Middle Eastern subsidiaries that would be unrecognizable as belonging to the same company save for their logo and reporting procedures. Often these are fundamentally different in the logic of their structure and the meanings they bring to shared activity."

Three aspects of organizational structure are especially important in determining corporate culture:

1. The general relationship between employees and their organization;
2. The vertical or hierarchical system of authority defining superiors and subordinates; and
3. The general views of employees about the organization's destiny, purpose, and goals and their places in this.

When we look at how this is depicted in a chart (see Figure 7), we look across several dimensions — equality-hierarchy and orientation to the person-task. This enables the definition of four types of corporate cultures, which vary considerably in how they think and learn, how they change, and how they motivate, reward and resolve conflicts. The four types are described as follows:

1. The Family,
2. The Eiffel Tower,
3. The Guided Missile, and
4. The Incubator.

These four metaphors illustrate the relationship of employees to their notion of the organization. Each description of corporate culture is the "ideal type," while in practice we know there is no such thing — but hopefully you will find this useful in terms of how employees learn, change, resolve conflicts, reward, motivate and so on.

1. The Family Culture — Personal, close face-to-face relationships, hierarchical, "father figure" management style.

This type of corporate culture is power-oriented where the "father" or leader knows better than the children or subordinates. Rather than threatening, this culture is often essentially intimate. The work of the corporation in this type of culture is usually carried forward in an atmosphere that in many respects mimics the home. The Japanese culture would be a regional culture that closely matches the "family" corporate culture.

2. The Eiffel Tower Culture — Bureaucratic, roles and functions defined in advance, hierarchical status is ascribed to the role not the person.

The Eiffel Tower was chosen to symbolize this cultural type because it is steep, symmetrical, narrow at the top and broad at the base, stable, rigid and robust. In general, its structure is more important than its function. At the top of German and Austrian companies, which are typically Eiffel Tower models, the titles of professor or doctor are common on office doors. This is extremely rare in the USA.

3. The Guided Missile Culture — Egalitarian, impersonal, task-oriented, focus on end versus means, team- or project-oriented.

In the Guided Missile culture what is important is how you perform and to what extent you contribute to the jointly desired outcome. As part of a team, the members share in problem solving. The relative contribution of any one person may not be as clear as in the Eiffel Tower culture where each role is described and output can be quantified.

4. The Incubator Culture — Organizations are secondary to the fulfillment of the individual, self-expression and self-fulfillment, creative, both personal and egalitarian, little structure.

Incubators often, but not always, operate in an environment of intense emotional commitment. However, this commitment is less towards people per se than to the world-changing, society-redeeming nature of the work being undertaken. Incubator cultures enjoy the process of creating and innovating.

Which countries prefer which corporate culture? Lets take a look at placing countries into this grid (see Figure 7).

Regardless of whether or not we agree with Trompenaars and Hampden-Turner on the names of these four classic corporate cultures or even the placement of countries into this grid, I believe it is critical as managers and human resources professionals that we understand the complexity of mapping the culture of our own companies (assuming we understand what that is) with that of a vastly different regional culture. Some matches like Japan for a Family culture work well together, but I wouldn't try the hierarchical dictatorial practices in Denmark or Switzerland.

Figure 8 gives some examples of how different practices — such as motivating and rewarding employees — work differently in each of these corporate cultures.

Figure 7. Four Classic Corporate Cultures.

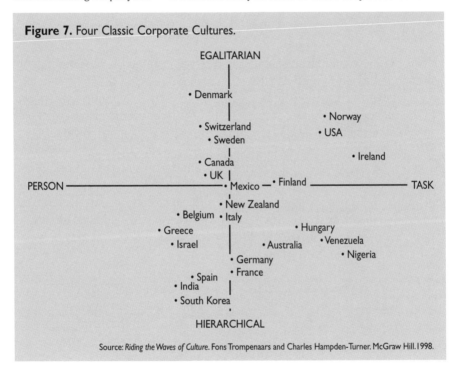

Source: *Riding the Waves of Culture.* Fons Trompenaars and Charles Hampden-Turner. McGraw Hill. 1998.

■ *Language in a Global Environment*

I am often asked what global companies do to address language when implementing a global HR solution. While there are some U.S. multinational organi-

Figure 8. Characteristics of Four Corporate Cultures.

	Family	Eiffel Tower	Guided Missle	Incubator
Relationships between employees	The whole	Specific role	Shared Objective	Spontaneous
Attitude towards authority	Parental	Superior role	Contributor	Entrepreneurial
Ways of thinking and learning	Holistic	Logical	Professional	Process oriented
Attitudes towards people	Family	Human resource	Expert	Co-creator
Ways of motivating and rewarding	Respect	Promotion	Pay for performance	Creation
Management style	Management by subjective	Management by description	Management by objective	Management by enthusiasm
Ways of changing	"Father" changes courses	Change rules and procedures	Shift aim as target changes	Improvise

Source: *Riding the Waves of Culture*. Fons Trompenaars and Charles Hampden-Turner. McGraw Hill. 1998.

zations that have established English as the system language, I believe that organizations truly interested in presenting a global persona will make information available to employees in their language of choice. Certainly, as we move toward self-service and more employee- and manager-centric processes, it will be more important than ever to accommodate the needs of the individual.

In the Feburary 2001 issue of *Human Resources Executive*, there was a very interesting article on training that specifically addressed the needs of the global workforce (specifically the technical workforce) regarding language. It is difficult enough for those not taught language skills at an early age to pick up a second or third language. But compound that with acronyms, technical terms and jargon. Michael Palm, marketing director for North America at Berlitz headquarters in Princeton, New Jersey says:

> "Two years ago, Berlitz International Inc. started getting feedback from corporate clients that some non-native workers knew English, but couldn't function in a simple business meeting. They knew gigabyte, hard drive, the English words for that. But they were unable to participate in meetings and express ideas or opinions...or digest and deliver solutions to meet requested requirements."

Training in general is probably the most important thing an organization can provide employees who need to work in a global culture or certainly on a global assignment. Training and exposure, not only to the language of the host country, but training on the cultural implications that we've looked at earlier in this chapter are critical if we expect success. Most failed global assignments occur primarily because the worker or family were not properly prepared for the changes they were going to face.

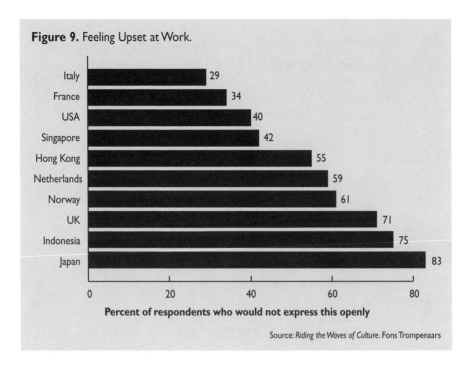

Figure 9. Feeling Upset at Work.

Percent of respondents who would not express this openly

Italy	29
France	34
USA	40
Singapore	42
Hong Kong	55
Netherlands	59
Norway	61
UK	71
Indonesia	75
Japan	83

Source: *Riding the Waves of Culture.* Fons Trompenaars

■ The Impact of the Economy on the Workforce and Culture

We started this chapter looking at the demographics of the workplace. I thought it appropriate to take a quick look at the international economic score-board to wrap this chapter up. After all, the two primary reasons today for global expansion are the need to grow business in a part of the world where the economy is thriving, not declining, and the need to look for human resources to supplement a staff that may not be readily available in our "home" countries.

I've taken my information from the year-end predictions of The Conference Board,[2] which provides valuable information to their customer base about the predictions of the economy on a global basis.

■ Outlook at a Glance

➤ **United States.** Federal tightening since early 1999 has at last begun to rein in the U.S. expansion, but the full impact in reducing consumer and investment

Figure 10. Quality of Life.

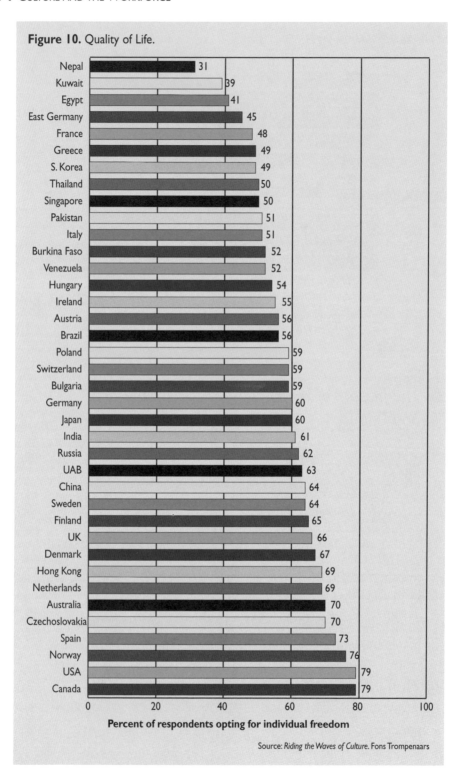

Percent of respondents opting for individual freedom

Source: *Riding the Waves of Culture.* Fons Trompenaars

spending growth will not surface until 2001. GDP growth will slip below four percent in 2001, while consumer inflation should ease after peaking above three percent.

➤ **Germany.** Credible corporate tax relief, labor market reform, and fiscal austerity measures have changed the economic outlook for the better. The anticipated boost to domestic consumption and investment points sustained economic growth comfortably above three percent through 2001.

➤ **Japan.** Enhanced corporate cash flows and efficiency in the wake of restructuring have set the foundations for recovery in business investment, while gradual improvement in personal income has begun to revive private consumption. These forces should sustain GDP expansion in a two to three percent range through 2001.

➤ **Regional overview.** Korea's double-digit annual GDP growth in 1999 and early 2000 should ease to a more sustainable six to seven percent pace in 2001, while the devaluation-driven surge in the current account surplus will dissipate next year as the won's undervaluation diminishes. Mexico is poised for the first crisis-free presidential transition in three decades, though growth will slow moderately next year in a restrictive monetary environment. Strong employment gains, sound public finances, and imminent tax reform will prolong a Dutch expansion already in its sixth year, fueling GDP advances of four percent this year and 3.5 percent in 2001. Austria's economic upswing remains solidly underpinned by robust job creation and exports, with most industries planning significant new investments through 2001.

■ Conclusion

A few tips to end on:

1. Use common cultural etiquette — in other words, treat others as you would expect to be treated in a different country or culture. In speaking situations and meetings, I found the following helpful:

➤ Do not use contractions like "don't" and "can't." Do not use two-word verbs like "come around."

Figure 11. What Makes a Good Manager.

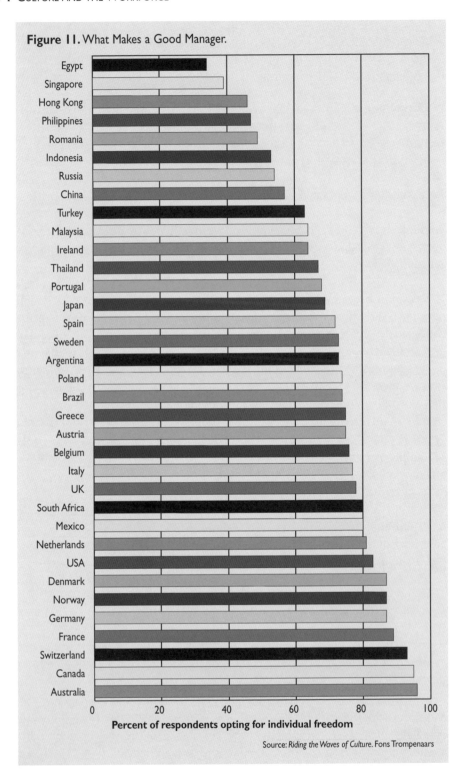

Percent of respondents opting for individual freedom

Source: *Riding the Waves of Culture.* Fons Trompenaars

➤ Be careful of the colloquial (especially because some cultures like Singapore like to copy American slang.) I once had someone say to me that they were going to "explode my brain" when they meant, "blow my mind."

➤ Do not drop words, like "that" and "which."

➤ Do not use abbreviations.

➤ If you are doing a presentation, make it available in printed form. Even better, have it translated into the language of the country you are presenting in.

➤ Learn to speak the language of the country you are working in or visiting. Even if you are there for only a few days or weeks, at least learn to speak the basics — "good morning," "good evening," "thank you," "my name is ..," "goodbye." If you can't speak the language — at least speak SLOWLY (not more loudly).

2. When implementing a global HRMS, decide what is important to your organization at both the global and local level, and then get buy-in from *both* parts of the organization. Get as much buy-in and consensus as possible and, if you are going to dictate a practice or process, be sure to explain why you made that choice. As with any other project, senior level support is critical. Understand that it is both important and critical to balance the local and global needs, according to your company's own culture.

3. Realize that each country has its unique cultural and legal sets of requirements that cannot be underestimated. Be sensitive to (and in compliance with) local cultures' views about data privacy.

4. Realize that being global is more than a word — it requires a great deal of hard work and patience and one cannot become "global" sitting in a corporate office. Get out and experience the real world beyond that of your comfort zone. I would encourage anyone working in a global environment to go on at least a temporary — if not long-term — assignment to a different country. It can be a rewarding experience for both the individual and the family.

5. Maintain the relationships you build on a global basis — they will come in handy often and be a constant source of reinforcement.

In summary, globalization of a company is more than merely expanding into another part of the world. It is important to train all employees — those going on an assignment to another part of the world or those simply exposed to different cultures as a part of doing business globally. You need to instill in your

Figure 12. Lewin's Circles.

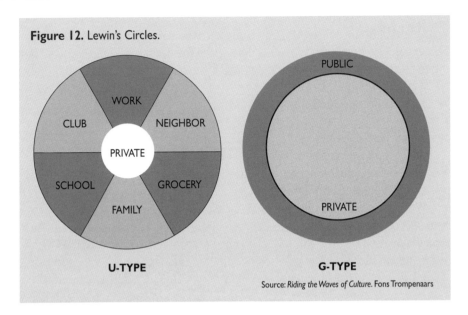

U-TYPE

G-TYPE

Source: *Riding the Waves of Culture.* Fons Trompenaars

workforce the importance of diversity both domestically and globally and that the characteristics and attitudes that make us all different also make us greater. The sum of the parts IS GREATER than the individual. Input from all parts of the organization will gain more buy-in from employees overall. This helps a company standardize when necessary, but also allows for local customization. With each part of a company sharing its knowledge within the corporate network, a successful globalization effort will result.

Row Henson has been involved in HR and HR management systems for the past 30 years. For eight years she held the role of Vice President of HRMS global product strategy at PeopleSoft where she was involved in setting the direction for their flagship HR product line. Before PeopleSoft, she spent fifteen years in the computer software industry with Dun & Bradstreet Software (previously MSA) and Cullinet Software, primarily focused on marketing, sales, support, and development of HR systems. Henson was voted one of the "Top Ten Women in Technology" by Computer Currents. In July of 2000 she received IHRIM's coveted Summit Award for lifetime achievement in her field. She has been a frequent speaker at HR associations, including IHRIM, IQPC, SHRM, APA, The Conference Board, AHRI, HRPS, and HR Technology. Additionally, she has been published in numerous personnel and software periodicals, including Personnel Journal, CFO Magazine, Software Magazine, IHRIM Journal *and* Benefits & Compensation Solutions Magazine. *She serves on advisory boards for Authoria and Exult. Prior to working in the HR software world, Henson was a Director of Personnel for seven years with a non-profit health agency. She holds a Bachelor degree in Business Administration, with an emphasis in Management and Insurance, from the University of Georgia. She "retired" from fulltime employment in July of 2000, but continues to be very involved in the HR field and serves as a PeopleSoft fellow, continuing to provide input and advice to them for their HRMS product line. She can be reached at* **row_henson@peoplesoft.com***.*

■ References

Trompenaars, Fons and Hampden-Turner, Charles. *Riding the Waves of Culture: Understanding Cultural Diversity in Global Business.* Second Edition, McGraw-Hill: 1998.

Attracting and Retaining Your Human Assets, A Look at the Recruiting Dilemma. PeopleSoft Whitepaper, December 2000.

Henson, Row. "Globalization of Human Resources." *IHRIM Journal,* Volume III, Number 3, September 1999, pp. 39-43.

Omae, Keniche, *The Borderless World: Power and Strategy in the Interlinked Economy,* Harper Business: April 1999.

Marx, Elisabeth. *Breaking Through Culture Shock,* Nicholas Brealey: June 2001

■ Endnotes

1 The sources of research for this chapter include a number of books and articles, which are referenced. However, I would like to give special acknowledgement to several other sources. The first is the book *Riding the Waves of Culture* by Fons Trompenaars and Charles Hampden-Turner, published by McGraw Hill in 1998. I found this to be extremely helpful in looking at culture and adapting culture to that of our own organizations. Secondly, I have borrowed a number of recent demographics on the global workforce from John Sumser, the founder and CEO of Internet Business Network. And finally, I'd like to give special thanks to my employer PeopleSoft who has given me the opportunity to both work and live in Europe and Asia and learn firsthand about "global culture."

2 The Conference Board. *International Economic Scoreboard.* Volume 8, Number 3 and 4 - 3rd/4th Quarter 2000. The Conference Board, 845 Third Avenue, NY 10022 USA.

Part Four:
The Global
HR Function

"When the group or civilization declines, it is through no mystic limitation of a corporate life, but through the failure of its political or intellectual leaders to meet the challenge of change."
— Will and Ariel Durant

"We must be the change we wish to see in the world."
—Mahatma Gandhi

• • • • • • • •

As the overall organization globalizes, so must HR. But its progress raises all kinds of questions. What sort of managerial mindsets should global HR foster? What strategic role can HR play as the organization globalizes? How does organizational size affect these concerns? And then, there is that thorny problem of data privacy, which becomes vastly complex in a global environment.

As the following authors point out, boundaryless HR is not the sort of field in which one-size solutions fit all problems. Indeed, a single global organization may need multiple approaches, roles, and mindsets, even within a single unit. These chapters discuss a number of issues with a sense of the wide range of responses we might need for successful HR in the globalized world.

Managers, Mindsets and Globalization

By Daniel Sullivan

Traditionally, discussing human capital management in the context of the global boundaryless economy revolved around the principal issues of human resource management (see sidebar). Anchoring analysis was the general idea that the asset value of managers grew as the corporation invested in their development — in this context, by posting them to newly opened markets, compensating them lavishly and trusting they would enrich their management repertoire to deal with the continued fade of national, market and institutional boundaries. Certainly, these issues still shape general issues of managing human capital in the context of a global market.

Other readings in this chapter, however, report events and trends that hasten the globalization of business in ways that confirm but also challenge these traditional tasks. Indeed, a cursory look around the business world shows that managers cannot pause; they must relentlessly question their thoughts, ideas and policies so that they can attract, develop and retain workers who are equipped for the challenges of the global economy. Consequently, we increasingly confront novel issues of managing workplace behaviors to optimize the value of people, both those who work abroad, as well as those who work at home. More precisely, there is a strong sense that managers must align human capital with the vision, core values and strategies of their firm. Formally aligning these conditions lets the company hold its human capital policies and practices to the standards of excellence and innovation of a brutally progressive global economy.

Effectively, then, the onset of globalization directs our attention to the matter of an individual's mindset and, importantly, its capacity for managing

PRINCIPAL ISSUES OF HUMAN RESOURCE MANAGEMENT

➤ The Selection and Recruitment of Qualified Individuals
➤ Training and Development of Personnel
➤ Assessment and Compensation of Performance
➤ Retention of Competent Personnel
➤ Management of the Interface between Labor and Management

knowledge to boost the value of human capital. Thus, this chapter submits that the vitality of human capital in a globalizing economy steadily escalates companies' sensitivity to the crucial role of managers' mindsets. Not surprisingly, companies that practice this principle see the remarkable value of human capital. For instance, John S. Reed, former chairman of Citicorp, noted "Our global human capital may be as important a resource as, if not more important than, our financial capital."

■ The Crux of Change

Not so long ago, the norm of the tightly bounded business world was many large, centralized companies that organized their human resource strategies on the basis of the easily applied criteria of technical competence. Meritocracy, narrowly defined, prevailed explicitly — managers, who moved the most products, moved upward and, by extension, moved outward to run operations in emerging markets. Practicality prevailed with the presumption that operational excellence eventually translated into executive enlightenment. While this has long been a successful approach, trends in markets, companies, cultures, technologies and institutions spur "gales of creative destruction" that rupture this orderly linkage.

Increasingly, the knowledge embedded in the design, development and delivery of most products and services constitutes a growing proportion of the total value of operations. For instance, succeeding in the microprocessor industry is not a function of tightly controlling traditional labor and material costs. Rather, victory follows from understanding how to position people to leverage the technological knowledge embedded in microprocessors, the knowledge embedded in highly specialized manufacturing equipment, and the knowledge of branding a product that is intrinsically a commodity. The ability to move an increasing volume of products out the door, consequently, fades in importance to managing the knowledge and inspiring the learning that create, sustain, and extend products. Setting a meaningful linkage between human capital and firm performance, therefore, demands adapting management to the game of globalization and its given technical competence and expectation of innovative mindsets.

For example, consider the experiences of a technology powerhouse like Sun Microsystems. In a break from the ethos of its engineering foundations, Sun rethought how it selects managers to run its growing overseas operations. During its initial international expansion in the early 1990s, Sun simply looked at the technical requirements of the overseas job and then found the successful person whose skills filled the gap. The poor track record of the first wave of Sun's expatriates prodded the admission that technical competency was a necessary but insufficient basis for getting the job done in loosely bounded economies. Sun found that a manager's softer skills and personal characteristics were often more important to defining and doing the job right. Hence, Sun's human resource executives recruited those managers with an open mind to the many exotic tasks that pop up when dealing with foreign governments, building local networks, negotiating across cultures, coaching local managers, and creatively navigating confusing market systems. Explained John Hall, Sun's vice president of international human resources, "More attention is being given up front to identifying the right assignments and the right people for them. We have quite a rigid process for getting an expat position approved and another for choosing the person to fill it. We want our people to think long and hard, not just about the experience and skills set, but about the whole situation and what type of people will succeed in that environment."[1]

These managers realized that communication skills, motivation, self-reliance and diplomacy, in addition to outright technical competence, developed the value of local human capital.

Plainly put, fading national, cultural and competitive boundaries link the value of human capital with managers' cognitive perspectives as much, if perhaps not more, than their technical aptitude. Various reports amplify this premise. The Harvard Business School and AMROP found that 96 percent of executives believed that personal leadership was the key ingredient of career success in global markets.[2] Asked why, most respondents noted that people in global markets often find themselves as a lead manager in remote locations. These managers realized that communication skills, motivation, self-reliance and diplomacy, in addition to outright technical competence, developed the value of local human capital. Similarly, a McKinsey and Company report said that technical competence is simply the foundation of human capital management in the global economy world. Building the actual structure for success, however, depends on the way that managers interpret, analyze and decide. That is, the McKinsey report concluded, "Global market pioneers must have a particular mindset,"[3] adding that "When you look behind the success stories of leading globalizers, you find companies that have learned how to think differently from the herd. They seek out different information, process it in a different way, come to different conclusions, and make different decisions. Where others see threats and complexity, they see opportunity. Where others see a barren landscape, they see a cornucopia of choices."[4]

"Global market pioneers must have a particular mindset,"[3] adding that "When you look behind the success stories of leading globalizers, you find companies that have learned how to think differently from the herd.

It is tempting to think that the advent of globalization releases one from traditional rules and policies of human resource. For example, the recent infatuation with the idea of a Net-based New Economy led some to argue that the principles of the brick-based Old Economy were moot, if not obsolete. However, given the tendency of limitless utopias to fall into entropy (as has befallen the New Economy), we hold that traditional policies and rules still prevail. No matter the scale and scope of globalization, the bedrock of human capital management depends upon effective recruitment, training, motivation and retention of people with the necessary technical skills. Nonetheless, expanding globalization spurs us to introduce the idea of mindsets and managers as the point of separation between able versus innovative human capital management.

■ The Idea of a Mindset

Every day we see events and read reports of developments in the world of business. For instance, Matsushita moves VCR production to low-cost East European plants, Nokia outlines its latest wireless device, or GM announces the end of the Oldsmobile brand. These sorts of things fit our particular understanding of the structure and behavior of consumers, companies, markets and institutions. Others, though, seem to challenge or confuse our interpretation of the business world. For instance, Napster threatens the foundation of the global music recording industry, U.S.-based McKinsey and Company appoints a native of India as its CEO, eBay sets out to change the means of international trade, or Japan reports yet another year of flat or declining corporate profits and prosperity. Generally, we try to make sense of the usual and unusual through our particular mindset — essentially the logic or interpretative framework that guides how we classify and discriminate changes in ways that let us understand what we perceive to be happening.

More formally, Peter Senge defines mindsets as "deeply ingrained assumptions, generalizations, or even pictures or images that influence how we understand the world and how we take action."[5] Essentially, then, a mindset represents a manager's elemental understanding of a situation. It helps him or her identify vital, trivial and irrelevant conditions. A mental model translates a fundamental understanding of how things work and what we believe ought to happen into the foundation for a decision. When we encounter a novel situation, we try to tailor our existing mindset to make sense of the new phenomenon — much like many executives' recent struggles to grasp the meaning and implications of the Internet to the business designs of the "Old Economy." Often, a person's mindset cannot sense the right signal amidst all the noise in the system. In such cases, cognitive dissonance moves us to question and, when necessary, abandon what we held to be true and timeless principles of business — again, much as the fascination with the New Economy paradigm did to conventional notions of business.

For our purpose, a manager's mindset frames what they see and, hence, how they try to interpret a situation. Consequently, a manager's mindset determines whether he or she notices a particular situation, how he or she will try to make sense of it, how he or she will communicate this understanding to colleagues, and ultimately, how he or she will deal with it. The fact that a manager's mindset frames what he or she sees, therefore, goes a long way in explaining why some executives quickly "see" the implications of nebulous situations while others ponder if something might be happening and, by extension, why the former seize the moment while the latter debate the mission and membership of the latest task force.

Managers and their mindsets in a world of falling boundaries are a growing curiosity. Research spotlights three principal types of mindsets to categorize managers: The ethnocentric mindset, the polycentric mindset, and the geocentric mindset. We look at each with respect to their implications to how managers interpret, analyze, and make decisions in a world of falling boundaries. Before starting, it is important to establish two conditions. First, if we asked 10 people to define the idea of the global economy, we would probably get 10 different replies. We would likely hear explanations of falling trade barriers, coordinated institutional policies, fewer competitors in more markets, greater standardization of products, and so on. In principle, we view the global market as containing each and all of these elements. With regards to managing human capital, we treat globalization as a euphemism for what we generally call international business.[6] That is, globalization is the outcome of the integration of nations in ways that permit and promote the freer movement of people, products and capital.

Second, as you review each mindset, keep in mind that there is no fundamentally superior outlook. Rather, each mindset has benefits and risks that make it, depending on the individual, company or situation, a useful way to manage human capital in the boundaryless world.

■ The Ethnocentric Mindset

The ethnocentric mindset holds that the values and practices of one's company and home country are intrinsically superior to those in others. Hence, the ethnocentric manager presumes that if my business design or national ethic has already proven successful, then it will work well anywhere for anyone.

■ Benefits of Ethnocentrism

1. Often, a technological innovation or hard-to-copy business design gives a firm an edge against better-positioned rivals — whether within a particular industry or emerging market. For the latter, transferring managers with ethnocentric mindsets from the home office to emerging market safeguards proprietary technology and ensures installing the idealized business design.
2. Sending managers to odd, exotic places (whether physical, such as a newly opened market, or abstract, such as a new product domain) poses cognitive challenges. An executive, guided by the ethnocentric mindset of his or her parent company's business design, endures less anxiety in making sense of unusual situations. Certainty of belief promotes leadership that inspires confidence and emulation by colleagues and subordinates.
3. In-depth understanding of an issue, task, design or nation makes the ethnocentric manager a proficient teacher. Helping fellow workers master the intricacies of the business enhances their contribution to performance. An ethnocentric manager can quickly seize opportunities to leverage human capital by building a focused workforce that reduces business risk.

THE ETHNOCENTRIC MINDSET IN PLAY

Many Japanese firms try to transfer their management mindset and business design directly to their foreign operations, regardless of where they might happen to be located. Japanese companies believe that the particular mindset of their company is the foundation for their success. In addition, Japanese managers often believe that their managerial innovations, such as lean "manufacturing" and "*kaizen*," are ideally supported by the principles of their homegrown and home-tested business design.

Japanese firms are popular examples, yet an ethnocentric mindset is not unique unto them. Successful companies from every nation, when expanding and operating abroad, often apply an ethnocentric outlook. For instance, MBNA America, one of the top credit card companies in the world, faithfully relies on its business design to guide its international expansion. Judged by many as the premier bank in the United States, MBNA America has staunchly transferred its founding design principles to organize its operations in Canada and the UK. Operationally, MBNA relies on carefully selected expatriates to imbue the local "people of MBNA" (by design, the company prohibits the term employee in favor of "people") to the company's guiding Statement of Purpose and train them in the intricacies of their prized business design.

■ Risks of Ethnocentrism

1. The effort to force all situations to fit the one and only way of doing business flirts with trying to slam circular pegs into the idealized square slot. Successful poundings can carry a high price in terms of falling morale, demotivation and lost opportunities.
2. An ethnocentric mindset is susceptible to cognitive blinders. Unchecked, design utopia may deteriorate into design failure as the ethnocentric manager fails to regulate the creative tension between those colleagues, customers and officials that apply different mindsets. This risk echoes the not-invented-here syndrome — rejection of an idea, regardless of its merits, because it originated elsewhere.
3. An ethnocentric mindset aggravates the difficulty of adapting to new places, people and processes. Anchored to his or her experiences back home, an ethnocentric executive can often struggle to absorb ideas or resolve cognitive dissonance.

■ The Polycentric Mindset

A polycentric outlook spurs an individual or organization to adapt to differences, both real and imagined, between people, businesses or nations. The polycentric manager tries to adapt to or, ideally, assimilate the values and attitudes of those who he or she deals with.

■ Benefits of Polycentrism

1. Polycentric mindsets bridge different groups by playing the role of empathetic interpreters and facilitator. Polycentric managers' sensitivity to the silent language of different groups — i.e., the nonverbal cues of communication — helps them improve decision-making, brainstorming and networking among people with various outlooks. As such, this outlook is particularly useful in companies expanding via acquisitions, alliances and mergers.

2. The purposeful bent toward empathetic flexibility can accelerate market entry, product adaptation and competitive positioning. Advocacy of rich opportunities in emerging markets expedites attracting and motivating people to venture into the void. This outlook works particularly well when expanding into newly opened markets where limited employment regulation hikes the influence of cultural issues.

3. Polycentric managers travel with a mindset attuned to the expectation of various customers, markets and institutions. They eagerly await the challenge to start the lines of communications needed to share ideas and best practices. Generally, polycentric managers eagerly venture into new markets, intently study situations and quickly transfer knowledge to others.

THE POLYCENTRIC MINDSET IN PLAY

A polycentric manager would reluctantly debate who ought to staff host country operations, as locals are intuitively familiar with the local business environment. Hence, they are an enormous competitive advantage. For instance, when operating outside the United States, Microsoft tries to hire foreign nationals rather than post-expatriate managers to overseas slots. Robert Herbold, the company's executive vice president and chief operating officer, explained that "You want people who know the local situation, its value system, the way work gets done, the way people use technology in that particular country, and who the key competitors are. If you send someone in fresh from a different region or country, they don't know those things."[9] Philosophically, Bill Gates, chairman and chief software architect of Microsoft, suggests a polycentric mindset is somewhat of a moral obligation, adding, "It sends the wrong message to have a foreigner come over to run things."

■ Risks of Polycentrism

1. A polycentric executive can direct his or her energy toward preferred products or markets to the rash exclusion of uninteresting ideas and places. Unchecked, polycentric managers frequently have limited territorial scope, often limited to their experience and knowledge of particular business or country.

2. A polycentric outlook often champions the ways of idealized foreign markets as, if not more, enlightened than the practices of his or her peers, company and home. This inclination can culminate in "going native" — the loss of a comparative perspective that leads to poor sensemaking of situations from both viewpoints.

3. The uncertainty triggered by falling boundaries can give undue credibility to the polycentric outlook — in the absence of objective metrics, one tends to rely on subjective interpretations. Risks arise when the polycentric manager generalizes his or her experiences in a small domain to a larger context.

■ The Geocentric Mindset

Geocentrism assumes nations have inalienable characteristics that are neither superior nor inferior but simply there. The geocentric mindset accepts the premise that bright people are doing bright things around the world. Therefore, wise management of human capital depends on understanding the interaction between the many things that are alike and the many things that are different. Once done, a geocentric manager can adapt his or her a mindset so that, while not perfect in any, functions well in all situations. More colorfully, there is talk of the goal of human capital management to develop so-called "cosmopolitans." These folks are viewed as a special type of men and women who are rising to leadership positions in their companies by "finding commonalities ... [and] spread[ing] universal ideas and juggl[ing] the requirements of diverse places."[7] Whether called geocentric or cosmopolitan, the outcome is the same — people and companies with this mindset seek and see commonalities across nations.

■ Advantages of Geocentrism

1. A geocentric mindset discerns the many beliefs, values, behaviors and practices of individuals and organizations. This outlook can help a manager assess

THE GEOCENTRIC MINDSET IN PLAY

As one of the world's leading multinational corporations, one could reasonably conjecture that Canon Inc. had developed a terrific geocentric outlook. Canon President Fujio Mitarai quickly objects to this popular portrayal. Under his direction, Canon will open regional headquarters for Europe and the Americas by 2002. These units will perform research that taps into the local design mindsets — i.e., engineers in California will pursue research in areas like digital and networking technology, while those in France will concentrate on telecommunications. Explained Mitarai, "Until recently, everything we did overseas was an extension of what we were doing in Japan. From now on, we want to give birth to new value abroad. We want to make the best of the different kinds of expertise available in different countries."[10]

workplace behaviors in ways that support integrating a diversity of human resources. The elemental benefit of boundaryless markets is exposure and an ever-expanding range of ways to do things better. Aggressive search for new learning opportunities sharpens the competitive edge of an individual or firm. This outlook prepares managers to merge business cultures and establish global standards for human capital policies that are sensitive to local employment practices.

2. A geocentric mindset taps learning opportunities around the world by pushing a manager to seek new ideas about running a business — no matter their national, cultural or competitive origin. The task is studying an event, identifying opportunities and threats, and gauging the degree that he or she can transfer the best practices to their business.

3. A geocentric mindset moves people to think of individual markets as part of the global community. Canon Inc., for example, tries to practice a philosophy calls *kyosei* or living together. President Fujio Mitarai of Canon explained that *kyosei* spreads with Canon wherever it goes because "When we work in different parts of the world, we want to be welcomed and respected. We have to live for the common good."[8] Thus, geocentrism encourages aligning your human capital strategies with your firm's culture, values and vision.

■ *The Risks of Geocentrism*

1. The geocentric outlook can result in some executives that know a little about everything but not much about anything. Learning processes can suffer as those with great expertise question the true usefulness of arguably superficial treatment of ideas.

2. The geocentric mindset is intrinsically difficult to develop and retain due to the challenge of preserving a sense of who you are while simultaneously refining your sensitivity to the ideas and attitudes of various peoples and processes.
3. The struggle to sense situations, interpret ideas and transfer knowledge can overwhelm the most able executive. Done well, a geocentric outlook can turbocharge human capital. Done poorly, a geocentric outlook can erode the sense of common purpose, ruin the clarity of task, and get lost in a hodgepodge of various mindsets.

■ Which Mindsets When?

While inviting, it is rash to make a blanket statement about which mindset is best suited for anchoring human capital management in the global economy. The default choice — all people in a company should aspire to the same mindset — reduces a complex question to a flimsy assertion. Granted, some managers might contend that an ethnocentric mindset, versus the polycentric or geocentric outlooks, best anchors a human capital strategy. Nonetheless, we believe that ethnocentric, polycentric and geocentric mindsets have strengths and weaknesses that preclude designating one the ideal.

More specifically, the fallout of falling national, cultural and competitive boundaries is quite simple: There are fewer and fewer universal rules about which mindset one should apply to interpret, analyze and decide. If anything, flexibility is the increasing order of the day. For instance, recall Canon President Fujio Mitarai's intent to liberate his company from the mindset shackles of conventional thought in Japan and access ideas around the world (see sidebar on page 21). Therefore, understanding the meaning of globalization to the design and development of human capital increasingly rests on an eclectic mix of ethnocentric, polycentric and geocentric mindsets.

Computer maker Dell shows the practicality of mixing complementary mindsets. Dell hires mostly local managers to run its international operations in the belief that they contribute terrific polycentric benefits. Still, Dell supplements these people with long-term expatriates from the United States who have exhibited a geocentric mindset. Dell also has "swat" teams, standing teams of specialized executives with intentionally ethnocentric outlooks. These teams roam the globe, establishing and fine-tuning overseas operations in line with the way they were setup and run in Texas, Dell's home base. So far, Dell's mixing of mindsets has boosted the value and performance of its human capital. Individuals have the freedom to slot themselves, given their sense of their skills and outlook, into their preferred mindset track. Dell, meanwhile, reduces the odds of personnel failure because of poor fit between the job and a manager's mindset. In addition, Dell gains the benefits of a self-motivating workforce by virtue of people tracking themselves into jobs that fit their outlook. Therefore, like many aspects of business, the "best" mindset often depends on what else is going on within the market, company or an existing career.

■ Mindset Traps

Simply segregating managers into like-minded cohorts is not the moral of Dell's experience. Rather, this example shows a way to begin building a pool of resourceful human capital that then permits designing an eclectic mix of mindsets. Before developing this point, we should note two intrinsic dangers of segregating mindsets. The first is groupthink, whereby pressures for conformity within a cohort installs and enforces the "correct" mindset. Groupthink often precludes critically evaluating, either when necessary or as an intellectual exercise, ideas about the way people and processes work. The second is the escalation of commitment, whereby managers steadfastly pursue a particular line of thought in the face of increasingly disappointing performance. Escalation typically ensues from managers' intent to justify the past or appear decisive about the future.

Therefore, clustering managers and mindsets creates a terrific resource — as long as the cluster actively preempts boundaries on the type, content and flow of information. Dell, for example, disciplines cohorts with committee reviews and best practice benchmarks. Similarly, we saw earlier that Microsoft tries to staff polycentric managers in local operations around the world. Still, Microsoft tries to control the risk that this group intentionally or inadvertently installs cognitive biases in decision making. For instance, many Microsoft teams operate globally, communicating by e-mail on projects, situations and trends. More powerfully, all groups are subject to similar human capital assessments, including an "organizational health index," in which employees rate their business units on 19 attributes, like overall job satisfaction, whether they feel their division has clear goals, and their general sense of intellectual fit.

The records of Dell and Microsoft highlight the importance of managing the mindset mix of your human capital with a formal bent toward integration. Whether the cohort in question endorses an ethnocentric, polycentric or geocentric mindset is moot — all add value to the human capital of a firm. The task incumbent on the managers of human capital is ably communicating the vitality of integrating information — both that which dovetails with, as well as that which may refute a particular mindset — during decision making. Research shows that effective leaders, irrespective of their particular mindset, entertain different points of view in interpreting scenarios and estimating outcomes. The reality of an enduring shortage of truly effective leaders calls for preempting cognitive bias traps within teams, task forces, and chains of command of competing mindsets.

■ Summary

The premise of this chapter is direct: globalization is a momentous agent of change that moves the basis of business activity and, hence, the basis of valuable human capital, from a hard-asset standpoint to a knowledge-based mentality. We are in the early stages of an era where knowledge, not labor, materials, or capital, determines and sustains competitiveness. The global economy continually amplifies the power of this link. Plainly stated, thriving depends on transitioning from treating human capital with an asset-based view to one that can apply an eclectic mix of ethnocentric, polycentric and geocentric mindsets to manage ideas, knowledge and learning. In the global economy, Peter Drucker cautions, "There will be no poor countries or industries, only ignorant ones."

As we earlier noted, technical competency has been, is, and will always be the foundation for success. Still, the falling boundaries that animate the global market inexorably call for mindsets that can handle contingencies in problem solving, motivation, leadership, use of power, and consensus building, to say nothing of the ability to make sense of trade rules and regulations, business designs, joint venture practices, and looming market realities. Overall, this expertise and outlook inspires the self-confidence to integrate the customs of technical competence with the catalyst of mindsets called for by globalization.

Daniel Sullivan is an Associate Professor of Management at the University of Delaware. His research looks at managers and mindsets, corporate strategy, corporate governance, and measurement theory. His work has appeared in, among others, Law and Society Review, Academy of Management Journal, Journal of International Business Studies, *and* Management International Review. *Presently, he is a member of the editorial boards of the latter two. Over his career, he has earned numerous teaching honors, notably being voted the Outstanding Teacher by seven consecutive EMBA classes. Sullivan has taught management course programs in several foreign countries, including England, France and Bulgaria. He, along with Professors John Daniel and Lee Radebaugh, are authors of* Globalization and Business, *(Prentice Hall, Fall 2001). Sullivan can be reached at* **Sullivad@be.udel.edu**.

■ Endnotes

1   Patricia Carey, "Coming Home," *CFO*, June 1998, p. 77.

2   Study entitled "The New International Executive Business Leadership for the 21st Century," Harvard Business School and Amrop International, 1995. Reported in Andrea Crisp, "International Careers Made Easy," *The European*, March, 1995, p. 27.

3   Tsun-Yan Hseih, Johanne Lavoie, and Robert Samek, "Are You Taking Your Expatriate Talent Seriously?" *The McKinsey Quarterly*, No. 3, 1999, pp. 70-83.

4   Jane Fraser and Jeremy Oppenheim, "What's new about globalization?" *The McKinsey Quarterly*, 2, 1997, pp. 168-179.

5   Peter Senge, *The Fifth Discipline: The Art and Practice of the Learning Organization*. New York: Doubleday/Currency, 1990.

6   John Daniels, Lee Radebaugh, and Daniel Sullivan, *Globalization and Business*. New York: Prentice Hall, Fall, 2001.

7   Rosabeth Kanter, *World Class: Thriving Locally in the Global Economy*. New York: Simon & Schuster, 1995.

8   Leslie Holstrom and Simon Brady, "The Changing Face of Global Business," *Fortune*, 140, Special Section, July 24, 2000, p. 5.

9   Jeremy Kahn, "The World's Most Admired Companies." *Fortune*, 140, October 11, 1999, p. 274.

10   Reported in Leslie Holstrom and Simon Brady, The Changing Face of Global Business: The Global Myth? Retrieved from www.fortune.com/sections/ April 1, 2000.

Reprinted from the *IHRIM Journal*, Volume V, Number 4, November 2001, pp. 18-23.

Mid-size, Nimble, and Going Global:
HR and Human Capital's Strategic Role in the Globalization of the Mid-size Company

By James E. Spoor

■ Introduction

Going global is not a one dimensional one-size-fits-all, strategy or event. Operating outside the home country of any enterprise can be done in various and differing ways. The alternatives differ widely and often are evolutionary in nature — one approach leading to another in a rational evolutionary manner as time and circumstances deem appropriate.

The primary focus of this chapter is to identify the more commonly used approaches to global business and to provide strategic perspectives, assistance and directional alternatives for the HR and human capital (HC) executive in the small to mid-size company that is planning to "go global."

Within the next several pages, a number of the HR/HC issues and challenges will be outlined for each of the predominant global operating strategies. These will include a high level examination of global business issues, cultural and cross-cultural issues, organizational and structural issues, governmental and regulatory compliance issues, and the supporting HR/HC policy and related systems issues of international and transnational operations.

This chapter focuses on outlining significant opportunities for the newly emerging breed of business-oriented HR and human capital leader who is committed to contributing in a truly strategic manner to the future direction and success of his or her enterprise. While it highlights some of the more significant issues, it must be recognized that endeavoring to more fully address the strategic issues of globalization of the mid-size enterprise is a topic that, if treated in greater depth, could easily become the subject of a comprehensive textbook.

■ Going Global — The Decision

In the past, decisions such launching operations outside of the home country of an enterprise were made by boards of directors and/or by a tightly knit group of executive insiders. This usually occurred with little or no input or discussion regarding the HR and human capital dimensions or consideration of the HR issues involved. The view commonly expressed was, we've decided, now it is an implementation issue. "Make it happen!" was the message to the HR organization and to the other support functions within the enterprise.

The price paid and the results achieved depended as much on stubborn tenacity, leadership commitment and serendipitous circumstance as they depended on the result of careful planning and effective execution.

Today, the global business environment has changed and matured. Business competition transcends any national borders. The workforce is truly a global workforce in which many professionals and managers simply have home addresses that reflect where they sleep, but not necessarily where their nominal office is located or where their work is really performed. It is a different world for the HR and human capital executive. Today, if the operating management of an organization believes that "going global" is the answer, the strategically focused HR executive must immediately raise a challenge and ask of the executive team, "If going global is the answer, what was the question?" The purpose of this challenge is not to be obstructive or resistant to the going global initiative, but rather to assure that the best approach is taken. That challenging probe and the implicit sibling probe, "What is the problem we are trying to solve?" may be couched in more diplomatic terms and positioned in a more constructive manner, but the question and the answers are essential if the HR and human capital executive is to do their job effectively and if that senior level HR person is to play a meaningful role in assuring a cor-

> *... if the operating management of an organization believes that "going global" is the answer, the strategically focused HR executive must ... ask ..., "If going global is the answer, what was the question?"*

rect strategic focus and tactical direction for what is potentially one of the most significant issues facing corporations today.

There is a vital aspect regarding global business that is too often not understood and the consequences of error in this arena are too significant to be ignored. The hard cold fact is that "going global" does not define a destination or business result. It does not define how to get there, or even suggest a routing. Going global is not a business goal. Going global is not a one dimensional one-size-fits-all strategy or event. Operating and conducting business outside the home country of any enterprise can be done in various and differing ways.

It is essential that the entire leadership team of any organization clearly understand that "going global" is simply one of many means that may help an organization get to a desired destination or achieve its intended goals.

■ What is the Problem that "Going Global" May Help Solve?

Why do organizations decide that global expansion is important?

What do people mean when they talk about global expansion?

What is it that these organizations are trying to achieve?

High-level corporate goals typically address one or both of two issues — market expansion with its related revenue opportunity and/or labor market related issues. These are often stated in broad terms such as "to achieve significantly increased revenue growth and profitability and to provide superior levels of service to our customers" or, on the labor side, they are stated using terms such as "to operate in labor markets that allow us to maintain competitive pricing through improved manufacturing costs." From those broad goals many "how and why" questions must be asked so that alternatives can be explored and evaluated. Global is one of the "how" alternatives.

Within that high level global decision, a series of "why" questions can be addressed and resolved. The results of that next level of drill down are usually articulated in specifics, which normally fall into the following categories:

➤ To expand market presence and position the enterprise as a global business in order to achieve market expansion and revenue growth;

➤ To open up new markets and establish a strong local presence in key national markets and to more effectively penetrate previously under-served markets;

➤ To better serve the support needs of global clients;

➤ To achieve more competitive cost structures for production and manufacturing functions as essential ingredients to maintaining competitive pricing of goods and services; and/or

➤ To expand the enterprise's potential labor pool for skilled professional and managerial staff skills that are in short supply or not available in the home country labor market.

While potentially inflammatory to those who choose not to accept an argument that low labor costs are appropriate pursuits for businesses or who feel that moving jobs offshore is wrong, these are all appropriate and legitimate business reasons for considering the extension of an existing business into the global arena. The next layer of decision centers around the alternative ways of making that global extension occur.

■ Alternative "Going Global" Forms of Business?

What are the alternative routes to the desired global goal?

What are the choices for achieving global business goals?

Why should an organization determine that operating in one manner or another outside of their home county is the best alternative?

Once the reasons for a global initiative have been defined and the desired results have been articulated, the new question on the table becomes, "How do we most effectively accomplish what we plan to accomplish?" While there is a predictable instinct to simply jump into the global business water and learn how to swim — the all or nothing approach — seldom does that approach work. The more astute and wise approach recognizes that there is a logical sequence of form-of-business alternatives to be considered.

Starting with the most basic and continuing on through the most complex and demanding, these going global alternatives normally can be defined as follows:

➤ **Going Global — Stage 1 — Transnational Selling of Products and Services.** In this alternative, the entity continues to operate from its home country base, but actively promotes its products and services on a global or targeted national basis. Ads are placed, the web site is modified to be less nationally-centric and to achieve a more global and transnational appeal, news releases and public relations promote the global value proposition, trade shows are attended, promotional efforts are focused at the desired market, international sales calls are made, orders are taken, and goods are shipped and/or services are delivered. At this stage, the "going global" enterprise has put little skin in the game and little change has occurred in the daily business operation of the enterprise other than people have learned how to deal with international payments and shipping. No real culture change occurs.

➤ **Going Global — Stage 2 — Independent National, Regional or Locally-based Distribution Channels.** In this alternative, individuals and/or entities are engaged as independent resellers to represent, promote and actively sell the product or service within a defined geographic area and/or industry sector. The reseller, by virtue of their independent status, may also represent other complementary, supplementary or even competitive products. The local distributor entity may engage in limited localization of the product or service and will normally handle installation, implementation, training and reasonable post-sale support functions.

At this stage the investment of time and effort to handle the recruitment of channel partners, training, and modification of operating procedures to accommodate the needs of the partner take on importance. On the HR side, there are no actual international employees and the HR/HC function's contribution is likely to be limited to assistance in dealing with high level cross-cultural issues.

➤ **Going Global — Stage 3 — Franchising or Product/Technology Licensing.** Under this scenario, the going global enterprise normally establishes formal strategic partnership relationships with established and respected nationally — or regionally-based businesses. These may be licenses or may be in the form of grants of a franchise or franchise-like rights to the national partner. The partner entity commonly is already established in a closely aligned business area, and will have the base of business contacts and relationships in place to provide reasonable assurance that they can introduce the new product and be successful. The locally-based "partners" will serve the market needs within a defined geographic and sometimes industry market sector specific area. The product or service may range from fast food, to technology, machinery or equipment, raw materials or even software. The local entity is given the business formula, the product, the needed knowledge and technology, the manuals and the how-to guidance, and they operate under a defined set of conditions and with defined result expectations and defined financial and reporting obligations to the grantor.

In this level of relationship the HR and human capital issues have increased slightly and may involve the facilitation of true knowledge transfer and the sharing of business intelligence. But no on-going employee issues exist to challenge the HR/HC staff.

➤ **Going Global — Stage 4 — Establishment of a formal corporate registered office or subsidiary to handle marketing and sales responsibilities for a defined geographic or national sector.** As the corporation reaches this level of involvement in doing business across national borders, there is an implicit and explicit commitment to the investment of resources, people and business development efforts. There is also an implicit recognition and acceptance of the fact that the organization is "taking on" not only other transnational/global competitors and surfacing as a competitive challenge, but it also signals that it intends to compete with respected local and regional providers of similar products and services.

Until this point, the level of commitment of the parent entity can be compared to that of the chicken in the ham and eggs breakfast analogy. The chicken lays the egg, which is eaten for breakfast, and the life of the chicken goes on. The pig, on the other hand, in contributing the ham portion of the meal has made an irreversible commitment. In this scenario, financial resources, people resources and reputation of the enterprise are on the line for the "going global" company.

The HR and human capital issues are now of a significant nature. The going global enterprise now has people employed in another country. It is necessary to assure that those people are properly recruited, trained, paid and managed in accordance with both corporate standards, as well as with new national employment standards and laws. As the operation grows, establishment of a local HR/HC function in the new country becomes a necessity.

➤ **Going Global — Stage 5 — Acquisition of a local entity, which may be a former business partner, competitor, distributor/supplier, synergistic manufacturer, sub-contractor or other strategically placed organization in the target market.** This means of "going global," is sometimes referred to as the jump start or accelerated mode by which organizations intend to rapidly achieve national or regional impact in a market. The advantages include the existence of bricks and mortar plants and facilities, the existence of a functioning labor force, the existence of a management team and leadership, an existing customer base, a support infrastructure and a corporate reputation. These all provide compelling support for this approach.

However, all is not upside, even in the best acquisition. The HR and human capital functions now have become major considerations. The descriptive analogy is not unlike that of adopting a teenage child. Once the initial euphoria and excitement is over, concerns and fears quickly surface and those responsible for blending and melding the separate parties together face the reality of dealing with differing deeply ingrained beliefs, personalities, differing cultural patterns, power structures, behaviors and value systems that are not to be taken lightly. Independence, power and values are not surrendered easily by either party. Yet the assets must be preserved.

If the new entity is to be treated other than as a totally independent operation with no ties other than financial reporting, the HR and human capital must deal with the issues of understanding and, if appropriate, rationalizing differing compensation and benefits practices, leadership and succession planning, expatriate issues, and a plethora of other issues. HR/HC then also becomes involved in addressing and resolving what are quickly perceived as guerilla warfare resistance to the fact that ownership has changed.

➤ **Going Global — Stage 6 — The creation, start-up and establishment of a full capabilities, subsidiary national entity with bricks and mortar as well as locally recruited staff at all levels.** Particularly for organizations seeking a full-blown production, marketing, sales and support presence in the targeted national marketplace, in the absence of a potential acquisition candidate for a jump-start as outlined in Stage 5, this approach, although the most costly and highest risk, often is the only viable alternative. The advantages are that the parent organization's corporate culture, business values and operating style, organizational structures, and ways of doing things that are already engrained in the corporate parent can, with effort, be promulgated within the new entity.

However, this approach and solution also requires substantial effort to deal with the realities of nationally specific cultural values, differing societal ways of doing business, differing legal and regulatory requirements, communication styles, standards of politeness and demeanor, and a host of "here's how it needs to be done in our country" issues. The challenges for the HR and human capital function are extensive.

■ What are the Unique Qualities and Issues with Stage 4, 5, and 6 operations?

Since the HR and human capital challenges are minimal in the first three of the above alternatives, it is appropriate to look more closely at the challenges of the last three alternative "going global" models. One of the early steps in the process of "going global," if these models are adopted, is to recognize that a global perspective is essential. But a global perspective is much more than thinking about geography. It involves being aware and conscious of a variety of differences of social values, cultural issues, political and economic differences, business standards and practices, and a host of other "soft" aspects that impact a stage 4, 5 and 6 transnational employer. This is a major mindset change — a bigger step than most individuals anticipate. The reasons for the difficulty are very understandable.

The difficulties are not nationally specific, although individuals from various countries will accuse other countries of being uniquely insensitive. The fact is that very similar insensitivities exist whether the parent "going global" entity is based in the United States, Canada, Germany, France, the UK, or any other country. Corporations that do business within their home country typically don't think twice about whether or not different operations are subject to differing linguistic, legal and regulatory requirements or to differing policies and cultural practices, Quebec being a notable exception within Canada. In most other instances, it is assumed that the same set of federal or national requirements permeate each entity, that a single language is used to transact business, and that common business principles, practices and standards apply almost uniformly across all business operations in that country. Where there are minor differences as a result of unique local requirements typically relating to mandated benefits and/or payroll taxation, the expectation is that the management of local operations and/or accounting and payroll will assure compliance as part of their normal conduct of business.

Consistency and commonality are assumed in a single nation setting.

These "normal growth" corporate expectations and behaviors become part of the framework, culture and processes of that business. Consistency and commonality are assumed in a single nation setting. So, it is not surprising, when that corporation begins to expand its operations across national borders, that individuals expect similar ease of migration of business processes, practices and systems. What this fails to take into consideration is that transnational operations are not as simple as opening up operations in another region of the same country.

The typical impulse is to endeavor to apply home country standards, practices, procedures and operating standards to the new international environment. What sometimes gets lost in the quest to meet senior management expectations and demands is the fact that international operations are impacted by a complex fabric of differing legal frameworks, political structures, social values, cultures, languages, business practices, employee/employer relationships, career expectations, family standards and expectations, religious infrastructures and beliefs, and deeply entrenched individual behaviors and traditions. Commonly expected practices and/or systems may or may not make sense, be doable, or even permitted in the new environment.

Yet, corporate management, including corporate IS/IT and HR, often expect that the same planning, reporting, analytical processes, policies, procedures, and control procedures, and the same systems and business applications can be and should be in place from country to country. This is sometimes referred to as the one-size-fits-all style of thinking.

■ What's the Reality?

In order to understand and put a perspective on the implications of these differences, it helps to break issues into two categories: the strategic components and the tactical/operational components. In trying to figure out what kind of solution is required and appropriate, it helps to determine whether the issues and problems being faced are strategic or operational.

Let's first deal with the high level strategic components — the basics around which a business is built. Transnational issues have a minimal impact here, and there are many commonalities. There can easily be a common strategic direction for most companies that is consistent across national borders. The corporate mission, business strategies, including how the organization intends to strategically address core human capital issues can be handled at a high strategic level. The ability to look at human capital assets on a global basis and the decision to utilize the knowledge and experience resources that are "packaged" in the minds of employees on a global basis is not only sensible, but essential.

On a tactical level there is no question about the need for local implementation of programs to support the strategy. It is also proper to expect the local entity to provide for reasonable, timely and accurate on-going corporate level financial and operational reporting. As information needs or requests move into progressively lower and lower levels of detail and into the direct/core operational and financial arena, it becomes increasingly necessary to find acceptable compromises on the extent to which, and the manner in which, the local operation can accommodate the unique and sometimes puzzling information desires/requirements of the parent entity.

From the corporate parent side it is essential to recognize that each country is different and that those differences must be understood and accommodated in order to operate successfully within each country. Even within the EU (European Union) common market countries there are national differences, particularly in the HR arena, that must be recognized and accommodated by the local business operations and by the systems used within that country. These differences impact the way businesses operate and their ability to report on some HR areas in a manner that is clear and properly interpretable.

■ Focusing on the HR Area

Accommodating local language and the most obvious nationally-based semantic differences in the HR area and being able to denominate pay in differing currencies is just the tip of the iceberg and are only a very insignificant part of the challenge for an international HR activity. To assist in understanding the scope of differences, even a person's name is not handled in a universally consistent manner. First, last, given, family, surnames, prefaces, preferred/ nicknames, salutations and name related titles all are handled differently in different cultures and countries. Other items as seemingly basic as address formats and structures, and telephone number formats vary widely internationally. Content that is essential in the home country to meet compliance reporting needs may be irrelevant in other countries. Yet, other information that is inappropriate or even illegal in the home country, such as tracking and reporting based on each employee's religious affiliation, may be required in some countries.

Organizational definitions also vary. The use of the term "department" or "division" has differing meanings and is used differently from country to country. Similarly, compensation structures, salary and grade structures, pay components, pay practices and payment methodologies vary widely from country to country. In some countries 12.5, 13, or even 14 or more monthly payments may make up an actual annual salary. In other countries, automatic adjustments based solely on government-mandated changes or to accommodate currency valuation and inflationary changes may be applicable.

Benefits practices vary radically. Providing benefits on a multi-country basis may be illegal or redundant in many cases. In some countries — typically emerging third world countries — there are few if any health and welfare benefits provided by many local employers and the transnational entity may be plowing new ground in granting those. In other countries, benefits as we know them in North America are totally meaningless since all welfare, medical and health coverages are provided by the state on a uniform basis.

Ethical standards, concepts of right and wrong, and even the relative value of a person's word, handshake and signature on a contract can vary radically. The differences could go on and on.

■ What are the Issues that Corporations Need to Address and Resolve when it comes to Globally-Focused HR Management, Reporting, Analysis and Control?

Effective corporate stewardship and the associated reasonable reporting of critical information is a legitimate need that must be addressed. The challenge is in defining what information is truly essential to meet that stewardship need and then how to handle that need from a systems perspective. A second, but related, dimension is to deal with the data privacy issues that may impact the ability of an employer to transmit employee data across national borders.

In general, the information areas that can be communicated without restriction and that can be effectively dealt with at the corporate level typically include the following:

➤ High level global headcount tracking, turnover trends and hiring activities by major business components and functional areas;

➤ Reasonable consolidated reporting that reflects trends and patterns that can impact operations;

➤ Periodic review of direct and indirect compensation plans and the administration of those plans;

➤ Review of meaningful trends and patterns in direct pay and benefits costs, and the interpretation of these in light of operating and financial information;

➤ Management of the performance assessment process and integration of that into staffing decisions;

➤ Identification of high potential key employees and their competencies, criticality and potential contributions to the growth of the organization; and the

➤ Establishment of a global skills and competencies bank and succession planning process for key positions.

■ What's the Best "Going Global" Alternative from the HR Perspective?

As suggested in the earlier statement, there is no "one-size-fits-all" answer. The challenge for the strategically focused HR and human capital executive is to assure that the leadership team carefully considers the strategic goals and objectives that are to be accomplished and then decide what the best "going global" strategy is, given both the short-term needs and the ability of the enterprise to adapt and change as those needs mature and change.

The fact is that businesses of all sizes, in all countries, and people at all levels within businesses, exist in an era of rapid massive change — social change, economic change, technological change, radical acceleration of information access, changes in how we communicate, changes in our expectations of others, and changes in what others expect of us, changes in how businesses operate and do business — massive changes in almost every aspect of our lives. These are the reality and underlying framework within which the "going global" decisions must be made.

Emerging global and transnational businesses are affected by myriad cultural and national specific issues and challenges. These affect the market place within each country, they affect the manner in which purchase decisions or employment decisions are made and they affect the ease with which business is done within that country. No matter how large or small, no matter what industry a business is in, and no matter where they are headquartered — New Brunswick, New York, New Delhi, New Guinea or Newcastle — the longstanding basics and fundamentals of how businesses operate, how they serve their existing markets, and how they expand the into new markets are being challenged and changed.

Today, as the realities of the new global economy become more and more evident and real, it is increasingly clear that resources of all types ... have all become globally available resources.

Today, as the realities of the new global economy become more and more evident and real, it is increasingly clear that resources of all types — financial, raw materials, energy, facilities, equipment, technology and intellectual capital — have all become globally available resources. No single country has dominance in any of these arenas. Money, materials, energy, equipment, technology and intellectual capital can all move around the world in an incredibly short time. These resources can be acquired in an open market environment. Even intellectual capital is now accessible with little regard to national borders. With the Web it is possible to employ virtual workers on a global basis. Even traditional concepts regarding the workplace are no longer applicable other than in true production and assembly settings.

In HR/HC, as in the operational aspects of a business, the nimble application of intelligence, a balance of sound business concepts and keen instincts are key to success. For the "going global" enterprise, human capital is now a global resource and in this new era — the digital era — the management of the human capital assets — the knowledge, experience and intellectual capital of the organization — is more strategically vital than financial resources or tangible assets, and it is locked up in the minds of the people of an organization. The challenge is that the asset walks out the door just before the lights are turned out at the end of each day.

Over the last 20 years the forced migration of focus for HR and for the systems that support the HR function has moved from traditional data capture and tracking and given way to a focus on providing information in an effective and convenient manner. But, in today's era of digital businesses operating on a global scale, information is no longer enough. Although many organizations are still struggling with the first transition, the next era of business is already upon us.

The business world is already entering a new era in which it is intelligence that supplies the spark for competitive advantage. Intelligence — the true intellectual capital of an enterprise — is where competitive advantage lives or dies.

Information may provide the fuel — Intelligence is the essential spark.

Time is now of the essence in global operations. In the past, facts could be gathered, opinions expressed, recommendations could be reviewed and decisions could be weighed carefully and deliberately. That has changed. In this new era of global competition in which decisions must be made and actions taken in "Internet time," the rewards will fall to the nimble and fast moving — to the cheetahs and gazelles — not to slow moving giants. Small and mid-size start-up organizations with passionately committed leadership and with similarly passionate, innovative and creative professional staff are uniquely positioned to exploit the opportunities presented in this new era. Exploiting these opportunities is the challenge. HR and its emerging successor, the human capital (HC) function, are key in this transition as enterprises "go global."

The challenge for the HR and human capital function of any organization — large, mid-sized, or small — and HR's new strategic role in the "going global" activity is to work with operational management in a highly strategic manner to maximize the value of its intelligence and intellectual capital. The platitudes of the past about people being the most important asset of an organization and the politically correct executive proclamations about the need to find ways to link HR programs and operating goals in way that optimize the organization's human capital and encourages employee loyalty and enhances shareholder value, all take on a new meaning in this new digital era of global competition.

Mid-size enterprises face unique challenges as they seek to become respected global players. These businesses typically have neither the magnitude of staff nor the breadth and depth of existing talent from whom to choose, nor do they have the existing infrastructure or the financial resources of their large existing global competitors. What they have is the differentiating ability to be nimble and fast — to be the cheetahs and the gazelles. The "going global" formula for achievement is complex and multi-threaded, but it all boils down to the effective use of human capital. It is in the human capital of an organization that strategic competitive advantages will be found.

Jim Spoor is founder, president and CEO of SPECTRUM Human Resource Systems Corp., a global provider of HR and human capital management software systems to high expectation HR organizations. Prior to forming SPECTRUM in 1984, Spoor had a very successful career that covered more than 25 years in both HR and line management with well respected internationally-focused Fortune 500 corporations where he had senior corporate executive responsibilities for global HR activities. His experience covers the energy, high tech and food processing industries. Spoor is regarded within the industry as a visionary, futurist, pioneer and tell it like it is innovator who focuses on exploiting technology in addressing strategic business issues. He has authored many articles, been a contributing author to several professional handbooks and textbooks, and has been a frequent speaker and panelist on diverse topics including HR and HR systems, entrepreneurism and emerging trends in technology. His professional involvements include serving on the Board of Directors of the International Association for Human Resource Information Management (IHRIM) and previously serving on the Steering Committee for the Global Special Interest Group of IHRIM. He is also a long time member of the Society for Human Resource Management (SHRM). He is Past National President and Chairman Emeritus of The Council of Growing Companies, an international organization for CEOs of rapidly growing companies. He has also served as Chairman of The Breckenridge Outdoor Education Center, a non-profit organization serving the outdoor experience needs of individuals with physical and emotional disabilities. He can be reached at **jspoor@spectrumhr.com**.

Reprinted from the *IHRIM Journal*, Volume V, Number 4, November 2001, pp. 36-41.

Managing Data Privacy Challenges in Global Systems(*)

By Donald Harris, Ph.D.

■ Introduction

Ask your average North American HR systems professional if he or she works with any controlled or regulated substances. Chances are, the response you receive will be a somewhat quizzical, but uncertain denial. The fact of the matter, however, is that anyone working with HR systems or applications is handling such substances on a daily basis, without realizing it. Employee information is that regulated entity.

As of February 2002, some 36 countries, both within the European Union and in every region of the world, have enacted national legislation protecting all types of personal information, including employee information (see Figure 1).

In these nations, personal information can *only* be collected, used and retained if such processing is conducted in a way that meets some very significant legal standards. You need to have a legal basis for handling personal information, and act in conformance with applicable laws, before you can process personal information in these nations.

Our perspective in North America is like a photographic negative of such a view; we tend to believe that we can do anything we want with personal information, as long as there is no law against it. We view personal information as we do water: as something abundantly available, that we are free to use as we see fit. Increasingly, other nations are disagreeing, saying that it is government's job to protect the use and flow of personal information in an ever more interconnected world.

Figure 1. Thiry-seven Nations with Omnibus Privacy Laws.

European Union:

Austria	Finland France	Ireland	Netherlands	Sweden
Belgium	Germany	Italy	Portugal	United Kingdom
Denmark	Greece	Luxembourg	Spain	

Canada (public sector and federally regulated private sector)

Elsewhere:

Argentina	Hong Kong	Latvia	South Africa
Australia	Hungary	Lithuania	Switzerland
Chile	Iceland	New Zealand	Thailand
Czech Republic	Isle of Man	Norway	
Estonia	Israel	Poland	
Guernsey	Jersey	Slovakia	

Until recent years, this divergence in perspectives towards employee data was moot. Most North American companies lacked either the motivation or the technical means to import anything more than aggregate headcount type information or limited data about employees overseas. Coupled with apparent low levels of enforcement of national data protection laws regarding international data transfers, compliance with these laws was viewed in North America largely as a concern of subsidiaries operating in local countries.

The European Union's Data Protection Directive, together with the emergence of the Internet, has changed all that. The Directive has driven public policy debates about privacy in nations around the world, at the same time the Internet has provided the means for companies to manage human resources on a truly global basis through global human resources programs supported by global HR information systems. Both have contributed to moving data privacy issues from the backburner to a position front and central in planning and operating global HR systems.

■ Defining the Challenge: Understanding Privacy

In order to understand the data protection and privacy challenges surrounding employee information, one must begin with an understanding of what privacy is and the types of privacy issues that come into play in the workplace. It is also important to recognize why privacy is important and that privacy is not an unlimited or unbounded right. Finally, privacy, security and confidentiality, although closely related, need to be clearly distinguished.

➤ **Definitions of privacy.** The classic, most-quoted definition of privacy comes from Justice Louis Brandeis, who, in 1928, described privacy as "the right to be left alone — the most comprehensive of rights, and the right most valued by civilized men." The stress here upon an *absence of interference* expresses a basic human need, to have control and enjoy what is one's own. While there are many dimensions to this need of individuals for a sphere of influence and for autonomy, Alan Westin captured one most relevant to what might be called *informational privacy* in his 1967 definition of privacy as "the claim of individuals, groups, or institutions to determine for themselves when, how, and to what extent information about them is communicated to others." As social beings, we want to control what we reveal about ourselves to others, how and when we reveal it, and to whom.

➤ **Types of privacy.** Informational privacy, which deals with how information about employees, applicants and others is collected and used, is the type of privacy most directly relevant to our focus. However, there are two other types that are significant in the workplace. The first of these is *communications privacy*, which relates to the tracking or monitoring of employee use of e-mail, telephones and the Internet as vehicles of communication. Invasions of privacy with respect to communications do not always resolve into issues of informational privacy, since the mere fact that one's communications are being monitored can be intrusive, apart from concerns about any disclosure of the content of specific messages. The other type of privacy most relevant to the workplace is *experiential privacy*, which typically involves an immediate intrusion occurring in one's presence, such as the experience of physical searches, overt video surveillance, drug and alcohol testing and the like.

Since the workplace is, in many ways, a microcosm of society, other types of privacy — medical, genetic, financial, etc. — also turn up in the employment context and must be addressed. In terms of broad categories of privacy, however, *informational privacy*, *communications privacy*, and *experiential privacy* are the major types of privacy that those involved with employee-related global systems need to be concerned about. While issues around informational privacy are naturally paramount when dealing with such systems, the other types of privacy issues are often closely related and can be ignored only at an organization's peril. Accessing an employee's PC remotely or using web cams to monitor facility security is as much subject to data protection laws as processing and transferring data in a global HR system.

➤ **Value and limits of privacy.** Privacy is clearly of value to individuals, for example in being vital to individual growth, autonomy and dignity. In its very simplest terms, privacy is basically about respecting individuals as individuals. At the same time, making allowances for privacy is critical in achieving desirable social objectives. The functioning of democracy, for example, would be impossible were it not for the secrecy of the voting booth, and employee attitude surveys would lose much of their effectiveness if respondents were not guaranteed anonymity. Privacy needs to be protected for social ends, as well as for the sake of the individual.

Recognizing social objectives is important in another way in dealing with privacy issues, turning on the fact that claims to privacy can never be absolute or unlimited. Just as the protection of information is important, so is the free flow and use of information. Just as the rights of the individual need to be taken into account, so do the rights of others. Just as the rights of employees need to be secured, so do the rights of employers. In other words, a balance is needed in dealing with privacy rights and claims. Finding the appropriate balance in dealing with privacy issues is a perennial, enduring challenge. It is not, and never will be, easy. But is unavoidable, and involves matters of the utmost importance to individuals and to society.

➤ **Privacy, security and confidentiality.** Some of the most common misconceptions about privacy arise from confusing privacy with security, and to a lesser extent, with confidentiality. The fundamental differences amongst these three related domains can be seen in the very first line of Figure 2, in terms of the major objective of each. Privacy is about *protecting data subjects* (*people*); security is about *protecting data*; and confidentiality is about *protecting companies*. The focus and character of the concerns in each domain also varies significantly, as can be seen in the figure. All three may involve personal information, even the same personal information; however, each involves a distinctive set of objectives, focuses and concerns.

The relationship of privacy and security is particularly close in a number of respects. In the first place, privacy associated with the collection and use of personal information can only be protected if adequate security for that information is provided. At the same time, while security is necessary to ensure pri-

Figure 2. Privacy, Security and Confidentiality.

	PRIVACY	**SECURITY**	**CONFIDENTIALITY**
Objective:	proect data subjects from misuse of personal information	protect data from unauthorized access and alteration	protect companies from misuse of sensitive information
Focus:	rights and responsibilities of data subjects and data users, including whether data should be collected in the first place	hardware, software and procedures needed to maintain control over information once obtained	controlling access to information that has commercial, proprietary or litigation value, which may include info about employees
Concerns:	social, ethical, legal	technical, organizational	commercial, legal

vacy, it is not sufficient. One can imagine a database of personal information maintained with the most sophisticated, state-of-the-art security, yet used in the most invasive, privacy-insensitive manner. Secondly, security constitutes one of the generally accepted principles of fair information practice. For example, the eleventh principle of the 1980 OECD *Guidelines* is the Security Safeguards Principle. More than just being a foundation for privacy, security is a vital part of privacy. However, reducing privacy to security is missing 80 to 90 percent of what privacy is all about.

■ *Defining the Challenges: Legal Protections for Privacy*

With this understanding of what privacy is, the next step in defining the challenges employers face is to consider current and evolving legal protections for privacy. For any responsible and reputable company, the need to comply with the laws of countries in which it operates is a given. We will begin with a review of legal protections for privacy in the United States and then provide an overview of the relationship of privacy and law in the European Union, Canada and the rest of the world.

➤ **United States.** Protection for privacy in the U.S. comes through a variety of vehicles and jurisdictional levels: the U.S. Constitution, federal laws, case law, state constitutions and laws, employment and labor laws, common law torts and class action suits.

• **U.S. Constitution.** The word *privacy* cannot be found in the U.S. Constitution or in the Bill of Rights. This does not mean that there are no protections for privacy based upon the Constitution or that there is no constitutional right to privacy. What it does mean is that a right to privacy is not directly or clearly provided for in the Constitution. Drawing largely upon the Fourth Amendment's prohibition of "unreasonable searches and seizures," constitutional lawyers and scholars have argued, with varying degrees of success, that privacy *is* protected by the Constitution. Against this backdrop, the debate over whether Americans *have*, or *should have*, a constitutional right to privacy is inconclusive.

• **Federal laws.** There are numerous federal laws that provide significant privacy protections including: the 1974 *Privacy Act*, which imposes a comprehensive set of requirements upon the collection and use of personal information by the federal government; the much-amended *Fair Credit Reporting Act*, which sets some very stringent procedures for organizations to follow when obtaining consumer credit reports (including employers conducting background checks); and, the *Video Privacy Protection Act*, which prohibits video rental stores from disclosing their customers' rental histories. Such laws are usually enacted in response to particular abuses, or patterns of abuse, that have occurred, and are typically very targeted and explicit in ruling out, or requiring, certain behavior.

- **Case law.** Privacy protections are also established through judicial interpretations of the Constitution, federal and state laws, and other cases. For example, in *Whalen vs. Roe* (1994), the court found a "penumbral" right to privacy in the U.S. Constitution. One needs to look beyond "laws on the books" in identifying legal protections for privacy and the remedies and consequences that may follow if those protections are not provided.

- **State constitutions and laws.** In several states, such as California, the right to privacy is clearly established at a constitutional level. California has also established an Office of Privacy Protection (web site http://www.privacyprotection. ca.gov/), which bears striking similarities to those of Privacy Commissioners in many nations. Some 17 states have created privacy task forces or commissions. State legislatures, which recently have been considering about 9,000 privacy bills each year, also have enacted significant legal protections for privacy, particularly in relation to issues of importance to individuals as consumers and citizens. It is important to note that these protections vary significantly state by state, and frequently lapse as one crosses state lines.

- **Employment and labor laws.** Although not usually perceived as being privacy laws, equal employment opportunity legislation and other laws forbidding discrimination on a variety of grounds contain some very stringent provisions governing proper and improper use of sensitive data, such as race, gender, age, and disabilities, by employers. Similarly, rulings of the National Labor Relations Board (NLRB) also set privacy standards for employers, even non-unionized ones, such as the recent ruling that prohibits companies from barring the use of company e-mail systems for purposes relating to union organizing and communications.

- **Common law torts.** Individuals also have legal protections in the U.S. through their ability to sue for invasion of privacy, embarrassment, defamatory actions, etc., resulting in harm or injury. Such cases often go before a jury, and recently have led to some huge awards against employers, such as US$1.65 million against Wal-Mart for embarrassing one employee in front of his neighbors, and US$2 million to applicants for jobs at Rent-A-Center, for inappropriately invasive psychological testing.

• **Class action suits.** The U.S. is one of only two countries in the world permitting class action suits (Canada is the other). Recently a number of such suits, seeking compensatory awards on behalf of a broadly defined category of plaintiffs, have been filed over disputes involving online privacy. These cases typically take considerable time to work their way through the judicial system, but the fact that privacy claims have emerged in class action suits indicates that the plaintiff's bar has its ear to the ground with respect to legally enforceable privacy rights.

• **Summary.** There are many strong legal protections for privacy in the United States. Some are far stronger in their specificity than those anywhere else, including the European Union. However, the laws providing these protections tend to be very specific in their applicability, often targeted to preventing the reiteration of clear abuses that have already occurred. Where incidents or patterns of abuse have not engendered sufficient outcries from the public to prompt elected officials to seek legislative solutions, U.S. law tends to be silent. The result is a system aptly described as providing "peaks and valleys" of legal protection for privacy. While the peaks may be very high and impressive, the valleys tend to be very broad and exposed.

➤ **European Union.** The European Union takes a fundamentally different approach to privacy protection than the United States. All 15 member states of the European Union have comprehensive national data protection laws, some going back to the early 1970s. In October 1995, a community-wide directive was passed for the purpose of strengthening and harmonizing these laws. The directive, usually referred to as the EU Data Protection Directive, bears the full title *Directive 95/46/EC on the protection of individuals with regard to the processing of personal data and on the free movement of such data.* As a framework document, the Directive gave member states three years, until October 1998, to transpose its provisions into national legislation. As of February 2002, three member states (France, Ireland and Luxembourg) are late in doing so and face significant fines for their delays. Nevertheless, through what is known as "the principle of direct effect," the Directive is in effect even in those nations.

What is different about the European approach to providing legal protection for privacy is that it centers upon omnibus privacy legislation, applicable to *all* types of personal information and *all* types of processing (collection, use, disclosure, storage, etc.), in *all* media (electronic, paper, audio, video, etc.), by *all* parties, in all sectors. Rather than relying upon a patchwork of highly specific laws as in the U.S., the Europeans have a single high-level law that must be followed by anyone processing personal information.

A chart highlighting the contrasting U.S. and European perspectives on these matters may be found in Figure 3. Two elements of this chart deserve special attention. The first is the fact that for Europeans, privacy is a well-established and fundamental civil right, whereas for Americans, privacy is at most an evolving civil right. Europeans attach the same irreducible, inalienable right to privacy that we attach to freedom of speech and expression. Having experienced first-hand the horrors of numerous wars in the last century marked by egregious abuses of personal information, Europeans concluded long ago that protecting privacy is a bedrock of the society they want to inhabit. The U.S. has yet to find consensus on privacy issues.

Secondly, the Europeans view personal information in the broadest sense, as any information about an identified or identifiable individual. This is a major paradigm shift from the traditional U.S. view of personal information as confined largely to matters relating to family, background or physical characteristics. The distinction we sometimes try to make between "personal information" (e.g., marital status, age, educational background, etc.) and "company information" (e.g., job title, office location, phone number, salary, etc.) is not one shared in Europe or in other nations with national privacy legislation.

➤ **Canada.** Until recently, legal protections for privacy in Canada by and large have followed the U.S. approach. Personal information collected and used in the public sector has been protected by the 1983 *Privacy Act*, as well as by provincial laws. Private sector processing of personal information was regulated, as in the U.S., only by selective laws in specific areas, with the notable exception of Quebec, which passed its *Act Concerning the Protection of Personal Information in the Private Sector* in 1994. Unlike the U.S. however, Canada, for two decades, has placed re-

Figure 3. Contrasting perspectives between European and American views of privacy and related issues.

Privacy	A fundamental civil right that cannot be waived	At best, an evolving civil right, possibly a commodity to be traded
Government	A trusted agent for larger social good, a protector	A necessary evil, to be kept at arm's length and minimized
How privacy should be protected	By government and law, supported by self-regulation	By market forces; by government and law only if there is a market failure
Nature of laws	Often high-level statements of principle	Typically very specific and targeted
Basis for processing personal information	Can only process with a lawful basis to do so	Can always process unless it is illegal to do so
Definition of personal information	Any information about an individual	Info relating to individual's private or familial life

sponsibility for overseeing and enforcing public sector privacy laws in the hands of independent privacy commissioners, at both the federal and provincial levels, leaning towards the European approach in this regard.

As of January 1, 2001, the effective date of its new federal privacy law, Canada set itself firmly on the path of adopting the European approach to legal privacy protections. The *Personal Information Protection and Electronic Documents Act*, also known as PIPEDA or Bill C-6, requires federally regulated companies, as well as those that collect, use or disclose personal information as a part of commercial activities, to observe all 10 principles of fair information practice set forth in the act. These principles more or less mirror the privacy principles found in the European Data Protection Directive. Oversight and enforcement authority, including the power to investigate complaints, conduct onsite audits and initiate judicial proceedings, is given to the Federal Privacy Commissioner.

... it will be up to each of Canada's provinces to decide whether to extend the scope of the newly legislated privacy protections to employees.

The coverage of the new act could create some significant issues for many Canadian companies importing employee data from Europe. Federally regulated companies, which include maritime shipping companies, inter-provincial railroad, bus and ferry companies, telephone companies, airlines and air services, radio, TV and cable stations and most banks, constitute only a small portion of Canada's private sector. PIPEDA contains a provision extending its applicability to the balance of the private sector on January 1, 2004, unless provinces enact similar or stronger legislation. However, because of a somewhat quirky limitation in the federal government's general trade and commerce powers, any such extension would apply to personal information of customers only, and not of employees. In other words, it will be up to each of Canada's provinces to decide whether to extend the scope of the newly legislated privacy protections to employees. Employers in the non-federally-regulated private sector in provinces that fail to do so may not have any legal underpinnings for the protection of employee privacy.

➤ **Elsewhere.** The 20 countries outside the EU and Canada that have enacted national privacy legislation (see Figure 1) are likely to be joined by many more in coming years since omnibus privacy laws are currently pending around the world in nations as diverse as Japan, Malaysia, Turkey and Brazil. The vast majority of nations that have either passed or are considering the passing of such legislation have been directly influenced by the EU Directive — often through the proselytizing efforts of European data protection commissioners. During March 2001 testimony before a Congressional sub-committee examining the impact of the Directive, Professor Joel Reidenberg of the Fordham University School of Law cautioned that if current trends continue, the U.S. may find itself regarded as a "privacy rogue" nation by most of the world in a few years. No matter where one looks, either within the U.S. or abroad, the prospects are for more and stronger legal protections for the privacy of personal information in the years ahead.

■ *Meeting the Challenge of the EU Privacy Directive*

Having considered the nature and legal environment of privacy, we turn to the major challenge facing companies planning, building or maintaining global HR information systems and applications: identifying and implementing a strategy for complying with the EU Data Protection Directive. Our focus is on companies that want to bring personally-identifiable European data to North America as data controllers, making decisions on their own about its use, as opposed to simply being data processors acting on behalf of others. We begin with a description of the challenge posed by the Directive.

➤ **The Challenge of the Directive.** Establishing a legal basis for transferring employee data from the European Union is the central problem the EU Directive poses for companies with global HR information systems. Justifying trans-border data flows constitutes only a small part of the total set of compliance requirements of the Directive; the largest burden of compliance, perhaps as much as 90 percent, falls upon host country companies, in terms of ensuring the legality and appropriateness of in-country processing. Nevertheless, the trans-border issues are critical. Without finding a lawful basis for data transfers, global systems cannot exist.

A key provision of the Directive, responsible for placing a huge question mark over the legality of transferring personal data out of Europe, may be found in Article 25:

> *The transfer of personal data to a third country, which does not ensure an adequate level of protection, must be prohibited.*

Given the European conclusion that the United States, with its patchwork of privacy laws and reliance upon self-regulation, does not have an adequate level of protection, this is very stark language indeed. Canadian companies covered by PIPEDA do not have to be concerned about this Article 25 prohibition because the European Commission has determined that the new federal privacy law provides an adequate level of protection.

The framers of the Directive, having devoted great effort to establishing protections for privacy in the processing of personal information within Europe, clearly were not prepared to see these protections ignored or eroded by transfers of data beyond European borders. Furthermore, Europeans view a transfer as any movement, accessing or viewing of data across a national border, whether by file transfer, the Internet, e-mail, paper or other means. The Article 25 prohibition drew a line in the sand that captured the attention of governments and enterprises around the world.

In order to make international data transfers possible, and thereby avoid disruptions in trade, Article 26 of the Directive goes on to allow the transfer of personal information to a country lacking an adequate level of protection if any one of a limited number of derogations or conditions, are satisfied. However, these derogations, which we shall consider shortly, are narrowly defined and those relevant to transfers of employee data are problematic.

Companies that do not comply with the requirements set forth in the Directive, or in the national laws implementing these requirements, subject themselves to regulatory and judicial enforcement actions including adverse publicity, damage to brand and reputation, civil and criminal penalties and data cut-offs. A sample of the maximum fines per offense set forth in national data protection laws in 2001 include US$3,000 in Italy, US$14,000 in Austria, US$50,000 in Germany, US$130,000 in Greece and US$600,000 in Spain. Furthermore, a wide range of parties have legal standing to initiate actions against companies for perceived violations of data protection laws, including individual citizens, residents and data subjects; privacy advocacy groups; independent data protection authorities established at the national level, as well as in Germany, at provincial levels; the member states; and the European Commission.

➤ **Enforcement.** With a fairly stringent set of data protection requirements to be met, and significant consequences for non-compliance, it is reasonable to ask why there have been so few enforcement actions against North American-based companies importing employee data from Europe. The lack of such actions has contributed to a "wait-and-see" attitude on the behalf of many companies with regard to how seriously they need to take the provisions of the Directive. After all, the Directive came into full effect in October 1998, with little discernible impact upon companies that have either ignored it or proceeded on a business-as-usual basis.

The primary reason there have been so few enforcement actions is that the U.S. government negotiated an enforcement standstill with the European Commission, during the period in which the two governments were engaged in bilateral discussions over how to bridge the gap between their conflicting approaches to privacy protection. These discussions, known as the Safe Harbor talks, lasted over two and a half years. Following the successful conclusion of the talks and the launch of the Safe Harbor program in November 2000, the European Commission agreed to continue the standstill in the form of an undefined grace period to allow U.S. companies time to evaluate and prepare for joining the program. That grace period is unlikely to continue indefinitely.

Another reason for the lack of publicized enforcement actions is that European data protection authorities, unlike regulatory agencies in the U.S., prefer to achieve compliance through quiet consultation and dialogue, rather than by wielding the hammer of press releases, public confrontation and court action. Limitations in staff and funding also contribute to a more low-key approach to enforcement than exists in the United States.

... four Deutsche Bank directors face possible imprisonment over their role in the company's monitoring of a Spanish employee's e-mail messages.

The official standstill in enforcement actions has not constrained all parties. In February 2001, it was revealed that Microsoft faced hundreds of thousands of dollars in fines by the Spanish government for improperly transferring employee data from Spain to a web server in the United States. Microsoft was subsequently successful in getting the fines reduced to about US$60,000. As further signs of significant employment-related data protection activism in Spain, in April 2001, it was reported that a court in Madrid ruled against the NCR Corporation for having U.S.-based staff remotely access a Spanish employee's personal computer and that four Deutsche Bank directors face possible imprisonment over their role in the company's monitoring of a Spanish employee's e-mail messages.

Enforcement aside, many North American-based multinationals have already been significantly inhibited by the Directive. A significant percentage of respondents to a 1997 IHRIM survey of members of its Global Special Interest Group reported that their companies had deferred or modified their plans for global HR information systems because of concerns about the Directive. Some companies have decided to transfer only aggregate headcount-like data, thereby avoiding the importation of personal information and all concerns about compliance. Others, like a major U.S.-based financial services firm, have decided not to transfer any employee data from Greece because they are unwilling to risk imprisonment of staff under what they view as complex and confusing provisions of Greece's national data protection legislation.

In addition, leading U.S.-based multinationals, including American Express, Compaq, Dow Corning, Dun & Bradstreet, McGraw-Hill, MasterCard, Hewlett-Packard, Pfizer, Phillip Morris, Baxter International and Boeing, have been actively addressing the issues around compliance with the Directive for a number of years. Most, if not all, of these companies are now in various stages of implementing programs to ensure that employee data transfers comply not only with the Directive, but also with increasingly globalized data protection regulations. Dozens of other large multinationals are in exploratory stages of dealing with this issue, as pressures for compliance continue to build.

➤ **Compliance Strategies.** There are five compliance strategies open to U.S-based companies that want to be data controllers and need to find a means of complying with the Directive. These alternatives are summarized in Figure 4. Although they are not eligible for the Safe Harbor Program, Canadian-based companies not subject to PIPEDA have the same options. Until recently, many companies have adopted, either intentionally or out of ignorance, the fifth alternative, which might be more appropriately called a non-compliance strategy. The viability of this posture, which is essentially to ignore the problem and hope it goes away, could vanish with a single major enforcement action directed against a large multinational. The other alternatives deserve serious consideration.

➤ **Utilizing an Article 26 Derogation.** The first two compliance strategies, involving consent and contracts, rely upon Article 26 derogations. Before discussing these strategies, it is worth considering the language in Article 26 upon which they depend. According to Article 26, transfers of personal information to countries lacking an adequate level of protection can still be made if the transfers are:

• Made with the unambiguous *consent* of the data subject,

• Necessary for performance of a *contract* between data subject and controller, or

• One in which a controller provides adequate *contractual safeguards* to protect the privacy of individuals and their freedom to exercise their rights and a Member State approves the transfer under those safeguards.

Figure 4. Strategies for Complying with the EU Privacy Directive.
1. Seek employee consent, where feasible
2. Develop and execute a model contract
3. Join the U.S.-EU Safe Harbor Program
4. Develop and implement a global code of conduct
5. Adopt a familiar No Problem strategy:
   • Take head
   • Insert in sand
   • Try not to wiggle big butt too much
   • Hope for the best

While there are a few other derogations in Article 26, these are the only ones relevant to transfers of employment-related data.

➤ **Consent.** At first blush, relying upon the consent of employees as the basis for the processing and transfer of their personal information seems promising as the notion of consent has clear grounding in the principles of fair information practice and in some European labor laws. Indeed, certain European nations, such as Germany, require employers to seek consent, both from individual employees and their collective representatives, i.e., the Works Councils. At least one major U.S.-based multinational, a well-known high-tech company, has adopted employee consent as the cornerstone of its compliance strategy, asking each of its employees around the world to provide consent for the transfer of their personal information to the United States.

However, the concept of consent in the employment context creates a number of profound difficulties. According to the Directive, consent, in order to be "unambiguous," must satisfy three conditions: it must be *freely given, specific* and *informed.* The typical imbalance of power between employees and employer prevents meeting the first of these conditions, since the actual or perceived pressure upon an employee to sign a consent form may be quite compelling. Consent that is freely given, it should be pointed out, can also be freely withdrawn. Secondly, any blanket permission for an employer to use employment data as it sees fit, "for normal employment purposes," would be unacceptably vague. Specifying the actual uses of HR data is not an easy undertaking, and could easily require multiple instances of obtaining consent. Thirdly, what assurance is there that an employee is sufficiently informed about the status of data protection in a distant nation to understand the risks involved in consenting to a data transfer? Are employers prepared to mount the educational campaigns necessary to ensure that employees are informed about these risks?

Consent that is freely given, it should be pointed out, can also be freely withdrawn.

The untenability of relying on consent as the primary legal basis for transferring extensive databases of employment-related personal information does not exist when there is a highly specific data set involved, such as the limited data required by law to administer a global stock option plan. Consent is a viable concept in such contexts. Likewise, it makes perfect sense to request employee consent by asking them if they want their home address included on the list that will be circulated in the office for the mailing of holiday greeting cards. It is reasonable in this situation because there is specificity, clear understanding, and an utter disinterest on the part of the employer in the choice that is exercised.

Confirmation of the very limited role consent may play when data subjects are applicants and employees may be found in an advisory paper on the processing of personal data in the employment context, issued by the Article 29 Working Party on September 11, 2001. The U.S. Court of Appeals for the Ninth Circuit reached a similar conclusion, in a February 4, 2002 ruling in *Circuit City Stores, Inc. vs. Saint Clair Adams*. In this case, the court ruled against Circuit City's requirement that job applicants agree to submit all claims and disputes to binding arbitration on the grounds that such an "agreement" was procedurally unconscionable because it constituted a contract of adhesion executed by a party with superior bargaining power. While this issue has not yet been tested in European courts, it is extremely unlikely that they will allow individuals to waive, or be effectively coerced into waiving, privacy rights viewed as fundamental under European law. Even apart from issues of legal viability, employee relations are hardly advanced by asking employees to do something about which they have real choice.

In those situations where the conditions for consent set forth by the Directive can be reasonably satisfied, or where consent is required by law, it is certainly reasonable and appropriate to seek it. However, using consent as the primary basis for justifying international data transfers, and in the process giving employees a degree of veto power over management's use of information technology, is a strategy that employers would be, in the words of the Article 29 Working Party, "ill-advised" to follow.

➤ **Contracts with Data Subjects.** Another way that North American companies may attempt to justify the transfer of employment data from Europe under the terms of Article 26 of the Directive is to argue that the transfer is "necessary for the performance of a contract" between the data subject, or employee, and the data controller, or company. *Employment contracts*, which are very common in Europe for all categories of employees, are sometimes viewed as constituting the contractual vehicles upon which lawful trans-border data transfers can be based.

However, if one contemplates adding language about data transfers to such contracts, the same considerations about the tenability of consent expressed above would apply, and even more pointedly, in that applicants understand that they must sign the contract if they want to get hired. Furthermore, from a purely practical point of view, employment contracts could not address establishing a basis for transferring the information of employees already hired, who did not execute contracts with the requisite language.

Some employers have pondered claiming that the employment contract provides a basis for transfers, not by virtue of any explicit consent contained therein, but in the larger sense that it is "necessary" for the employer to transfer the data in order to carry out its responsibilities as an employer. The problem with such an approach is with the notion of "unambiguous consent," European data protection authorities take the word "necessary" very seriously. Saying that the transfer is "necessary" because of the way the company chooses to structure its operations, or "necessary" to achieve certain efficiencies, would not be persuasive.

To make the argument about what is "necessary," an employer would have to prove that there was no alternative arrangement that would work except to export the data, in much the same way as a credit card issuer can argue that transferring a name, credit card number and mailing address is necessary for trans-border purchases using credit cards. Since most employers have a history of carrying out their responsibilities as employers before trans-border data transfers were even contemplated, this is a difficult, if not impossible, case to prove. For this reason, European data protection authorities have rejected reliance upon employment contracts as a way for justifying transfers of employee information.

▶ **Contractual Safeguards.** *Inter-company contracts* are commonly used to control data transfers from the exporting segment of a company to another company, either within the corporate group or to an external data processor, and are required under European law. However, while they establish important protections for the data, particularly with regards to security safeguards and restrictions on onward transfers or unauthorized uses of the data, they do not address the rights of any data subjects whose information is transferred. For this reason, inter-company contracts do not meet this standard, set forth in Article 26 of the Directive, for exporting personal information to third countries lacking an adequate level of protection.

Model contracts attempt to remedy the lack of standing of data subjects in intra-company contracts by explicitly incorporating the subjects, as third-party beneficiaries with independently enforceable rights under the contract, into their provisions. Model contracts take their inspiration from a contract entered into in the mid-1990s by the German and North American subsidiaries of Citibank, to allow for the legal processing in North Dakota of information about holders of Citibank-issued German rail cards. The contract was sometimes referred to as "extra-territorial" in character, because it sought to extend all of the rights and protections enjoyed by purchasers under German law, via a contract, to operations performed upon their data in the United States. During the few years that the contract was in effect, it operated successfully, even involving several unannounced onsite inspections in North Dakota by German data protection authorities; however, for business reasons, Citibank withdrew from its rail card operations.

One of the underlying rationales of model contracts is that there could be a standard framework and language (the "model" in "model contracts") that all companies could use in providing contractual safeguards for trans-border data flows. Data protection authorities, in reviewing the contracts, could thereby focus upon any provisions unique to the data processing operations referenced by the contract. Since European data protection authorities are established, or at least coordinated, on a national basis, any model contracts approved for use in a particular case would likely be usable throughout the nation in question.

In the mid-to-late-1990s, at least three model contract projects were active, sponsored by the Confederation of British Industry, the International Chamber of Commerce and by Privacy and American Business. However, no model contract developed through any of these initiatives was actually executed, as companies waited to see how the U.S.-EU Safe Harbor talks would turn out and also waited for European Commission approval of model contract language. A Commission-approved model contract would have the advantage of being trans-union in scope and applicability, thereby sparing companies the burden of seeking the approval of data protection authorities in each EU member state.

On June 15, 2001, after a long gestation period, the Commission issued model contract language, known as "standard contractual clauses for the transfer of personal data to third countries." All EU member states are obligated to recognize these clauses as providing adequate minimum safeguards for transferring personal data to data controllers in third countries lacking adequate levels of privacy protection. However, additional requirements or specifications may be added, depending upon the laws of a particular member state, and the supervisory authority in a member state retains the right to override the contract and suspend data flows under certain conditions.

The model contract, executed by the exporting data controller and the importing data controller, defines the duties and responsibilities of each, and commits both to follow the data protection laws of a designated member state. Each party must agree to process personal information in accordance with nine "mandatory" data protection principles: *purpose limitation; data quality and proportionality; transparency; security and confidentiality; rights of access, rectification, erasure and blocking of data; restrictions on onward transfers; special categories of data; direct marketing; and automated individual decisions.* The meaning of these principles is spelled out in the model contract itself, as well as in an accompanying set of FAQs.

In a nod towards criticism that the draft model contract language set a higher standard than required by the Safe Harbor Program, which was finalized earlier, the Commission ruled that "relevant" Safe Harbor Principles may be substituted for the nine mandatory data protection principles. However, it also singled out three of the nine principles as being non-replaceable: *purpose limitation; rights of access, rectification, erasure and blocking of data; and restrictions on onward transfer.*

The model contract also provides that data subjects have legal standing as third-party beneficiaries to seek redress and compensation from the data exporter, the data importer or both. Aggrieved data subjects have the right to refer a dispute to an independent mediator, a supervisory authority, arbitration body or the courts. The data exporter and the data importer must accept joint and several liability for any damages to data subjects. Data subjects are also entitled to a copy of the contractual safeguards, and to being informed in advance of any transfers of sensitive data.

➤ **Advantages and Disadvantages of Model Contracts.** A model contract offers a number of advantages and disadvantages to companies that decide to develop and execute one as the primary basis for legitimizing the transfer of employee data. These are summarized in Figure 5.

Amongst the advantages of model contracts, flexibility and their usefulness in multi-lateral data flows rank at the top of the list. Companies can add additional language to the contract, can decide how to implement the required principles, and can choose which member state's law will be applicable. They can also use the contract they develop through global iterations, achieving compliance in transfers extending from beyond those from the EU to the United States. In terms of disadvantages, there is significantly less clarity about exactly what is required by a model contract than by Safe Harbor. This arises from both the substitutability of the relevant Safe Harbor principles and the lack of guidance about what needs to be done to implement the principles. In addition, contract administration — keeping contracts current and reflective of evolving business practices — could become a nightmare for a large or complex company.

As of February 2002, there have been no reported uses of the model contract language approved by the European Commission. However, this situation is likely to change, as many multi-nationals are now evaluating the desirability of pursuing this compliance option. The Commission has also indicated that it is considering alternative model contract language proposed by a half-dozen organizations.

➤ **The Safe Harbor Program.** By virtue of being first out of the starting gate, the Safe Harbor Program is currently the only officially approved compliance

Figure 5. Advantages and Disadvantages of Model Contracts.

MODEL CONTRACT TRADE-OFFS

Pros	Cons
• Commitments are private	• Lacks public relations value
• No commitment to oversight authority of the FTC	• No back-up, support by U.S. government
• Sets standards to be met, without performance measures	• Standards not entirely clear (e.g., substitute Safe Harbor principles)
• Flexibilty in what else goes into the contract	• Multiple and overlapping channels of redress (no preclusion)
• Can choose which member state to transfer data from	• Advance notice and approval may be required for data transfers
• Useful with any third country	• Contract administration could be burdensome

option actually known to be used by companies as a legal basis for transferring employment-related personal information from the European Union to the United States. The program, negotiated by the U.S. Department of Commerce and the European Commission, was prompted by the need to bridge the differences between the European and American approaches to privacy protection and thereby avert a trade war. In streamlining and simplifying compliance, it represents a political solution to the challenge of the Directive, rather than one that follows from a reading of the Directive itself.

The core concept of the Safe Harbor program is that companies that voluntarily adhere to the seven Safe Harbor privacy principles (Notice, Choice, Onward Transfer, Security, Data Integrity, Access and Enforcement) and accompanying Frequently Asked Questions (FAQs) will earn the presumption of adequacy with respect to data imported from the European Union. The program only applies to data transferred from the EU after joining the program, and does not need to be extended to employees in other countries.

➤ **Requirements for Participation in Safe Harbor.** Safe Harbor involves significantly more than a voluntary affirmative of some basic principles, imposing at least seven substantial requirements upon participants, including:

• **Annual self-certification of compliance with the Safe Harbor Principles and FAQs.** Companies fill out a certification form which is then posted on a public web site maintained by the Department of Commerce. Information that is made public includes identification of the nature of the data covered, a description of the company's activities with the data, a description of its privacy policy, a point of contact for inquiries and complaints, an indication of how the company's compliance claims will be verified, and a description of the independent recourse mechanisms it will use to resolve complaints.

• **Published privacy policies conforming to the Safe Harbor Principles and FAQs.** Companies must have written policies governing their activities related to the data imported from the EU that conform to the Safe Harbor Principles and FAQs, and must indicate where these policies can be viewed.

• **Training of employees and disciplinary procedures.** Companies have to train their employees to follow company policies and procedures with respect to data transferred from the EU, and must have disciplinary procedures for employees who fail to do so.

• **Verification of compliance.** Companies may choose to verify their compliance with the Safe Harbor Principles and FAQs either through internal audits and self-assessment, or through compliance reviews conducted by external parties. In either case, compliance must be verified on an annual basis, with summaries of the findings of the audits or reviews made publicly available.

- **A program to facilitate and respond to inquiries and complaints.** Companies must have points of contact and internal programs in place to handle inquiries and complaints about their policies and practices for handling personal information received from the EU, and they must make good faith efforts to resolve any complaints brought to their attention.

- **Agreement to cooperate with the EU data protection authorities.** Companies must agree to cooperate with European data protection authorities in the investigation and resolution of any complaints brought to the authorities' attention that the company is unable to resolve internally. Part of the resolution of complaints may involve providing redress and compensation to data subjects as recommended by the authorities.

- **Acceptance of oversight and enforcement by the FTC.** Companies participating in Safe Harbor make themselves subject to the oversight and enforcement authority of the Federal Trade Commission, under its Section 5 powers to take actions against "unfair and deceptive acts or practices" in or affecting commerce.

➤ **Advantages and Disadvantages of Joining Safe Harbor.** There are both advantages and disadvantages to joining the Safe Harbor Program with respect to employee data. The pros and cons of joining are summarized in Figure 6.

A few comments are in order for those considerations that are not self-evident. Amongst the advantages of joining Safe Harbor is realizing a form of due process should significant complaints arise, involving notification by governmental authorities that a problem exists, a period of time and opportunity to address the problem, and possible intercession by the Department of Commerce, as opposed to abrupt and unexpected enforcement actions that might

Figure 6. Advantages and Disadvantages of Joining Safe Harbor.

SAFE HARBOR TRADE-OFFS

Pros	Cons
• Only officially sanctioned compliance option today	• Voluntary acceptance of liability and FTC oversight
• Due process if problems or complaints arise	• High public exposure
• Being held to an easier standard	• Costs of compliance
• Avoids advance notification requirements of Directive	• May have to join for all data
• Opportunity for public privacy leadership	• Impact of special protections and rights for certain employees
	• Uncertain legal standing and future of Safe Harbor program

otherwise occur. Another advantage is that the Safe Harbor requirements are easier to meet than those in the Directive, a fact confirmed by critics of the agreement, who disparagingly refer to the Safe Harbor Principles as "EU Directive Light." Finally, by joining Safe Harbor, companies free themselves of the need to provide advance notification to national data protection authorities before actual data transfers occur, which is required by the laws in certain EU member states.

Amongst the disadvantages of joining Safe Harbor is the possibility that a company may need to join for all types of data, not just for human resources data. This was the original intent of the negotiators, but in their actual self-certifications, companies are exercising more latitude. Whether such selective certifications will lead to pressure in the future to join for all data remains to be seen. Another disadvantage for companies that decide to have separate policies for European data and non-European data is the impact upon employee relations of having some employees enjoy rights and protections that others don't. Finally, Safe Harbor is an unprecedented type of bi-lateral political agreement with uncertain legal standing, and no established forum to resolve differences of interpretation, such as over what data needs to be covered. With strong critics in Europe, and to some extent in the U.S., the Safe Harbor Program could easily be derailed by either side.

➤ **Future of Safe Harbor**. As of February 2002, 150 companies have signed up for the Safe Harbor Program, including 61 (41 percent) for human resources data. While some of the participants are small, many well-known companies have joined, including Aligent, Baxter International, Bechtel, Compaq, Doubleclick, Dun & Bradstreet, Eastman Kodak, Gateway, Hewlett Packard, Intel, McKesson, Merck, Microsoft, Perot Systems, Proctor & Gamble, Seagate, Sybase and TRW. Furthermore, of these major companies, all but four (DoubleClick, Dun & Bradstreet, Intel and Microsoft) have joined for HR data. The number of participants is likely to grow, as companies see the names of their peers and competitors appear on the publicly available Safe Harbor List.

The Safe Harbor Program also received a boost from the new chairman of the Federal Trade Commission, Timothy Muris, who announced in October 2001 that the FTC would give priority to investigating any complaints received under the program. The Direct Marketing Association has also endorsed it by offering members an independent third-party dispute resolution mechanism and other support under its own DMA Safe Harbor Program.

The European Commission and Parliament are committed to reviewing the Safe Harbor Program at some point, and could decide to withdraw support for it in light of previous European criticisms and a less than overwhelming response from the American business community. However, the probability of this happening decreases with each new participant self-certifying for the program. Legal challenges to the program, either in Europe or the U.S., could also derail it. Ultimately, the success of Safe Harbor will depend upon the extent of participation by U.S. companies, the effectiveness of the self-regulatory measures participants commit themselves to, and continued political support both in Europe and in the United States.

➤ **Corporate Code of Conduct.** The last compliance option, adopting and implementing a worldwide corporate code of conduct governing the processing of personal information, is also the newest possibility to emerge from years of debate and work on how companies can achieve compliance with the Directive. This strategy is being actively promoted in Germany by Daimler-Chrysler, Unilever and other parties, who believe that a practice-oriented corporate privacy code, adequate in its provisions and effectively implemented, is a superior means of delivering the protections envisaged by the Directive with respect to employment data, in comparison to either the legalistic approach of model contracts or the political agreement reached in the Safe Harbor discussions. The goal of the advocates of this approach is to first secure the approval of German data protection authorities, and then the approval of the European Commission.

A number of questions arise that need to be satisfactorily answered before official European endorsement of this compliance strategy is likely. These are not presented with any implication that they are showstoppers. On the contrary, the approach of relying upon a corporate code of conduct is enormously appealing, and any efforts required to resolve these matters are worthy of encouragement.

… what safeguards would a data subject have if a company failed to follow its own code and provide adequate redress?

The first issue to be addressed is the need to find support for the strategy within the Directive, which cannot be simply ignored. Would that be in Article 25, 26, or 27? Would it be Elsewhere? Secondly, how much detail should be in the code? Should it be confined to a high level of generality, or reach down towards day-to-day matters? Should it be short or long? Thirdly, what would the implications be if different companies came up with different codes of conduct? Fourthly, how will the adequacy of a code, as a code, be established? Fifthly, how would conformance to the code be assessed, and by whom? And lastly, what safeguards would a data subject have if a company failed to follow its own code and provide adequate redress?

Each of the two viable compliance options, i.e., model contracts and Safe Harbor, took years to mature into acceptability. If the corporate code of conduct approach is on a similar trajectory, companies seeking a bona fide compliance strategy in the near term may need to look elsewhere.

■ Compliance with National Laws

As a framework or harmonizing document, the EU Privacy Directive sets minimum standards that member states are obliged to transpose into national legislation. At the same time, the Directive allows member states considerable discretion as to how they go about this. Member states may adopt a higher level of protection, by setting additional requirements beyond those contained in the Directive. For example, they may require data controllers to register with the national data protection authority, or to notify the authority prior to initiating a data transfer. They may require employers to obtain the consent of the Works Council for cross-border transfers of employee data.

Can companies seeking a lawful basis for transferring data from Europe to the U.S., by meeting the requirements of the Directive via standard contractual safeguards or though participation in the Safe Harbor Program, ignore the provisions of national legislation? The answer is no. Companies still need to attend to the national data protection and labor laws of each EU member state in which they operate. The only exception to this general rule occurs in connection with the Safe Harbor agreement, and only to the extent that there is specific language in the Principles and FAQs explicitly superceding the provisions of national legislation. Such points are relatively minor.

■ Adopting a Global Approach

The traditional approach to data protection challenges of most multi-nationals was to manage privacy issues locally. In other words, to make compliance with local data protection laws, which were largely European, the exclusive responsibility of local management, working with data protection authorities and Works Councils as necessary, obtaining consent from employees when required to do so, and using intra-company contracts to protect data involved in trans-border data flows. The Directive changed the regulatory environment dramatically, however, forcing management to adopt at least a regional view of compliance needs.

Every company planning, implementing or assisting in the operation of global HR information systems or applications now needs to meet the challenge of the EU Data Protection Directive. However, given the worldwide proliferation of countries with national data protection regimes, it would be a mistake to let privacy developments in the trans-Atlantic theater dominate the approach to what is truly a global issue. Many leading multi-nationals that have examined the regulatory landscape have determined that it makes sense to look beyond Europe and to take a broader view, one that tackles compliance challenges on a global, rather than a piece-meal, basis. They have recognized that multi-national companies that want to operate across national borders, using global business practices and HR programs, supported by global IT systems to reach global customers, need global data privacy standards.

The real privacy challenge over the next decade is ... about moving personal information from any country to any country ....

From this perspective, meeting the challenge of the Directive is but one component of a larger strategy and approach. The real privacy challenge over the next decade is not about bringing European personal information into North America, but about moving personal information *from* any country *to* any country, and complying with regulatory requirements relating to personal information throughout the world.

➤ **Components of a Global Approach.** Adopting a global approach to meeting privacy challenges means creating a culture of respect for privacy throughout a company. The foundation of such a culture, as well as the starting point for creating it, is a single, comprehensive set of employee privacy principles, issued on a worldwide basis, applicable in every country in which a company operates. Such principles are at the heart of any corporate policy or code of conduct.

The core principles are best developed by taking into account internationally accepted principles of fair information practice, as well as leading national privacy legislation and human resource codes of practice. Doing so ensures that the principles are sufficiently robust to set a standard of internal privacy practices and protection that will satisfy 80 percent to 90 percent of the regulatory requirements likely to be encountered. Getting one's privacy house in order in this way, by shifting the focus from complying with particular laws, to doing the right thing with respect to the privacy of employees, simplifies compliance activities. It also makes it possible to manage human resources in a consistent manner across national borders.

Once a set of employee privacy principles is established, these principles need to be translated into privacy policies, procedures and programs that will be implemented on a worldwide basis. Managers and employees alike need the guidance and structure provided through these mechanisms to bring the employee privacy principles down to earth in terms of day-to-day operations. Once the privacy policies, procedures and programs have been developed, they need to be rolled out throughout the enterprise through employee communications and training.

Important privacy programs that need to be created include one to address employee privacy concerns and objections, and to find a reasonable accommodation for those concerns, as well as a program to handle and attempt to resolve complaints. The complaint program needs to have an internal component, feeding into an independent alternative dispute resolution (ADR) mechanism should attempts to reach a resolution internally be unsuccessful. Another important program to be created is an audit or review program, to ensure that privacy principles and policies are being followed in practice.

Companies proceeding along this path have found considerable value in designating corporate and regional privacy officers with responsibility for overseeing and coordinating the company's privacy programs and initiatives. Having an ongoing management structure in place to deal with privacy issues is important to ensure that privacy policies and programs are properly implemented and maintained. A privacy management team is also needed to ensure that these policies and programs are kept up-to-date and responsive to new privacy challenges generated by technological, business, legal and social changes.

An overview of this approach, adopted by a leading U.S.-based pharmaceutical company, may be found in Figure 7.

Figure 7. The Global Approach of a Leading Pharmaceutical Firm.

Global Business
Practices

**Customers
and Employees**

Global IT Systems

Global Data
Privacy Standards

- Recognition of importance of privacy to business success
- HR taking the lead, driven by new global HR info sytem
- A comprehensive worldwide set of employee privacy principles
- Articulation of principles into privacy policies and procedures
- Global implementation of employee privacy program (employee awareness, training, internal certification, complaint programs, audits, etc.
- Designation of corporate and divisional privacy officers
- Participation in the Safe Harbor Program

◼ Towards a Single Global Standard for Handling Employee Data

Adopting a global approach to employee privacy issues, and building an internal culture of respect for privacy, is the best course of action open to a multinational corporation that wants to act as a global employer in the current regulatory environment surrounding the collection and use of personal information. In the long term, however, what is needed is a single, internationally agreed upon standard for respecting privacy in the handling of employee data. Business processes and systems are increasingly globalized, with diminishing differences across regions and industries. How employees in large enterprises are or should be treated, at least in democratic societies, is increasingly pointing towards common standards and approaches. From the point of view of both equity and efficiency, having a single global standard with respect to employee personal information makes enormous sense.

We are beginning to witness the evolution of such a single global standard. National standards for handling employee information are being established in a number of countries. Hong Kong has had one in place since September 2000, a code of practice for employers that has the force of law. The United Kingdom is expected to issue its overdue final code of practice for employers in pieces during 2002. Germany is also exploring development of an HR code of practice. Finally, but certainly not least important, after years of rumors and suggestions, the European Commission was reported in December 2001 to be actively polling member states as to the possible development of a new EU directive addressed to data protection in the employment context.

> **What is missing from the scene is a U.S. or North American privacy code for employers.**

What is missing from the scene is a U.S. or North American privacy code for employers. If North American companies want to have a say in the creation of the emerging international standard for handling employee data, they need to step up to the plate. Unless time and resources are devoted to common efforts in the form of an industry consortium dedicated to the collaborative production of a homegrown HR privacy code, standard-setters in other regions of the world — or, perish the thought, in our own legislative capitals and regulatory agencies — will write that code for us. One way or another, however, a single global standard for handling employment data is coming into existence.

Dr. Donald Harris (donaldharris@hrprivacy.com) is president of HR Privacy Solutions, a New York-based consulting practice that has assisted a dozen leading multi-national employers and employment services providers in meeting the challenges of regulatory requirements surrounding employee informa-

tion. Don is internationally known as a leader, expert, author, speaker, and conference producer on issues relating to privacy and data protection in the employment context. As founder and chair of IHRIM's Privacy Committee, he was invited by the U.S. Department of Commerce to participate in the first session of the Safe Harbor talks, and subsequently advised the Department on HR issues. Prior to establishing his own practice, Don managed HR systems and information, and developed privacy policies, for major private and public sector organizations, during a 25-year career in HR, payroll and labor relations. He holds an MBA in Computer Applications and Information Systems from NYU, and a PhD in Philosophy from Columbia University. He can be reached at **donaldharris@hrprivacy.com**.

■ Endnotes

*   The opinions expressed in this chapter are offered solely for educational purposes, and are neither intended, nor should be taken, as legal advice. Any conclusions about what particular companies should do in particular circumstances should be reviewed by counsel.

Part Five:
Global Human Capital Management Systems

"We used to think that we knew how to run organizations. Now we know better. More than ever they need to be global and local at the same time, to be small in some ways but big in others, to be centralized some of the time and decentralized most of it."

—Charles Handy

• • • • • • • •

The familiar concerns of HR management-system development and implementation are magnified and given new twists when you globalize. Your clients may have operations in different parts of the world that interact little or not at all. Gaining buy-in from all parties (notably management) requires a degree of coordination and of wide-angle vision that exceeds what's required in domestic business.

The problem goes beyond the sheer size of a global operation; it's also the astonishing diversity. Practices or rules that apply in one country may fail (or even be illegal) in another. Users speak different languages. An onscreen icon that conveys exactly what is intended in one country can deeply offend users in another. The list goes on.

This section gives an idea of the range of issues you must deal with in HRMS development — from strategic planning and vendor selection to implementation — and provides some guidance to help ensure success.

Getting the Best of All Worlds:
Strategies for Successful Global HRMS Projects

By Jenni Lehman and Synco Jonkerson

On the same day, the vice president of human resources for an international toy manufacturer receives two requests: one from the company's CEO and another from the Hong Kong field office. The CEO wants to know how many administrative assistants the company employs worldwide, and the Hong Kong offices needs help assembling an international project team to optimize the company's product distribution process. Both requests require that the vice president access data about his global workforce. Unfortunately, the information resides in multiple systems across the globe, over 20 different job function codes appear to exist for administrative assistants, and skill information is disparate and not aligned. Without a consolidated view of the worldwide workforce, the VP of HR becomes a bearer of bad news — he can't help his boss or the Hong Kong office.

For companies operating on a global scale, global HRMS implementations are no longer an option; they're a necessity. As advances in communication technologies erase boundaries and collapse distances, businesses are stretching into new territories to remain competitive. While expanding into global markets often promises lucrative benefits, companies that fail to prepare for the operational impacts of globalization may face a rude awakening when they begin to integrate each new country's operations. For a human resources department, aligning employees and best practices from disparate cultures, languages, and priorities with corporate objectives can seem daunting. Any benefits an HR department may reap from worldwide operations — reducing costs, increasing efficiencies, optimizing the global workforce, ensuring global alignment to corporate objectives, reducing IT errors and simplifying maintenance

"After the merger, our organization was much larger, and we needed an effective way to communicate and collaborate — to give ourselves a platform for collaboration between the two employee bases," said Scott Ramsey, Supervisor of HR and Corporate Administrative Systems at Anadarko Petroleum Corporation. *"We have operations in the Congo, Gabon, Georgia in the former Soviet Union, Canada and Guatemala. Basically, we realized that if we were going to keep growing internationally, we needed a platform through which to communicate."*

—may be overshadowed by the monumental task of managing simple HR functions across a fractured organization.

Operations in different countries can quickly become islands unto themselves. Your French HR headquarters may have no visibility into your operations in Malaysia or Brazil, for example. Standardization of technology and best practices can seem impossible as each country has business practices unique to its culture, not to mention disparate regulations, languages and currencies. With hundreds of systems in as many countries, you may not be able to consolidate your data — such as employee profiles, workforce skills, turnover rates and compensation information — making it difficult to manage human resources from a global perspective. Many companies are beginning to implement global Human Resource Management Systems (HRMS) to combine local functionality with a global architecture that provides collaborative business processes and a consolidated view of the worldwide workforce. Yet, while global HRMS projects can prevent some of the challenges inherent in running a global enterprise and offer tremendous benefits such as cutting costs, optimizing global business processes and increasing productivity, they require careful planning to be most successful.

■ The ABCs of Successful Global HRMS Projects

A few words of advice on how to reap maximum benefits from your global HRMS implementation: First, in order for your global initiative to be successful, it is important to secure ground-up support from managers in each locale. With careful planning, a global HRMS project will enable each country to maintain specialized operations while also gaining access to a greater depth of resources and information such as surveys and data from throughout the company, analytic applications that provide insight into trends and practices, HR policies and procedures, and financials that can only come from a single, centralized system.

Second, an HRMS project should match HR and IT requirements with the right technology. Planning jointly with the IT department, you must define the objectives most important to the company, including:

➤ Does your company plan to continue expanding into new countries?

➤ Are mergers and acquisitions occurring regularly?

➤ Do employees need anytime, anywhere access to their personal information?

➤ Does your HR department need to analyze data across the entire enterprise?

➤ Do you require better visibility into the worldwide competencies available?

➤ Is your HR department trying to automate or push down tasks to managers and employees, regardless of their location?

By carefully answering these questions, you can provide the IT department with a blueprint for technology functionality that will facilitate the joint process of choosing the right vendor. For example, if it is important that your HRMS solution supports the country rules and regulations of satellite offices, you would choose a vendor with a flexible product that can easily be localized.

Finally, it is tantamount that you have a sound strategy for implementing a successful global HRMS project. Different goals will drive different strategies. There are three basic approaches to HRMS projects: IT-centric, process-centric and workforce-centric. Considering one or more of these strategies can help you set your organization's parameters and priorities for implementation, while defining the metrics by which your project's success may be judged.

➤ An IT-Centric Strategy

An IT-centric approach recognizes the strain global expansion has on the IT function, and focuses on reducing IT costs and complexity. Using a single HRMS application worldwide, the IT department implements the same system in multiple locations, consolidating global HR information into one database. By using the Internet, an HRMS can facilitate browser-based access of multiple users regardless of their location, dramatically reducing IT maintenance and upgrade costs. This approach recognizes the value of a single platform; it pro-

Figure 1. Global HRMS Implementation Strategies.

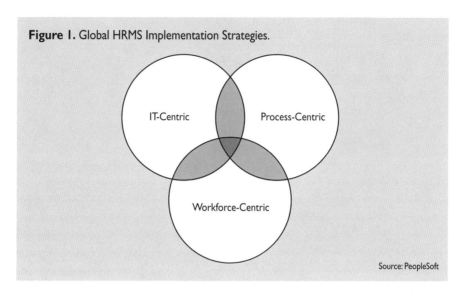

Source: PeopleSoft

vides repeatable IT practices for maintenance and upgrades, economies of scale through shared services, and easy knowledge transfer. An IT-centric strategy may make architecture flexibility a main priority, opting for a technology solution with one alterable code line rather than a hard-coded solution, or a single rules-based engine with country extensions rather than multiple country-specific engines.

While an IT-centric strategy focuses on using technology to cut costs, it also poses some risks. One potential risk is that it may be harder to support HRMS practices in smaller locations, putting a dent in your objective to consolidate business processes worldwide. Another is that your HR department can be cut out of decisions that ultimately impact operations. For example, if each country is allowed to choose its own vendors without considering the needs of the global organization, the HRMS implementation may ultimately fail to produce the expected cost benefits across the organization. On the other hand, if a global solution is selected without proper consultation with all of the impacted regions, it may prove difficult to get user acceptance and could fall equally short of reaching its goals. To minimize these risks, it is important to carefully assess the organizational goals for the HRMS implementation at all levels and for all regions and determine whether an IT-centric strategy captures all of your objectives. For example, if one of your organizational goals is to better leverage your workforce skills throughout the enterprise, you may choose to augment your IT-centric approach with the workforce-centric approach outlined below.

➤ A Process-Centric Strategy

Rather than looking at saving costs by focusing on technology economies of scale, the process-centric approach focuses on maximizing efficiencies by improving business processes and standardizing best practices. With the process-centric strategy, the HRMS is ultimately a tool for imposing best practices and business rule compliance through application implementation. For many HR professionals, the process-centric approach may offer particular appeal, since it is designed to delegate administrative functions and enable corporate HR to be more strategic.

With elaborate self-service functionality, the HRMS entrusts employees and managers with using the system to conduct online tasks that were once paper based and routed through the HR department. An organization adopting a process-centric strategy may choose a technology solution based on an architecture that fully leverages the Internet. Web-based self-service applications provided through a comprehensive portal would allow employees to collaborate and manage their own benefits, procurement and travel. Rather than making requests for training through HR, employees would access their personal profile via the Internet and sign up for company or third-party training online. Research from the Cedar Group shows tremendous savings; self-service, Internet-enabled applications reduce cycle times and error rates by 60 percent and headcounts by up to 70 percent. The same study also demonstrated that savings for base HR processes such as approving a promotion or benefits enrollment can be as high as 80 percent.[1] In addition to these substantial savings, corporate HR resources are no longer drained with basic administration; instead, they're reserved for strategic initiatives that can help the company maintain a competitive edge.

Like all strategies, the process-centric approach introduces its own risks. Those adopting this approach may fail to consider the variety of needs within an organization in an effort to standardize practices. Changing processes within a large organization can be slow, costly and painful. For example, offices accustomed to using their own job codes may resist a move to consolidate job codes company-wide. The process-centric approach may not be the answer if your organization has many different lines of businesses, each with its own particular processes, embedded many layers deep. Careful due diligence can help you determine whether the process-centric approach is right for your organization. Achieving success with this approach requires the cooperation of managers and employees throughout the global enterprise, so it is important that you rally worldwide support for the changes you advocate.

➤ A Workforce-Centric Strategy

Human capital is typically the most important and costly asset of any business. How well you manage global human capital can tip the scales of success or failure. The workforce-centric approach to HRMS projects aims to obtain a global view of the workforce to support your business objectives. By analyzing performance indicators, simulating scenarios to determine the impact of change, and managing the allocation of human resources, you can leverage human capital to its full potential.

With a workforce-centric strategy, the HR department identifies which HRMS data is relevant to support business decision-making. For example, the ability to view granular details about human capital all over the globe would enable you to efficiently disperse skills throughout the enterprise. If a project manager in the Japan office needed to speak with an engineer specializing in wireless network components, you could simply search the central data repository to find employees around the world with that particular skill-set. The workforce-centric approach recognizes the value of focusing at a global level on human resource management, and constantly realigns the workforce investment with business objectives.

Without setting up proper metrics to measure outcomes, however, the workforce-centric approach can fail to articulate a compelling business case for the HRMS project. This strategy will appeal to knowledge-intensive organizations more than to companies dependent mostly on manual labor. To minimize the risks inherent in the workforce-centric strategy and ensure that the strategy works for you, it is important to consider how you can show the impact of improved workforce management on the bottom line.

➤ A Hybrid Strategy

It is quite likely that you will combine the elements and perspectives of each approach outlined above to arrive at a hybrid strategy uniquely yours. Because HRMS projects have the potential to impact so many facets of corporate oper-

BENEFITS OF THE THREE GLOBAL HRMS IMPLEMENTATION STRATEGIES

IT-Centric Strategy:
• Reduces costs by using a single HRMS application worldwide,
• Ensures repeatable IT practices for maintenance and upgrades,
• Captures economies of scale through shared services, and
• Eases knowledge transfer.

Process-Centric Strategy:
• Increases process efficiency and reduces process costs,
• Standardizes best practices and business rule compliance,
• Improves data integrity and quality, and
• Decreases redundancy.

Workforce-Centric Strategy:
• Provides global view of the workforce to support business initiatives,
• Integrates global workforce information with business processes,
• Aligns workforce investment with business investment, and
• Enables strategic deployment of workforce on project basis.

ations, it is important to prioritize your objectives and carefully consider the benefits and risks of each strategy prior to choosing an approach for your global HRMS implementation.

A hybrid strategy combining elements from IT-centric and process-centric approaches may appeal to many organizations. In this case, a company's objectives may be twofold: to streamline operations around the world by implementing a single technology platform and create standard business processes and best practices that will improve efficiencies. For example, a global shipping corporation that has just acquired 10 smaller companies around the world wants to align the practices of each newly acquired operation with those of the corporate office, while at the same time standardizing on a single HRMS application. With a hybrid approach to its HRMS project, the shipping company uses elements from both the IT-centric and process-centric strategies to achieve the implementation's dual objectives.

For other organizations, managing human capital effectively and improving business processes on a global scale may take precedence. These organizations may choose to combine a process-centric strategy with a workforce-centric approach. For example, a global pharmaceutical company dependant on its intellectual capital wants to improve the way it assigns employees to R&D projects and streamline its best practices across offices in five countries. Combining process-centric and workforce-centric strategies ensures that the pharmaceutical company's HRMS project will focus on both issues.

Because every company has its own special needs, your company may not fit neatly into one strategy. Therefore, it is important that you carefully consider

HP ADOPTS A HYBRID APPROACH FOR IMPLEMENTING ITS GLOBAL HRMS

Hewlett-Packard Company (HP) wanted to standardize its HR technology, cut operational costs, and give employees instant access to the global HR information they needed to make strategic decisions. The company decided on a pure Internet HRMS that would streamline HR processes in eight languages for over 90,000 employees in over 120 countries.

Despite the IT-centric advantages, Steve Rice, director of HR global enterprise programs and technology at HP, reveals that his company also adopted a workforce-centric approach. "This implementation isn't just about software. It's about changing the way we deliver HR services across our enterprise." He continues, "We wanted to push information out to employees and managers and put them at the center of what we call the HP ecosystem."

HP's HRMS project allowed it to transition from four geographic instances of HR software to one; save US$3 million annually in hardware, software, databases and maintenance costs; and drop from 25 servers to 10. How will HP take advantage of the workforce management benefits? "I've already re-deployed forty developers from our organization," said Rice.

which combination of strategies will best help you achieve the benefits a global HRMS implementation offers.

■ Assessing Risks

Global businesses are complex because they encompass a multiplicity of languages, regulations and cultures and operate on an immense scale with diverse regional policies. Regardless of the implementation strategy you select, you may face challenges that fall into three main risk areas: those associated with an inadequate business case, a lack of project momentum or an overspent budget. Avoiding these risks should help you stay within budget, receive continuing support from executives, and realize the full benefits of your HRMS project.

➤ Inadequate Business Case

Many HR organizations lack experience in justifying large-scale technology projects. Even for the savvy HR manager, building a feasible business case to defend a significant HRMS investment is not easy. However, a compelling business case — one that quantifies the benefits of a global human capital management strategy — should help secure full corporate commitment to your global HRMS project.

To build a strong business case, first assess how the global HRMS project will impact your company. For example, an HRMS with a solid self-service component would allow HR officers to recruit online and would reduce the calls that managers make to the HR department. Second, calculate the savings in time, money, and human capital resulting from these changes. It is important to emphasize these quantitative benefits in your business case.

It is also helpful to include less tangible benefits, such as improved employee satisfaction and increased quality of business processes, to bolster your business case. While time-consuming to build, a strong business case can help you receive the financial and operational support you need to implement an HRMS project on a global scale.

➤ Lack of Project Momentum

Global HRMS implementations are long-term projects with many phases. For some companies, maintaining momentum can be a challenge. The project may exceed its projected budget or implementation deadline, tempting the company to rush through the deployment or cut it short. However, if a project is prematurely concluded, it may not produce all of the expected benefits. It is important to remember that for most companies, HRMS projects aim to impact multiple aspects of the business — including critical changes to existing processes. Implementing the technology is just the first step.

For example, a multinational retailer implements a global HRMS project to standardize on a single system, streamline administration, provide better training, and conduct recruitment over the Web. After completing the technology implementation, the retailer loses momentum. In this case, the company has met only one of its four objectives — standardizing on a single system. Without further effort, the retailer is unlikely to improve its administration, training and recruitment processes. Thus, it is important to remember throughout the long implementation process that an HRMS project is not a simple technology fix, but rather a vehicle that can positively impact the way your entire organization does business.

➤ Overspent Budget

Staying within budget is never easy. With a global implementation, the sheer scope of the project can make it difficult to rein in costs. However, the total cost of ownership for the HRMS must be carefully monitored and controlled since it has a direct relationship to the system's expected return on investment (ROI). During the implementation and production stages, it is important to set realistic cost assumptions that correlate accurately to the envisioned benefits. If a one-year project becomes a two-year project, the ROI is delayed. The most severe impact to ROI results from a change in the "I," or the cost of investment. If you decide mid-project that you need local interfaces for an additional 20 countries, the cost of your investment skyrockets and upsets the ROI equation.

BEA SOLVES TECHNOLOGY INTEGRATION ISSUES WITH HRMS PROJECT

One of the world's leading e-business infrastructure software companies, BEA Systems Inc., needed a scalable human resources infrastructure to foster collaboration across the enterprise, reduce cost of ownership, and deliver access to its employees and managers across the globe.

With a scalable, integrated HRMS, BEA adopted infrastructure to help it grow from a US$3 billion to a US$5 billion company. According to Jeanette Pereira, BEA's IT director for G&A business solutions delivery, "Integration is key — not having to worry about application compatibilities and additional integration costs when we upgrade." The employee portal built on this integrated platform offered additional advantages. Pereira explains, "We are implementing single sign-on and one-stop shopping. We don't have to teach every employee different login procedures. We're setting up single processes across the company."

BEA's global HRMS implementation helped the company lower maintenance costs, transition from time-consuming paper-based to simplified web-based HR processes, eliminate 13 stand-alone information silos, and establish a unified look and feel for its HR system. "Before, it was like, 'This is my system, that's your system.' Today it's our system," said Pereira.

To maintain control of your budget, it is important to clearly define your needs before you embark on the HRMS project. A global bank avoided altering its project scope midstream by sending project teams to each country before it began implementation. After conducting workshops for a week, the team defined the project scope and cost for each country. By carefully planning and soliciting local support, the project team eliminated the chance that the countries would request changes in the project during construction. With careful planning, you can ensure that your global HRMS project stays on track and on budget.

■ A Sample Implementation Methodology

After considering various strategies for implementing your global HRMS projects and assessing the potential risks, you may want to spend time considering a methodology for undertaking the implementation. Global implementations can be complex, with the success or failure of one phase potentially influencing the next. Therefore, it is essential that an implementation methodology target the entire project lifecycle. A successful implementation methodology recognizes the following phases:

- Strategy,
- Planning,
- Structure,
- Construction,
- Transition, and
- Deployment.

➤ Strategy

As discussed above, the choice of strategy is an important component of a successful global HRMS project. During this phase, a company determines the appropriate strategy for the project — IT-centric, process-centric, workforce-centric or some hybrid of these — considering factors such as global corporate objectives and expected ROI. The strategy phase becomes the foundation for the project and involves executives who will ultimately champion the project within the organization.

➤ Planning

In the planning phase, a company conducts a technical feasibility analysis, defines project member roles and sets realistic timelines and budgets. This is the phase when all practical issues are considered. For global implementa-

Global HRMS Implementation Process.

During global HRMS implementations, it is particularly important to secure participation of regional and local offices during the beginning (strategy and planning) and final (transition and deployment) phases.

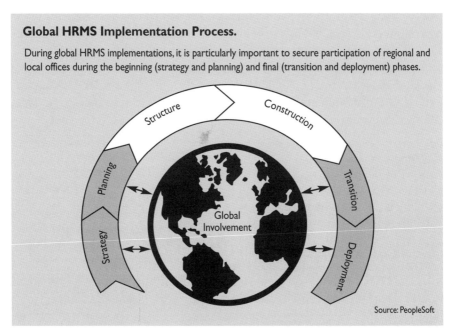

Source: PeopleSoft

tions, this may mean determining how and when different countries will get involved in the project. Fastidious attention to detail and scope in the planning phase should allow you to anticipate and address potential challenges before they occur. To keep the entire organization aligned behind the same objectives, it is important to communicate project goals and phases to the appropriate executives. This phase also acts as another checkpoint for ensuring that the plan supports your organization's overall business objectives.

➤ Structure

A solid implementation approach pays particular attention to the structure phase of the process. Essentially administrative in nature, the structure phase builds the skeleton for your global HRMS project. You assemble project teams, define roles and responsibilities, and build structures for conducting quality assurance, communicating effectively, providing consistent feedback, and comparing business needs with the project's progress. Many companies choose to form an international project team or steering committee to oversee the human capital management and project implementation at a global level. The goal of the structure phase is to ensure that the project will actually deliver the business solution promised. While scope changes in this stage are acceptable, surprises down the road are not.

➤ Construction

In the construction phase, all of your diligent strategizing and planning begins to pay off. The actual construction of the global HRMS project is under way. Monitoring progress is a key element of this phase. Throughout construction, maintaining open communication with project teams ensures that the process moves smoothly — on budget and on time. To ease the transition to the final phases of the implementation process, you may also choose to concentrate on future-oriented activities, such as building disaster recovery plans, during this phase.

➤ Transition

Once your HRMS is in place, it is time to start involving different categories of users. In the transition stage, a company will employ various users with disparate job functions and expertise to test the system. By watching users interact with the new system, you can set up specialized training for all employees who will access it throughout the global organization. In this way, the HRMS will meet the requirements of all countries, cementing support for the system on a local level. Countries that have invested personnel and provided input to the process will be more likely to encourage employees to take full advantage of the HRMS.

➤ Deployment

Finally, the payoff arrives. In the final stage, the HRMS project is deployed across the entire enterprise. Often, companies adopt a phased-deployment approach defined by geography. For example, the company may train users, cut over to the new system, install quality assurance, and conduct project reviews in Europe before it tackles the United States. By deploying the system at regular intervals, a relatively small team can perform user training and handle the actual changeover. A stepped-deployment approach renders the deployment process more manageable and helps companies avoid risks associated with simultaneous global deployments. However, it also delays the benefits offered by the HRMS system.

■ Conclusion

Implementing an HRMS offers tremendous benefits to global companies. It cuts costs through economies of scale, optimizes global business processes and streamlines best practices; empowers employees by giving them universal access to important information; enables managers to assemble talent for projects from all over the enterprise; and allows each country to meet unique regulations and still integrate operations and data across the global corporation.

Undertaking a successful global HRMS project requires the cooperation of your entire organization. Thus, it is important that you plan carefully, considering which blend of implementation strategies — IT-centric, process-centric, or workforce-centric — will help you meet your corporate objectives. With assiduous planning, you can address sensitive areas that may undercut a project, such as building a strong business case, maintaining momentum throughout the life of the project and staying within budget. If you understand the implementation methodology from the beginning, you can monitor progress with each phase, from strategy to deployment, ensuring that you meet all of the project goals. With an HRMS in place, you will have the tools to effectively manage your global HR operation while delivering remarkable benefits that impact all departments of the organization.

Jenni Lehman is vice president of global product strategy for PeopleSoft HRMS. She joined PeopleSoft in January 2002 as vice president of global human resources management systems (HRMS) product strategy. In this role, Lehman is responsible for leading the strategic direction for the entire HRMS product marketing division. Prior to joining PeopleSoft, Lehman served as vice president and research area director at Gartner Research Group, a leading strategic consulting services firm based in Stamford, Connecticut. While at Gartner, Lehman was responsible for the ERPII business applications area. She managed a team of analysts covering enterprise resource planning (ERP) systems, and corporate financial and HR applications. Lehman was also previously employed at Cyborg Systems, where she played a lead role in defining global product strategies for advanced technology products. In addition, Lehman held a senior leadership position at Akron General Medical Center. Lehman earned a bachelor's degree from the University of Akron. She can be reached at **jenni_lehman@peoplesoft.com**.

Synco Jonkeren,director, HRMS product strategy Europe for PeopleSoft, is responsible for ensuring that all the products in the PeopleSoft HRMS suite meet the requirements of European customers. He is also responsible for building and leading a pan-European team of product strategy managers. Jonkerson joined PeopleSoft when it embarked on its programme of international expansion in 1993. Following a period in the customer services division, working as an account manager for multinational customers, he joined the product development organisation in 1996. Prior to taking up his present position, he was European development manager for PeopleSoft HRMS. From 1988 to 1993, Jonkerson worked with IBM, where he became leader of a project to develop a new international HR system for use in all of the company's European offices. He has given presentations at a variety of conferences, focusing mainly on personnel management and its relationship with corporate organisational structures and information technology (IT). He has a master's degree in social sciences. He can be reached at **synco_jonkerson@peoplesoft.com**.

■ Endnote

1   The Cedar Group, Human Resources Self Service Survey 2001

Leading Practices in Global Implementations

By John Johnston

Best practices can often be misleading if they are applied blindly to a company without considering the unique cultural and organizational issues specific to the company. Leading practices are ones that, based on experience, will assist any organization in the implementation of a global HRMS system. In this chapter, we outline some of the key leading practices that should be considered in the implementation and comment on how they can be tailored to the organization to achieve success.

■ What are Leading Practices

Why not call this chapter *Best Practices in Global Implementations*? Everybody loves best practices. After all, they are the best — right? They are not merely good or better, they are the best! You can't tell your boss that you are putting in pretty good practices; they must be best.

Best practices are those that have been used by others who have achieved success on their implementations. The practices and processes, which they credit for their success, become "best practices." Organizations believe "if they worked for Ford, IBM or ABB, they will work for us."

Best practices, if used without understanding the complex interplay of process, people, technology, structure and culture, can result in disaster somewhat akin to the saying "the operation was a success but, unfortunately, the patient died."

Leading practices tend to be more generic. They represent the experiences gained from multiple projects among many different companies. They are not specific to a particular organization. They represent "truisms." If leading practices are followed, they assist in project success.

Project success is defined as the project being:

➤ Delivered on time,

➤ Delivered on budget, and

➤ Meeting the objectives for which the project was chartered.

Other criteria for success include user satisfaction with the delivered solution, the sustainability of the project, and the satisfactory experience of the team working on the project.

Leading practices are the focus of this chapter. These are based on the experience of others and my own experience in the successful implementations of global human resource management systems (HRMS) projects. Leading practices also represent a form of risk management. None is mandatory. Missing a leading practice will not cause your project to be a dismal failure and bring shame to all associated with the project. Not using them will, however, increase the chances of project failure. Leading practices become a barometer of project success, indicating that there is clear weather ahead or storm clouds on the horizon. The more leading practices you use, the greater your chances for smooth sailing. The fewer you use, the greater your risk for volatility and storminess.

> *Leading practices become a barometer of project success, indicating that there is clear weather ahead or storm clouds on the horizon.*

This chapter is not an exhaustive compilation of every leading practice, tool or technique used in a global implementation. Technology savants will be concerned that nowhere do I mention software, touch only briefly on hardware, and seem to spend most of my time talking about the "soft stuff." Largely this is because projects don't fail because the technology was wrong or the team members incompetent. They fail because insufficient focus was placed on dealing with change or ignoring the culture of the organization in an HRMS team's haste to prove themselves to senior management.

Projects fail on the simple things.

■ Project Governance

➤ Project Charter

The first leading practices occur long before the project kick-off. They address the way in which the project is chartered and the construction of the project's governance structure.

Global HRMS projects are chartered for different reasons. The primary reason is a corporation's commitment to manage their human assets on a global basis. Global systems provide the ability to derive management information about people and productivity. Better information should result in better decisions about items such as staffing and talent management. It should result in lowered cost through reductions in administration and turnover. It should also result in improved service to the employee and management populations.

There are other reasons for putting in a global HRMS, among these are:

- A desire to capitalize on the investment in a major vendor package,

- A desire to reduce duplication of effort and systems costs,

- A desire to put in place the enhanced functionality global systems can deliver, and

- A belief that employees in all countries should be provided with global career opportunities.

All too often, however, a global HRMS project is put in because a vendor oversold the benefits. They are also put in because it is coincidently a pressing need in the home country, and a global system will help to position the return on investment by incorporating a larger user population.

➤ Strong Sponsorship

The sponsor of global HRMS projects is often the human resource department or the top HR executive when he/she has been convinced of the value of such a system. Sponsorship from only the HR department is likely the "kiss of death" for any HRMS project. At the first sign of a downturn or when the project experiences any difficulty, the project will be shut down.

HRMS systems must be regarded as *business systems* that apply to the entire enterprise — not as a system for the human resources department. Sadly, in many enterprises, the top HR position may not have sufficient business impact and personal business support to sustain a large global program. When conflicting priorities arise and cause a re-assessment of systems development funds, HR systems may lose out.

A leading practice among global implementations is to have both the top HR person and the top operations person as sponsors. Having the COO or CEO aligned with the project will likely result in sufficient drive to see the project through to completion even in the event of competing priorities. In order to obtain such sponsorship, there must be a compelling business case for the HRMS. Although we deal with this issue later under its own framework, the business case is crucial to obtaining the required sponsorship.

... the top HR person must have the marketing skills and savvy to line up the support of the CEO in framing not only a logical business case but also an emotional response.

In addition, the top HR person must have the marketing skills and savvy to line up the support of the CEO in framing not only a logical business case but also an emotional response. Unless the financial component of the business case is exceptional, a significant part of the case should be the depiction and vision of how the system will change the business lives of both employees and managers. The marketing skills of the project initiator can carry the business case and make it real for the CEO/COO.

In addition, it helps to use those same skills to garner support from the CFO and operating division heads. Framing the system in terms of the benefits to be returned to the organization is not enough. Cogent examples of how this will create a financial return, reduce administration, increase sales and create more appropriate use of human capital will increase the likelihood that a system will be implemented, even in the face of issues and concerns.

Earlier, the terms Project Sponsor and Project Initiator were used. The two are not interchangeable. Each has specific roles and responsibilities. The Project Initiator is the person who brought the project forward to the Project Sponsor. The Project Initiator has ensured that the research and the business case present a compelling story. The Project Initiator has prepared the groundwork and developed alternate visions of the future with and without the system. They must convince the sponsor that this is the right — the only — course of action that makes sense, and they must believe it.

The Project Sponsor, as mentioned earlier, must be an exceptionally powerful business ally. He or she should be able to drive the project even in the face of unforeseen circumstance. This person must have been convinced of the necessity and benefits of having a system. The two roles are not interchangeable. If the Project Sponsor becomes the champion of the system, then the Project Initiator must be the cheerleader and the coach.

Top executives have significant pressures on their time and attention. Major systems implementations may take upward of two years. For executives accustomed to addressing the business quarter by quarter, as do external analysts, two years is an eternity. The Project Initiator must continue to reinforce the reasons for the project and ensure that routine and regular updates are provided to the Project Sponsor along with evidence of short-term wins.

➤ Global Steering Committee

Global projects need to be sponsored by each division and geographical executive who will be impacted by the project. Much in the manner of the Project Sponsor, the Project Initiator must also enlist the support of the key customers.

Corporate systems forced down the throat of a geographic region without any discernable business benefit to the region (and, in fact, probably a business impediment) will likely cause the project to fail. The only exception to this rule is when the system is critical to the survival of the organization and the Project Sponsor has the influence to override the objections.

One of the leading practices in reducing resistance in global projects is the use of a project steering committee that includes the top officers of the geographic regions. By preparing the groundwork on an individual level and then proposing a global steering committee, the project will reduce the degree of resistance by providing an element of control for the regions.

This also makes good business sense, as the global steering committee members will be invested in achieving project success. This will reduce objections and reduce the number of requests for non-legislative software localizations.

Projects implemented by consensus in all of the countries impacted by the system will lead to greater support, lessened resistance to change and higher enterprise return on investment (ROI).

Much like the Project Sponsor needs regular updates on the project, the global steering committee needs to meet regularly to monitor the progress of the project, conduct financial due diligence and to arbitrate between conflicting priorities. Often project charters outline that the steering committee is also responsible for project scope changes. This may not be a wise course of action as the steering committee may not meet often enough to understand the issues leading to a scope change or be timely enough to keep the project moving forward.

If the global steering committee is focused on the global plan, the funding, and the reduction of conflict, then their plate is full enough.

Having regular global steering committee meetings and ensuring the meetings are focused on high-level strategies for completion is a practice that will enhance the chances of success.

➤ Funding Mechanisms

A critical item in ensuring that a global HRMS project will succeed is the issue of funding for the project. Many organizations have policies that deal with the funding of local and global projects. This is a good idea as it reduces the conflict in establishing a new policy for each project. This is particularly true of global infrastructure projects that may not bring immediate local benefits.

The three primary methods of funding global projects are outlined below, along with the strengths and drawbacks of each for a global project. In some cases, the funding mechanism will reinforce the project deployment strategy that should be aligned with the business structure (more on this later).

The first funding approach is the *corporate funded* approach. Essentially the project is funded and paid for by the corporate body. The benefits of such an approach are numerous. There is reduced conflict between geographies as to the relative price that each will pay. There is greater corporate control over the project, as "he who pays the piper gets to call the dance." Finally, there is less likelihood that the project will be stalled in a particular region due to short-term business conditions. Steering committees may find that under this approach a drawback is determining which area will be deployed first and how much functionality will be in place.

Another drawback is ensuring that scope creep does not occur. If someone else is paying the bill, there is often a natural tendency to insist that all the bells and whistles be included in the first phase. In later phases, the business unit might have to pay for items that have not been implemented in the first phase. The third drawback is that the regions have no "skin" in the game. A corporately-funded initiative may not be considered as high a priority in the minds of local management as other projects. Getting the crucial time and human resources to contribute to the project may be more difficult. As most consultants will attest, clients pay attention to things that they have to pay money to get.

As most consultants will attest, clients pay attention to things that they have to pay money to get.

Another funding approach is *local funding by the Business Units*. In this approach the local business units each pay a portion of the costs for the system and for the localization of the system to the region. One advantage is that the region has a strong business interest in seeing the project through to completion. For this model to work, the region must see a business benefit to the implementation. It will allow the region to put in place the enhanced functionality that it needs to run its business. Corporately, it ensures that the beneficiary of the system will fund the money invested in the system. Accountability for success rests in the region.

The drawbacks are less control over the system by the project team since the regions control the purse strings and will demand their priorities be addressed sometimes at the expense of the project. The regions may defer crucial decisions due to a downturn in their business conditions. This will drag the project out and reduce the likelihood of co-operation between the regions. Regions will also try to reduce their portion of the necessary infrastructure costs or may find it prohibitively expensive in the first place and opt out of a global approach in favour of a local system.

The last option involves a mixed strategy where the *core system is funded corporately and the local deployment is funded locally* by the region. This ensures that the system and infrastructure are put in place and the local deployments are suited to the local business conditions. This puts the onus on the corporation and the "host" country.

A leading practice is to ensure the funding for a project is consistent with the culture and business structure of the organization. Review the history of successful projects and ensure the governance structure is modelled in a similar manner and funded accordingly.

■ Alignment with the Business Structure

The company structure dictates organization of a successful global systems approach. As in the funding, there are several choices to be made as to the approach and systems architecture. In reviewing the systems model you should ensure the systems approach follows the culture of the organization.

The first decision dictates whether multiple vendors are used in a mixed environment or a single vendor platform is selected and the regions be mandated to comply with a corporate decision. Both approaches have merit.

In the first instance, it becomes easier to put in place a system where the local regions select a platform consistent with their business needs. The globalization occurs after the systems are implemented, using a data warehouse strategy to gather common information from all systems, which is housed in a central system available to the corporate decision makers. This requires laying out which fields will be collected and fed to the parent organization. A common data format is specified and a regular interface schedule developed.

In this scenario, local areas are responsible for funding their own project and providing the required information interface. Using a separate reporting system ensures that the regions transaction systems are kept free of the reporting requirements and storage costs. This results in a more responsive system with fewer delays in systems response time for the users. The corporate body still has the benefit of a global system, but reports may not be as up-to-date as with a single platform. Interface requirements become more difficult and will require ongoing maintenance as versions are upgraded to ensure the data feed is consistent.

These costs can be reduced if a single vendor is selected. The field and data maintenance processes are simplified as field translation and manipulation are reduced. There may also be significant economies of scale in purchasing with the single vendor providing larger volume discounts. Each country still funds the development, but they can implement according to their own schedule as business conditions warrant.

If a single vendor is chosen, there is yet another decision to be made. The decision is whether to have a single global system with local deployments, or multiple systems feeding into a single instance in a "host" area. There are arguments for both sides. A significant factor is the cost associated with acquiring a number of systems and then operating them in multiple locations.

A leading practice is to ensure that the decisions around vendor platform and delivery model are consistent with the existing IT infrastructure and the strategy of the organization.

■ Delivery Model

Global HRMS systems are a balancing act. At best they are a compromise when viewed from a regional perspective. From a corporate perspective, they may be critical to the organization and consequently require that standards and consistency of format be maintained. The key consideration is how to keep the corporate group happy with a global system while providing the local functionality to make the system a boon to the regions rather than another administrative requirement.

One leading practice is the development of a "template" of required corporate functionality and to then use it as a model in rolling the system out globally. Like a methodology from a consulting firm, this template approach provides a framework and plan without being overly restrictive and pedantic.

The template should address the policies and practices that the organization wants to enforce globally but also allow some room for non-standard processes. As part of the template development, considerable time should be spent on mapping the major HR business processes across countries and establishing a standardized set of processes *before* committing to automate them.

With a template in place, the next issue becomes one of localization. This refers to the practice of configuring the system using a generic approach and then refining the set-up to address local issues, such as legislative requirements, additional fields required and critical local practices.

The greater the amount of localization the more significant the costs will be both on installation and on maintenance and upgrade. Most Global HRMS systems come with some delivered functionality for selected countries, but depending on the country and on the legislative environment, almost all systems will fall short of complete coverage.

A significant differentiation here is between *localization* and *local preference.* The distinction is that localization refers to compliance with the legislative and cultural components of a geographic region (or country), whereas local preference refers to local business practices and customization to fit local business requirements.

Leading practices in global implementations focus most of the attention on the template followed by localization and then by local preference.

It is necessary in a global implementation to pay attention to local preference as this will assist in regional business units "buying into" the use of the system. Inclusion of local requirements will also assist in improving the expected ROI on the system.

A leading practice rule of thumb in global HRMS delivery is to spend 70 percent of the available budget on Global Template activities, 20 percent on localizations for legislative compliance and 10 percent on local preference items.

■ *Strong Business Case*

The success of a project is greatly enhanced by the preparation of a strong numbers-driven business case. This business case should provide both the direct savings to be recouped and the indirect savings that result from such items as reduced turnover and improved management satisfaction.

The business case should not only address the cost savings resulting from such items as staff reductions, reductions in paper/printing, etc., but should also include the impact on key HR performance metrics.

A strong business case will often carry a project even in the face of stiff opposition because the financial numbers and the ROI analysis will garner support at the executive level which can carry a project through when there are minor delays or "turf" issues which might cause the project to stall.

Prior to the commencement of the project, HR Management should determine and put in place a significant effort to establish operational, financial, customer satisfaction and learning/innovation measures, and establish a baseline response for analysis purposes.

Over the course of the project, a regular program of measurement and comparison to benchmark data should be conducted in addition to normal project management activities. This measurement program will, if properly developed, be able to lead directly to conclusions regarding the overall effectiveness of the system.

➤ Stabilization Periods

It is critical over the course of a project to ensure that a period of time be explicitly labelled for system stabilization. Over the course of many projects we have watched the project team disband soon after go-live and consequently seen the user community suffer through the stabilization period alone. On one project, the project team was disbanded and returned to their normal positions one week after the first payroll go-live. The project team left behind a lengthy list of noncritical but, nonetheless important issues in the project log. Some issues addressed year-end payroll processing concerns that would not surface for months, others addressed user requests that had been shuffled to the bottom of the priority list.

In these cases, the projects are not deemed successful. The user struggles with the system and ultimately the system is blamed when the solution required only an extra month of funding and resources. This is also true in staged or phased releases where countries (or functionality) are released one at a time.

It is a leading practice that after each go-live there be a minimum one-month period of stabilization before the team goes on to the next stage or is returned to their business unit. The same is true of project funding — do not end the project without including stabilization.

■ Team Formation

Global implementation teams require special attention. Due to the time that global implementations take and the geographic distances involved, these teams will work together for longer periods than those experienced in local implementations. On one hand, this is a good thing as the teams have a longer period to gel and work together effectively. On the other hand, if the teams fail to perform it means that minor issues can be blown out of proportion and the longer time period the team is together seems to stretch into eternity.

The first area to consider is the composition of a global implementation team. Surprisingly, many companies attempt to implement a global system with a team comprised entirely of staff from the "parent" company and only a token nod to the "global project." Depending on the nature of the project, the company culture, and the funding and delivery model noted above, this can be a recipe for disaster. Why would a company consider a using a team made up entirely of employees from "head office?"

The first reason is simple ignorance of the unique nature of global projects. The initial implementation is done in the company's corporate offices and then they use the same team to roll out the project overseas — after all, these are the most experienced employees with the new system. Unfortunately, these team members may not have sufficient cultural sensitivity and knowledge of the host country to effectively interact with the local regions. Secondly, companies tend to continue to use the team that was successful, and it is the lowest cost option in conducting the implementation. This team composition can result in lowered acceptance of the system in the new region or worse, a project where the users reject the new system due to missing or lesser functionality.

This problem can be easily addressed by having a global steering committee and team members from all of the countries involved in the global project. These employees should be involved from the beginning during the planning stages and be required to participate in regular team activities such as conference calls.

These teams require specific training upon formation. First, the team should be assembled in one location if they will not be co-located throughout the whole project. While together, they should be provided with intense team training to get them to the "performing" stage as quickly as possible. This familiarization and friendly interaction, far from being a costly frill, is critical in reducing later confrontations and friction over simple misunderstandings. In one project, communication issues were created that actually brought the project to a standstill until the team was brought together and allowed to air and explore their differences. It is harder to stay angry with someone when they are three metres away from you than it is when they are three time zones away from you.

Having brought the team together to allow them to develop a rapport, ensure that the differences do not grow through neglect. Generally, a project team should meet face-to-face at least every six months during the project and more frequently by conference call and videoconference. Encourage team members to communicate with each other via e-mail and consider collaboration tools such as instant messaging to allow informal interaction between teammates.

When forming a global project team, these four leading practices need to be considered:

➤ Create a multinational project team including members from each country.

➤ Consider carefully the mix of personalities to ensure they can work together over a lengthy period of time.

➤ Bring the team together during the planning stages to ensure they learn to work as a team before the development effort begins.

LEADING PRACTICE SUMMARY

➤ Have a detailed business case that outlines the project's costs and benefits on a country-by-country basis to garner senior management support.

➤ Select a strong executive sponsor, preferably someone outside the HR function, responsible for the global operations (or with the most to lose if the system is not implemented).

➤ Select a global Steering Committee incorporating both those countries involved in the initial operation and others who might join in later stages.

➤ The Steering Committee should deal with strategic issues and concerns. They should never involve themselves in the tactical details of the project. Key activities include defining the reporting structure and financial management considerations.

➤ Projects with a strong global mandate and a clear set of criteria supporting the decision to put in a global system will be more successful than those without such a mandate.

➤ Have both the top HR person and the top Operations person as sponsors.

➤ Provide examples of how the Global HRMS will result in a financial return, lessened reduced administration, greater sales, and more appropriate use of human capital applied to individual business functions.

➤ The top HR person must use marketing skills and be savvy to line up the support of the CEO in framing not only a logical business case but also an emotional response.

➤ Continually reinforce the reasons for the project.

➤ Ensure that routine and regular updates are provided to the Project Sponsor along with evidence of short-term wins.

➤ Global projects need to be sponsored by each division and geographical executive who will be impacted by the project.

➤ Use a project steering committee that includes the Top Officers of the geographic regions.

➤ Have the project steering committee meet regularly to monitor the progress of the project, to conduct financial due diligence, and to arbitrate between conflicting priorities.

➤ Ensure the funding for a project is consistent with the culture and business structure of the organization.

➤ Review the history of successful projects and ensure the project governance structure is modelled in a similar manner and funded accordingly.

➤ Ensure the decisions around vendor platform and delivery model are consistent with the existing IT infrastructure and the business strategy of the organization.

➤ Continue to have the team interact informally together and meet face-to-face at least twice yearly.

A consideration in bringing together a multinational team is the use of a common vocabulary around the project issues. One of the tools regarded as very successful on global projects is the development of a shared lexicon of terminology. Developing and using a glossary will reduce the misunderstandings and communications issues between team members from different countries.

LEADING PRACTICE SUMMARY (continued)

➤ Develop a "template" of required corporate functionality and use it as a model in rolling the system out globally.

➤ Map the major HR business processes across countries, and establish a standardized set of processes before committing to automate them.

➤ Spend 70 percent of the available budget on global template activities, 20 percent on localizations for legislative compliance, and 10 percent on local preference items.

➤ Business cases should address the cost savings and the impact on key HR performance metrics.

➤ HR should establish operational, financial, customer satisfaction, and learning/innovation measures, and establish a baseline response for investment analysis purposes.

➤ Establishing a regular program of measurement and benchmark data will lead directly to conclusions regarding the overall effectiveness of the system.

➤ After each go-live, ensure there is a one-month period of stabilization before the team goes on to the next stage or is returned to their business unit.

➤ Do not end the project funding without ensuring a period of system stabilization.

➤ Include on the project team members from all of the countries involved in the global project.

➤ Involve regional team members during the planning stages.

➤ Co-locate the project team in one location.

➤ If they will not be co-located, bring the team together and provide team training to increase cooperation.

➤ Ensure the project team meets face-to-face at least every six months during the project. Encourage frequent informal interaction.

➤ Use a common methodology for the project.

➤ Develop a shared lexicon of terminology for the project team.

➤ Gradually transition team members to ensure there is continuity on the project and that team members do not become "stale."

➤ Have a dedicated person on the team responsible for managing the human aspects of change.

➤ Use the change person to conduct pre-implementation change readiness analysis and post-implementation reviews.

➤ Training documentation must be translated into the languages of the countries being implemented.

➤ Have a communications plan and monitor it over the course of the implementation.

Typically, most organizations install in one country (if using a template, the template is developed in one country and them moved in successive waves to other regions) and then the project is rolled out to other regions. For example, the project is implemented in the United States and then implemented in the UK, Germany, Italy, France and Japan.

A leading practice is to include team members from these countries as noted above, but then as the project emphasis changes from the United States to the UK, some of the members of the U.S. team would roll off of the project and return to their normal duties or be assigned to another project. The other team members would be recruited from the UK pool of talent and then implement the system in the UK. This gradual shifting of team members by regional implementation will ensure that there is continuity on the project but that the team members do not get stale or burned out. Constantly adding new members to the team will ensure greater buy-in on the project and will also allow each country to complete its localizations more efficiently with team members from the country.

■ Change Management

Having a dedicated person on the team who is responsible for managing the human aspects of change on a project is a leading practice. Often change management is viewed as a frill or the project sponsors have the impression that "if the new system is implemented we just need to tell people to use the new system." This approach is akin to the story "Field of Dreams" where the belief is "If we build it, they will come." In real life, however, without a crisis, nothing is further from the truth.

Other organizations take the position that change management activities are the responsibility of the project manager. The project manager has a real job juggling resources, timetables and budgets. Without support, the change initiatives will be pushed into the background until the risk of project failure increases to a dangerous level.

Change management involves many different areas including management of sponsor involvement, coordinating communications, scheduling training, and identifying stakeholders and appropriate strategies for each stakeholder group. A trained change practitioner should be made a part of the team and charged with the management of these issues.

Another leading practice is the use of the change person to conduct change readiness analysis and post-implementation reviews. The change readiness activities will determine how aware employees are of the need for change and can help determine the communications effort necessary to build the case for the project with the end user. Post-implementation reviews will identify those areas where the project team should apply more effort in subsequent phases of the project.

The change management team member can arrange the team building activities that are used in the initial team formation. They can also monitor the team members to ensure that early signs of burnout and project frustrations are recognized and addressed before the project gets into trouble.

■ *Communications*

Project communications on global implementations are complicated. Not only must the different global stakeholder groups be identified, but they must be communicated with in a language appropriate for the group. In some cases this may mean translation of documents from one language to another. In developing the training documentation, it is essential that the documents be translated into the language of the country being implemented. Although this may add to the price, it will ensure that the training is accepted and makes sense to the end user. Unfortunately, it also means that documentation must be maintained in several languages. In the future, we hope that translation software might make this task less onerous.

A leading practice is to create a communications plan by project activity and by stakeholder group and then monitor the plan over the course of the implementation. Projects often err in having massive amounts of communication early in the project and then trailing communications activities off as the project progresses. Having a communications plan will ensure that you balance communications over the course of the project.

These are some of the leading practices that lead to success on global HRMS implementations. There are many more than can be covered. In fact, Leading Practices In Global Implementations could be a book all on its own. However, these examples will start you along the path.

The best way to determine leading practices is to talk with other users of your system who are further along the implementation path. Networking will uncover all manner of leading practices and offer you the opportunity to benefit from the experience of others. Participation in industry-specific organizations such as the International Association for Human Resource Information Management (IHRIM) or, in the SAP world, The American SAP Users Group (ASUG), will provide you with a number of networking opportunities. Articles and books will also provide insight into what others have experienced. Lastly, the Web is becoming the repository of choice for archiving best practices. Monitoring and searching for articles and white papers can pay off in short order.

John Johnston is the Director Strategic Consulting and E-HR Solutions for Arinso International. He is responsible for assisting clients in creating a more effective and efficient Human Resource function incorporating the use of technology. John has a bachelor's degree from McMaster University and has been accorded the designation CHRP from the Human Resources Professionals Association of Ontario. John is a member of HRPAO, SHRM, the Toronto Board of Trade and is a former IHRIM Board Member. He can be reached at **john.johnston@Arinso.com**.

Reprinted from the *IHRIM Journal*, Volume V, Number 4, November 2001, pp. 29-35.

Global HRMS:
Making the Selection
Work for You

By Catherine Veinbachs

Your company is going global, or has acquired new business units around the world. Or, after years of operating multiple, independent business units, your company has decided that it needs some means of consolidating HR information. A new HR information management system is required. This new HRMS, it is determined, must better support HR customers, provide more accurate and meaningful reporting and position the organization for future business initiatives.

There are many options out there; how do you know which one will provide the best value for your organization? Is there a structured process you should use to reach the right decision, and if so, what is the process? What factors do we need to consider? How can you be sure that the solutions you consider can really support the global organization?

This chapter will outline a suggested process for evaluating the various solution options, and will identify some of the key issues to consider. It will also include a high-level examination of some of the implementation considerations.

Before getting started in earnest, it is important to clarify several key issues. These include:

➤ Why are you seeking to implement a new HRMS?

➤ What are the business drivers when looking for a new solution?

➤ What countries will be involved, and to what extent?

➤ What benefits is the company seeking to derive from implementation?

The answers to these questions will form the basis of the strategic rationale and viewpoint behind the selection process and will guide your efforts through implementation and deployment. We will also highlight some of the unique challenges inherent in a global vendor selection.

The ultimate goal of the project is to provide true HR service to all HR customers, regardless of location. We need to unify our employee populations — not assimilate, not integrate, but align them to our corporation's mission and operating style. Successfully doing this will ensure our place at the strategic business table.

■ The Vendor Selection Process

The typical vendor selection process follows a series of steps; each designed to increase the understanding of the company's requirements, vendor options and the best fit between the two. This typical process can be shortened or lengthened, and the level of detail is solely at the discretion of the user organization. In addition, a number of "expedited" approaches exist that streamline the process in various ways. What I have presented here, however, is the "standard" approach from which most others are derived.

The major steps in the standard vendor selection are these:

➤ Visioning,

➤ Current state assessment,

➤ Solution definition, and

➤ Solution selection.

Each major step has several sub-steps within it, which will be described in greater detail below. We will also discuss the major issues and factors to consider within each step, and also present areas where the vendor selection process might be expedited.

The process overview is depicted in Figure 1.

Figure 1. The Global Vision: How Do We Get There?

Take a hard look at where you are today:	Open your mind to where you want to be:	Identify the tools to create your new reality:
• Organization design	• Business strategy alignment	• Information/education
• Process design	• New role of HR	• Data
• Technology infrastructure	• Redesign of processes	• Interactive tools
• Communication strategy and processes	• Reinforcement of infrastucture	• Transactions
	• Refocusing of communication strategy	• Collaboration
		• Global Community

AND THE CYCLE CONTINUES

■ Step 1 — Visioning

The first step, visioning, is the most fundamental, but is often the most over-looked. Many companies, in their rush to achieve results, storm forward without taking the time to properly assess what they're trying to achieve. This is like driving across the country without a map. Although this trend was more common in the rush to implement solutions before Y2K, this disturbing omission continues today.

The vision, in its simplest form, is a "model" of what the future environment will look like. This includes the HR service delivery goals and objectives, as well as the key initiatives that HR is trying to accomplish. It may also include a high-level diagram of the operational model, the service delivery structure and key tools and enablers to allow efficient management and administration of HR services. It is important to note that this vision defines what HR services will be delivered via the HRMS and may begin to address how, but does not delve into the detailed specifics of process design.

Moreover, it is during this step that the company begins to formulate an idea of what its boundaries are relative to HR service delivery. That is, areas where compromise is possible versus where it is not.

The visioning step has several important objectives, including:

➤ Identify and confirm business drivers, critical success factors and strategic and tactical business plans;

➤ Set expectations and promote buy-in for future processes and systems;

➤ Define the model for the evolution of systems, organization and business processes;

➤ Develop a high-level "roadmap" for how this vision will be achieved;

➤ Establish how business units and geographies will operate in the future state; and

➤ Establish early buy-in and commitment to the future state.

Of course, reaching consensus on what this vision should be is not a straightforward event. There are numerous factors to consider, and each impacts what form the vision ultimately takes. For example, the business strategy must play a key role in developing the HRMS vision. In what areas does the company expect its growth to occur, and how? Is heavy merger and acquisition activity planned, or is a certain geographic area targeted for expansion?

The company's style and culture must also be considered during these early weeks. For example, does the company operate (and desire to continue to operate) in a highly centralized manner, or is the organization comprised of a number of disparate business units that operate autonomously? What are the business drivers pushing the search for a new HR system (and, by extension, a potentially new view of HR service delivery)? Is the new HRMS — and its affiliated components — going to support a more robust version of today's operating style, or will it be the catalyst for a new HR strategy? What is the strategy around global workforce management?

To what extent will managers and/or employees be allowed to manage their own information? What is the company's position on work/ life balance — will non-work related features be allowed into the employees' view, for example, allowing them to apply for a mortgage through the company's system? What is the status of the company's technical infrastructure? Are global standards in place? Are technical capabilities similar around the globe, or will vast differences need to be considered? Finally, does the company stay in the forefront of technology and HR issues, or does it tend to be conservative?

This is also the time to consider, at a high level, global and country-specific standards and requirements. For example, is payroll better administered locally, or will it be run through one integrated unit? What countries are being supported (note: this is not necessarily each country in which the company is doing business) and what are the language requirements?

The answers to these and other similar issues are critical to understanding the environment in which the new HR system must operate. Through cross-cultural interviews, focus groups, surveys and/or facilitated discussions, a view will begin to emerge of how the future environment must be structured. This will include:

➤ Identifying the HR vision;

➤ Determining expectations for HR, HR service delivery and HR systems;

➤ Determining the interaction of country-specific visions with the global view;

➤ Evaluating various components that will enable the HRMS; and

➤ Assessing the cultural readiness of the organization for various enabling technologies.

The resulting vision consolidates the information and forms a cohesive view of the new HRMS operating environment. As noted above, this is supportive of the business objectives — for example, if a company has, as its key strategy, heavy M&A activity, a "traditional" control-oriented, highly centralized HRMS model will not work. The appropriate HRMS vision considers the business drivers and culture of the organization and its implications on HR and the HRMS.

Understanding what the business units and local operations need, and delivering it in a timely, cost-effective manner, is a global requirement. Some HR enablers that allow us to achieve this goal include deployment of flexible HR systems that include work process automation and are able to support local business requirements, as well as satisfy corporate reporting and analysis needs.

In addition, the key goals of the HRMS will be articulated through the establishment of the vision. These may include elements such as establishing a lower cost of operations, increasing emphasis on the HR customer and customer service, leveraging HR information as a strategic resource to support the business, and leveraging economies of scale while recognizing local requirements. Finally, this vision will form the foundation for the business case and justification of the new HRMS, including identifying the metrics and measurements that will be required as the vision is deployed.

■ *Step 2 — Current State Assessment*

The second step, Current State Assessment, is needed to establish the baseline from which the vision will be achieved. In short, it helps the organization understand where it is today so it can be positioned to make the vision a reality. Although this step may be accomplished to varying degrees of detail, it should not be skipped in its entirety.

The Current State Assessment has the following objectives:

➤ Develop an understanding of the current systems and operating environment;

➤ Recognize globally common and country-unique business and functional requirements;

➤ Determine key areas of "pain" and other critical and/or unique requirements;

➤ Identify immediate and short-term opportunities for process improvement (the "low hanging fruit"); and

➤ Document key processes, includ-ing cycle times, blockages and gaps.

The degree of detail needed during this stage will vary by organization, and this must be determined early in the process. For example, if the organization will require a full, detailed financial analysis and cost justification for acquisition of the new HRMS, then full documentation of the current state is typically required (along with detailed development of future processes, which will be discussed below).

Many organizations, however, do not require this level of detailed current state analysis. For them, a higher-level review of current processes will suffice. This high-level review must allow, at a minimum, an understanding of how work is currently performed, where, and by whom. This will facilitate the identification of key areas of concern and/or areas that must be the targeted focus of process and system change during the next step.

In either case, the ultimate purpose of this step is to develop a reasonable understanding of the organization's current operational environment so that the "gaps" between this and the vision can be identified.

This current state assessment utilizes cross-cultural, cross-business unit and cross-functional teams to gather and share information on the current state processes and technology as well as potential change management issues. These teams provide a common foundation for discussions and comparisons across the organizational units and provide input into the identification and prioritization of the critical activities and functions. They define areas of commonality and areas of difference, and identify how these similarities and differences factor into the future vision.

These teams also identify opportunities for immediate action — processes and/or technologies that can be transitioned to an improved operational state with minimal investment (yet are on the path to achieving the vision).

The technical infrastructure and current systems capability is also reviewed during this step. This identifies technical components already deployed worldwide, including redundancies and interactions. This is the time to identify the varying degrees of technical capability found around the globe, such as

Internet access and speed, desktop tools and standards, and workforce acceptance of technology solutions.

As a result of these activities, the organization can:

➤ Develop an understanding of the organizational culture and business environment of the corporation and its organizations;

➤ Globalize key processes to leverage economies of scale while recognizing local/country autonomy;

➤ Identify opportunities to recognize immediate and short-term operational improvements; and

➤ Determine elements of the current processes and/or systems that can be leveraged to support the future vision.

This step provides a baseline from which the more detailed view of the future state can be developed, and facilitates understanding of the kinds of changes that need to be managed.

■ Step 3 — Solution Definition

Step 3, Solution Definition, is where the more detailed view of the vision is created. This includes the process, technology and people components, all of which must come together to create the future of the global HR organization. It is during this step that the organization will create a more detailed view of what the future looks like, including new processes that will be enabled by the new HRMS.

The purpose of this step is to:

➤ Develop re-engineered processes to support the vision, including a view of best practices and their fit to the organization;

➤ Assess alternative service delivery models that might be appropriate to support the vision;

➤ Develop an understanding of the technical infrastructures available in each location and develop a global strategy to support them;

➤ Identify technologies to be deployed to support the re-engineered processes and service delivery model; and

➤ Identify components of the current technology environment that can be leveraged to support the vision.

During this step, the most critical caveat is, of course, no sacred cows. However, it is important that each geography's unique requirements be recognized and validated. This is a fine line — an important part of managing this process is developing sensitivity to cultural nuances that may impact the degree to which current processes may change. Thus, the importance of maintaining the cross-cultural teams discussed above is magnified here.

It is also important, during this step, to include a discussion of global best practices around technology, service delivery and processes. This can serve as a starting point in discussions of how the organization can achieve its vision. These best practices should by no means be taken on blind faith, however, what works for one organization may have no place in another. Therefore, while these best practices should be considered and evaluated, they should be tempered by, and adapted to, fit where the organization is and where it wants to be.

It is during this step that the actual service delivery model, the technology tools and enablers, and the process flows are designed. Through a series of facilitated focus groups and brainstorming sessions, a number of operational service delivery models are developed that will fit the vision and allow HR to meet its objectives. These models are developed to a reasonable degree of detail and the fit and impact of each is determined.

For example, the organization may have established a vision that HR processing will occur as close to the operating units as possible, and field HR representatives will have access to all information. Several operational models can be developed around this objective — outsourcing to local vendors with data feeds into a central reporting repository, or outsourcing or hosting to a single vendor with web-based access to name two. Each of these models must be assessed for general feasibility, ability to support the vision, technical impact and cultural fit. An early view of the potential vendors capable of providing this support must also be developed. RFIs (requests for information) may be issued at this point to gain more information about potential solution providers and additional research, such as attendance at trade shows, may also be conducted. Note that not all companies need to go through this step of developing several service delivery models — some companies already know what services they're delivering and how, so this step is articulated as part of the vision.

These operational models — the possible service delivery solutions — will then be narrowed down to one or two (each of which may have variations), which will then be driven further out. A more detailed view of the processes and enabling technology will be developed, again with an understanding of where changes or deviations are acceptable. The feasibility of each service delivery solution will be ascertained at this more detailed level. Since the organization does not yet know specifically what technology and/or application will provide support, the processes are designed with a general understanding of what needs to happen to drive out the vision, but the highly detailed process design will occur much later (typically, during actual implementation so product-specific adjustments can be made). However, it is important that the general process flows and information requirements be identified at this stage.

Additional meetings, discussions and focus groups are held to discuss and confirm the most viable service delivery model, and to define the specific impacts and implications of implementing it. At this point, the beginnings of a high-level deployment strategy are developed. This deployment strategy begins to identify activities that need to occur to move the organization from the current state to the desired future state. The short-term improvement opportunities identified above are incorporated and integrated into the deployment strategy. Finally, the change management implications — globally and locally — are identified and clarified at this point, and change management activities should begin in earnest.

Through all these activities, a more detailed view of the future environment that fit the vision will emerge. This includes:

➤ A view of best practices that might be applicable to the organization;

➤ Integration of these best practices with in-house capabilities and organizational culture to develop and assess future state operating models supporting the vision;

➤ The definition of the technology requirements necessary to support the future state operating models, taking into consideration local and global capabilities;

➤ The development of a strategic action plan that identifies activities and the timing necessary to achieve the vision; and

➤ An understanding of the impacts of implementing the vision locally and globally, and the development of change management strategies to support the effort.

Documentation produced during this step typically includes service delivery model structures and approaches, process maps to a reasonable degree of detail (more or less depending upon the specific organization — again, if the organization is pursuing an industrial engineering-like approach, the future process flows may need to be quite detailed to recognize potential process impacts), technology enablers to be deployed (and how), and a deployment strategy.

■ Step 4 — Solution Selection

The last step, Solution Selection, is when all of the pieces fall into place. This is the step when the service delivery model is finalized and technology components are selected. Specifically, the objectives of this phase are to:

➤ Develop functional and technical system requirements based upon the vision and future state service delivery models;

➤ Identify specific technology components necessary to support the vision and future state service delivery models;

➤ Determine vendors capable of meeting corporate and individual, country-specific requirements and their relative "degree of fit;"

➤ Select the vendors most capable of delivering required functionality; and

➤ Develop the deployment strategy and prepare for implementation.

This step is typically the longest in elapsed time due to vendor response times, but it is important to maintain a reasonable project timeline so "analysis paralysis" does not set in. It is important to recognize that there is no silver bullet, and that trade-offs will be made regardless of the service delivery and technology solution chosen. As noted above, the key is to understand where compromises are possible and what the implications of those compromises will be.

A key activity in this step is the development of the general, functional and technical requirements necessary to support the vision, current and future processes and requirements. These requirements answer the basic question — what capabilities need to be supported?

The degrees to which these requirements are articulated vary by organization. Some companies, in their zest to be all-inclusive, will detail all possible requirements. Most organizations find this process to be too cumbersome, however, and will settle for a somewhat less rigorous requirements document. This requirements document, which may be formatted into a full request for proposal (RFP) or the more informal RFI, often lists the major processes and activities that must be accomplished along with the general structure for accomplishing them. They will then delve into more detail only for those processes that are mission-critical, unique to their business or are areas where no compromise is possible.

It is important to note that this requirements document will also include technical requirements, including how the solution must be architected and how various solution components will interface or integrate. It will also include specific items around web deployment, employee and manager self-service, call center capabilities, reporting capabilities and analytical tools, security, ability to handle multiple languages and any other technical issues that may be of concern. Technology access around the world is a particular concern here. The organization must consider the workforce demographics — are employees mobile, or do they have access to the desktop (or wireless)? Is the Internet generally available at all sites (and in all countries)? What connection speeds are possible? The organization must consider the technical infrastructure of all operating units in all locations and build this knowledge into the technical requirements.

The organization must consider the technical infrastructure of all operating units in all locations and build this knowledge into the technical requirements.

The general requirements — not functionally or technically specific, but key to ability to support the vision — should also be articulated. They also include cost and implementation considerations.

Regardless of the level of detail covered in the requirements, the next key activity is the prioritization of them. This is important in solidifying the organization's understanding of each major requirement's importance in achieving the vision. Again, the degree of detail will vary by organization — some will prioritize each line item and will rate them on a one-to-five scale, while others will prioritize by subject area and will simply list a "mandatory" or "desired" rating. This prioritization activity is critical for vendors, as it helps them focus their answers and respond in the most appropriate manner.

This prioritization is critical to the organization for another reason. It will roll into a structured tool, which should be employed to make the evaluation process more objective. Based on the organization's prioritized requirements and taking into consideration any additional components (support, global structure and support, etc.), this structured decision tool will quantify results from the vendors, from on-site demonstrations and for the overall evaluation process.

Typically completed concurrently with the above activities, the final slate of vendors to whom the RFI/RFP will be issued is developed. This final list — typically short with no more than five vendors, depending upon the technology solution — is derived based on the research conducted to date on possible vendors, and will vary depending upon the service delivery model chosen. For example, if the organization is looking for one global HRMS, the short list may total three. However, if the organization is seeking to deploy local solutions, or is looking for niche applications within the service delivery model, the number of finalists may be larger. It is important to note that various solution set scenarios — combinations of tools and enablers — should be considered. That is, which sets of potential vendors fit together to form a potential solution, and what is the anticipated interplay between them. Thus, there may be several "sets" of RFP/RFIs issued, each referring to a different solution set.

Once RFPs are issued, vendors respond to the best of their ability. The issuing organization may conduct a bidders conference or may allow inquiries from the vendors to clarify any confusing issues.

As vendor responses are returned, the organization evaluates them for "fit" to requirements. Using the scoring tool developed above, the responses will be scored and the general feasibility of the proposed solution assessed. The fit being assessed is according to the vendors' view and is subject to their ability to understand the requirements. It will also be infused with a degree of "salesiness" — so be warned! It is sometimes helpful, when possible, to enlist the aid of someone with more detailed knowledge of the products in question, but without a vested interest in the outcome, to assist in removing the rose-colored glasses of vendor responses.

Following the RFP scoring, the finalists (or a subset of them) should be invited in for a more structured, formal product demonstration. This can take several forms, from a detailed product overview to a scripted demonstration where specific requirements of the organization are developed into scenarios and the product must demonstrate how it will handle those. Some vendors may also allow a pilot session or a hands-on test drive. Again, the approach may vary. The key here is to make the experience objective and meaningful to the organization. The product demonstrations should not be driven by the vendor, but by the organization. In whatever form it takes, the detailed product demonstrations should be scored using the same scoring tool noted above. The resulting combination of scores will prioritize the finalist vendors according to fit to the organization and ability to deliver on the vision.

Additional due diligence should now be conducted. This may include site visits, a visit to the vendors' corporate headquarters and reference checks (including those not supplied directly by the vendor) to confirm or refute the general impressions. Note that various pieces of due diligence can be completed earlier in the process if desired.

Finally, the organization is in a position to make the HRMS decision based on all factors, including fit to the vision, solution set integration, cost, technical capabilities and implementation considerations. The final piece is the de-

Figure 2. Bringing the Pieces Together.

ORGANIZATION DESIGN	e-HR	PROCESS REDESIGN
Redefining the roles and responsibilities of HR, employees and managers to support the HR service delivery strategy	Designing an electronic communication network of fully integrated HR-related data, information, tools and transactions available to HR, employees and managers	Redesigning the network to support the strategy and underlying business model
Shared Services	HRMS	Streamlining HR Processes
Call Centers	Supporting Applications	Performance Measures
Centralization/ Decentralization	Employee/Manager Self-Service	Comparison to Benchmarks
Workforce Reallocation	Outsource Vendors	
	Interface Design and Usability	
	HR Portals	

OUTCOMES

- Increased Service
- Decreased Costs
- Efficient Administration

- Strategic Focus
- Alignment with Business Objectives
- Increased Shareholder Value

velopment of an Impact Analysis (IA), which may include the following elements: a summary of the business issues, the vision and associated goals and objectives, a high-level implementation plan and approach, process impacts and improvement recommendations, staffing and resource implications, change management implications, critical success factors and implementation risks. As discussed earlier, this will likely include some degree of financial impact and/or justification (although the degree of detail will vary based on the organization).

The keys to success in this step include:

➤ Translating the future state service delivery models into business requirements and prioritizing them;

➤ Identifying a short list of vendors capable of providing the required functionality;

➤ Customizing the decision support tool based on the organization's weightings and business drivers;

➤ Structuring vendor demonstrations according to the organization's business requirements and drivers;

➤ Hosting demonstrations corporately and/or locally utilizing cross-functional and cross-country resources;

➤ Identifying risks, costs and benefits of pursuing various solution alternatives; and

➤ Developing a cohesive, integrated plan for implementing the solution model.

Once the decision is reached, it is time to make the vision into reality!

■ *The Global Impact*

While each step of the process outlined above has implications for and is impacted by the global organization, there are a number of specific considerations that must be addressed by organizations seeking to undertake a global vendor selection. These include:

➤ Technical readiness,

➤ Language requirements,

➤ Multi-cultural project team work styles,

➤ Time differences, and

➤ Regulatory requirements.

We've already talked about the issue of technical readiness and access channels. As we've noted, this has a direct bearing on the technical solutions that can be deployed.

We also need to be cognizant of the language issues — certainly whether each country's language is supported, even if English is the "corporate" language. Some countries require/encourage the use of the local language and the willingness to comply (or not) sends a strong message. Translations, and even the use of certain phrases and graphics, must be handled with care (think of the famous Chevy Nova and it's import into Mexico, where "Nova" literally means "no go!").

Certainly, involving a multi-cultural project team can help avoid some common cultural missteps. But, a global project team can have its own set of issues to handle. For example, time differences and work schedules can be difficult to manage (did you know, for example, that the Israeli work week runs Sunday - Thursday?).

There are also culturally embedded work style differences that must be managed. For example, while Germans are extremely time- sensitive and are rarely late for a meeting, Latin Americans, Hispanics, Spaniards and Middle Easterners often are. These differences must be respected and taken into consideration when managing the project.

Some business units and geographies will embrace a strong corporate presence in their operations and others may not. Many geographic units have especially strong feelings (either positive or negative) about U.S. control. These issues must be recognized and handled with a strong, sensitive and dynamic change management program.

Finally, each country or geographic region has its own laws, regulations, policies and requirements that must be recognized and incorporated into the new HRMS.

■ Critical Success Factors

A successful vendor selection can be characterized by a project in which a solution set capable of supporting the organization now and into the future is defined and selected for implementation with the full support of the organization's stakeholders. There are several key issues to remember during this process to maximize the likelihood of a successful vendor selection, including:

➤ Enlist a strong executive sponsor for the project;

➤ Encourage active user involvement and commitment;

➤ Develop a vision of the future HR/payroll processes;

➤ Identify a viable strategy for achievement of the vision;

➤ Understand the mission-critical and geographic requirements;

➤ Work within the organization's technology strategy, but consider technical differences;

➤ Focus on the gaps;

➤ Provide for global functionality while supporting local business requirements;

➤ Invest in change management and communications;

➤ Present a good business case for the investment; and

➤ Assure project success by structuring the process and driving it to meet the organization's needs.

There are several additional considerations which merit special attention. First, there must be a common denominator for the technical environment for a globally deployed solution. The technical environment differs and includes a varying level of sophistication that must be incorporated into the vision and communicated. This means, quite simply, that the solution must operate across all business units and geographies.

The concept of inclusion is also a key element in any global project. Including all parties in a cross-cultural team will go a long way towards establishing creditability and buy-in. This relates to the issue of change management — involving as many business units and geographies as possible demonstrates the commitment to providing a truly global solution. Likewise, special needs and requirements must be recognized; this is inherent in a global project. However, even in instances where the U.S. dollar is the core currency, or English is the standard language, discussing the business rationales for these decisions, as well as the implications on the geographies, will again facilitate change management issues.

It is important to be clear about corporate strategy versus business unit strategies, as the same company may operate very differently across units and/or geographies. Understanding the real business drivers, as well as the history of the corporate culture, will help ensure that the new solution is positioned correctly. It is also helpful to drill down into the business units to discover their business and drivers and, if possible, the cultural ramifications as well. This will facilitate understanding of the sometimes contradictory needs of the two, and how best to reach a middle ground.

Finally, the need for a business case tailored to the needs of the organization cannot be overstated. A good business case articulates where the HR organization is headed and what it will take to get there. It forces the HR group to evaluate its goals and, more importantly, why it wants to reach them. This, integrated with an actionable strategy, makes a compelling statement that HR has done its homework and has sound business reasons for making the change. As projects can sometimes get sidelined, it serves as an important reminder of why this HR transition is so critical to the organization.

■ Conclusion

A successful global vendor selection can pave the way for a new model of HR service delivery and increased productivity and HR customer satisfaction. It facilitates an understanding of the organization and its key business drivers, culture and people strategies in a way that few other projects can.

The structured, four-step approach outlined above can serve as a template from which each organization's project can be structured. It includes the following key elements:

➤ Visioning,

➤ Current State Assessment,

➤ Solution Definition, and

➤ Solution Selection.

This utilization of a structured approach leverages the broad spectrum of employees, managers, business units and geographies to provide the foundation for improved delivery of HR services. By recognizing the global and multicultural aspects of the project and striving for inclusion to the extent possible, we can maximize early buy-in and commitment to the new solution. This will ease the transition to the new HR service delivery model and will help ensure alignment to the organization's goals and objectives. A successful vendor selection project, followed by successful solution deployment, will facilitate HR's transition to a strategic business partner for the organization.

Cathy Veinbachs is a senior consultant in the HR Technologies practice at Watson Wyatt. She specializes in working with companies to design and deploy enterprise-wide and specialty technologies as enablers to improve operational efficiencies. She has more than 15 years of experience in human resource management, HR service delivery models, strategic HR and systems alignment and HR technology applications. Prior to joining Watson Wyatt, she was the north region practice leader of management consulting for The Hunter Group, and she has written and lectured locally, nationally and internationally on topics relating to human resources and human resource technologies. She has a bachelor of arts degree in Industrial Psychology from Temple University and a master's of business administration with a concentration in Management Information Systems from Bentley College, and currently serves on the IHRIM Board of Directors. She is the vice president of the IHRIM Global Special Interest Group, past president of the New England Chapter of IHRIM and a member of the Human Resource Planning Society. She can be reached at **cathy_veinbachs@watsonwyatt.com**.

■ References

Axtell, Roger E. *Do's and Taboos Around the World.* New York: John Wiley & Sons, Inc. 1993.

Axtell, Roger E. *Gestures: The Do's and Taboos of Body Language Around the World.* New York: John Wiley & Sons, Inc. 1998.

Carr, David K., and Johansson, Henry J. *Best Practices in Reengineering.* New York: McGraw-Hill, Inc. 1995.

Currid, Cheryl. *The Reengineering Toolkit.* California: Prima Publishing. 1994.

Gubman, Edward L. *The Talent Solution.* New York: McGraw-Hill, Inc. 1998.

Hammer, Michael, and Champy, James. *Reengineering the Corporation.* New York: HarperCollins Publishers. 1993.

Reprinted from the *IHRIM.link*, Volume VI, Issue 6, December 2001/January 2002, pp. 28-35.

Part Six:
The Virtual Connected World

"All thought draws life from contacts and exchanges."

—*Fernand Braudel*

• • • • • • • •

Fernand Braudel, an esteemed historian, gives the principle that lies behind the key competitive advantage of the global age: leveraging a worldwide knowledgebase. But how do we put the principle into practice? A change in organizational structures and incentive systems is critically important — but so are abilities that have previously been left to chance. Consider social networks and networking skills: boundaryless HR must proactively foster and develop such competencies, rather than letting them take care of themselves. Being able to stay "in the loop" is no longer something that's merely desirable; it has become critical for the success of everyone in the organization.

But as with most things in life, connectedness has dangers as well as advantages. Potential reward always brings potential risk. As Valdis Krebs points out, the computer virus is a metaphor (and example) for how networks can sabotage you just as surely as they can "give life." To maximize the advantages of connectedness while minimizing the risks will be one of HR's central tasks in the next century. The following chapters explore how HR can accomplish this.

Building
Social Capital
as an
HR Competence

By Wayne E. Baker, Ph.D.

"Nothing is more powerful than an idea whose time has come," said Victor Hugo. Social capital is one of those ideas. With the rise of the network society and the informational economy,[1] building social capital as a personal and organizational competence is more important than ever before. "The new currency won't be intellectual capital," says James Kouzes, chairman emeritus of the tompeters!company and co-author of *The Leadership Challenge*. "It will be social capital — the collective value of whom we know and what we'll do for each other. When social connections are strong and numerous, there is more trust, reciprocity, information flow, collective action, happiness, and, by the way, greater wealth."[2]

In this chapter, I describe the importance of social capital and the role HR leaders can play in building it as a competence for themselves and their companies. I begin by defining the concept and outlining the business case for social capital — scientific evidence gathered from many studies that demonstrate the importance of social capital for personal and organizational success. I also present the case beyond the business case: the links between social capital and happiness, health, and a meaningful life. Next, I describe the most important social capital principle: reciprocity. Reciprocity is the engine of networks. It is the ethical and practical answer to the question, How do I "use" social capital? I conclude with some of the challenges to HR leaders who want to develop social capital as business competence.

■ What is Social Capital?

Social capital is a venerable concept. Its roots go back many years, when the term was used to describe the trust, cooperation, and collective action necessary for vibrant local communities. Political scientist Robert Putnam brought the concept of social capital to popular attention with his studies of the link between social capital and democracy. For example, he learned in his 25-year study of democracy in Italy that the regions with rich social capital — networks of cooperation, norms of civic engagement and a spirit of trust — enjoy strong economic development and responsive local governments while the regions with poor social capital suffer.[3] Recently, Putnam traced over time the American propensity to join voluntary groups and associations, coining the phrase "bowling alone" (from the observed rise of solo versus team bowling) to represent the downward trend in this form of social capital.[4] While other analysts dispute his claims of a decline of American social capital,[5] no one argues with his contention that social capital is critical for democracy.

During the past 20 years or so, sociologists and organizational researchers have focused on the role of social capital in business performance for individuals and companies.[6] While this line of research recognizes social capital as trust, cooperation and goodwill, it also emphasizes social capital of a different type; access to information and entrepreneurial opportunities. These are two sides of the social capital coin. Together, the original definition of social capital and the more recent provide a general definition of social capital: "the resources available in and through our personal and business networks. These resources...include information, ideas, leads, business opportunities, financial capital, power and influence, emotional support, even goodwill, trust and cooperation."[7]

Economists think of social capital as a personal asset, much like "human capital" (one's knowledge, skills and experiences). However, sociologists emphasize that no single person owns the resources in networks. Rather, these resources reside in the networks themselves. Building the right kinds of networks — as a person or an organization — provides access to these resources. Fortunately, it is possible to improve networks. Social capital, like other forms of capital, is a productive asset; by investing in it, we are better able to get things done, achieve our goals and fulfill our missions in life. As I discuss in the last section of this chapter, social capital assessment, training, and changes in the architecture of the organization improve networks and build the social capital of individuals, groups and companies.

■ The Business Case for Social Change

The business case for social capital stands on a scholarly foundation.[8] Human resources and organizational behavior are often considered to be "soft" and unquantifiable. However, the facts about social capital that I summarize below are based on hard evidence — scientific findings from rigorous, quantitative research studies conducted by sociologists, psychologists, economists and political scientists. Here is a sample of benefits for individuals and companies:

➤ **Attracting, Keeping and Developing Good People.**

This is the number one pressing problem of business today, according to a recent survey of over 1,700 mid-level and senior executives, conducted by the University of Michigan Business School. Most people find jobs — and most employers find good people — by tapping networks. This finding is supported by a long line of scientific research, starting with Granovetter's seminal study.[9] Job-person matches realized via networks yield better paying, more satisfying jobs that people stay in longer. Some companies boost the power of networks by creating employee referral programs, or ERPs, which reward employees who refer their contacts to the company.[10] ERPs are the single most effective way to recruit new talent, according to a 1999 American Electronics Association (AEA) survey.[11]

Once you get new employees, you have to keep them. Building social capital keeps new employees because it creates emotional bonds to the company, meaningful connections to others, and aids personal growth and professional development. Natural talent, for example, does not blossom in isolation; it is developed and expressed through relationships with other people. Human capital (such as knowledge) is created via social capital.[12] In fact, as much as 70 percent of organizational learning takes place via informal networks and social interactions.[13] Even the emotions are relational.[14] Happiness, Victor Frankl argues, ensues from the pursuit of worthwhile, meaningful activities.[15] The best companies create an environment in which their people flourish, finding satisfaction and meaning in their work and relationships.

➤ **Earning Higher Pay, Faster Promotions, Better Evaluations and Bigger Bonuses.**

Several studies show that people with rich social capital are paid better, promoted faster, promoted at younger ages, receive better evaluations and earn bigger bonuses.[16] Why? The cynical interpretation is that these people "schmooze" the boss, getting rewards they haven't earned and don't deserve. Such behavior does take place, and it earns "networking" a well-deserved bad name. We've learned, however, that rich social capital is associated with pay, promotions, evaluations, and bonuses because these are rewards for creating value. People with rich social capital are better informed, better problem solvers, more creative and more efficient — and they are rewarded accordingly.

One of the main findings from this line of research is that people who receive rewards have networks with lots of "structural holes" or gaps.[17] A "structural hole" means a person is linked with two other people who are not directly connected to one another. For example, your network contains a structural hole if you are the link between two departmental silos, A and B. A structural hole is an opportunity to create value by introducing people, linking problems with solutions, sharing information and so forth. For example, if you discover that department A has solved a problem that department B is working on, you can create value by filling the hole, introducing the appropriate people from the two departments. Filling structural holes is one of the main ways to create value by "using" one's networks.[18] Those who fill holes repeatedly are rewarded because they continually create value.

The holder of a structural hole has an advantage — superior knowledge. A structural hole presents a choice between two possible strategies for using one's network of opportunities: the "union" strategy versus the "disunion" strategy.[19] The unethical alternative to filling holes (the "union" strategy) is to leave them open and exploit the opportunity for personal gain (the "disunion" strategy). Reconsider the scenario above. Instead of introducing people from the two departments, one could take the solution from department A and foist it off on department B as one's own, taking the credit for oneself.

This disunion strategy dominates in traditional, fear-based cultures that measure and reward only individual performance. In contrast, the best companies create a culture that encourages and rewards the union strategy. At GE, for example, if you discover a scenario such as the one described above, it is your duty to close the structural hole and share information. The widespread practice of the union strategy in an organization creates a culture of cooperation and boosts efficiency and productivity.

➤ Shifting Sources of Power and Influence.

Traditionally, the main sources of power and influence were the formal authority and control of rewards and punishments (coercion) that came with a position in an organizational hierarchy.[20] These traditional sources are declining, due to the transformation of organizations, which have downsized, delayered, outsourced, and restructured into flexible network designs,[21] and the "individualization" of work — the replacement of long-term careers in the same company with a sequence of employers over time, short-term projects, flexible working time, telecommuting, part-time and temporary positions, contract work and so forth.[22] For example, as one knowledge worker put it, "My work is a series of projects. My life is a series of moves. My parents had institutions they could connect to. What can I connect to? My community."[23] In this brave new world, what we know (our human capital) and who we know (our networks) are the only real sources of power.[24] Building human capital and social capital are the keys to success in the network society.

➤ Securing Venture Capital and Ongoing Financing.

How do most startups and new business find angel financing? It's not through the formal venture capital market. Rather, 75 percent of startups and new businesses get financing in the "informal capital market" — the social networks of capital seekers and angel investors.[25] Networks are also critical for established companies. For example, mid-sized firms that cultivate personal ties with their bankers get lower rates compared with firms that have arms' length relationships.[26] Even economists have come to realize that social networks play a central role in investing. Investing is an intensely "social activity."[27] Instead of relying on technical analysis of stock prices or investigating the fundamentals of a company, most institutional and individual investors make decisions to purchase stock based on information from a friend or business associate, or because they know someone who bought the stock.[28]

➤ Selling via Word-of-Mouth Networks.

How do people decide to buy products and services? Advertising is not so influential. Advertising increases awareness but doesn't lead to purchase. Rather, most of us buy products and services that have been recommended to us by our friends, colleagues and acquaintances. There are more than 4,000 empirical studies that show conclusively that products and services diffuse through word-of-mouth networks.[29] So, the best marketers make "word-of-mouth marketing"[30] one of their key methods, tapping social networks to sell their products and services. Given the rise of the network society — and the consequent growth of personal and organizational networks — this form of marketing can only become more powerful in the future.

➤ Building Strategic Alliances.

The network design is the organizational blueprint of the network society and informational economy. Allying with other companies is part of the design. Indeed, it is difficult — if not impossible — for a single company to go it alone and succeed. Access to new technologies, markets, capital, distribution networks, manufacturing specialties, and so forth demands the use of strategic alliances.[31] For example, small high-tech firms boost their status by allying with prestigious partners, while their partners gain access to new technologies.[32] Social capital plays a central role in finding new alliance partners and making alliances successful.[33]

All the elements of the business case I reviewed above fit into a well-researched theory about the best way to achieve business success. Put simply, this theory argues that "putting people first" — or, as I put it, developing social capital — builds profits and market share. The cover of the January 2001 issue of Fast Company makes the same point albeit a bit more colorfully: "Yes, you'd better rethink the Web. Sure, the stock market looks scary. But the best leaders know where all the great companies start. (It's the people, stupid!)."

➤ Knowledge Management and Organizational Learning.

The easy availability of computer-mediated communication (CMC) technologies lures many companies into investing huge sums in formal knowledge management systems. Many don't get much return on their investments. Why? Knowledge resides in the network, not a computer. Most knowledge management systems, argue Pfeffer and Sutton, "rarely reflect the fact that essential knowledge, including technical knowledge, is often transferred between people by stories, gossip, and by watching one another work."[34] Indeed, a 1998 study by the Center for Workforce Development reports that 70 percent of learning takes place via informal networks.[35] Knowledge management is a social activity. "There's a personal paradigm shift," argues Jon Sidoli, principal of Knovus Communications, "that says I am more of a node on the network than anything else."[36] Knowledge managers generate and share knowledge in their social networks.

An organization is "a network of intersubjectively shared meanings that are sustained through the development and use of a common language and everyday social interaction."[37] Change and complexity call for an increase "intersubjective sense-making," Weick argues.[38] People make sense of change and complexity by interacting and talking about it, developing shared meanings and definitions of the situation. Narratives and storytelling are central to the sense-making enterprise. Given the relentless change that defines our times, face-to-face interaction — networks — is critical. The challenge is that people interact more and more via their computer screens than face-to-face. Requisite intersubjectivity is lost when managers stop walking around (MBWA) and start doing what Tom Peters calls "management by screening around."[39] The more complex the world becomes, the more organizational learning depends on developing rich social networks to support sense-making, propagate stories and narratives and create shared meaning.

➤ Building Profits and Market Share by Putting People First.

All competencies are important but different ones rise to prominence in different eras. As the world changes, so do the sources of competence. For example, finance was the preeminent competency in the business world of the 1980s. But in the emerging network society and informational economy, social capital is the key competence. Recognizing and acting on this change is critical for personal and organizational success. As Jeffrey Pfeffer warns, "If you seek success in the wrong places, you are likely to waste a lot of effort, focus on the wrong things, and, in the end, overlook some of the real sources of competitive leverage — *the culture and capabilities of your organization that derive from how you manage your people*. This is a more important source of sustained success than many of those so commonly mentioned, because it is much more difficult to imitate or understand capability and systems of management practice than it is to copy strategy, technology or even global presence."[40]

A host of research demonstrates that so-called "high commitment" or "high performance" HR systems yield higher labor efficiency, improved productivity and quality, reduced employee turnover, better equipment efficiency, higher sales and faster sales growth, increased return on assets, increased return on equity, and higher market share.[41] These systems include the HR practices that build social capital as an organizational competence: self-directed teams, job rotation, decentralization, training, skill development, performance appraisals, collective incentive systems, information sharing systems, quality circles, attitude surveys and so forth. In the last section of this chapter, I provide a list of the top 10 interventions used to build social capital as an organizational competence.

■ The Case Beyond the Business Case: The Quality of Life

There are good business reasons for learning how to build and use social capital, but there are even more important ones. Studies in the fields of medicine, psychology, neuroscience, and epidemiology demonstrate the relationship between social capital and the quality, purpose and meaning of life. For example, a series of studies show that happiness comes from only two sources: meaningful work and the quality of relationships with others.[42] Indeed, the new "relational theories" of psychology show we grow and develop not by gaining independence from one another but by participating in relationships.[43] Social networks, psychologist Barton Hirsch says, "involve far more than provision of narrow categories of 'help.' Instead, networks reflect the nature and value of our participation in the major life spheres."[44]

Building and participating in networks improves mental and physical health. People with solid networks lower their risks of everything from the common cold to serious illnesses.[45] Surprisingly, it's not the size of the networks that counts but the diversity of the relationships. For example, an article in the *Journal of the American Medical Association* reports the findings of an experiment designed to study resistance to the common cold. As the researchers put it, "More diverse social networks were associated with greater resistance to upper respiratory illness."[46] This held true even when they controlled for factors such as age, sex, season, body mass index, education, and race, as well as for health behaviors such as smoking, sleep quality, alcohol intake, and dietary intake of vitamin C. Other studies show that when people do get ill, those with good networks recover faster.[47]

And, people with good networks live longer.[48] A series of more than a dozen studies around the world, beginning with Dr. Lisa Berkman's study of the social networks, lifestyles, and health behaviors of 7,000 residents of Alameda County, California,[49] show that those who are well-integrated in their communities are less likely to die. For example, during the nine years of Dr. Berkman's study, isolated people were three times more likely to die than the well-connected. The life-lengthening effect of networks persists even in the presence of unhealthy practices such as smoking or obesity.[50] And, like resistance to the common cold, diversity matters more than size. Having a variety of ties and connections is the important factor, as Dr. Hallowell summarizes in *Connect: 12 Vital Ties That Open Your Heart, Lengthen Your Life, and Deepen Your Soul.*[51]

■ Using Social Capital: Power of Reciprocity

Probably the most common question I get when I give talks and workshops about social capital is this: How should we use social capital? The idea of using social capital invokes a lot of negative connotations and unsavory images. Everyone knows people who initiate relationships for the purpose of getting something. This common practice is what gives "networking" a bad name. Similarly, attending events or joining associations for the primary purpose of making contacts backfires. Most people see right through such behaviors.

The best way to use social capital involves a paradox. The more we put our resources into action for the service of others, and the less we think about how we will be rewarded in turn, the greater the benefits we receive. This paradox is documented in both scientific research and ethics.[52] The best prescription is to focus on contributions to others. For example, Fred Manske, Jr., CEO of Purolator Courier, a CDN$1 billion Canadian company, attributes his success to the application of his "servant-leadership philosophy." Leaders are more successful when they focus on serving and helping others.

Focusing on contributions to others works because it invokes a fundamental social principle: *reciprocity*. This principle is universal, including both animal and human societies, and ranging from interpersonal to international relations.[53] Reciprocity is the engine of social capital. Its basic form is two-person reciprocity. For example, if you want people to share information with you, give information to them first and they are likely to reciprocate. This is a powerful social psychological principle and it works.[54] But the highest form of reciprocity — and the most powerful — is generalized reciprocity. Here, the focus is contributions to others without expectations of a return. Paradoxically, the more we focus on helping others, and the less we are concerned with getting something, the more we are helped in return, often far in excess of what anyone would expect. There are many examples of this level of reciprocity.[55] The sidebar presents an example from banking. I call it "Janet's story." Janet isn't her real name but she's a real person. And she achieved great success by focus on contributions to others.

When the practice of reciprocity is instilled in a company, it creates a powerful *network of reciprocity* that reaches far and wide. It means that people are more

JANET'S STORY: THE POWER OF RECIPROCITY - A CASE STUDY

I am acquainted with a bank loan officer in Chicago, Janet, whose behavior is the epitome of what I call "the paradox of taking yourself out of the equation." Janet was successful, but she wanted to be extraordinarily successful. Her job was to make loans, and she was evaluated on the volume of loans she "produced." One day she experienced a shift of perspective. She stopped trying to make loans and started trying to help. Instead of looking at the person across from her desk as a "loan" to be made, Janet saw the person as someone with needs that she might be able to help satisfy. If she thought they didn't need a loan, she would tell them so, even if they "qualified" for one. If she thought her potential customers could do better by getting a loan at a competitor's bank, she would give them the name of a loan officer at the bank. Eventually, she engaged potential customers in a broad conversation about lives, families, and their needs, and then worked hard to help them, no matter what kind of help they needed. She even began the practice of sharing cab rides with strangers, just so she could strike up a conversation and see if there was some way she could assist them. What happened? Everyone she helped was so grateful that they did everything they could to help her. Even if they didn't get a loan at her bank, they would recommend Janet to all of their friends, family, neighbors, business associates, colleagues, and just about anyone else. The result was an explosion in Janet's "loan productivity." She made more loans, and made more money, than over before. She had become extraordinarily successful by taking herself "out of the equation" — helping others without regard to how it might help her.

The ethics of social capital requires us to recognize our moral duty to consciously manage relationships. We can't evade our duty — not managing relationships is managing them. Our only choice is how to manage our networks of relationships. To be an effective networker, we can't directly pursue the benefits of networks, or focus on what we can get from our networks. The best prescription is to take ourselves out of the equation, focusing on how we can contribute to others. For us, "using" social capital means putting our networks into action and service for others. The great paradox is that by contributing to others, we are helped in return, often far in excess of what one would expect or predict.

Source: Baker, Wayne. 2000. Achieving Success Through Social Capital (Jossey-Bass): pp. 22-24.

likely to get information when then need it, often without asking for it. It means that problems are solved quickly and efficiently, as people see and close structural holes with regard to how it will help them. It means people work productively because they get the information, ideas, leads, opportunities, and other resources they need when they need them as people unselfishly share them. Acts of contribution help to build long-last, profitable customer relationships. Creating a network of reciprocity turns a crowd of individuals into powerfully organized human activity.

■ HR Challenges

Social capital is the key competence for both personal and organizational success in the network society and informational economy. Like any competence, building this one presents challenges. My research and consulting show that two levels of work are required to build social capital as a competence. The first aims to change individual behavior through education, evaluation and training. The second aims to create an organizational environment that enables people to build the personal and business networks they need. As Noel Tichy and Ram Charan prescribe, "The role of the leader is to *architect* these networks in a way that will lead to success in tomorrow's environment."[56] Business leaders at all levels have to become social architects, helping themselves as they help others build their social capital.

➤ Social Capital Education, Evaluation, and Training

Social capital is an old concept but it's a new idea for business. Most business people are not aware of the concept of social capital, the need to evaluate it, or the many ways to build it. The first challenge, therefore, is education and advocacy: increasing awareness of the concept and benefits of social capital. Next comes evaluation. As I describe below, evaluating social capital is necessary because most people don't have a good sense of their networks. Training helps to instill proper social capital principles, such as reciprocity, as well as practice and modeling.

Social capital is often mistaken as "networking." Networking is only as small corner of the world of social capital. Better synonyms for social capital are contributing, relating, interacting, connecting, helping, reciprocating, and so on. Many people are aware of the traditional use of social capital — getting a job — but most are not aware of the business case and all the business benefits social capital produces. Reviewing the business case helps to answer the question most people have in the backs of their minds — "What's in it for me?" I've found that telling the case beyond the business case — the link between social capital and the quality of life — is just as important. Indeed, getting people to think about the relationship of social capital and health, happiness, and meaning helps to move people beyond the what's-in-it-for-me perspective and consider their larger roles as participants in and contributors to the world.

Education and advocacy are also necessary because common cultural myths stand in the way of social capital. For example, an obstacle to the practice of reciprocity is the myth that competition is natural and cooperation is not. After reexamining Darwin's theory and evidence, social scientist and philosopher Helena Cronin concludes that the fittest who survive are *altruists*. "Doing what's immediately good for oneself has been understood by Darwinists for a long time," she says. "But what hasn't been understood until recently is that you can actually do better for yourself by being cooperative and altruistic than you can by selfishly refusing to cooperate with others. It's not that you do as well. You actually do better — and all of you do better than if you had gone off on your own and refused to help others."[57] This is a tough lesson to learn for anyone who was schooled in the social virtues of self-interest and all-out competition.

A related obstacle is the myth of *individualism*: The cultural belief that everyone succeeds or fails on the basis of her or his own individual efforts and abilities.[58] Sociologist James Coleman calls individualism "a broadly perpetrated fiction in modern society." "This fiction is that society consists of a set of independent individuals, each of whom acts to achieve goals that are independently arrived at, and that the functioning of the social system consists of the combination of these actions of independent individuals."[59] Individualism is a prized American principle but we have to unlearn the lessons of individual achievement[60] to survive and thrive in the network society.

Evaluating social capital is as necessary as educating about it. Research shows that people's mental maps of their networks are inaccurate.[61] While most people can recite their human capital (the facts on the résumé) with ease and accuracy, few can accurately describe the networks around them. Overconfidence confounds the problem of inaccuracy — most people think they know their networks but most people don't. Inaccuracy and overconfidence create the need to evaluate social capital. Fortunately, an entire field is devoted to the measurement of social networks and social capital.[62] (To learn about this field, visit the web site of INSNA, the professional association of social network analysts, at www.heinz.cmu.edu/project/INSNA/.) I have developed an online social capital assessment tool for Humax Corporation, an assessment and training firm (www.humaxnetworks.com) (See sidebar). This tool surveys "egocentric networks" (a person and his or her direct contacts) as opposed to "whole networks" (all the connections among the members of a defined population). (See www.orgnet.com for tools that analyze whole networks.)

The Humax Assessment — An Online Social Capital Assessment Tool

The Humax Assessment is a web-based tool that diagnoses social capital along three dimensions: structure, composition, and focus. Structure refers to the pattern of connections in an egocentric network. It ranges from cohesive, closed networks to expansive, open networks. The latter have lots of structural holes (defined above) and hence opportunities to create value by closing them. Composition refers to the demographic characteristics of people in the network. It varies from homogeneous to diverse. Focus is the concentration of a network in certain areas or activities. Focus varies from internally focused networks to externally focused networks.

The Assessment produces an "individual profile" for each person who takes it, along with a "composite profile" for the group or company as a whole. A profile is composed of three letters that correspond to the three dimensions of structure, composition, and focus. Each dimension is continuous but divided into thirds to provide categories for profiling. Figure 1 describes the dimensions and categories. Three dimensions and three categories yield 27 possible profiles. The two fundamental types are Profile CHI (the first column in Figure 1) and Profile XDE (the right column in Figure 1). Profile CHI is a cohesive, homogeneous network with an internal focus. This network profile represents social capital in the form of trust and cooperation among a closed network of similar people. This network is helpful for building group loyalty, identity, and a sense of common purpose. This network may make it difficult to get new information or other resources, or for influencing people outside the network. It is subject to group-think and an us-versus-them view of the world. Profile XDE is an expansive, diverse network with an external focus. It represents social capital in the form of entrepreneurial opportunities. This profile is helpful for getting new information, learning about new opportunities and finding resources. But it may make it difficult to build consensus, produce consistent expectations, or develop a sense of common mission. It can be subject to conflicts and tensions.

Which profile is "best"? One size does not fit all; the best profile depends on one's needs and goals. Generally, however, I've found that most networks are too closed, homogeneous and internally focused. In today's business world, networks closer to Profile XDE produce superior business performance. This prescription doesn't mean that everyone should build the largest, most diverse, most externally focused networks possible. Rather, it means that most people can benefit from moving in the direction of XDE.

Technologies exist now to conduct "social network audits" of organizations (see sidebar). It is possible now to assess the current state of social capital in a company, as well as to benchmark and to monitor and track social capital changes over time. Network analysis can be applied to evaluate a host of HR issues. For example, network analysis can reveal patterns of inclusion and exclusion in a company's informal networks. With this knowledge, the company could take remedial action to create more inclusive networks. In fact, ignoring the network analysis could lead to charges that a company could have measured and improved networks but didn't. Network analysis could provide evidence to back a person's claim that he or she was excluded from the informal networks.

Figure 1. The Three Dimensions of a Humax Profile.

Dimension 1 Structure	**C**ohesive network of closely connected people; strong relationships; below average number of people.	**V**ersatile network of somewhat interconnected people; mix of strong and weak relationships; average number of people.	**EX**pansive network of mostly unconnected people; weaker relationships; above average number of people.
Dimension 2 Composition	**H**omogeneous set of people with similar demographics, such as age, education, gender, ethnicity.	**B**lended set of people with a mix of similar and different demographics.	**D**iverse set of people; most demographics are different.
Dimension 3 Focus	**I**nternal focus; your network is focused on work or family; network tends to be domestic; few ties to outside organizations or associations.	**EQ**ual internal and external focus; a balance of work and family ties; mix of domestic and global ties; some ties to outside organizations or associations.	**E**xternal focus; most relationships are not work or family related; network tends to be global; many ties to outside organizations and associations.

Copyright © 1999 - 2001 by Humax Corporation. Reprinted with permission.

Evaluating networks also provides direct insights into issues that before could be measured only indirectly. For example, how diverse is your organization? Demographic statistics tell only part of the story. An organization could be split 50:50 with respect to gender, for instance, but the informal networks could be segregated and separate. Do men and women actually interact with each other? Do you have what I call "relational diversity?" One company that used the Humax Assessment was proud to discover that their employees' networks were diverse. Men and women included each other in their core networks of work, advice, assistance and informal socializing.

Of course, it is possible that some employees might argue that tracking their social network "signature" is an invasion of their workplace privacy. This problem is averted when a third-party assessment company conducts the evaluation. Employees know their privacy is protected. For example, the Humax Assessment is password protected. Each person creates his or her own user name and password. Unless the person gives it out, no one at the company can view the person's reports. From a managerial point of view, the proper focus is the group or the company, not an individual.

Finally, experiential training is necessary to introduce, learn and reinforce new behaviors. This is true generally, but the principles of social capital, such as the highest level of reciprocity (helping others without expectations of return), are counterintuitive for many, so the principles need to be experienced to be learned. Training for social capital can't be done via computer. Even today there are software programs that claim to build "community" but community is built face-to-face, working together to build networks and contribute to one another. Social capital training has to be experienced with others, preferably with groups that can benefit from building their social capital during the training experience. For example, post-merger integration is one of the biggest HR challenges after the two companies are combined. Training on social capital can help bridge the chasm, creating integrative social networks and the reciprocal relationships required to convert two cultures into one. Software programs may improve the *efficiency* of an existing network, but they don't change the *incentives* for investing in the network. Community can't emerge if the incentive remains "What's in it for me?" Only after social capital training provides a new principle, rationale, and model of community — the highest level of reciprocity — can software help to reinforce the community.

➤ Building the Architecture for Social Capital

The companies that thrive in the future will be those that recognize the growing importance of social capital and build the architecture to support it. HR can and should play a leadership role in promoting awareness of social capital and establishing the mechanisms and practices that build social capital as an organizational competence. It won't be long, I predict, until we see an enlightened company creating the position of Chief Social Capital Officer! The Chief Social Capital Officer would be responsible for eliminating the mechanisms and practices that destroy social capital and for creating the mechanisms and practices that build it. This person would be the chief network builder and social network nurturer of the organization.

There are many mechanisms and practices that build social capital as an organizational competence. With Humax Corporation, I have identified over 55 "best practices." In the last chapter of my book on social capital, I describe 10 main interventions, which I list here. You can use this as a checklist for an "easy" measure of the richness of social capital in your organization. These and others could be added to the "balanced scorecard" movement that is commonly used today.

1. **Facility design and location.** Proximity is (almost) everything, even in these days of computer-mediated communication. Co-location, open offices, the absence of physical barriers, and "campus" office designs facilitate the formation of social capital. "Hoteling" and similar practices inhibit it.

2. **Hiring.** Most people are hired on the basis of what they know, even in a world where networks are more important than ever before. Hire networks, not just on the basis of intellectual capital.

3. **Multidisciplinary teams.** It's commonplace to argue for the use of multidisciplinary or cross-functional teams. But it's still good advice. Multidisciplinary teams are the social architect's basic building blocks.

4. Rotation programs. Rotation programs have been around for a long time and are even more important now. They are natural vehicles for building networks that crisscross organizational units, transfer knowledge across boundaries, and develop a global mindset. The trick is to avoid what Snyder and Duarte call *chaotic role movements*: "the rapid movement of professionals and managers into new roles within a company in which the number of roles exceed the number of qualified people available."[63]

5. Education and training. Education and training are necessary, as I discussed above, to build social capital as an individual competence. Making social capital an *organizational* competence requires a comprehensive and orderly program rolled out to all units and levels.

6. Communities of practice. The original communities of practice arose spontaneously. Today, companies that build social capital as an organizational competence actively foster, nurture, and invest in the construction and communities of practice. This is especially important in large companies where it's easy to feel lost and alone. Communities of practice make the cold, big world of a global company much warmer and more personal. A community of practice gives people a home. Employees are happier and work smarter because they learn and share knowledge in their community of practices. Another benefit is employee retention: When people feel an emotional bond to others at work, they are more likely to feel committed to the company and stay.

7. Participatory processes. The regular and routine processes of the corporation — budgeting, continuous improvement, quality programs and so on — contain great opportunities for building social capital. This potential often goes unnoticed and untapped. Making these processes participatory by involving people from various units and levels can build social capital naturally.

8. Management networks. A management network includes people who "are drawn from across the company's functions, business units, and geography, and from different levels in the hierarchy."[64] Jack Welch's Corporate Executive Council is a good example.[65] These are natural vehicles for building ties and bonds across units, departments, levels and location.

9. External networks. Companies rarely go it alone any more. Those at the leading edge, like Corning, are evolving into a complex network of alliances with competitors, customer relationships, and supplier partnerships.

10. Incentive systems. The incentive system is often the biggest single obstacle to building social capital in a company. When people are measured and rewarded for individual performance, it's difficult to practice the highest levels of reciprocity. Progressive companies use a combination of individual and collective rewards. These encourage bridge-building, sharing, helping, and contributing. That's what builds social capital.

One by one, these interventions don't work. They are powerful in combination — components of an overall organizational redesign that focuses on social capital as an organizational competence. Together, they help to build the *network organization*. One of the chief lessons of organizational theory is the importance of congruence: the design of an organization should fit its environment. The architectural blueprint for success in the network society is the network organization.

■ Conclusion

We really are living in a time of change. "We are living through one of the most fundamental technological and social changes in history," says sociologist Manuel Castells. "The revolution in information technologies that took shape in the early 1970s, and diffused throughout the economy, society, and culture in the last quarter of the twentieth century, has profoundly transformed the way we live, work, produce, consume, communicate, travel, think, enjoy, make war and peace, give birth, and die. It has also transformed, as have all major technological revolutions, the material foundations of human life, time, and space."[66] What this means, as he writes in his monumental trilogy on the Information Age,[67] is the rise of a new form of society: the network society. Building and using social capital is the key to surviving and thriving in the network society.

Wayne E. Baker, Ph.D. is Professor of Organizational Behavior and Human Resource Management and Director of the Center for Society & Economy at the University of Michigan Business School. He is a Faculty Associate at the Institute for Social Research at the University of Michigan. Baker puts his knowledge into action through his work with Humax Corporation, an assessment and training firm specializing in personal and organizational development (http://www.humaxnetworks.com). His newest book, Achieving Success Through Social Capital: Tapping the Hidden Resources in Your Personal and Business Networks, *was published by Jossey-Bass in August 2000. Since November 2000, it has been on every monthly business best-seller list compiled by 800CEOREAD. His first book,* Networking Smart, *was named "one of the thirty best business books of 1994" by* Executive Book Summaries. Networking Smart *was a main selection in the Newbridge and Business Week Book Clubs. Baker's research on social capital, networks, organizations, and culture is published in the* American Sociological Review, the American Journal of Sociology, the Journal of Mathematical

Sociology, *the* American Behavioral Scientist, *and other places. Baker teaches courses on social capital and networks, organizational behavior, organizational design, and general management in all of the University of Michigan Business School's programs: Executive Education, Ph.D., MBA, and BBA. He won the Emory Williams Award for Excellence in Teaching, and the Max Weber Award for Distinguished Scholarship. Baker was a post-doctoral research fellow in finance and organizational behavior at Harvard Business School, and a partner and senior manager of TSG, Inc., a Washington, D.C.-based management consulting firm. In 1981 he earned his Ph.D. in sociology from Northwestern University. He has a M.A. in sociology (1976) and B.S. in finance, summa cum laude (1974) from Northern Illinois University. He can be reached at* **wayneb@umich.edu**.

■ Endnotes

1   Manuel Castells, *The Rise of the Network Society,* second edition (Malden, MA: Blackwell, 2000)

2   James M. Kouzes, "Link Me to Your Leader." *Business 2.0.* October 10, 2000. Electronic publication, http://www.business2.com/content/magazine/ideas/2000/09/29/19123

3   Robert Putnam, *Making Democracy Work* (Princeton, NJ: Princeton University Press, 1993)

4   Robert D. Putnam, "Bowling Alone: American's Declining Social Capital." *Journal of Democracy* 6:65-78. Robert D. Putnam, *Bowling Alone: The Collapse and Revival of American Community.* (New York: Simon & Schuster, 2000)

5   See, for example, Pamela Paxton, "Is Social Capital Declining in the United States? A Multiple Indicator Assessment." *American Journal of Sociology,* 1999, 105:88-127.

6   For example: Paul Adler and Seok-Woo Kwon. "Social Capital: The Good, The Bad, and the Ugly," Working paper, University of California at Los Angeles, Business School, 1999. Wayne E. Baker, *Networking Smart: How To Build Relationships for Personal and Organizational Success,* (McGraw-Hill 1994). Wayne E. Baker and David Obstfeld, "Social Capital by Design: Structures, Strategies, and Institutional Context," chapter 4 in R. T. A. J. Leenders and Shaul Gabbay (eds.), *Corporate Social Capital and Liability.* Kluwer Academic (1999). Ronald S. Burt, *Structural Holes: The Social Structure of Competition.* (Harvard University Press, 1992); "The Social Capital of Entrepreneurial Managers," *Financial Times* (European Edition, May 5, 1996; "The Network Structure of Social Capital," working paper, University of Chicago Graduate School of Business (1999). James S. Coleman,. "Social capital in the creation of human capital." *American Journal of Sociology,* 1998, 94:S95 - S120.

Jane E. Fountain, "Social Capital: Its Relationship to Innovation in Science and Technology." *Science and Public Policy,* 1998, 25:103-155. Jane Jacobs, *The Death and Life of Great American Cities.* (Penguin, 1965). Nan Lin, "Building a Network Theory of Social Capital," *Connections,* 1999, 22:28-51. Janine Nahapiet and Sumantra Ghoshal, "Social Capital, Intellectual Capital, and the Organizational Advantage," *Academy of Management Review,* 1998, 23:242-266. Pamela Paxton, "Is Social Capital Declining in the United States? A Multiple Indicator Assessment," *American Journal of Sociology,* 1999, 105:88-127. Joel M. Podolny and James Baron, "Resources and Relationships: Social Networks and Mobility in the Workplace," *American Sociological Review,* 1997, 62:673-693. Robert D. Putnam, *Making Democracy Work,* (Princeton University Press, 1993); Robert D. Putnam, "Bowling Alone: America's Declining Social Capital." *Journal of Democracy,* 1995, 6:65-78; G. Walker, B. Kogut, and W. Shan, "Social Capital, Structural Holes and the Formation of an Industrial Network," *Organization Science,* 1997, 8: 109 - 125.

7   Wayne Baker, *Achieving Success Through Social Capital.* (San Francisco, CA: Jossey-Bass, 2000), p. 1.

8   For example: Paul Adler and Seok-Woo Kwon, "Social Capital: The Good, The Bad, and the Ugly" Working paper, University of California at Los Angeles Business School, 1999; Wayne E. Baker, *Networking Smart: How To Build Relationships for Personal and Organizational Success,* (McGraw-Hill: 1994); Wayne E. Baker and David Obstfeld, "Social Capital by Design: Structures, Strategies, and Institutional Context," chapter 4 in R. T. A. J. Leenders and Shaul Gabbay (eds.), *Corporate Social Capital and Liability Kluwer Academic,* 1999; Ronald S. Burt, *Structural Holes: The Social Structure of Competition,* (Harvard University Press: 1992); "The Social Capital of Entrepreneur-

ial Managers," *Financial Times*, European Edition, May 5, 1996; "The Network Structure of Social Capital," working paper, University of Chicago Graduate School of Business, 1999; James S. Coleman, "Social capital in the creation of human capital," *American Journal of Sociology*, 1988, 94: pp. S95 - S120; Jane E. Fountain, "Social Capital: Its Relationship to Innovation in Science and Technology," *Science and Public Policy*, 1988, Vol. 25, pp. 103-155; Jane Jacobs, *The Death and Life of Great American Cities*, (Penguin, 1965); Nan Lin, "Building a Network Theory of Social Capital," Connections, 1999, Vol. 22, pp. 28-51. Janine Nahapiet and Sumantra Ghoshal, "Social Capital, Intellectual Capital, and the Organizational Advantage," *Academy of Management Review*, 1998, vol. 23, pp. 242-266; Pamela Paxton, "Is Social Capital Declining in the United States? A Multiple Indicator Assessment," *American Journal of Sociology*, 1999, vol. 105, pp. 88-127; Joel M. Podolny and James Baron. "Resources and Relationships: Social Networks and Mobility in the Workplace," *American Sociological Review*, 1997, vol. 62, pp. 673-693. Robert D. Putnam, *Making Democracy Work*, (Princeton University Press, 1993); Robert D. Putnam, "Bowling Alone: America's Declining Social Capital," *Journal of Democracy*, 1995, vol. 6, pp. 65-78. G. Walker, B. Kogut, and W. Shan, "Social Capital, Structural Holes and the Formation of an Industrial Network," *Organization Science*, 1997, vol. 8, pp. 109 - 125.

9   Mark Granovetter, *Getting a Job* (Cambridge, MA: Harvard University Press, 1973).

10   For example, Roberto M. Fernandez and N. Weinberg, "Sifting and Sorting: Personal Contacts and Hiring in a Retail Bank," *American Sociological Review*, 1997, vol. 62, pp. 883-902.

11   Study cited in Wayne Baker , "Using Social Capital to Attract and Retain Good People," *Lightwave* (in press), 2001.

12   James S. Coleman,. "Social Capital in the Creation of Human Capital," *American Journal of Sociology*, 1988, vol. 94, pp. S95-S120.

13   "The Real Meaning of On-the-Job Training," *Leader-to-Leader*, Fall 1998, vol. 61. Cited and discussed in Jeffrey Pfeffer and Robert I. Sutton, *The Knowing-Doing Gap*, (Boston: Harvard Business School Press, 2000) p. 18.

14   Kenneth J. Gergen, *Realities and Relationships* (Cambridge, MA: Harvard, 1994), chapter 9.

15   Viktor E., Frankl, *The Will to Meaning* (New York: Meridian, 1988).

16   For example, see Ronald S. Burt, *Structural Holes: The Social Structure of Competition* (Harvard University Press, 1992); "The Social Capital of Entrepreneurial Managers," *Financial Times* (European Edition, May 5, 1996; "The Network Structure of Social Capital," working paper, University of Chicago Graduate School of Business, 1999; E. A. W. Boxman, P.M.D. Graaf and H.D. Flapp, "The Impact of Social and Human Capital on the Income Attainment of Dutch Managers," *Social Networks*, 1991, vol. 13, pp. 51-73; , H. Flap and E. Boxman, "Getting a Job as a Manager," 1999, chapter 11 in R.T.A. J. Leenders and Shaul Gabbay (eds.); *Corporate Social Capital and Liability*, (Kluwer Academic, 1999); Rebecca Sandefur, Edward O. Laumann and John P. Heinz, "The Changing Value of Social Capital in an Expanding Social System: Lawyers in the Chicago Bar, 1975 and 1995," chapter 12 in R.T.A. J. Leenders and Shaul Gabbay (eds.), *Corporate Social Capital and Liability*, (Kluwer Academic, 1999).

17   For example, see Ronald S. Burt, *Structural Holes: The Social Structure of Competition* (Harvard University Press, 1992); "The Social Capital of Entrepreneurial Managers," *Financial Times* (European Edition, May 5, 1996; "The Network Structure of Social Capital," working paper, University of Chicago Graduate School of Business, 1999).

18   Wayne Baker, *Achieving Success Through Social Capital*. (San Francisco, CA: Jossey-Bass, 2000) pp. 150 - 159.

19 Wayne E. Baker and David Obstfeld, "Social Capital By Design: Structures, Strategies, and Institutional Context." Chapter 4 in R.T.A.J. Leenders and Shaul Gabbay (eds.) *Corporate Social Capital and Liability* (Boston: Kluwer Academic Publishers, 1999).

20 The classic statement is John R. P. French, Jr. and Bertram Raven, "The Bases of Social Power," pp. 259-269 in Dorwin Cartwright and Alvin Zander (eds.), *Group Dynamics*, third edition, (NY: Harper and Row, 1968); For an update and elaboration, see Part II in Pfeffer (1992). For an empirical test, see Noah E. Friedkin, 1993; "Structural Bases of Interpersonal Influence in Groups: A Longitudinal Case Study," *American Sociological Review* 58:861-872.

21 For example, Wayne E. Baker, "The Network Organization in Theory and Practice." pp. 397-429 in Nitin Nohria and Robert G. Eccles (eds.), *Networks and Organizations: Structure, Form, and Action* (Boston, MA: Harvard Business School Press, 1992).

22 Chapter 4 in Manuel Castells, *The Rise of the Network Society*, second edition, (Malden, MA: Blackwell, 2000).

23 Quoted on p. 104 in Bill Breen, "Where are you on the talent map?" *Fast Company*, January 2001, pp. 102-108.

24 Wayne E. Baker, and Aimee Arlington, "Serving Two (or More) Masters: The Challenge and Promise of Multiple Accountabilities," chapter 2 in Robert E. Quinn, Regina M. O'Neill, and Lynda St. Clair (eds.), *Pressing Problems in Modern Organizations* (New York: AMACOM, 1994).

25 For example, Robert J Gaston and Sharon Bell, "The Informal Supply of Capital." Final Report submitted to the U.S. Small Business Administration by the Applied Economics Group, Inc., 1988.

26 Brian Uzzi, "Embeddedness in the Making of Financial Capital: How Social Relations and Networks Benefit Firms Seeking Financing," *American Sociological Review*, 1999, vol.

64, pp. 481-505. Brian Uzzi and James J. Gillespie. "Corporate Social Capital and the Cost of Financial Capital: An Embeddedness Approach," 1999, pp. 446-459 in Roger Th.A.J. Leenders and Shaul M. Gabbay (eds.), *Corporate Social Capital and Liability*, (Boston: Kluwer); Wayne E Baker, "Market Networks and Corporate Behavior," *American Journal of Sociology*, 1990, vol. 96, pp. 589-625.

27 Robert Shiller, *Market Volatility* (Cambridge, MA: MIT Press, 1991).

28 Robert J. Shiller and John Pound, "Survey Evidence of Diffusion of Interest and Information Among Investors," *Journal of Economic Behavior and Organization*, 1989, vol. 12, pp. 47-66. Robert. Shiller, Market Volatility (Cambridge, MA: MIT Press 1991).

29 Everett M. Rogers, *Diffusion of Innovations*, fourth edition. (New York: Free Press, 1995).

30 Baker (1994: chapter 11).

31 Wayne E. Baker and David Obstfeld. "Social Capital by Design: Structures, Strategies, and Institutional Context," chapter 4 in R.T.A.J. Leenders and Shaul Gabbay (eds.), *Corporate Social Capital and Liability*, (Norwell, MA: Kluwer. 1999).

32 Toby E. Stuart, "Technological Prestige and the Accumulation of Alliance Capital," chapter 20 in R.T.A.J. Leenders and Shaul Gabbay (eds.), *Corporate Social Capital and Liability* (Norwell, MA: Kluwer. 1999).

33 Ranjay Gulati, "Social Structure and Alliance Formation Patterns: A Longitudinal Analysis," *Administrative Science Quarterly*, 1995, vol. 40, pp. 619-652.

34 J. Pfeffer and Robert I. Sutton, *The Knowing-Doing Gap* (Boston: Harvard Business School Press, 2000).

35 "The Real Meaning of On-the-Job Training," *Leader to Leader*, Fall 1998, vol. 61.

36 Quoted in Steve Barth, "The Power of One," *Knowledge Management*, December 2000, pp. 31-36.

37   James P.Walsh and G. R. Ungson, "Organizational Memory," *Academy of Management Review*, 1991, vol. 16, pp. 57-91.

38   Karl Weick, *Sensemaking in Organizations* (Thousand Oaks, CA: Sage) pp. 70-71, 174.

39   Weick makes this point on p. 73 in *Sensemaking in Organizations* (Thousand Oaks, CA: Sage), drawing on Tom Peter's discussion of MBWA versus Management by Screening Around on pp. 432-434 in *Liberation Management*. (New York: Knopf, 1992).

40   J. Pfeffer, *The Human Equation: Building Profits by Putting People First*. (Boston: Harvard Business School Press, 1998). p. 5. Emphasis added.

41   M.A Huselid, S. E. Jackson and R. S. Schuler, "Technical and Strategic Human Resource Management Effectiveness As Determinants of Firm Performance." *Academy of Management Journal*, 1997, vol. 40 (1), pp. 171-188; C. Ichniowski, *Human Resource Management Systems and the Performance of U.S. Manufacturing Businesses* (Boston: National Bureau of Economic Research, 1990); M.J Koch and R.G. McGrath, "Improving Labor Productivity: Human Resource Management Policies Do Matter," *Strategic Management Journal*, 1996, vol. 17, pp. 335-354; J.P. MacDuffie, "Human Resource Bundles and Manufacturing Performance: Organizational Logic and Flexible Production Systems in the World Auto Industry," *Industrial and Labor Relations Review*, 1995, vol. 48; T.M. Welbourne and A.O. Andrews, "Predicting the Performance of Initial Public Offerings: Should Human Resource Management be in the Equation?" *Academy of Management Journal*, 1996, vol. 39 (4), pp. 891-919; P.M Wright, G.C. McMahan, B. McCormick and W.S. Sherman, "Strategy, Core Competence, and HR Involvement As Determinants of HR Effectiveness and Refinery Performance," *Human Resource Management*, 1998 vol. 37 (1), pp. 17-29; M.A. Youndt, S.A. Snell, Jr., and D.P. Lepak, "Human Resource Management, Manufacturing Strategy, and Firm Performance," *Academy of Management Journal*, 1996, vol. 39 (4), pp. 836-866. T. Baker, *Doing Well by Doing Good: The Bottom Line on Workplace Practices* (Washington DC: Economic Policy Institute, 1999). T. Kochan, and P. Osterman, *The Mutual Gains Enterprise* (Boston, MA: Harvard Business School Press, 1994); J. Pfeffer, *Competitive Advantage Through People: Unleashing the Power of the Work Force* (Boston: Harvard Business School Press, 1994); J. Pfeffer, *The Human Equation: Building Profits by Putting People First* (Boston, MA: Harvard Business School Press, 1998).

42   Mihaly Csikszentmihalyi, *Flow: The Psychology of Optimal Experience* (New York: Harper & Row, 1990).

43   For example, see Jean Baker Miller and Irene Pierce Stiver, *The Healing Connection* (Boston: Beacon Press, 1997); Joyce K. Fletcher, "Relational Practice," *Journal of Management Inquiry*, 1998, vol. 7, pp. 163-186; Joyce K. Fletcher, "Developing an Interactive Self" *Social Policy*, Summer 1998, pp. 48-51; Edward M. Hallowell, *Connect*, (Pantheon, 1999).

44   Barton J. Hirsch, "Social Networks and the Coping Process: Creating Personal Communities," pp. 149-170 in Benjamin H. Gottlieb (ed.), *Social Networks and Social Support* (Beverly Hills, CA: Sage, 1981), p. 169.

45   For example, S. Cohen, W.J. Doyle, D.P. Skoner, B.S. Rabin and J.M. Gwaltney, Jr., "Social Ties and Susceptibility to the Common Cold," *Journal of the American Medical Association* June 25, 1997, vol. 277, pp. 1940-1944; James S. House, Karl R. Landis and Debra Umberson, "Social Relationships and Health," *Science*, 1988 vol. 241, pp. 540-545; J.A. House, *Work Stress and Social Support* (Reading, MA: Addison-Wesley, 1981); S.S. Jouard, and T. Landsman. *Healthy Personality: An Approach From the Viewpoint of Humanistic Psychology* (New York: Macmillan, 1980); Charles Kadushin, "Social Density and Mental Health," 1982, pp. 147-158 in Peter V. Marsden and Nan Lin (eds.), *Social Structure and Network Analysis* (Beverly Hills, CA:

Sage); Benjamin H. Gottlieb, (ed.), *Social Networks and Social Support* (Beverly Hills, CA: Sage, 1981); R.S. Lazarus, "The Health-Related Functions of Social Support," *Journal of Behavioral Medicine*, 1981 vol. 4, pp. 381-406; S.E. Taylor and J. Brown,, "Illusion and Well-Being," *Psychological Bulletin*, 1988, vol. 103, pp. 193-210. K.A Wallston and B.S. Wallston, "Who Is Responsible for Your Health? The Construct of Health Locus of Control" pp. 65-95 in G. Saunders and J. Suls (eds.), *Social Psychology of Health and Illness* (Hillsdale, NJ: Erlbaum, 1982).

46 S. Cohen, W.J. Doyle, D.P Skoner, B.S. Rabin and J.M. Gwaltney, Jr., "Social Ties and Susceptibility to the Common Cold," *Journal of the American Medical Association*, 1997, vol. 277, pp. 1940-1944.

47 Benjamin H. Gottlieb, (ed.), *Social Networks and Social Support* (Beverly Hills, CA: Sage, 1981).

48 Lisa F. Berkman, and S. Leonard Syme, "Social Networks, Host Resistance, and Mortality: A Nine-Year Follow-up Study of Alameda County Residents," *American Journal of Epidemiology*, 1979, vol. 109, pp. 186-204; James S. House, Karl R. Landis and Debra Umberson, "Social Relationships and Health," *Science* 1988, vol. 241, pp. 540-545; Robin M. DiMatteo and Ron Hays, "Social Support and Serious Illness," chapter 5 in Benjamin H. Gottlieb, (ed.), *Social Networks and Social Support* (Beverly Hills, CA: Sage, 1981).

49 Lisa F. Berkman and S. Leonard Syme, "Social Networks, Host Resistance, and Mortality: A Nine-Year Follow-up Study of Alameda County Residents," *American Journal of Epidemiology*, 1979, vol. 109, pp. 186-204.

50 M.D Hallowell and M. Edward, *Connect* (New York: Pantheon, 1999) pp. 5-6.

51 *Ibid.* Hallowell

52 Wayne Baker, *Achieving Success Through Social Capital*. (San Francisco, CA: Jossey-Bass, 2000), chapter four.

53 Robert B. Cialdini, *Influence: The Psychology of Persuasion* (New York: Quill/ William Morrow, 1993); Alvin. W. Gouldner, "The norm of reciprocity," *American Journal of Sociology*, 1960, vol. 25, pp. 161-178; "Reciprocity and Autonomy in Functional Theory," pp. 241-270 in Llewellyn Gross (ed.), *Symposium on Sociological Theory*. 1959. Evanston, Illinois: Row, Peterson and Company. Levi-Strauss, Claude. [1949] 1996. "The Principle of Reciprocity." pp. 15-26 in *The Gift: An Interdisciplinary Perspective*, edited by Aafke E. Komter (Amsterdam: Amsterdam University Press); Helena Cronin's work on reciprocity in the animal world was reported in Harriet Rubin, "Only the Pronoid Survive," *Fast Company*, November, 1999.

54 Robert Cialdini, *Instant Influence* [audio tape], (Dartnell Audio, 1995).

55 Wayne Baker, *Achieving Success Through Social Capital* (San Francisco, CA: Jossey-Bass, 2000), chapter 4.

56 Ram Charan and Noel M. Tichy, *Every Business a Growth Engine* (New York: Times Business/Random House, 1999), p. 296. Italics added.

57 Quoted in Harriet Rubin, "Only the Pronoid Survive." *Fast Company*, November 1999.

58 Wayne Baker, *Achieving Success Through Social Capital* (San Francisco, CA: Jossey-Bass, 2000), pp. 3-9.

59 James S. Coleman, *Foundations of Social Theory* (Cambridge, MA: Harvard University Press, 1990), p. 300.

60 Pfeffer also makes this point in Jeffery Pfeffer, *Managing with Power* (Boston, MA: Harvard Business School, 1992), pp. 17-18.

61 Ronald S. Burt, "A Note on the General Social Survey's Ersatz Network Density Item," *Social Networks*, 1987, vol. 9, pp. 75-85. I review the need for evaluation and the field of network analysis in chapter two of Wayne Baker, *Achieving Success*

Through Social Capital (San Francisco, CA: Jossey-Bass, 2000).

62 Stanley Wasserman and Katherine Faust, *Social Network Analysis: Methods and Applications* (Cambridge: Cambridge University Press, 1994).

63 Nancy Tennant Snyder and Deborah Duarte, "Chaotic Role Movement in Large Organizations: From Planning to Dynamic Management," Chapter six in Robert E. Quinn, Regina M. O'Neill and Lynda St. Clair (eds.), *Pressing Problems in Modern Organizations.* (New York: AMACOM, 2000) p. 113.

64 Ram Charan, "How Networks Reshape Organizations — for Results." *Harvard Business Review*, September-October, 1991, pp. 104-115.

65 Slater, 2000, pp. 82-83.

66 Manual Castells, "The Informational City is a Dual City: Can It Be Reversed?" pp. 26-41 in Donald A. Schön, Bish Sanyal and William J. Mitchell (eds.), *High Technology and Low-Income Communities* (Cambridge, MA: MIT Press).

67 Manuel Castells, *The Rise of the Network Society*, second edition, 2000a. Volume 1 of The Information Age: Economy, Society, and Culture (Oxford: Blackwell; 1996). *The Power of Identity*. Volume 2 of The Information Age: Economy, Society, and Culture (Oxford: Blackwell. 2000b). *End of Millennium*, second edition. Volume 3 of The Information Age: Economy, Society, and Culture (Oxford: Blackwell).

■ Recommended Readings

Baker, Wayne. *Achieving Success Through Social Capital: Tapping the Hidden Resources in Your Personal and Business Networks.* San Francisco, CA: Jossey-Bass, 2000.

Putnam, Robert D. *Bowling Alone: The Collapse and Revival of American Community.* New York: Simon & Schuster, 2000.

Leenders, Roger Th. A. J. and Shaul M. Gabbay (eds.). *Corporate Social Capital and Liability.* Kluwer Academic Publishers, 1999.

Wasserman, Stanley and Katherine Faust. *Social Network Analysis: Methods and Applications.* Cambridge University Press, 1994.

Castells, Manuel. *The Power of Identity.* Volume 2 of The Information Age: Economy, Society, and Culture. Oxford: Blackwell 1996.

2000a. *The Rise of the Network Society*, second edition. Volume 1 of The Information Age: Economy, Society, and Culture. Oxford: Blackwell.

2000b. *End of Millennium*, second edition. Volume 3 of The Information Age: Economy, Society, and Culture. Oxford: Blackwell.

Reprinted from the *IHRIM Journal*, Volume V, Number 2, April - June 2001, pp. 98-109.

Working in the Connected World

BY VALDIS KREBS

"*There is a central difference between the old and new economies: the old industrial economy was driven by economies of scale; the new information economy is driven by economics of networks...*"

Information Rules
by Carl Shapiro, Hal R. Varian

• • • • • • • •

Managing Connected Assets

The new economy operates on the complexities of connections. Human resource (HR) professionals in the past focused solely on the individual and recently on collections of individuals called teams. The economics of networks has no place for independent (i.e., unconnected) objects whether they are individuals, teams or computer systems. All individuals, communities, systems, and other business assets are massively interconnected in an evolving economic web. No man, woman, team, or organization is an island. In the connected economy, each network actor (individual, team, or organization) is embedded in a larger economic system that affects each participant and, in return, is influenced by each participant. In such an interdependent system we can no longer focus on individual or single team performance. If they are to be effective in improving the effectiveness of their organizations, HR professionals must see that they are helping to manage connected assets, not unconnected individuals.

Efforts at making sense of this new world are beginning to reveal some basic principles at work in the complex human systems we call our organizations, work groups, and economic webs. Recent research on productivity and effectiveness in the knowledge economy provides insight into what works in the connected workplace. Certain patterns of connections appear around both effective individuals and successful teams when performing knowledge work. Other research shows us how to provide the "missing links" that change a poor economic network into a better conduit for information, influence, and knowledge.

■ Social Capital

Is it "who" you know (social capital) or "what" you know (human capital) that leads to success? This has been often debated with good arguments on both sides. With its focus on education, training and job experience, HR has usually sided with the "what you know" crowd. In the old economy this strategy worked more often than not.

In the late 1980s and early 1990s management researchers were starting to notice that effective managers were better at accomplishing objectives through their relationships than less effective managers. John Kotter[1] discovered that effective general managers spend more than 80 percent of their time interacting with others. Other management scholars were also starting to see the importance of conversations and relationships in managerial work. Individual mastery was no longer the key – "what" you knew actually depended on "who" you knew! Relationships were the key for general managers in accomplishing their goals – they did not "own" the knowledge to get things done, they kept it in their network!

Arent Greve, a researcher at the Norwegian School of Economics, was intrigued by this social capital versus human capital debate[2]. How did this effect productivity? He studied project managers in a knowledge-based services company in Europe. He viewed human capital as the knowledge and skills attained by the individual over his/her career. Social capital was defined as a property of personal networks – the ability to reach others, inside and outside the organization, for information, advice and problem-solving. He found something very interesting. Both individual competency and social capital had a positive effect on productivity, but the effect of social capital was noticeably stronger! Project managers with better personal networks were more productive – they were better able to coordinate tasks and find the knowledge necessary to accomplish the goals of the project.

■ Improving Team Effectiveness

Meanwhile, across the Atlantic in a high-tech firm, Morten Hansen of Harvard Business School, had a similar research agenda. The key difference was that Hansen was interested in the productivity and effectiveness of teams[3]. Hansen found very similar results with project teams. Those teams that could easily reach other teams and access the knowledge they needed were more successful than teams with poor network connections. Both Greve and Hansen found that the ability to reach a diverse set of others in the network through very few links was the key to success.

Hansen took his research one step further. He examined the difference between those teams that had many direct connections to other project teams and those that used both direct and indirect ties to reach the resources they needed. Hansen found that those teams that used direct ties to seek and find information were soon overwhelmed with too many connections. The teams that used the power of the indirect tie, while at the same time limiting their direct ties, were more successful – they did not spend as much time interacting with the network to get what they needed. A sparse, radial network, in which your direct ties are connected to others that you are "not" connected to, has been shown to provide many benefits and opportunities. A dense, local network, where all of your ties are connected only to each other, is a poor structure for accessing information and knowledge found in distant parts of the organization.

Hansen discovered one other insight that is key for knowledge management[4]. A diverse, radial network, with many unique indirect ties is good for monitoring what is happening in the organization and for discovering pockets of knowledge and expertise. Yet, this type of network may not be useful for transferring knowledge. Although indirect ties help you cast a wide net and "see" far into the organization (and beyond it), these ties are not always efficient for transferring knowledge once it is discovered. It depends on what type of knowledge needs to be transferred. Explicit knowledge can be easily codified and transferred via many technologies available today such as e-mail, FTP, WWW or documents through interoffice mail. Complex experiential knowledge cannot be easily codified. This tacit knowledge requires direct interaction and sharing of experiences. To transfer tacit knowledge a direct tie with the knowledge source(s) needs to be established. Trust and understanding must be built – this is similar to apprenticeship. Indirect ties monitor the environment; direct ties mine the environment.

■ *Improving Information Flow*

Network ties are distributed unevenly. People that work together form networks together – clusters emerge around established work relationships. Engineers working on Project X form a cluster, those working on Project Y form a cluster, and those working on Project Z form a cluster. Everyone knows everyone else within the local cluster, and yet only a few individuals have boundary spanning ties to other clusters. Strong, frequent, ties are usually found within clusters, while weaker, less frequent ties are found between clusters.

Clusters of concentrated connections appear throughout an organization and throughout industries. Some clusters have many ties to many others, while other clusters have only a few ties. Poor connections between clusters result in very long path lengths throughout the greater network. In such a network it is easy to access those in your cluster but not those in other clusters. This often results in distant clusters not having access to information and knowledge that is available in the organization.

Often the knowledge you need is in clusters other than your own. Networks have a "horizon" beyond which it is difficult to see what is happening. Research by Noah Friedkin[5] at UC Santa Barbara has shown that this horizon of observability is usually two steps in a human network – your direct contacts and their direct contacts. Around three steps out, things are real fuzzy – you do not have a good idea of what is happening there. Beyond three steps, you are blind to what is happening in the rest of the network.

In a network of very long path lengths between clusters, your ability to find the knowledge or information you need is constrained. If the knowledge that you seek is not within your "network horizon", then you assume it is not available and you reinvent it or pay for it on the outside. Exasperated with this network horizon in his organization, a former CEO of HP once lamented, "If we only knew what we know."

The natural response in many organizations is to throw technology at the problem. A very poor, yet quite common, solution is to "mine" the knowledge from employees, codify it, and store it in a knowledge database. Many large consulting firms tried this approach in the early to mid-1990s with usually poor results. They found that people were not always willing to make pubic their best knowledge and that codifying tacit knowledge was like trying to nail jelly to the wall. A better use of technology is to keep a database of "who knows what" and add a table of "who knows who." In other words, store "pointers" to the knowledge, not the knowledge itself. A hybrid solution may be to store both pointers and summary information chunks.

Why not use the power of the network itself to create a solution? Improve the organizational network and then use technology to help people communicate across wide spans of the human network. At first blush, improving an organization-wide network may seem an overwhelming task. Where do we start? First, look at the networks and communities of practice/interest/knowledge that have organized around a specific topic, product, service or customer. Usually the whole organization does not have to be included in the problem space. Second, map out the network nodes and their connections (who goes to whom for expertise/knowledge/advice on X?). From this network map, you can see the various clusters and how they are connected. Figure 1 shows a network map of project teams. A line connecting two teams indicates a two-way information flow or exchange of knowledge.

This network of 17 project teams all work on sub-assemblies to a larger product. The teams are composed of mostly engineers, technicians, and project managers. All teams have less than ten members. Three clusters are evident with the cluster composed of teams N, O, and P connecting the other two emergent clusters.

Figure 1. Project Team Network Map.

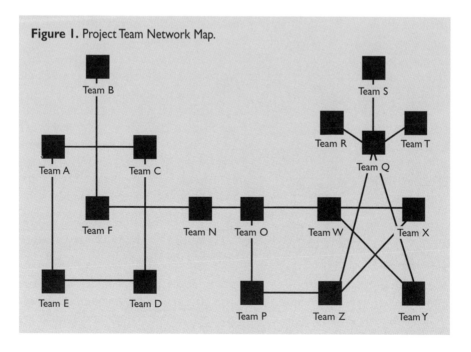

Before we look at how to improve the overall connectivity of the network, let's digress back to social capital. Which team has the best social capital in this network? Which team can access all of the knowledge and resources in the network quicker than the others? (Hint: this network is drawn to reveal the answer.)

Common wisdom in networks is "the more connections, the better." This is usually not true. What is always true is "the better connections, the better." Connections that provide the most network benefits give you access to nodes that you currently do not have access to. Although Team F and Team Q have many connections each and have excellent local access (to the nodes near them), they have only fair access to the rest of the network. Team O has the best social capital (aka network benefits) in this network of project teams. Team O achieves this with only three direct ties — it is connected to others who are well connected.

The average path length in this network is 3.9 with many paths longer than the network horizon. Even in this small network there are nodes that are nearly blind to what is happening in other parts of the network.

In the summer of 1998, quite a stir of excitement was generated by two mathematicians from Cornell, Steven Strogatz and Duncan Watts, writing in the scientific journal, *Nature*[6]. *Business Week*, *The New York Times*, NPR, and many others reported on this research. After they published their results they received a flood of emails from epidemiologists, computer scientists, marketing people, economists, engineers, government agencies and at least one management consultant (me). What attracted professionals in all of these diverse fields? Part of the attraction was the simple elegance of the solution. While investigating small-world networks (those with many clusters), they discovered that a few randomly added cross-cuts (network links) would improve the average path length significantly – very small adjustments could cause large positive changes. On top of that, the benefits were not just local, but spread throughout the network — changes far away could benefit you!

Looking back on our project team network in Figure 1, how can we improve the connectivity with just one added link? Which two nodes would you connect to bring everyone in the network closer together? Although many combinations will increase the access of everyone to everyone else, the greatest measurable effect is when we add a cross-cut between Team Q and Team F. The average path length drops from 3.9 steps to 2.6 - an improvement of 33%! Information flowing from any node in the network to any other node in the network now arrives much sooner and with less distortion.

The connection between Teams Q and F may be the optimal connection in network efficiency, but it may not be a "practical" connection. Both of these teams already have many ties and may not have the time and energy to support another one (remember Hansen's research above). What is an alternative connection? If you cannot connect the highly connected nodes, how about connecting their respective network neighbors? Instead of connecting Q and F, how about connecting D and Z? This connection will not reduce the path length as much, but it is between nodes that are not overburdened with connections.

This dynamic reveals one of the counter-intuitive aspects of networks – you can decrease by adding! We are all well indoctrinated by the recent management efforts of downsizing, rightsizing, total quality management, and business process reengineering. All of these efforts were aimed at decreasing time and expense within the organization. They followed the intuitive approach of removing "unnecessary" people and steps from work flows — decrease by subtracting. Networks often reveal their logic to counter-intuitive reasoning — add redundancy to improve information flow. Networks, with some redundancy, but not too much, function better than those with little or no redundancy. Networks without redundant paths are very brittle (remove one node or tie and the network fragments) and are usually very inefficient in transporting knowledge and information from one end to another. Very often adding ties, decreases the path traveled and decreases the probability for failure.

■ Leading Edge HR

One of the benefits of consulting in network dynamics is having leading edge clients. Not only are they open to new methods to improve their organizations, they usually end up teaching me quite a bit. One such client is Vancho Cirovski, Vice President of Human Resources at R. P. Scherer-Hardcapsule. Vancho, an expert soccer player and coach, first noticed an interesting phenomenon on the playing field. Teams that were more integrated and communicated well amongst themselves on the field, more often than not, beat a collection of individually superior players who were not interacting well on the field.

Vancho saw the same effect in project teams inside organizations. He has summarized these concepts of managing connected assets using Einstein's famous formula:

E = MC2

♦ E is Effectiveness of the team or organization
♦ M is the Mastery attained by each individual (human capital)
♦ C are the Connections that joins the individual into a community (social capital)
♦ C is the Communication that flows amongst the individuals

The effectiveness of a team or organization is based on personal know-how (mastery), enhanced by communications (feedback and new knowledge) from both direct and indirect connections (diverse networked resources).

A common reason for the failure of many mergers and acquisitions is the failure to properly integrate the two combining organizations and their cultures. Although a formal hierarchy combining the two organizations may be in place, the right work relationships are never formed and the organizations remain "disconnected." Ralph Polumbo, Vice President of Integration for Rubbermaid's 1998 acquisition of its European competitor, Curver, wanted to make sure the two organizations were combining effectively. He wanted to map and measure the melding of information flows, work relationships and knowledge exchanges – connections that help cultures combine. His vision was one of a boundaryless organization with no fragmentation along former constituencies. He wanted to see where integration was happening and where it was not occurring. By examining his human and social capital concurrently, he was able to monitor the integration process and focus attention on areas that needed help.

How can HR make connectivity work in the organization? Here are a few places to get started:

➤ Look beyond the individual — see their connections and multiple group memberships. Performance and productivity in the new economy results from the interplay of individuals, their connections, and their conversations. How does this affect performance management and succession planning?

➤ Know the difference between tacit and explicit knowledge and how it is shared and transferred — discover how this changes training and knowledge management.

➤ Reward people for directly sharing their know-how.

➤ Design computer systems that facilitate conversations and sharing of knowledge – think communication, not storage/retrieval.

➤ Help women and people of color connect to key knowledge flows and communities in the organization. This may help eliminate the "glass ceiling".

➤ Recruit new hires through the networks of current employees – they will be happier, adjust quicker, and stay longer.

➤ When transferring employees keep in mind their connections. Exchanging employees with a diverse network of ties can create short-cuts between departments or teams and greatly improve the information flow.

➤ Ensure better coordination of behavior between departments or projects by adding cross-cuts to minimize the path length of their information exchange networks. To reduce delays you want some redundancy in the paths – if one is blocked, then alternative communication paths are available.

➤ It is no longer sufficient to just hire the best. You must hire and wire! Start new networks, help employees and teams connect – be a matchmaker – connect the unconnected!

In the 1992 U.S. presidential race, one simple phrase refocused and re-ignited a jumbled campaign effort by Bill Clinton – "It's the economy, stupid!" Adaptive businesses see the benefits in managing connected assets – those they own and those they do not. In the current economy we can adapt the old campaign slogan to reflect a new reality – "It's the connections, stupid!"

• • • • • • • •

■ Endnotes

1   John P. Kotter, "What Effective General Managers Really Do," *Harvard Business Review*, March/April 1999.

2   Arent Greve, "Comparing the Influence of Human and Social Capital on Performance" (paper presented at Sunbelt Social Networks Conference XIX, February 1999).

3   Morten T. Hansen, "Combining Network Centrality and Related Knowledge Explaining Effective Knowledge Sharing in Multiunit Firms" (Harvard Business School Working Paper 98-081, 1998).

4   Morten T. Hansen, "The Search-Transfer Problem: The Role of Weak Ties in Sharing Knowledge Across Organization Subunits," (Harvard Business School Working Paper 98-011, 1997).

5   Noah Friedkin, "Horizons of Observability and Limits of Informal Control in Organizations," *Social Networks*, September 1983.

6   Duncan J. Watts and Steven H. Strogatz, "Collective Dynamics of 'Small-World' Networks," *Nature*, 4 June 1998.

Reprinted from the *IHRIM Journal*, Volume III, Number 2, June 1999, pp. 64-67.

Mining for Knowledge

In the network, your pattern of connections reveal who you are and what you are trying to accomplish. We don't need to see inside the node, we can deduce much from how it is connected to other nodes and in return how they are connected. By looking at the patterns in the network we can answer these questions:

➤ Who is a leader? Who is a follower?

➤ Who is included? Who is excluded?

➤ Who has power? Who will be ineffectual?

➤ Who belongs to an emergent community? Who ties diverse communities together?

➤ Who will soon be friends, collaborators, knowledge co-creators?

➤ Who has common interests? Who has similar goals?

➤ Who will blossom? Who will struggle?

➤ Who will stay? Who will go?

No psychoanalysis, Meyers-Briggs, or [insert latest management fad here] are necessary to answer these questions. Just look at the emergent pattern of ties that an individual, team, or organization develop as they strive to reach their goals. These insights also work for networks that are not composed of solely humans, such as computer networks, power grids, WWW, supply chains/webs, and trade networks. Want to understand your competition? Look at their connections! Want to find your community of interest? Look for connections similar to yours.

Want to find your community of interest? Look for connections similar to yours.

Understanding an individual or group by investigating their connections is not a new science. It has been going on for a few decades. The CIA uses patterns of connections (called "pocs") to reveal terrorist organizations and uncover spy rings and conspiracies. The FBI and Treasury Department use pocs to discover and track money laundering. Insurance companies uses pocs to detect fraudulent claims, the Los Angeles Police Department uses pocs to detect the "hidden organizers" behind staged auto accidents, and NATO used their knowledge of connections within the Serbian supply and communication networks to choose which targets to bomb first. How does this "spook stuff" relate to HR? These same methods can be applied within organizations to enable and invigorate knowledge sharing and innovation.

◼ Emergent Patterns

How does this work? Analyzing patterns of connections is based upon three simple behaviors found in all human networks. The first behavior is recognized around the world. Many say it is the basis of community — "birds of a feather flock together." People with similar interests, problems and goals usually find each other and form emergent communities for support, affiliation and learning. Often similar people find similar others through connections they have already made.

Once explained, the second behavior is very intuitive. Diane knows Mark and Lisa, but Mark and Lisa do not know each other. This is the unfinished triangle in Figure 1.

In most cases Mark and Lisa will eventually get to know each other — they have a common friend. This is the completed triangle in Figure 2. Friends of friends become friends. Colleagues of colleagues become colleagues.

The third behavior is based upon the principle of structural equivalence. Through many years of sociological research, it has been shown again and again that people with similar problems, interests and goals will show ties to similar resources whether these resources are people, documents or

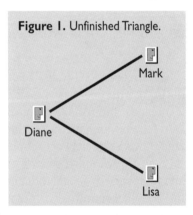

Figure 1. Unfinished Triangle.

Mark

Diane

Lisa

Figure 2. Completed Triangle.

Mark

Diane

Lisa

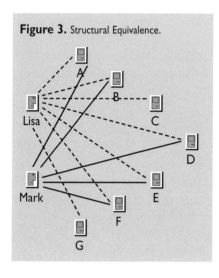

Figure 3. Structural Equivalence.

databases. Two individuals can be structurally equivalent if they have the same or similar connections. Two structurally equivalent people do not even need to know each other! In Figure 3, Mark and Lisa are structurally equivalent because they both have connections to the same 5 out of 7 resources [A,B,D,E,F].

They are structurally equivalent even though Lisa has connections to two resources that Mark does not [C,G], and they are not directly connected to each other. They have enough of an overlap to suggest a common goals, problem or interest.

■ *Do we know what we know?*

Often people with similar problems, interests and goals are either introduced or stumble across each other. They form communities to share their challenges, interests and insights. Through community interaction existing knowledge is exchanged, combined in diverse ways and new knowledge is created. Knowledge networks support learning throughout the organization. This process of knowledge sharing and creation may happen with adequate speed and frequency in a small organization or professional community. What about the large decentralized corporation? Does the right hand know what the left hand is doing? Are they reinventing the wheel? Are they utilizing the lessons learned in previous projects?

Can this informal discovery process scale to large decentralized organizations? Usually not. The quick adaptation required in today's economy out-runs this slow unearthing of new knowledge and new collaborators through face-to-face interaction. If we could only speed up, and expand, this natural networking that occurs in organizations.

Organization size provides both good news and bad news. The good news is that the larger the organization in which you work, the greater the possibility it contains the knowledge and expertise you need to accomplish your goals. The bad news is the larger the organization the more difficult it is to find the knowledge you need when you need it.

The common solution to this knowledge discovery problem has been to mine the organization's knowledge and dump it into a computer. This worked fine for data and other structured information — which is sometimes referred to as explicit knowledge. Unfortunately data and explicit information do not provide competitive advantage — it is available to most players within the competitive arena. The seed of competitive advantage is the interpretation and creative use of data and information. This requires analysis, learning and wisdom — tacit knowledge, which is usually found within emergent communities within and across organizations. It's the context not the content!

As many organizations began to realize that the key to the effective use and sharing of knowledge was not in capturing structured data, they began investigating how to find and capture tacit knowledge. Structured databases failed to hold tacit knowledge, so many firms tried unstructured data storage such as Lotus Notes, intranets and corporate portals. These solutions had their place — they were great at providing access to various types of content, but they still could not handle the contextual aspects of meaning, relevance, and possibility in learning. Not only was tacit knowledge difficult to store, it was even more difficult to extract. Employees and managers did not want to devote much time to mining employee brains when the use and outcome was not clear. In organizations of low trust, with a culture and history of not sharing, employees flat out resisted giving up what they thought was their only value added — their wisdom and experience.

Capturing content works. Capturing context is like nailing jelly to the wall. After many failed attempts the pioneers of knowledge management realized that people's connections and communities were going to be critical in sharing existing knowledge and creating new knowledge. Even though technology is not the direct answer to developing and utilizing tacit knowledge, it plays a key indirect role in discovering knowledge and in building communities of interest.

■ *Discovering and Utilizing Knowledge*

How do you discover who has the knowledge you need in the organization? How do you find who else is working on similar products and services? How do you find those employees who have already done what you are trying to do? I have worked on many projects that attempted to answer these questions by throwing the latest technology at the problem. First, there were skills databases, a pet project of many an HR VP trying to show how HR supports the business. These databases usually ended up being shelfware upon their release. Not only was it difficult to populate these databases with accurate information, it was almost impossible to keep them updated. They always appeared inaccurate and out-of-date. The data collection process was like pulling teeth. Not only did employees have to fill out long surveys, but the completed surveys had to be verified by their managers, and then the approved surveys had to be parsed by HR to fit into the correct database structure. In a few months everyone was mad at a process that took time away from real work, caused great stress, and was inaccurate on the day it was delivered.

A slightly improved process was played out in developing corporate yellow pages, resume databases, and knowledge repositories. Although the process of extracting and storing knowledge was improving over time, it was the wrong process! Many companies were starting to do the wrong thing fairly well — which just kept them on the wrong path longer. Only data and structured information can be codified and efficiently stored. Knowledge and wisdom cannot. Knowledge and wisdom do not require a new storage medium in the organization — they already have one. They are stored in the individuals, relationships and communities that make up the organization and its economic environment. The key is not storage of knowledge, the focus should be on access to knowledge.

How do we utilize the knowledge of those who went before us? How do we utilize the learning of those who have similar goals to ours? The first step is to find them. As we learned above, finding the right resource in a large organization may be difficult. Even those with wide reaching personal networks may not be aware of key knowledge pockets inside the organization. The answer is, throw technology at the problem! This time we will not build an elaborate database or system. We will use a common technology in an uncommon way.

What's the first thing you do when you have to find out about a new product, process or person? You check the WWW! Inside the organization you check the corporate intranet. People seeking new information and knowledge spend much of their time surfing from one site to another, linking from one document to another, trying to find the right resources to meet their goals. Those with effective personal networks also check with their contacts — who do you know that's knowledgeable about X? Often the answer contains a few names of people and web sites.

As people surf and search the WWW or the corporate intranet, they leave tracks in various web logs. The access log reveals who looked at what and when. Following the user id through the web log, a path is revealed. One can almost see a train of thought — first they looked here, then there, then back to here, and then over to this department's documents. From this list of documents visited |path through the web site(s)| this person must have been interested in X. There are many traversals of an intranet. Soon common paths appear — people interested in a similar topic choose similar links to similar documents. These overlapping trails of knowledge and information seeking begin to reveal the goals of a group individuals. These insights can help employees find experts, possible collaborators and communities of interest that have similar goals and may hold the knowledge they seek.

■ Patterns in the Net

The larger and more diverse your organization's intranet the more effective this method of pattern mining will be. Two employees, Mary and Sean, visiting the internal Marketing home page may not have any goals or interests in common. Two other employees, Lisa and Mark, visiting a document that explains the roll-out plan for a UNIX-based currency analysis software in Germany, may have a common interest. The more rarely visited documents they both access in common, the more likely it is that they should be talking to each other. If Lisa and Mark's path through very specific and unique documents overlap greatly and if Lisa's path through the documents occurred 12 month's ago, then Mark may have found someone who has been there, done that. Mark may be able to take advantage of Lisa's learning and not repeat the mistakes she made.

Not only has Mark found a potential knowledge source in Lisa, he may have found other documents to visit that he has not seen yet (refer back to Figure 3). Notice that Lisa, in her search, had visited documents F and G. Mark had not seen these documents. Since Lisa had viewed these documents in the same paths that took her to the documents that she had in common with Mark, chances are that these documents may hold some value for Mark also. This is similar to the service that amazon.com provides: "people who bought this book, also purchased..."

Although Lisa has exhibited interest in many documents that Mark has also viewed, she may not be the resource he was looking for. If she is not, chances are she knows who is. Remember, birds of a feather flock together. Lisa may belong to a community within the organization with similar interests. She can then introduce Mark to the right person. After talking to Mark about his project and his needs, Lisa may also point Mark to a former project team member of hers who better fits the expertise and experience Mark seeks.

■ Networking in Internet Time

Without the assistance of this pattern discovery method, Mark may have used his personal network to find Lisa and then through Lisa to discover other resources. If Mark and Lisa were only one link apart (refer back to Figure 2), then this discovery process may have happened quickly enough for Mark to find the knowledge he needed within his deadline. Yet if Mark and Lisa were separated by two or more intermediaries, as is quite frequent in large organizations, then they probably would not have discovered each other on a timely basis. In large networks, individuals who are separated by more than one intermediary usually are unaware of the other's knowledge, interests and goals. The pattern discovery method described here is way for us to speed up the traversal of the knowledge network to find the resource we need when we need it.

Here we have an unobtrusive and adaptive method to keep knowledge flowing and employees learning from each other. Analyzing patterns of knowledge access can be broken down into three steps:

1) monitor and model an employee's access patterns in real time to various documents and other knowledge resources,

2) compare an employee's interest model against the access patterns of other employees,

3) based on equivalent patterns, suggest to the employee:
   a) new collaborators or topic experts to contact, and
   b) new documents or other knowledge resources to investigate.

Not only can this pattern analysis be applied to web browsing, it can also be used to analyze databases access logs, emails sent and received, and phone logs. Finding the paths and patterns in these logs will reveal how the organization really works, and how information and knowledge flow between people via various technologies.

The only drawback is a perceived invasion of privacy. But this method does not invade an employee's privacy any more than current monitoring methods already in place in many organizations. Many companies already track an employee's web surfing habits — to keep them away from sports, gambling and sex sites during work hours. E-mails are also monitored — not just who sends to whom — but what is said in the message. Now video cameras assist security personnel in monitoring an employment facility. And finally, the use and misuse of the ubiquitous office telephone has been monitored for decades. The notion of complete privacy in the workplace is just an illusion. This pattern analysis approach does not create any new privacy breaches.

As we progress in our relationship with technology, we see an interesting pattern. Our early focus on technology centered around computation and data. Our emerging view of technology is now turning towards knowledge and communication.

• • • • • • • •

Reprinted from the *IHRIM Journal*, Volume III, Number 3, September 1999, pp. 105-108.

Social Capital:

In the 20th century, the human resources (HR) function became quite adept at managing human capital, defined as the skills, knowledge, and experience of individual employees within the firm. Just as HR was gaining competencies in this arena, the new economy came along and moved the goal posts. It is no longer sufficient to manage individual assets. The HR professional of the 21st century must manage connected assets[1] with many of these not being employees of the firm!

In the knowledge economy, content is no longer sufficient. . .everyone has access to multitudes of content. You cannot compete on what everyone knows. The new advantage is context — how internal and external content is interpreted, combined, made sense of, and converted to end product. Creating competitive context requires social capital, the ability to find, utilize and combine the skills, knowledge and experience of others.

HR used to focus only on within-employee factors. The new competitive landscape requires focussing on between-employee factors, the connections that combine to create new processes, products and services. Social capital encompasses communities of practice, knowledge exchanges, information flows, interest groups, social networks and other emergent connections between employees, suppliers, regulators, partners and customers. Social capital is what connects various forms of human capital. It is these patterns of connections that produce advantage for one group, and constraint for another. In the networked economy the one with the best connections wins!

■ Winning the Connections Game

Although many HR professionals have not often heard the term "social capital" used in conversations about organizational effectiveness, research shows that it will become increasingly important. Ron Burt, a leading researcher and professor, at both The University of Chicago and INSEAD (France), predicts that managing an organization's social capital will become one of the core competencies in knowledge-based organizations.[2] This will [finally!] be the road to respect for HR. In addition to being one of the leading academicians in this field, Burt keeps abreast on practices by advising executives at General Electric,

Raytheon, several investment banks and other leading-edge organizations. Burt has developed some of the key theories in the field of social capital[3] and writes often and contributes the most respected academic publications. In these articles he cites research on social capital and how it affects recruitment, retention, performance, compensation and creativity in organizations.

The following is a list of outcomes and goals that are the focus of HR. All are significantly influenced and enhanced by better social capital both within the firm and across its borders. People with better social capital:

➤ Find better jobs more quickly,[4]

➤ Are more likely to be promoted early,[5,6]

➤ Close deals faster,[7]

➤ Receive larger bonuses,[8]

➤ Enhance the performance of their teams,[9]

➤ Help their teams reach their goals more rapidly,[10]

➤ Perform better as project managers,[11]

➤ Help their teams generate more creative solutions,[12]

➤ Increase output from their R&D teams,[13]

➤ Coordinate projects more effectively,[14]

➤ Learn more about the firm's environment and marketplace,[15] and

➤ Receive higher performance evaluations.[16]

The affects of social capital do not contribute to just the success of individuals and teams. Organizations with better connections in the network of industry alliances and joint ventures report higher patent outputs,[17] a higher probability of innovation[18] and higher earnings and chances of survival in rapidly innovating industries.[19] Social capital within the firm and across the firm's border to other firms, seems to be a prerequisite for organizational learning, adaptability, and agility.

When the HR focus was on human capital, the goal was to hire the best individual for the job. In today's knowledge organization, the goal expands to "hire-

and-wire"— to hire the best people with the best network and integrate them into the value chain so that their combined human and social capital provide excellent returns.

■ The Network is the Employee

Sun Microsystems has long extolled that "the network is the computer" — it is not the individual box that gives you computing power, but many interconnected computers that exponentially increase the power of a single processor. The network effect is more than simply additive. With the advent of the Internet we have clearly seen how true this view of the future was. Social capital has this same effect on productivity and innovation. It is not the sum of individual employees know that provides competitive advantage. It is the unique interconnectivity of human capital, available inside and outside of the firm, that will provide some economic players with an advantage over those who are not so well connected. HR will not focus on individual employees but on emergent networks of employees.

How should HR usher in the age of the connected employee? Burt sees four key areas where HR will need to map, monitor and mold social capital:

1) Identification,

2) Development,

3) Retention, and

4) Enhancement.

The first step is to identify the social capital in the organization. How is the company connected internally? Are the critical people/teams/projects connected? Is information flowing between these entities? Is knowledge being exchanged? The next area for identification is across the borders of the organization. Is knowledge of the environment flowing in to the right parties inside the company? Are customers and suppliers included in knowledge networks? Is the company effectively monitoring developments and trends?

The development process emerges from the identification process. Is there an identified lack of social capital? How does the company compare to benchmarks? Who needs to be trained to develop more social capital, a product of the relationship between individuals and between groups. It is not held by any one party. The recipient of human capital development is the individual. The targets of social capital development are individuals and their group/team/community. This relational aspect adds a whole new dimension to training and learning.

Social capital is a key driver in employee retention. Ron Burt has identified patterns of social capital that indicate, with a high probability, who will stay and who will go. Knowing who is in danger of leaving allows early HR intervention before losing a key knowledge resource. A similar process, developed by the author for TRW Space & Electronics revealed that women and minority engineers needed better connections to key knowledge communities. Inclusion in these communities was viewed as a sign of "commitment" to employees. In return, employees felt greater commitment to the organization. Employees who are included in key information flows and communities of knowledge are more dedicated and have a much higher rate of retention.

The final factor in effective social capital is enhancement. How do we weave a better organization? HR is accustomed to examining at prescribed, vertical relationships inside the organization — who works where and who reports to whom? Going forward, HR must also consider horizontal and diagonal relationships. The focus is shifting from strictly internal connections to internal and external connections to all stakeholders. The key to enhancement is knowing where you are now and where you want to go. With this information, the gaps and holes in the networks are easy to spot. For example, if we want to develop a product for X market, we might determine that departments 4 and 15 need a better working relationship and knowledge exchange. We also need access to knowledge outside the organization — who has links to the communities in which this knowledge resides? Who can access and transfer that knowledge?

■ It's not Ownership, but Access

It is apparent that the definition of human capital has changed and continues to form new forms. It is no longer spelled e-m-p-l-o-y-e-e. The human assets that an organization uses to reach its goals include full- and part-time employees, contractors, consultants, partners and increasingly suppliers and customers.

Organizations rely less frequently on owned assets. Today's fluid environment does not reward ownership, including the old employment relationship. The agility needed by today's organizations requires finding the right assets and combining them into the right structure to meet short-lived goals. It is not "what you control," but "what you can access" that is the key link in the value chain. This shifting landscape will drastically alter the HR function and the systems used to track assets both within-employee and the between-employee as-sets, a totally new concept to explore. Even though HR's realm is becoming more chaotic, this complexity and increased dependence on human and social capital will provide HR an opportunity to more directly influence an organiza-tion's results. As HR's role grows, so will the role of HRIS/HRMS in monitoring and modeling of these new capital structures.

• • • • • • • •

■ Endnotes

1   Valdis E. Krebs, "Managing Connected Assets," *IHRIM Journal*, Volume 3, Number 2, June 1999.

2   Ronald S. Burt, personal conversation with the author, March 2000.

3   Ronald S. Burt, Structural Holes — *The Social Structure of Competition* (Harvard University Press, 1992).

4   Mark S. Granovetter, *Getting a Job* (University of Chicago Press, 1995).

5   Ronald S. Burt, "The Network Structure of Social Capital," *Research in Organizational Behavior*, edited by Robert I. Sutton and Barry M. Staw, (JAI Press, 2000).

6   Shaul M. Gabbay, *Social Capital in the Creation of Financial Capital*, (Stipes, 1997).

7   Mark S. Mizruchi and Linda B. Stearns, "Strategic Social Capital and Deal Making in a Large Commercial Bank" (paper presented at the International Sunbelt Social Network Conference, XX, April 2000).

8   Op. Cit.

9   Elizabeth A. Rosenthal, "Social Networks and Team Performance," Ph.D. dissertation (University of Chicago, 1996).

10   Morten T. Hansen, "Combining Network Centrality and Related Knowledge Explaining Effective Knowledge Sharing in Multiunit Firms" (Harvard Business School working paper, 98-081, 1998).

11   Arent Greve, "Comparing the Influence of Human Capital and Social Capital on Performance" paper presented at the International Sunbelt Social Network Conference. XIX, February 1999).

12   Deborah G. Ancona and David F. Caldwell, "Bridging the Boundary: External Activity and Performance in Organizational Teams," *Administrative Science Quarterly* 37: 634-665: 1992.

13   Ray Reagans and Ezra W. Zuckerman, "Networks, Diversity and Performance: the Social Capital of Corporate R&D Units," Carnegie Mellon University, Unpublished Paper, 1999.

14   Martin Gargiulo and Mario Benassi, "Trapped in Your Own Net: Network Cohesion, Structural Holes, and the Adaptation of Social Capital," *Organization Science* 11 (in press) 2000.

15   Shawn M. Lofstrom, "Absorbtive Capacity in Strategic Alliances: Investigating the Effects of Individuals' Social and Human Capital on Inter-firm Learning," Paper presented at the Organization Science Winter Conference, Denver, CO (February 2000).

16   Ronald S. Burt, Joseph E. Jannotta and James T. Mahoney, "Personality Correlates of Structural Holes," *Social Networks*, 20:63-87: 1998

17   Gautam Ahuja, "Collaboration Networks, Structural Holes, and Innovation: A Longitudinal Study." Paper presented at the annual meetings of the Academy of Management, 1998.

18   Toby E. Stuart and Joel Podolny, "Positional Causes and Correlates of Strategic Alliances in the Semiconductor Industry," Reserach in the Sociology of Oraganizations, edited by Steven Andrews and David Knoke, (JAI Press, 1999).

19   Kenneth Koput and Walter W, "Not Your Stepping Stone: Collaboration and the Dynamics of Industry Evolution in Biotechnology." Paper presented at the 2000 Organization Science Winter Conference, 2000.

Reprinted from the *IHRIM Journal*, Volume IV, Number 2, June 2000, pp. 89-91.

Seeing Patterns
in the Connected World

The pendulum between centralization and decentralization is swinging out of control. In the past we could expect a predictable, periodic motion. The rapid change of the recent past has created a chaotic cadence that we can only watch in amazement. Five years ago the Internet changed everything; five months ago the terrorists did the same. In the last decade, we eliminated redundancies from our business processes — now it looks like we need to put redundancy back in. We used to focus on just-in-time. Maybe now "just-in-case" is more important. We had a sharp focus on efficiency. Now it looks like we will have to trade some of that efficiency for security. We used to centralize our key resources for economies of scale. Now decentralization looks like the business topology of the future.

Recently every information technology publication has experts singing the praises of decentralization and redundancy. The CEO of a health insurer, which was previously headquartered in the World Trade Center, was quoted in *Computerworld*:

> "More and more we are getting away from a centralized model to a decentralized enterprise characterized by smaller units linked to one another in a variety of ways."[1]

It looks like the topology of our businesses will be changing rapidly, as we all adapt to a dangerous world. The links within, as well as between, our organizations will change. The old process flows, supply chains, and computer networks will look different — they will have fewer clusters of concentrated resources and more redundancy. Our old business taboos appear to be our new friends. What a strange world we work in.

Our old business taboos appear to be our new friends. What a strange world we work in.

Yet one trend will not change — the Internet and the global interconnectivity of money, work, resources, ideas and information will remain and continue to grow. Networks and connectivity are here to stay, it's their shape and structure that will change, not their ubiquity and usefulness.

■ Network Patterns

In order to live and work successfully in the connected world, we need to understand our connections and the network patterns that we are embedded in. Where are we safe in our networks and where are we at risk? How can we mitigate the risks without breaking the bank or the business relationships we have worked so hard to establish? Which network patterns are resilient in most situations? Which network structures stand up to random failure? Which ones crumble under deliberate attack?

There are several simple patterns found in all networks. To operate successfully in a networked world we must understand what these patterns are how they come together to form more complex structures.

All networks are made up of nodes and links. The nodes are the resources — individuals, teams, organizations, computers or other physical business objects. The links connect the resources in many ways, providing flows, exchanges, and relationships, which form various reoccurring patterns. Knowing the collection of network patterns, and your place in them, tells you what opportunities, constraints and dangers you face given your location in the network and the structure of links and resources around you. In the networked world, much of your fate is determined by where you are embedded in the network of transactions, flows and exchanges.

We will look at the most frequent patterns found in business networks — human networks, computer networks and organizational networks. Forming a project team, building a corporate wide area network (WAN), or integrating a supply web are tasks that assemble basic network patterns into a more complex whole. Network patterns are the Legos™ for the new economy.

The most basic network pattern is the chain shown in Figure 1. This simple structure is easy to build and easy to destroy. In strands of short length, the chain is useful. The longer the chain, the less efficient and the more dangerous it becomes. Disable any node or link in the middle of the chain and you instantly fragment the network into two components that can no longer reach each other. An intelligent attack on the network in Figure 1 would focus on node #005 or the links surrounding it.

Hook both ends of the chain together and you get a ring — a big improvement in efficiency, but only a small improvement in resilience. Figure 2 shows a simple structure that is easy to build.

The ring falls apart after two nodes or two links are disrupted. An intelligent attack on a ring structure would focus on two nodes or links opposite one another on the ring — nodes 001 and 006 or any other such combination would be likely targets.

Probably the most common structure seen in business networks is the star topology as shown in Figure 3. In computing, this is the client/server or host/terminal model. In human networks this is the leader and a group of followers.

Figure 1. Chain Pattern.

In energy infrastructure, this is the refinery or the power generation plant and the distribution points. This is commonly called a hub and spoke pattern.

This is a very efficient design that maximizes economies of scale. It only has one glaring weakness — a single point of failure. When a terrorist or hacker disables node 005, the system collapses immediately and completely. There is no gradual decline when this topology is attacked at the obvious point of vulnerability. Sure, you can protect node 005 with a fortress, but if your attack comes from within, then your external moat is useless.

The normal knee-jerk reaction to these models is to connect every node to every other node and create a full mesh design. This pattern does prevent any single node from being a rich target, and it minimizes the path length between any two nodes in the network. When under attack, network performance degrades gradually, allowing for opportunity to repel the attack before the network is completely disabled. Although a full mesh network is the most efficient and most resilient, it is also the most expensive to build and to expand. Is there a network pattern that gives us good efficiency and acceptable resilience?

A partial mesh blends several of the previous network patterns and gives us an effective combination of efficiency, resilience and cost. Figure 4 shows a partial mesh pattern.

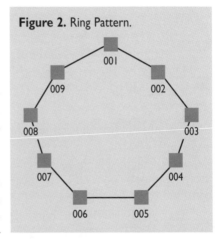

Figure 2. Ring Pattern.

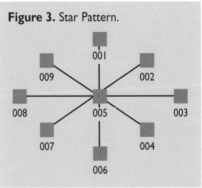

Figure 3. Star Pattern.

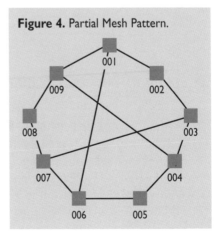

Figure 4. Partial Mesh Pattern.

A partial mesh design has another benefit. It is more difficult for the attacker to uncover the most vulnerable nodes and links to attack — there are no simple rules to follow. The attacker must know the full topology of the network and must then calculate network metrics in order to discern the best target(s).

■ Combining Patterns

Most large networks such as WANs, supply webs, distribution grids, roadways, and social networks are complex combinations of basic network patterns. Combining many simple patterns, in unique ways, gives us complex networks like the Internet. Figure 5 shows a very small part of the Internet mapped in late 2001. In this map we see many of the patterns shown in Figures 1 through 4. The black links form the backbone of this section and are in the pattern of a partial mesh. We also see chains, stars and rings.

A common fear is that one day the Internet will be attacked and brought to a halt. Is this possible? I think it is very unlikely that the whole Internet can be disabled, but it is very likely that parts of the Internet can be dislodged from the whole.

Like many large, emergent networks, the Internet follows a core and periphery structure. The core of the network is very densely connected resulting in a high redundancy of links and a tight coupling of systems and devices — almost a full mesh. Attacking the Internet at its core will not do great damage. Even widespread, repeated attacks at the core will not fragment this worldwide structure. On the other hand the periphery of the network is vulnerable. Looking around the edges of Figure 5 we see many of the patterns that we found to be vulnerable.

■ Location, Location, Location

The same law as in real estate — location, location, location — governs networks. Value and security are largely determined by your location in the network. In real estate it is the physical geography. In networks it is the link structure that determines good or poor location. Where are your company's knowledge resources and information assets located? Can they be easily pruned from the network? Are they at the end of a single spoke? How many

Figure 5. The Internet Network as Mapped in Late 2001.

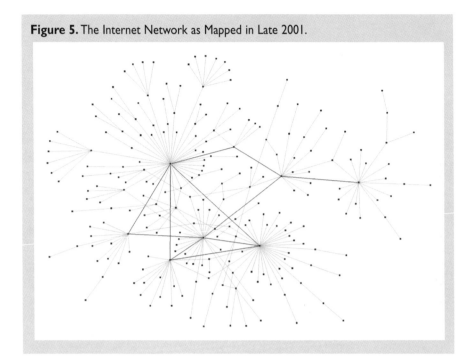

paths do they have to the backbone? How long are these paths? Do your paths travel along cables that all go through one vulnerable physical structure such as a bridge or tunnel or a skyscraper?

No matter what type of network you are building you will create a better topology by knowing the patterns that make up the greater whole. Given the chaotic complexity of the world, gaining insight into how patterns are assembled to build more complex structures represents a competitive advantage in the new economy.

Valdis Krebs is an organizational consultant and the author of Inflow™, *a software-based social systems analysis methodology that maps and measures knowledge exchange, information flow, informal networks, communities of practice and emergent groups within and between organizations. Krebs is a collaborative researcher with Ernst & Young's Center for Business Innovation and has degrees in Mathematics, Computer Science and Human Resources. He can be reached at* **valdis@orgnet.com**.

■ Endnotes

1   "September 11 Attacks Prompt De-
centralization Moves," *Computerworld,* Volume 35, Number 51, December 17, 2001,
p. 10.

Reprinted from the *IHRIM Journal,* Volume VI, Number 2, March 2002, pp. 37-39.

Part Seven:
Our Global Future

"Fasten your seat belts, the turbulence has scarcely begun. Unless evolution has radically changed its ways, we are facing an explosion of societal diversity and complexity hundreds of times greater than we now experience or can yet imagine. If we think to perpetuate the old ways, we should try to recall the last time evolution rang our number and asked consent."

—Dee Hock

• • • • • • • •

The emergence of the boundaryless business world raises numerous questions that resist quick, much less definitive, answers. Solutions (which will likely be somewhat provisional) are achieved through dialogue between differing viewpoints. Such dialogue exemplifies one of the principles of globalization: that the organization's collective knowledge grows through the interaction of a range of expertise. That principle motivates this entire book.

Hardly anyone doubts that globalization is the defining condition of business in the 21st century. But there is room for disagreement about its implications. In this final section on boundaryless HR, two important thinkers in the field differ on how to balance the local and the global in the organization. We hope you'll find the counterpoint illustrative of the need to manage and reconcile the paradoxes that exist in the business world — indeed throughout our every day lives.

Global Networks, Local Systems

BY ROBERT H. STAMBAUGH

"They've paved paradise and put in a parking lot."

—Joni Mitchell

• • • • • • • •

■ Introduction

A year or so ago, I wrote a series of four articles for the IHRIM *Journal*,[1] each one addressing some aspect of post-modern HRIS behavior and environments. I introduced the term "post-modern" to describe the overall information ecosystem we in HRIS are creating and nurturing as soon as we migrate to systems that use the Internet and tools associated with it to extend, expand, and make accessible the knowledge about HR that exists in the enterprise today and will be added in the future.[2] The terms "create" and "nurture" are critical to understanding our new relationship with such systems, because these systems take on a virtual life of their own as soon as the human constituents in their networks achieve a certain critical level of "connectedness." They become "self-aware;" they begin to exhibit patterns of behavior similar to those in living organisms. These quasi-living systems are becoming an object of study by both hard and soft sciences, and they are collectively referred to as CAS, short for "complex adaptive systems."[3] The connectedness in question can be local, national or worldwide; geography, proximity and boundaries make little difference to networks.

Once this critical level is attained, information systems managers not only lose control of the people who use (and thus make up) the systems, but also of the systems themselves. This loss of control means that, except in very artificial and short-lived circumstances, we are no longer able to consciously "engineer" our systems for increased productivity, efficiency, precision or reliability.[4] We can, however, influence their content, direction and reach — most of the time.[5] And such influence allows us to guide the systems in a direction that benefits the organization as a whole. When we exert our influence wisely, we are usually able to amplify the HR environment's potential for creativity and participation across the entire enterprise, and — at a minimum — we set the stage for a learning organization. Conversely, when we attempt to "optimize" and "engineer" these same systems, we undermine their promise and rob them of their vitality.[6] Along with the systems, we regress to pencil pusher status and begin a long, slow decline to marginality in the business world of the 21st century.[7]

… when we attempt to "optimize" and "engineer" these same systems, we undermine their promise and rob them of their vitality.[6]

My earlier articles focused on the evolutionary pressures that delivered of our circa-1999 HRIS environment and the myriad satellite systems that had accumulated at its periphery, especially where our systems intersected other niches in the larger corporate ecosystem. The increase in "intersections" or collisions due to the expansion of the Internet was only beginning. Although I viewed Internet-based systems as different from their predecessors, primarily because of the way they influenced behavior in areas like individual employee communication, collaboration and creativity, they were not yet evolved enough to exhibit many traits of a mature HRIS, and the shape of their challenge to older-era systems was not clear. Hosted systems and ASP use were minimal at best and didn't offer enough specifics to justify their inclusion as a "center" or scaffolding for a new tier of HRIS functionality. Thus in earlier analyses, the differentiator of Tier Three systems remained the less-than-tangible nuances of functionality created by the inter-workings of the Net and its far-flung users. Things were informal — even fluid — and Tier Three systems were a work in progress.

Two years later, we are more frequently faced with the prospect of separate and unique, but competing, HRIS systems and environments that are — or could become — functional equals to our primary HRIS. Potential competitive systems nearby (those from a renegade division, a merger/acquisition, etc.) have been joined by more geographically dispersed systems in other countries. For the first time, the HRIS ecosystem is becoming crowded — overpopulated, in fact — and is experiencing real evolutionary pressures and competition along lines other than vendor differences or simple tier versus tier functionality.

From a pre-Internet perspective, of course, the impact of this competition or "race" was moot in 1999; the financial costs and management challenges associated with encouraging or maintaining two "peer" HRIS were overwhelming. Multiple systems were seen as inefficient. So, when potential competitors emerged, massive pressures from the old "control" core and even later ERP installations were brought to bear, and numerous promising and locally responsible new HRIS initiatives were stomped out before they could take root. At least two Fortune 100 semiconductor companies pulled back from "separate but equal" systems developments in Asia in favor of less popular but more politically correct ERP "solutions" emanating from North America. The self-knowledge they might have gained via internal development was lost forever, just as the meaning of fossils and the remnants of early cites are compromised when excavation values only the old artifacts, not their interrelationships.

But at the leading edge of today's technology, new systems options for managing an organization's HR "assets" or associates have continued to emerge, and the timing of their debut is no coincidence; they're appearing just in the nick of time, as out current models begin to fray around the edges. They are especially suited to their local ecosystem — the people, cultures and work expectations that prevail in their home countries. The Net enables them. Informal communities create and use them. They are a factor of 21st century business life, and they cannot be eradicated. Instead of adopting a non-changeable "outside the scope of discussion" approach to these multiple systems, we now need to re-examine how we treat and co-exist with other non-U.S.-centric HR ecosystems, whether or not they (and we) benefit from standardization and engineering. We need to revisit how our overall strategies contribute to or undermine emerging corporate issues like effectiveness of asset utilization, intellectual property and human asset management[8].

Issues like these are especially relevant as our physical networks expand and HRIS increases its embrace of a "global system" approach to managing employees and associates in multiple sites, countries and regions around the world. To understand the globalization challenges we face during such a shift, it's helpful to look a little more deeply at what's really going on in the postmodern, multi-tier environment of today's post-modern systems.

■ Multi-Tier Systems, Multi-Polar Practices

The HRIS complexes we work with today all comprise multiple levels or tiers of operating HRIS. There's always the basic record-keeping/control system that sits at the core of the HRIS environment. The core is not all that comprehensive — it gets by with about one hundred data elements,[9] and few, if any, of its functions provide competitive advantage to the organization as a whole in emerging 21st century HR and business environments. These "core" systems are a little like the autonomic nervous system in higher order animals; they allow us to breathe and conduct a lot of other necessary functions *unconsciously*, and they do it so well that, apart from specialty areas where we introduce expanded capabilities via neuro-linguistic programming or advanced yoga, there's little we can do to improve on nature's design. So we don't keep tinkering with it. Companies occasionally exchange one of these core systems for another, and outsourcing of core functions is becoming more common. The motivation for such shifts, however, isn't strategic but rather operational — a little like having a pacemaker installed to provide some "out of sight, out of mind" assistance in everyday tasks.

This core system exerts control at every turn. Where its definitions and practices go unquestioned, its influence is absolute. Processes are designed around it. That's true at headquarters and everywhere around the globe. The problem is, the black-and-white issues the core system was created to handle have become less distinct; we're now working in grayscale and color, and thus a newer tier of newer systems like client/server and ERP have been introduced to override or counter-balance some of the older core's

We — and our systems —

experience distress

at both individual

and organizational levels.

signals and decisions. Thirty years ago, for example, any applicant tracking system would have been expected to reject an applicant with more than two previous jobs in an 18-month period. Today's systems reflect a different reality, and we would expect them to flag the applicant for special processing due to his/her wealth of recent experience!

When the rules for care and feeding of the two systems environments diverge, two conflicting sets of orders start pulling us in different directions. We — and our systems — experience distress at both individual and organizational levels. We usually override the demands that emanate from the core, instead trusting more sophisticated and specialized "second generation" responses to the problem at hand. For example, we don't just organize all our reports according to a "chart of accounts" sequence or to reflect how a payroll is processed, since that's not how more evolved HRIS operations are organized. Instead, we add a new layer of functionality to deal with newer business and environmental conditions, and we sort reports based on department or location. Or, stakeholders go to an informal system and detour around the one-right-way-to-organize "rules" we've been given. This ambivalence is the state of the HRIS today. Our centralized "core" systems can't keep up with the demands of multiple, simultaneous, divergent external business environments or the communities that form part of the system itself, and so the core shrieks for additional control — and we sometimes respond with more of what isn't working, more control, more reporting, more integration and less diversity!

This layering approach was satisfactory for a while, as we can see by looking at client/server expansion in the 1980s and ERP growth curves in the second half of the last decade, but as the pace of change in the business world increased, even ERP support couldn't keep up with the pace of change or different demands from multiple, different parts of the system. We're seeing a mild example of this phenomenon today, with battles back and forth on the subject of privacy — not just narrowly defined employee information privacy, but broader worldwide consumer privacy practices. Pure ERP monoliths have evolved through vertical versioning (special configurations for the energy business, the shoe business and local government), alliances and plug-ins or personalized portals.

You can actually interpret the history of HRIS in the 1990s through the lens of these repeated efforts of this core system to re-exert its one-size-fits-all control approach over many different and newer ecosystems and the data/information the latter groups required. In some instances, like ERP, they've experienced temporary success (as long as we define success according to the preferences of denizens of the old core system — once we ask today's stakeholders about success, the answer is usually different). Just like the dinosaurs' lizard descendants today, the ERP's in their own "control" ecosystems appear to be flourishing; but they're still dinosaurs, with the same "reptilian brain" at their center, and the same pre-programmed responses (read "best practices") that they exhibited from the start. That's *always* a problem, but in a "global" environment where speed and change are factors, it's becoming a real handicap. In fact, as they have attempted to respond to multiple, localized demands, ERP's have evolved and now offer some of the more flexible processing capabilities needed for the newer business world. This development reveals another underlying complex adaptive systems principle (CAS) — co-evolution. ERP's have become so tightly connected to how business works that they have no choice but to evolve as business changes. So much for stability and predictability in business.[10]

And just as it appears that an early collision between the earth and comets or meteors led to climatic shifts that doomed the dinosaurs to extinction or to shrinkage in size of geckos and iguanas today, so the rise of the Internet and its internal extensions seriously compromised the viability of ERP in its original jumbo systems format. The ERP strategy was automation, end-to-end process linkage and central control — not a particularly successful recipe in the face of broad, discontinuous, systemic change. After all, what we have succeeded in automating with our systems up to now is the *easy, basic, predictable* part of HR — those three terms describe what we used to call "clerical work" in a less politically correct era. We're now dallying with employee self-service and its big cousin, managerial self-service. Big deal — they're still part of the autonomic system. They're not strategic. They don't direct business activity. Our systems have scarcely touched the higher order functions, and if we remain tightly linked to the precepts of ERP, it's unlikely we will do so in the next decade or so. Why? It is because the real world just changes too fast *for our systems* to keep up.[11]

Nevertheless, we — *the human stakeholders of these systems* — do keep up. We manage to get by because we communicate with each other and learn from each other — we network. We each see things differently, we reach different conclusions and solutions to problems, and we share the differences among our communities of practice (COP). We pick things apart, not because we think we can understand how they work when they're reassembled, but because we're searching for new threats and opportunities that have emerged from the changing world in which we live and work.[12] This CAS issue of emergence is pivotal to us and to our systems. Without this human ability to recognize patterns that presage an emerging problem (as opposed to a problem the "engineers" identified and for which they developed practices and data structures in response), we're in the same fix as the dinosaurs. Thanks to the Net, however, we have both our individual capability and the expanded system — nervous system if you will — to deal with these new threats.

What we need to do now is embed and *internalize*, not just use, networks and network tools as a part of our HR and HRIS everyday practice. This means more than adding a browser interface to a "Tier Two" system, although the browser route isn't a bad way to start building a bridgehead away from Tier Two operations. To use a biological analogy again, we need to pursue consciously the same strategy singled celled organisms, like amoebas, followed billions of years ago; recognize other organisms that function well and exploit a part of the same overall environment we inhabit, and then appropriate their "secrets" simply by engulfing them intact into our own cellular structure. That's how humans acquired chloroplasts and mitochondria and, perhaps, even DNA as a part of their makeup.[13] Our cells allowed these foreign bodies to keep working at what they did well in their local environments — we didn't "re-engineer" them for tight linkages to our own space and needs, because that would have created such a specialized entity that even very minor changes in the ecosystem would have killed the entire population overnight.

In general, this appropriation of other approaches is what's happening in leading edge companies as they start to create Tier Three systems. However, you won't see much overt activity associated with change in corporate charters and ROI summaries. That's because the newer systems and their users are *informal*, hidden in the interstices of current systems, and preoccupied with creating locally effective results, even when they have to maintain a different system and interface for the "corporate" world. We all know people who use such personal systems.[14]

Notice that the biological processes at work here didn't require reworking the mitochondria to do everything like their hosts — that would have been a waste of a good-fit response to the environment, and it would have reduced the diversity of options for the cell instead of the other way around. Nature — which appears to be mighty efficient in the long view — doesn't like to work that way — it makes use of what it finds. It much prefers *increasing* variety and difference, even if it's a little messier than any of the "engineered" alternatives.[15] Enough scientists have watched this phenomenon in action that they have elevated it to an accepted part of their science — what's termed the "principal of requisite variety." In short, if a system isn't more varied and complex than the environment in which it exists and has to exploit, it's doomed to gradual starvation and death. Later, we'll apply that thought to the emerging global environment and examine whether a "global" strategy that removes variety to make administrative activity easier is effective — or just an efficient way to insure disaster down the road.

So that's where we are today, three parallel, co-existing systems: Tier One control systems, Tier Two standards guardians and emerging Tier Three connective groupings. Each is a little less control-oriented than its predecessor, each attempting to advance its special functions in this uneasy HRIS partnership, and each now challenged by the need to come to terms with whole new ecosystems — different shareholders, business practices and definitions. When we look at HRIS operations globally, we need to recognize that all three tiers of activity are always at work. It's not as simple as choosing a model for organizing far-flung processing. In fact, it's enormously more complex.[16]

■ Global Reach

Here we are in 2002, addressing the creation, reorganization or support for "global HRIS." I'm really not sure how to define that term, other than I will know a global system when I see it. However, in the interests of brevity, I'll accept Karen Beaman and Al Walker's definitions of the "global" entity in a recent issue of the IHRIM Journal[17] and reprinted in this volume. The authors identify four approaches to such systems and differentiate them along the lines of centralization, responsiveness to local issues, and the ability to leverage and share "innovation and learning" on a worldwide basis.

Specifically, they identify:

➤ Multinational,

➤ Global,

➤ International, and

➤ Transnational.

These are variations on the basic global theme. While this segmentation is an excellent starting point for understanding the options available to architects of a "modern" system environment (one that is based on formal organization, believes in "standards," and has a bias toward innovation as opposed to break-through creativity and learning), it stops at the near edge of Tier Three thinking and opportunity. In other words, it fails to address most of the components of the "post-modern" ecosystem and the special demands these components generate among HRIS practitioners today. It also minimizes the personal and organizational prerequisites to "breakthrough" knowledge creation — as opposed to innovative behavior— and dissemination/sharing of the "learnings" that result.[18] Likewise, there's a failure to account for the already significant and still growing role of informal networks in this process.

Again, this is not to say that "global" systems such as the authors describe are not appropriate responses to a particular stage of corporate development and HR management; in fact, they are the lynchpin or centerpiece in Tier Two HRIS evolution. They are perfectly positioned to benefit from and balance the Tier One and Tier Two structures noted earlier in this chapter.

They do not, however, define the future individual support and HR-ecosystem goal toward which leading edge companies today should aspire. In fact, some of their more efficiency-oriented attributes are rapidly becoming a strategic handicap. Let's look at the reasons for this assertion.

■ Connections in a Networked World

Let's return for just a moment to HR systems "by the numbers" — those multiple tiers of older and newer systems that are functioning in today's operating environment as well as the playing fields we will be using long into the future. I introduced and explored above the concept of the core or foundation tier, where basic data resides, where retrospective analysis and reports are prepared for "control" purposes, and where interfaces exist to other similar systems in our organizations and beyond our walls. (The IRS and the OFCCP are examples of these external links.) By the mid 1990s, we were well along the way to outsourcing many components of this core: benefits administration, pension, payroll, and EEO reporting. Part of the reason for this shift was to remove the systems and processes in question from proximity to higher-level corporate issues — quarantining Tier One systems to prevent undue exercise of control.

For the most part, these older systems process *data*. It's interesting to note that almost all of the foundation systems treat people as interchangeable — we identify them as "numbers," not as names. I generally place them under the catchall title of "smokestack" systems since they were developed for the data-processing based management styles of the mass-production manufacturing era.[19] The kind of "associates"[20] they're meant to track are interchangeable. Today's "data model" approach to systems is a more sophisticated approach to the same problem.

I also introduced the idea of a related second tier of systems — LAN's, C/S, etc. — that essentially replicates the earlier "core" function and composition, but with significant differences. First, these systems have been freeze-dried and shrunken so they are affordable by smaller companies. They're less powerful than some of their predecessors, but they can be maintained by local IT specialists. And they're all anti-control if used discretely. Corporate specialists are neither required nor wanted. Again, system evolution parallels nature, where the dinosaurs' brute force couldn't match the speed, diversity, and ingenuity of smaller competitors when the overall ecosystem began to change. Second, Tier Two systems are relatively expandable, and can be combined with or used in conjunction with "best-of-breed" offerings for non-core functionality. They *appear* responsive, at least in a relative sense. Although it isn't part of their definition, the profile of such systems usually reveals a few separate "companion" systems that don't even link directly with the main "core" package, but do share (through interface or duplicate entry) some baseline data for each employee. More important, they provide the "receptors" that allow us to append other, newer, richer data related to the employee himself/herself and how he/she relates to the business unit. These can be the beginnings of information, not data, processing complexities.[21]

Although it may not appear so at first, ERP systems are just another variant on this Tier Two system approach; they combine some of the richer functionality from LAN and client/server options with their "velvet glove" approach to increased control via "right way" practices. They automate more and thus deliver significant increases in corporate efficiency — at a price[22]. Their price is eradication of many areas of discretion where daily issue-resolution calls for creative HR problem solving—where HR people can make an immediate real world difference by personalizing and balancing their actions between "associate" needs and corporate strategic direction *according to local needs and conditions, not global or "HQ" norms.*

In pre-Internet days, each time the system encounters a danger or an unexpected business condition, the response included detailed analysis, re-engineering and retrofit with "sound" IT practices. I've labeled this Tier Two systems area "status quo" because it acts as a leveler; systems here maintain things as they are, or with only the minor, incremental improvements possible in their slow-moving, non-volatile, homogeneous world. The problem is that world began to disappear in the 1970s and was completely gone in most parts of the world by the mid-1990s. Even when they deliver "same day" information to their stakeholders, by the time those deliveries are personalized and applied, the opportunities they represented are generally gone.

Tier Three systems utilize a wider range of tactics for getting beyond the 1990s.[23] A few forward-looking firms have developed true data warehouses that combine information from multiple sources and thus present analysts with the immediate "requisite variety" needed for learning. Other leading-edge software in areas like compensation management or workforce planning are beginning to offer prospective — forward looking — analysis instead of the old, "yesterday's news" reporting. This encouraging trend in business today is occurring thanks to new players in the HRIS arena,[24] often via ASP's, aggregators and the like. In this tier, we also see linkages between different HRIS and their plug-in extensions, warehouses and analytic/graphic offerings — all via the Internet.

With the arrival of these systems, and their linkage via the Internet, we in HR are finally *poised* for a contribution to the knowledge creation business and the learning organization — two key components in the organization of the future. But the old control mentality kicks in yet again, with the IT/engineering approach to knowledge management and storage (that is, "rules" and control!). But this new knowledge can't be produced on schedule, according to a Gantt chart and list of deliverables. Most of it will be uncovered accidentally, not by design. Nobody at a corporate headquarters is prescient enough to know what local breakthroughs will have downstream organizational meaning. In short, knowledge — except for run-of-the-mill stuff — will not become a commodity, and it won't be managed — period. According to the old rules, it will be deployed quickly and efficiently around the enterprise precisely to the extent that it doesn't threaten the status quo, challenge data definitions and best practices and the like.

In short, the very structures that finally allow knowledge creation and true innovation in the enterprise run the risk of continued suffocation from the "gravitational pull" of the older systems on which they rest. If we concentrate on ERP and its hallmark reports, standards and "one best way" logic, we lose an immense amount of knowledge and insight about the company and its problems. This dichotomy between control and "open" knowledge management initiatives has been around for years; it is becoming pivotal to our futures in the global, connected workplace we are creating today.

■ Global Initiatives: Specific Threats and Concerns and Countermeasures

That's the prospect in the abstract. Let's look at it specifically as it impacts the issue of global systems. Why should we be afraid of old Tier One and Two systems and the infrastructures they have spawned? Why should we be afraid of the collateral damage they can cause?

First, because there's a very real threat of what's basically U.S., British, German and Canadian "electronic colonialism," there's hardly a system out there that doesn't begin with a business model whose foundation is North American or Western European business and IT practice. The last time I looked, that base represented less than one-fifth of the world's population and only one particular slant on business. Our approach (especially the accounting/ROI orientation we're all familiar with today) has been around with only minor variation since it was first invented in fifteenth century Florence. Since most of the rest of the world is only now embarking on "modern" trade, human resource practice, we need to allow other groups as much "slack" as possible in their development. We have to minimize the "best practices," assumptions, definitions and organizational forms we impose on the rest of the world and let them develop what's effective — not just efficient — locally.[25] Many of our best multi-national companies and most of our experienced expatriates understand the need for local creativity in business dealings, including HR dealings. We need to extend that mindset to systems and reporting as well. This ties directly to what the information in our systems actually means and what we use it for. Anyone who has spent time in the Far East, Scandinavia or Latin America will tell you about some of the special information they need to cope with business demands locally. (U.S. and European Union privacy concerns, for example, aren't anything like those in India or China. And data meaning/interpretation needs no further comment than the recent U.S.-Chinese quarrel over the Orion spy plane incident.)

In short, global systems thinking as practiced today is condescending, and it is often blatant colonialism.[26] We need to rethink the entire HR and HRIS model framework we use, up to and including their basic building blocks — the "individual employee" focus that forms the base for HR systems everywhere, , or individually defined roles and competencies for reward and recognition purposes. Who's to say that the most telling insights into good business process and practice in China or North Dakota aren't hidden behind the imposed-from-above, Tier One "employee" façade, ready to emerge if we recast our artifacts to focus on, say, work teams as the primary organizational unit?

Second, when we "globalize," we do so in large part as a means of increasing system speed and efficiency. That's a learned type of goal-seeking behavior; once we carry out initial automation — that is, once we get beyond a few "dumb" processes, we are rarely successful at either goal. We struggle for speed because management wants information "now," but the infrastructure we have built up and engineered to meet that demand ensures delays and out-dated information. Worse yet, our approach to streamlining and downsizing has left us without many mid-level managers — the very part of the workforce that wields the "sense-making" capability that observers like Karl Weick[27] have identified as a primary role of organizations everywhere. It should go without saying that until we know our overseas allies, fellow associates and subsidiaries' working conditions a lot better, we ought to protect and enable global middle managers as a part of developing global systems capacity.

Third, we standardize and summarize the information or data that arrives from the field. It's long been generally accepted practice to scrub what's submitted by remote sites, both as a precaution to prevent the introduction of bad data into the core repository or warehouse, and as a means of keeping report recipients focused on what's happening in the "mainstream" business. In the post-modern world, we need to split the input stream into two equally valuable information sources. The first — with the traditional edits and aggregation — feeds the Tier One "control mechanisms" of the organization. The second stream, however, emphasizes the anomalies and outer data. It allows us to harness what Kevin Kelly calls the "power of the swarm" — all the individual associate's sensors as they pick up and report on minute changes in the operating environment they personally encounter.[28] It's critical to remember the underlying assumption from the complexity theory — that tiny changes anywhere on the periphery of a system can quickly balloon into a threat or opportunity for the entire system. In other words, big changes emerge from small, unexpected, and seemingly inconsequential happenings — exactly what we screen out as "noise" in multinational and global systems.

Fourth, we concentrate on streamlining *formal* channels of communication. Headcount reports "roll up" by division or by region. Salaries are grouped by region or project. We organize according to organizational charts and charts of accounts. We even compare performance of one entity against "similarly situated" business units elsewhere in the organization, although it's doubtful that any two entities anywhere are "similarly situated" today. There is all this to consider despite our lip service to diversity! We know from studies of knowledge creation that new learning stems from diverse groups sprinkled throughout the company and even beyond its boundaries, specifically from how multiple groups interact with each other. They identify, weigh, discuss, and adopt different behaviors and pass them on to other groups. Centralized control — globalized presence — intimidates these groups and relegates their contributions to back alleys of the organization. We need to bring them more visibility instead[29]

Fifth, the power of the center impacts the ability to communicate quickly and directly from the boundaries of the organization to those in central "power" positions. "HQ" is, in most instances, a "black hole" when it comes to communicating among far-flung parts of the organization. Like real black holes, messages (and their meanings) are swallowed up when they get close to a corporate function. Bad information is discarded, "good" information is bent by "gravity" — the interests of the powers that be — and the resulting garbled messages seldom reach their designated targets unscathed. A classic "catch-22" situation is thus perpetuated; we get rid of the informal information because it doesn't meet our formal IT expectations — which it could do only if IT didn't remove the questionable content, which is what leads IT to conclude the information is of little value for corporate uses.

Again, the prescription is to move away from the models or global "reach," and embrace instead the potential for ubiquity and flexibility of the Net, leaving the choice of how and what to communicate to each separate, local group — and allowing it all to be open to revision each time local conditions change. Proponents of the "control" side global approach argue that such laissez-faire attitudes make it costly, difficult, and inconvenient to aggregate and summarize multiple pieces of information about behavior and operating reality in line operations. Proponents of this less structured approach reply that we should stop looking at what we did well or badly and instead concentrate on what we have the opportunity to improve in the future. Again, this is efficiency versus effectiveness.

> *The only sure way to "share" knowledge today is from one local group to another local group; enough local sharing simply adds up to global knowledge dissemination.*

Next, we utterly *decimate* knowledge creation by trying to manage and manipulate its subsequent valuation, dissemination and use from any central place.[30] The idea that we can somehow package local knowledge as "best practice" and then export it for broad consumption elsewhere is rapidly losing credibility, because in the new HR environment, the flexibility of the Internet allows us to create tailored personal workspaces. The only sure way to "share" knowledge today is from one local group to another local group; enough local sharing simply adds up to global knowledge dissemination. Best practice may have worked for transactional systems processing in the core areas of payroll and benefits administration, but it's not for workforce planning, logistics and strategy. Instead of this control-"global" approach, we need further localization and then better, more open networks and networking to allow more and more COP's an opportunity to encounter, discuss and improve practices that work in there space. If the networks are available, COP's and other informal structures will use them to disseminate and share learning better than any centralized unit could hope to do.

Whether we think about swarms of gnats or piranhas that, in groups, have devastating affect on humans, or swarms of mini-earthquakes that appear to precede and thus predict earthquakes, there's no denying the overall cumulative impact of many small and independent actions. They reach a critical mass and — bang! — we're suddenly and often painfully aware of their presence. At local levels, that awareness sets in sooner than at higher levels of the hierarchy — the "pain" threshold is lower. "Managing" and interpreting global HR behavior from a distance uses techniques that impede the natural actions of such swarms. According to the practices associated with the models of global systems noted above, we smooth out aberrant behaviors. We clean bad data. We lose specifics among averages. Instead, we need new analytic tools that are sensitive to small changes — and again, we need the network bandwidth so different groups can discuss and diagnose little events and then test countermeasures locally as well.

Next, Tier Two global systems appear to function best when they minimize or eradicate boundaries. While that is a goal of efficiency-oriented twentieth century operations, it's another hurdle in the race for innovation and knowledge creation. Once again, here's the rationale: we learn best and most when we encounter new and different ways of looking at, describing and working with the same general problems. When we standardize things first (as with data models or business models), we eliminate the very differences we should be examining as possible threats or opportunities in the future.[31] The prescription here is to open up access to the Internet and World Wide Web, encourage its use through provision of enough slack time to encourage exploration, and then develop virtual, online "fairs" where netizens display their learnings for other to use.

... we learn best and most when we encounter new and different ways of looking at, describing and working with the same general problems.

Cultural frictions present another problem. This issue shares many characteristics with the "neo-colonialism" theme I introduced earlier, but it's also alive and well in another guise. Global systems (actually, any of the organizational forms/models noted in the Beaman/Walker article) are built to optimize management and control of the workforce in a particular combination of corporate and geographical cultures.[32] Similarly, regional systems, where they exist, optimize a regional view of business, commerce and human value. North American/Western European systems all emphasize variations on a theme of quantitative analysis, efficiency, short term planning and results-oriented behavior. In the U.S., there are classic examples of misfit at regional levels (regions are, after all, global entities as well — just with truncated horizons). Silicon Valley versus Route 128 offers one example.[33]

Another issue stems from the efficiency versus effectiveness battle that lurks just beneath the surface of every multi-tier surface. Efficiency and control go hand in hand. Effectiveness doesn't happen without practices that are, by their nature, inefficient. Given today's information technology— we can't afford effective global systems in economic terms, and we cannot afford the institutional impoverishment that accompanies all-out efficiency.[34]

Older systems were created in a period of relative stability in the world economy and even greater calm at national and local levels. Most of their reporting conventions are designed to help keep operations on an even keel in the face of small and somewhat predictable change. And that goal is supported via control-oriented systems and the models noted in Beaman and Walker's article. Most of the familiar tools of our trade, like mainstream compensation planning and administration, are exquisitely sensitive to minor shifts in the compensation world, and it's not overly difficult to make annual adjustments to an ongoing program. But trade yesterday's compensation world for what we're facing today, or for the "auction block" buying and selling of mercenary talent we're starting to encounter now, and we're again back to local experimentation, local strategies, Net-based sharing, and differential adoption when it makes sense to do so.

Last and worst is the cumulative effect of all the issues I've surfaced in this chapter. We aren't just a new generation of colonizers whose practices severely constrain workplace choices in 2002. *We are also colonizing our own, and others' futures.* Our attempts at standardization of approaches and definitions and by-the-book allocation of responsibility among local/regional/and global systems managers collectively straitjacket our planners. When we tell our global stakeholders how things should be, we marginalize every other approach to what futures could be for us all. We are precluding choice and creativity in favor of standards and uniformity. We are giving up the struggles and mistakes that lead to understanding and knowledge.

We need to look at each site and facility in a country or region as a new opportunity to learn from how people and work interact in this new and constantly changing century. We need to concentrate on the contracts and equations between and among workers and employers at the most basic levels; are there emerging needs and support patterns? Will scientific management and the Western faith in reductionist approaches to understanding complex systems yield the knowledge we need to innovate and adapt in other parts of the world? Can we learn from isolated groups and cultures how to leverage apprenticeships, guilds and the like? What exactly does a U.S. definition of turnover mean in a culture where people work seasonally and have never experienced regular jobs? Sometimes, we'll find a fit and other times a miss. Gradually, local communities and systems will gravitate towards like systems and like problems — wherever they are. Political scientists term this pattern bi- or tri-multipolarity, depending upon the number of "super sites" or corporate concentrates smaller systems cluster around.

Those of us lucky enough to work with or in a global company where you can experience this level of uncertainty, lack of structure, and ebb-and-flow network coalescence will probably be *the last* HR *professionals ever to encounter "un-engineered" and un-Westernized work cultures* face-to-face with real-life "what-if" scenarios from which we can learn. Let's connect these sites and redefine global systems very simply: local HRIS that use networks to trade data and information back-and-forth, each according to needs of the moment. That way, we can keep looking and learning from the diversity that exists out there. Let's forget about leveraging, fine-tuning, standardizing, and otherwise sucking the creative life out of them.

■ Conclusion

I suppose it is possible to doubt this somewhat pessimistic view of global and control-oriented systems. But before you dismiss it outright, let me leave you with a single image.

Several years ago, during a visit to Australia, I was passing the time before lunch in a colleague's office — looking at his various mementos, pictures and maps. One of the maps was especially interesting: a photograph of our earth, blue and white and green, suspended against a black backdrop of space and stars. At the top of the globe was — you guessed it — Australia! It was the first time I had consciously realized how parochial we (the American/Europeans) and our artifacts really are, believing that it's "right" to have our country at the top and in the middle of a map. The reason I never questioned the positioning before, and the reason I had never seen that interpretation of cartography before, goes directly to the kind of global systems we in HR and HRIS want as a part of our knowledgebase.

We never saw "Oz" at the top because we only had access to the standard maps, the standard definitions, and the best practices of the whole cartography business. That's just for maps. Think how many more opportunities we miss when we apply "global" thinking and management structures to people and communities and networks, and the solutions "unmanaged" groups have created for many of the problems we all face in our own uncertain future.

Give these groups a network, and you'll get a functioning global system in return — at no extra cost.

Bob Stambaugh is president of Kapa'a Associates, where he has explored the role of emerging technologies in future work environments with more than 50 Fortune 1000 clients. He was previously employed as a financial industries analyst and project leader at SRI International. He has also developed and managed HRIS *capabilities and* HR *information centers at Crocker Bank,* Intel *Corporation, and Atari. He was vice president of* VRC *Consulting Group and was western region manager and vice president of the* Hunter *Group. With more than 30 years experience in* HR *and* HRIS, *Stambaugh is a co-founder of* IHRIM *(formerly* HRSP), *whose first meeting occurred in his office in San Francisco about 20 years ago. He is a former Bay Area* IHRIM *chapter director and president, and has served four terms as a member of* IHRIM's *Board of Directors. In 2000, he received* IHRIM's *Summit Award for his lifetime contribution to the* HRIS *discipline. In addition to* IHRIM, *he is a member of* ACA, ACM, AHRI, AMA, HRPS, IEEE, SHRM, *and the* World Futures Society. *He is a frequent speaker and leader of seminars dealing with alternative futures and the use of hard/soft science tools and techniques in leading-edge* HRIS *initiatives for organizational effectiveness. He is the author of more than 75 reviews and articles and the editor of* 21 Tomorrows, *a recently published book of articles about the future of* HRIS. *His own book about managing post-modern human resource information environments is slated for publishing in 2002. He can be reached at* **bobstambaugh@earthlink.net**.

■ Endnotes

1 Stambaugh, Bob, "Post Modern HR Systems," *IHRIM Journal*. This four-part series began in March 1999 and ran through December 1999. Reprints are available from IHRIM.

2 For a comprehensive treatment of this issue, see Thomas H. Davenport's *Information Ecology: why technology is not enough for success in the information age*, Oxford University Press, 1997.

3 Following the initial migration of CAS from mathematical/hard science realms, its application in the soft sciences and organizational behavior is perhaps best exemplified by the works of Ralph Stacey and Margaret Wheatley. For an introduction to Stacey's work, see *Complexity and Creativity in Organizations*, Berrett-Koehler (1996). Meg Wheatley's *Leadership and the New Science: Discovering Order in a Chaotic World*, 2nd ed., Berrett-Koehler (1999) is a particularly easy-to-read introduction to this field. Interestingly, Stacey has begun to push beyond the organizational level CAS approach, and is now exploring the concept of "complex responsive processes in organizations," in a book by the same title, issued by Routledge in 2001.

4 This overall concept of self-awareness is referred to in CAS circles as autopoiesis. See Maturana and Varela's *Autopoiesis and Cognition: The Realization of the Living*, Reid, (1980).

5 This concept is a recurrent theme in Wheatley (1999) and in Michael McMaster's *The Intelligence Advantage: Organizing for Complexity*, Butterworth-Heinemann, 1996. McMaster's *The Praxis Equation: Design Principles for Intelligent Organisation* (1997) expands his concepts and introduces a number of easily applicable action plans for their use.

6 The best treatment of this phenomenon is Etienne Wenger's *Communities of Practice*, Cambridge University Press (1998).

7 We are seeing this phenomenon from an HRIS perspective not only with the shift of processing to third party administrators in the Benefits arena, but also with the wholesale outsourcing option pioneered by companies like Exult. As these barriers fall, we're likely to see Tom Stewart's *Fortune Magazine* discussion of total HR outsourcing become a reality.

8 It's interesting to note the progression in thinking represented by one of the true gurus in the "quantitative" HR field, Dr. Jac Fitz-Enz. His original book, *How to Measure Human Resources Management* (McGraw-Hill, 1984) has been a "bible" for Tier One and Tier Two managers since its original publication. As HR practice and systems have matured, he's added books such as *Human Value Management* (Jossey-Bass, 1990), and *The ROI of Human Capital* (AMACOM, 2000). His forthcoming book demonstrates a pronounced shift to the qualitative issues associated with our emerging "eWorld" — and our Tier Three systems.

9 The author's projects with nearly a dozen companies in various industries between 1987 and 2000 have all yielded counts of approximately 100 "core" data elements. Most additional data elements are discretionary. I suspect many such discretionary additions can be traced by Tier One control influences.

10 The differences between the Tier One "tight ship" efficiency approach and the looser, more relaxed stance required to profit from today's business opportunities is eloquently presented in Tom Demarco's new book, *Slack: Getting Past Burnout, Busywork, and the Myth of Total Efficiency*, Broadway: (2001).

11 Arthur Battram's *Navigating Complexity*, The Industrial Society, (1998) is a good introduction to the full range of dynamics at work in these processes.

12   This concept of learning and its basis in the concept of ba is well described in my "The Knowledge Creating HRIS: Learning to Live in the Messy World of Work," *IHRIM Journal*, March 2000, pp 8-18. A more scholarly presentation can be found in Nonaka and Takeuchi, *The Knowledge Creating Company*, Oxford 1995. See also Nonaka and Konno, "The Concept of ba: Building a Foundation for Knowledge Creation," *California Management Journal*, Spring 1998.

13   Recent research, summarized in several issues of *The New Scientist*, all point to a further wrinkle in this approach: the complexity needed to create the entire genetic makeup of a human comes not from many separate components, but from relatively few building blocks that are sequenced and resequenced via networks.

14   Electronic recruiting seeks to automate some or all tasks associated with the entire hiring process — and sometimes beyond. While the best of such systems offer real advances in recruiting, informal surveys show that "critical" hires and special situations are dealt with by informal, manual systems and shadow networks of stakeholders in the recruiting process. As long as we're recruiting people and not machines, this dichotomy will continue.

15   At this writing, much of the U.S. upper Midwest is underwater — a result of spring rains and thaws and the subsequent flooding of the Mississippi and other rivers. All this is courtesy of the Army Corps of Engineers, who "improved" many of the wetlands along the river out of existence. Once the absorptive capacity of the wetlands was gone, only the Corps' inadequate levee system prevented flooding. The same situation occurs when forestry personnel "manage" forests to prevent the annual fires that, if left to burn, prepare the area for better growth and protect against disastrous mega-fires.

16   See Bennett Reddin's "Reflections of the Landscape" in *IHRIM Journal*, 2001, Issue 2.

17   Karen Beaman and Alfred Walker, "Globalizing HRIS: The New Transitional Model," *IHRIM Journal*, October-December 2000.

18   A non-CAS approach to these issues can be found in Nitin Nohria and Sumantra Ghoshal's *The Differentiated Network: Organizing Multinational Corporations for Value* Creation, Jossey-Bass: (1997).

19   Demarco (2001) discusses, in detail, the idea and implications of fungal resources, see pages 13-21.

20   I've heard this term used before as a synonym for "employee," but it has never stuck. Jac Fitz Enz's forthcoming book uses the term so pervasively and persuasively that it may well become the preferred descriptor for workforce members in the new decade.

21   A number of early adopters of client/server (CS) systems overplayed the customization card as the extended CS reach to geographically remote parts of their organization. They attempted to customize core data, rather than developing parallel structures for core and local usage. When core reporting needs appeared to be in danger, the client/server experiments ended abruptly.

22   Again, see Demarco (2001) for a condemnation of "the myth of efficiency." More to the point for HRIS and HR professionals, see the recent *The HR Scorecard*, by Becker, Huselid, and Ulrich. There's an early and frequently reinforced admonition that efficiency is a necessary prerequisite in today's organization, but that effectiveness is where competitive potential resides.

23   Fitz-Enz (2001) and Becker, Huselid, and Ulrich (2001) both address this issue.

24   There are many top tier newcomers to choose from, but I recommend reviewing the approaches of Deploy, Icarian, Kadiri, and Workscape as representative of innovative and potentially "breakthrough" packages and capabilities today.

25   While the source is somewhat dated, Mary O'Hara-Devereaux and Bob Johansen's *Global Work: Bridging Distance, Time, and Cultures*, Jossey-Bass (1994) to understand the true magnitude of what a "global" system must balance. Ironically, the Internet doesn't appear to minimize these differences. In cultural contexts, it allows "small" cultures to act "large" — and this exacerbates the differences in the field.

26   *Building Cross-Cultural Competence: How to Create Wealth from Conflicting Values*, Charles Hampden-Turner and Fons Trompenaars' recent (Yale, 2000) addition to the "global" bookshelf illustrates this issue quite well. *Managing With a Global Mindset*, by Jean-Pierre Jeannet (Prentice Hall/Financial Times, 2000) is another fertile source for ideas that run parallel to many of the concepts I have introduced in this chapter. Jeannet's book is full of terrific diagrams and charts to help clarify this whole area of interest. Hampden-Turned and Trompenaars are more informal, but equally useful in this area.

27   Karl Weick's classic *Sensemaking in Organizations* (Sage, 1995) offers a pre-Internet description of what really needs to get done at an organizational level if values, culture, action plans, etc. are to be successful and strategically in line with overall company goals.

28   Kevin Kelly's "power of the swarm" and a raft of other powerful and often counter-intuitive notions are all included in his *Ten Rules for the New Economy*, Viking (1998).

29   See my article "Visions of the Future," in the *IHRIM Journal*, 2001, Issue 1.

30   See Wenger (1998)

31   See "Lessons From an Island's Knowledge," by Jeff Angus, in *Knowledge Management*, March 2001.

32   Once in a while, corporate management successfully reflects a marriage of two different cultures. I do not believe it to be an accident that Royal Dutch Shell, with its anglo-British mix of management styles and goals, has not only prospered for several centuries, but has consistently respected the people and the local cultures with which it interacts. See *The Living Company*, by Arie de Geus (Harvard Business Review Press, 1997).

33   Annalee Saxenian's doctoral thesis turned book, *Regional Advantage*, Harvard University Press (1994), details the broad differences that separate two cultures in the same country and, arguably, the same industry segment. Yet, there's rarely a satisfactory compromise when systems "for all of us" are the subject of debate for organizations with plants along Route 128 and in the Silicon Valley.

34   We can see this principle at work in attitudes toward government. In the U.S., we rail at inefficient governmental practice and processes, but we accept them as long as the overall government appears to be effective. We just don't want the kind of efficiency that is needed to deal with fuzzy issues like privacy. Cross "the pond" to Europe, where the EU data privacy regulations offer efficient approaches to privacy guarantees, and where citizens in Europe appear willing to accept them — a level of governmental interference in personal life that's absolutely anathema to many Americans. This kind of split is even more pronounced between Western and some non-Western cultures.

The Future of HR — Globalize or Perish
(the steps in transforming HR into a global powerhouse)

BY JOHN SULLIVAN, PH.D.

◼ A Changing Business World Demands Globalization

CEO's and business leaders have known for some time that if you are to succeed in the "new" business world it is essential that your firm expand its production, product design and sales efforts around the world. Cheap travel and communications, the Internet and the growth of third world economies means new and expanding markets for businesses. Mere expansion is not enough though. In order to globalize in the "new" business world, businesses must also learn how to use the evolving business and management practices that are necessary in order to do business in different countries around the world. Globalization does not mean that everyone in the organization must think and act the same way around the world. The key to globalizing effectively is to offer some percentage of required consistency and some degree of latitude for local managers. Much like the avocado, where the inside core is hard but the outside portion is flexible. Companies that do not expand their global reach or that fail to understand the need for global variations in management practices, are doomed to fail.

Many years of advising HR leaders on globalization efforts have made me a cynic, so proceed reading at your own risk. Globalization is invariably in the top three on any CEO's priority list, unfortunately it rarely has the same strategic priority for HR...and when it's even on the strategic radar screen, it is often approached as an independent "HR program" rather than a new way of thinking that permeates all of HR. My purpose here is to lay down the globalization gauntlet, offer a strategic versus tactical perspective and some out-of-the-box approaches to guide HR towards offering real value-added direction and services.

■ HR'S Changing Role in Globalization

A major part of any effort to understand global management practices includes knowing how to attract, retain, develop and increase productivity at numerous sites around the world. Developing and implementing global management practices is a shared role between HR and managers. Unfortunately in most cases, HR has failed to do its part. While globalization has been an HR buzzword for many years, in reality what HR actually does when it globalizes is frequently relatively simple and transactional in nature. For example, most HR programs that directly relate to globalization are primarily just relocation and expatriate programs. HR efforts involve mostly administration and even then, vendors, consultants or lawyers do most of the actual work.

At one large high-tech firm when we polled the international managers about what they thought about corporate HR, the responses were uniformly negative (no translating difficulties here). They ranged from "they never listen to us" to "we are the last to get new HR programs and when we do, they are barely modified versions of the U.S. program." It is also not surprising to find that few HR programs measure management's satisfaction with HR's contribution to productivity. We could not find a single HR department that polled international managers about HR's contribution to productivity. Even after extensive benchmarking, we couldn't identify a single HR function that even attempted to measure (employee) productivity variations between the different countries in which they had facilities. It's obvious that you can't improve productivity using HR programs, if you don't even measure its impact!

■ What's Wrong with Most "Globalized" HR Efforts

Businesses are seeking leadership in the process of globalization. Senior managers expect HR to take the lead rather than being a follower. But HR is seldom proactive. Rather than seeking out opportunities to assess new countries and new global opportunities, HR generally waits for management to tell it where it's going, and after the decision has already been made, it then builds programs to fit. As a result of this follower's approach, when it comes to globalizing, most HR professionals and functions are not major players. The programs they offer and the skills that they have are limited in scope and U.S.-centric at best.

■ The "one-size-doesn't-fit-any" HR Approach to Globalization

Everyone would like the world to be a simple place where simple solutions can be applied. Unfortunately though, the world is becoming increasingly complex. And as a result, rather than needing a single solution, most global situations require a range of solutions to fit the unique set of circumstances in that place and at that time. It might be true that all HR solutions (and their processes) need to share a common base (e.g., technologies and metrics), but the remaining portion of the solution must be customizable to fit local needs. Only accountants, fools and bureaucrats believe "one size" is ideal for every situation and in every region of the world. While most HR solutions are developed in a "one-size-fits-all" model, what is actually needed is a mass customized approach where "one-size-fits-one." The need for customization in HR and management solutions comes from a variety of factors that I call the "big eight."

➤ The "big eight" factors that create the need for flexibility in globalized HR operations

1. *Variations in business practices* — Stereotyping a country and its people can be a huge mistake. Even within U.S. borders, there are huge variations in what it takes to be a successful manager. Variations occur even between cities in the same state. For example, managing in San Francisco is entirely different than managing in Weaverville, even though they are only 100+ miles apart. Just as customer needs vary, so do the needs of managers and employees, whether they are in the same state or in a different country!

2. *Speed of change* — HR fails to recognize that corporate divisions as well as different regions of the world change at different paces. Their willingness to rapidly adopt "outside ideas" also varies significantly.

3. *Employee power* — HR fails to recognize that the power relationship between employees and managers varies dramatically, depending on local laws and the

local unemployment rate. The power relationship directly impacts recruiting and retention efforts.

4. *Rate of Economic Growth* — HR practices tend to be static and they fail to change with economic conditions. Programs that are designed for a constant rate of growth are destined to fail because economic growth rates vary even between regions in the same country as well as between countries.

5. *Skill level* — The level and range of management and employee skills varies throughout the company and the world. Programs designed for more sophisticated managers and employees will probably fail in regions where the managers and employees are less skilled.

6. *Local practices* — The firm's and the country's culture as well as past management practices vary dramatically within business divisions, regions and continents. Almost no HR programs allow for variations in either corporate or regional cultures.

7. *Technology* — The level of technology that is available within regions and between continents varies dramatically. Programs that work where there is a high level of IT support may "sputter" in other areas.

8. *Team focus* — The focus on teamwork, as opposed to individual contributions, varies between regions and divisions. Most corporate environments are strongly team focused, while isolated offices might function in a strong (often male) culture. HR departments often fail to allow for these variations in their programs.

■ *A List of Common Problems with HR Globalization Efforts*

As we have just seen, a single "one-size-fits-all" approach can doom many international programs to mediocrity. However, there are many other problem areas and weaknesses with most HR efforts to globalize. Here is a list of some of the common problems that can occur. Later on in this chapter, the positive steps you can take to improve your globalization efforts are outlined.

➤ Focus
• Failure to integrate all HR functions into the global effort — most global efforts just include compensation and relocation but globalization efforts also

need to emphasize recruiting, training, performance management and productivity improvement

• HR has a tendency to develop its programs in the U.S. first and then transfer them to their international sites, rather than vice versa. This often tends to make non-U.S. employees feel like second-class citizens.

• Many HR globalization efforts have focused on developing standardized processes and policies around the world. In fact, this is the exact opposite of what is needed. What managers really need is a range of policies and procedures that allows each manager to apply a personalized solution that fits their unique needs. A "one-size-fits-one" solution is needed rather than the all too common "one-size-doesn't-fit-any" approach!

• Most existing HR programs over focus on relocation programs. Moving U.S. employees to and from non-U.S. assignments, as well as moving foreign nationals in the U.S. while important, has little real impact on productivity.

➤ **Information Collection and Metrics**
• HR professionals often fail to do competitive intelligence and market research in order to identify the unique aspects of each region. If remote units are to beat their competition they need to know what people practices work and don't work, as well as the best people practices that are employed by the competitors. Most HR functions do no competitive intelligence, benchmarking or market research on worker expectations outside of the U.S.

• It's difficult to observe the work of people at remote locations. As a result, the primary key to success in "remote" management is to develop extensive performance metrics, which allow managers to identify problems early and to increase productivity as errors are spotted. Performance metrics and rewards allow managers to vary the approach they take to solving problems (depending on regional differences), as long as they produce the desired results.

➤ **Knowledge and Learning**
• Most HR professionals have a minimal knowledge of international business, remote management and the HR practices and norms in other countries. HR often makes the assumption that U.S. business practices are the norm and as a result they can be easily implemented "as is" in any country.

• Most recruiting functions are U.S. centric. Few have studied labor practices, competencies and labor surpluses in different countries in order to identify sites for future business expansion.

• Almost all corporate training programs are designed from the English-speaking "U.S. perspective." Unfortunately people from most cultures don't think and learn in the same fashion as most U.S. residents. Some training programs teach international business practices, but few teach you how to actually "think" globally. Many firms send their managers to global learning seminars and international assignments. But few corporate HR professionals involved in international HR have had that opportunity.

• Most HR professionals in U.S. firms are U.S.-born. They often know only one language, have never had an international business course, and as a result, they are ill equipped to be leaders in international business.

• Mergers and acquisitions are a major tool for corporate growth. Most HR functions are not capable of identifying international firms (with teams of experienced talent) that would be great takeover targets.

➤ **Recruiting and Retention**
• Few U.S.-based corporations have taken the time to do the research on which unique set of factors increase retention, productivity and recruiting success in different regions of the world.

• Most experienced recruiters know that it requires market research to identify candidate acceptance criteria. Unfortunately, the staffing function has failed to do research to show how these acceptance criteria vary with the culture, the local economic situation and with the changing power balance between managers and employees.

• Using U.S. concepts and definitions for diversity around the world is common in HR, even though the definition of and the demand for diversity vary significantly throughout the world. In a global market, diversity is not just a legal issue it is an economic one. A firm must have a diverse workforce in order to successfully design and sell its products around the world.

• Almost all corporate college recruiting programs (at U.S.-based firms) recruit only in the U.S. Such limited efforts seem to infer that all non-U.S. colleges, and their graduates, are undesirable!

➤ **...and Another Thing**
• Most compensation programs aim for market equity by using salary surveys. Unfortunately that approach fails where salary surveys are either unreliable or non-existent. Compensation also tends to focus on the "money" while ignoring the non-monetary aspects of motivation. This error is compounded when they

fail to identify the unique non-monetary motivators that are found in different cultures and regions of the world. The same can be said for failing to change benefit offerings to fit the local region.

• The employee relations function tends to view employee issues through "U.S. eyes." Unfortunately legal issues, past practices and the power relationship between employees and management vary significantly in different localities.

• HR re-engineering efforts often focus on process standardization with the implied inference that consistency is superior in all cases. Outstanding results do not always come from standardized processes.

Now that we have identified some of the common problems that occur when globalizing HR, it's time to shift our attention toward solving them.

■ Steps in Globalizing Your HR Function

There is no standard "roadmap" for successful HR globalization efforts. The first move is to, of course, avoid all of the errors (see the above list) that others have made before you. The next thing to do is to identify best practices and ideas. Here are some solutions to consider:

➤ Focus, Program Design and Planning

1. *Develop a new "attitude" where everyone thinks globally* — The first step in an effective globalization effort involves a massive change in attitude inside HR. Globalization cannot just be the name of a department or part of someone's job title. Globalization is everyone's job. Rapid transportation, cheap communications and the growth of the World Wide Web have brought us all closer together but they have also simultaneously increased the speed of change in the world of business. Globalized business has also increased the number of opportunities to sell products around the world. In contrast to this rapid growth, the failing economy in the U.S. has reduced HR budgets so that it is now essential that every person, program and function in HR is continually increasing it's effectiveness. And not just on the home front but in every region of the world. All of these drastic changes combined require HR to dramatically shift its approach, as well as the attitude toward globalization of everyone who works in HR. HR leaders must develop a set of "filters" which automatically

screen out programs, any new HR hires and all ideas that fail to meet the "globalization test."

2. *Agile HR solutions with a range of options* — Managers both within and outside the U.S. need people solutions and tools that fit their environment. HR must strive to develop approaches which are either directly tailored to the region or that allow local leeway for local variations. "Agile" HR programs must be designed in a format that allows for a central core of practices that are consistent throughout the world, while at the same time, allowing some percentage of most programs content (usually a quarter to a half) to be "mass customized" to meet the unique needs of the local managers and employees. I call this approach the "one-size-fits-one" approach. This "one-size" approach requires that managers be given a range of options in all HR programs. Options allow managers to "tweak" programs to fit local needs. Agility must be "written into" all programs so that they can change to meet the differing social, legal and speed of change conditions in different regions around the world. Programs must also anticipate the extremes in unemployment, slow medium or rapid economic growth and the availability of technology solutions.

3. *Have a narrow plan* — Globalization requires forward thinking and a clear strategy that is outlined in a written international HR plan. It's easy to get sidetracked, so it's important to know what HR programs have the most business impact. As a result, the best firms narrow their focus to productivity improvement and the recruiting and retention of top performers while allowing managers to make most compensation, benefits and training decisions at the local level. The three most essential elements of a successful international HR plan are forecasting, performance metrics and performance rewards.

4. *HR must be a business leader* — Taking a leadership role within HR is not enough. HR must broaden its approach to influence business results and also to be a role model for line managers. It must take the lead in identifying problems and in providing training and the necessary tools so that managers can get the most productivity from their workers in remote locations.

5. *Once you move them a mile* — Global management is essentially the same as "remote management." As more and more workers are physically located away from their U.S. corporate offices (at remote offices, at home or continually on the move), HR needs to develop remote tools to effectively manage them. These same tools can also be applied to the global work force. Whether you move the employees one mile or ten thousand, a manager will not be able to ensure that the employee can reach and maintain their productivity goals if they continue to rely on the current "face-to-face" approach to management.

6. *Anticipate* — An essential element of HR planning is forecasting the future. Forecasting is difficult just within the U.S. alone, but it is even more essential globally because economic growth varies much more across regions than it does within a single country. Unfortunately, most HR is backward looking. Most HR reports tell managers what happened "last year" or at best, what is happening today. However, what managers really need are accurate forecasts of what the competitors are planning and how technology and economic factors will change, so that they can prepare for the future.

7. *Utilize the global hand-off* — One of the most effective tools for increasing productivity is the global "hand-off" of projects. A global hand-off is where parts of a project are completed during normal working hours in a particular location and at the close of business they are then "handed-off" to the next time zone towards the west. This continues on to other time zones all around the world. This allows projects to be worked on continuously 24 hours a day. As firms acclimate to this hand-off method, it can result in a rapid improvement in product development cycles and in time-to-market.

8. *Equity is local* — The equitable treatment of employees is a difficult issue anytime, but it is especially difficult in a global company. It is an impossible task to "guarantee" equity around the world. A better approach is to define equity as a local issue. Trying to equalize all practices, pay and treatment is a time- consuming task. All you can reasonably expect is for the local manager to provide equity within their region. It is a fine goal to attempt to provide equity globally, but it is a monumental task and a goal that is almost impossible to reach. Providing opportunities for those that wish to move to regions where they "fit better" is often a superior option than striving for global equity.

➤ Information Gathering and Metrics

9. *Competitive intelligence and "what works" sharing* — HR must expand its competitive intelligent capability to include international firms and regions. HR must know about the best people practices everywhere in the world and provide managers with a toolkit full of productivity improvement tools. Equally important is the rapid sharing of "what works" rapidly between managers. HR must treat successes, failures and learning like a hot potatoes and rapidly pass them around the organization in order to ensure that all managers have access to them.

10. *Two-way communications* — Top down communications are slow and can frustrate remote managers. Honest two-way communication and feedback are essential for effective globalization and remote management. HR must take an

active approach in seeking out the opinions and the ideas of managers and employees from remote locations. Without rapid learning and upward communication, the company faces the risk of repeating the same mistakes around the world. Just as those who ignore history are bound to repeat it, those that fail to learn from "local" mistakes are bound to have them repeated in numerous locations. One of the primary goals of HR globalization is to develop a process that allows us to identify the unique needs of global/remote customers (managers and employees). This can be accomplished in a variety of ways including e-mail surveys, "pulse surveys" telephone focus groups, "Net meetings" and with individual telephone interviews.

11. *"Repeat back" communications* — HR must learn to frequently ask international managers to "repeat back" what was just said and what it meant to them. This "repeat back" feature helps to minimize errors due to cultural and language differences and to ensure that the message got through clearly. In a similar light, HR leaders need to learn how to listen to global managers "first" before you tell them about the "conclusion" that you have already reached!

12. *Metrics not culture* — Corporate cultures vary significantly in their strength around the world. If you want to change behavior rapidly it's essential to use "what you measure and what you reward," rather than culture, as the driver of change. In addition, metrics can help us rapidly understand which people practices are the most effective in the different regions. As the world gets more competitive, metrics and rewards can ensure that we drop ineffective practices rapidly so that we get the best return from our people investment.

13. *Business connections* — Almost without exception HR databases work in isolation. When sales (and sales forecasts) increase, that information needs to be shared with recruiting (so that they can begin sourcing) just as much as the information needs to be shared with production. In a similar light externally, when the government in an area announces low unemployment and inflation, retention and compensation programs need to begin to modify their efforts accordingly.

Unfortunately, most HR information is obtained independently from the rest of the business (and the economy) and as a result HR can only be a "late reactor" to events. HR databases have some other faults in that they do not "learn" or anticipate. When an error is made in one international location the databases need to learn and as a result offer a modified solution in the future. They also need "analytics" to help forecast and anticipate events in one sector of the world as a result of experiences in other sectors.

➤ Quality and Competencies of the HR Staff

14. *Hire globally within* HR — HR must determine the essential competencies for a global thinking HR person. Then HR must test to see if these competencies can be developed through training or whether the competencies can only be obtained through experience. If the latter is true, HR needs to hire a significant number of non-U.S. nationals to work in the HR function. This probably also means that a significant percentage of the department's HR professionals will work full-time outside the U.S. while they remain an integral part of the HR team. You can't be globalized without employing people from around the globe and not all HR professionals can or wish to reside in the U.S. In most cases HR needs to begin to hire professionals that speak different languages, have traveled extensively and are open to change and a new way of thinking. HR needs to increase its tolerance for diverse thinking and different approaches to HR. This means understanding the needs of managers and employees that are physically located in a different environment. HR professionals also need excellent listening and communications skills, which will allow them to understand the different linguistic nuances of people who speak English as a second language.

15. *Learning rapidly* — Above all, if every HR service and function is to become a global service, everyone in HR must begin to learn rapidly. This learning must begin by reading international business journals, visiting international business web sites and learning about the business practices of each of the countries in which your firm currently (or may soon) do business. HR professionals must also develop their own international e-mail learning network. A global learning network will allow them to benchmark and learn rapidly about international business practices. Online translators can assist in learning from non-English speaking sources.

16. *Internationalizing* HR *program development* — Learning and program development must be a two-way street. Everything can't start "at corporate" and then generate outward. Globally developed programs and learning must also flow into and be adopted by "corporate" on a regular basis. HR must make a concerted effort to ensure that non-corporate ideas are recognized, rewarded and promoted just as often as those developed "at corporate" to ensure that remotely located managers and non-corporate based HR professionals don't feel like second-class citizens.

➤ Recruiting and Retention

17. *Put the work where the talent is* — In a world where talent can be difficult to acquire and retain, it is essential that we learn to put "the work where the talent

is." Instead of automatically moving work to the U.S., the global approach is to gather data on where there are labor surpluses and easy labor laws. Then move some or all of the work to those talent surplus areas.

➤ Technology in HR

18. *You can't globalize effectively without technology* — As technology improves and becomes more accessible, remote management becomes much easier. As new technology like Net meetings, file sharing and the Web become more common around the world, managers can be provided with desktop decision tools. They can use these tools to make more effective "localized" decisions and thus reduce the need for much of the current centralized HR decision-making.

■ Conclusion

As more companies move from "U.S.-only" to "world" companies, it is essential that each and every business function also become globalized. This new trend gives HR an exciting chance to move from the "caboose" role (often the follower of change) to the locomotive role, leading the change. As a leader, the HR department has two distinct roles in globalization. First it must re-design its own systems to function globally and second it must develop "global" tools that help managers do their job more effectively all around the world.

In order to accomplish these two goals HR must develop a new attitude and new "DNA" within HR. By changing the way we learn, develop programs, communicate and hire we can transform HR's traditionally transactional role into that of a global leader. HR can become a function that not only globalizes its own programs, but one that also assists managers and business units in becoming more effective around the globe. As a result of this "new" business focus, HR must begin to measure its globalization success not just on internal HR measures, but also on how well global business units perform and meet their business goals.

Unfortunately many HR professionals are ill equipped both in attitude and in skill level to take on this daunting task. If they are to be effective, they need to rethink their approach, change their attitude and increase their learning speed so that they become global business experts. Only then can they truly make the transition into becoming global business leaders!

Dr. John Sullivan is a professor of HR and the head of the Human Resource Management Program in the College of Business at San Francisco State University. He just completed a stint as the chief talent officer for Agilent Technologies (43,000 employee HP spinoff). He is a well-known international speaker, author and advisor to Fortune 500 and Silicon Valley firms. He specializes in making HR "THE" competitive advantage for firms. He has served as a consultant and advisor to numerous hi-tech and Fortune 500 companies including Microsoft, HP, Nike, National Semiconductor, Cisco, Sun Microsystems, Charles Schwab, McDonalds, and Pac Telesis. His current consulting interests include employee retention, 21st century HR, technology and "e-HR," strategic HR, thinking outside the box, making organizations "agile" and measuring and increasing HR's business impact. Sullivan is also a frequent contributor to HR-NET (a Worldwide Internet information exchange), writes a weekly column for the Electronic Recruiting Daily and is on the IHRIM Journal Editorial Advisory Board. He has authored over 30 articles, reports and book and is a frequent and dynamic presenter. In the corporate world he has recently been a speaker at HP, the Charles Schwab Corporate Staffing Conference, the Abbott Labs/Lucent Employment workshop, the National Semiconductor's Retention Workshop and the Ameritech IS Leadership Conference. He is often quoted in leading HR publications (most recently in HR News, Workforce Magazine, Team-Leader and Network World Magazine) and on the Internet. He was recently interviewed by Fast Company on 21st century recruiting strategies, Fortune Magazine and Businessweek on recruiting and the World Wide Web, Workforce Magazine on HR planning and HR Executive on technology in HR. He was the Workforce Magazine's online "web" expert on Workforce planning and was called the "Michael Jordan of hiring" by Fast Company magazine. He has trained over 1,000 international managers and has completed a lecture tour in China for the Chinese Government. During the summer of 1998 he did a four-city speaking tour of Australia on 21st century recruiting and HR practices. He was the founding executive director (and is still on the advisory board) of the California Strategic Human Resources Partnership, a consortium of 31 leading HR Senior Vice Presidents from Fortune 500 firms. He is also head of the HR Strategic Forecasting Project, whose goal is to forecast and anticipate HR issues and opportunities. His management experience includes three years as a CEO, seven years as a research manager and three years as a director of training. He has been an advisor to senior management for more than 25 years. Dr. Sullivan has a Ph.D., an MBA and a BSc, all in Human Resource Management, from the University of Florida. He can be reached at **johns@sfsu.edu**.

About the Editor

KAREN V. BEAMAN is division vice president and general manager for ADP Professional Services (also known as AGConsulting), a global HR/Payroll consultancy focused on providing strategic planning, best practice innovation, and system implementation services to Global Fortune 500 corporations. Previously based in Paris, France, she was responsible for building and leading ADP's professional services business in Europe and for launching the company's professional services in Latin America. Beaman has more than 20 years of experience with information systems and human resource management specifically in the development, integration, and management of enterprise-wide HR systems. She has been responsible for all aspects of the business, including strategic planning, international business development, sales and marketing, product and services development, client delivery and customer satisfaction, administration, recruiting, hiring, training, and staffing. Beaman has degrees from Old Dominion and Georgetown Universities and was promoted to Ph.D. candidate in Sociolinguistics and Historical and Computational Linguistics. She is an internationally recognized speaker and has published works in the fields of both Linguistics and HRIS. She is currently the editor-in-chief of the IHRIM *Journal*, past-chair of the IHRIM.*link* magazine Editorial Committee, and a former member of the IHRIM Board of Directors. She can be reached at **Karen_Beaman@adp.com**.

"To be the leading global source of knowledge for the application of human resource information and technology to improve organizational effectiveness." While that mission statement may seem a mouthful, it very much reflects IHRIM's focus for serving the global community.

Achievement of this mission comes from the delivery of a wide variety of products and services offered to customers around the globe. One of our newest products is a book series focusing on a variety of topics. While written with a focus on human resource management, the series is of interest to the entire business community. Fifth in the series, this book on global HR gives a glimpse of the incredible current and future scope of opportunities of human capital management in a global economy.

We hope you enjoy the book and invite you to order one or more books and periodicals from IHRIM Press. For more information about publications, membership, conferences, education, and other programs, visit **www.ihrim.org**, e-mail **moreinfo@ihrim.org**, or call **+1.800.946.6363**.

Sincerely,

Robert Loller
Chairman of the Board and President
International Association for Human
Resource Information Management

IHRIM Publications

■ *E-learning: Expanding the Training Classroom through Technology*

Edited by Lynne Mealy and Bob Loller
Preface by Tina Sung, CEO and President, ASTD

A collection of articles by the pioneers of e-learning, this book provides diverse opinions and definitions, all of which are correct. Whether you are just beginning to explore e-learning or have worked in the field for a while, you will find material that will add to your knowledge base. Even if you are an e-learning expert, this book contains information that will cause one or two "ah-ha's." The book is available to IHRIM members for **US$29** — a discount of US$10.00 off the cover price.

■ *21 Tomorrows: HR Systems in the Emerging Workplace of the 21st Century*

Edited by Robert H. Stambaugh

The first in a series of IHRIM books, 21 *Tomorrows* is a collection of original essays by HRIS thought leaders. The authors address new systems, people and management challenges we will all confront in the 21st century HRIS environments. The chapters provide the short- and long-term predictions that practitioners will need to make sense of what's happening in our industry today — and tomorrow. The book is available to IHRIM members for **US$29** — a discount of US$10.00 off the cover price.

■ *Knowledge Management: Clarifying the Key Issues*

By Scott I. Tannenbaum, Ph.D. and George M. Alliger, Ph.D.

This IHRIM book is designed to stimulate dialogue and foster a shared understanding of relevant knowledge management (KM) issues among HR professionals, information technologists and business leaders. The authors emphasize a few recurring themes that reflect their core beliefs about KM — smaller can be better, technology is not KM, start with business needs and understand the big picture. Each chapter addresses a key question and highlights a pitfall to avoid. The book is available to IHRIM members for **US$29** — a discount of US$10.00 off the cover price.

■ *E-work Architect: How HR Leads the Way Using the Internet*

Edited by Al Doran
Forward by Jim Carroll

Packed with and exciting set of essays, this IHRIM book describes how HR is not only using the Internet, but in many ways is leading the way in business today. HR is throwing out the binders and moving volumes of information to Internet/intranet sites, enabling employee and manager self-service applications to improve organizational effectiveness. It would seem that the Internet and intranet were created specifically for human resources and they have embraced the technology and used it to their strategic advantage. This book poses as many questions as it provides answers, but the one common theme is progress. Share this information with senior-level decision makers and strategic planners — they will thank you for it. The book is available to IHRIM members for **US$29** — a discount of US$10.00 off the cover price.

■ *IHRIM.link*

This bi-monthly magazine is provided as a member benefit and is available by subscription to non-members for an annual price of **US$60**. Whether you're exploring the human resource information management field as a beginner, or you're an expert thick in the trenches of its technology, the IHRIM.*link* is a significant resource. Innovative fea-

ture articles, relevant columns and case histories as well as current marketplace news are found in each issue.

■ IHRIM Journal

Published bi-monthly, the Journal is available by subscription only; **US$70** to IHRIM members and **US$120** to non-members. The Journal is written by recognized experts in the field for current and emerging thought leaders and senior management. Each issue features global industry trends and international perspectives, engaging readers to think in strategic business terms and position themselves in writing the new rules of fast-changing business.

■ IHRIM Go-to-Guides

The Foundation and the Advanced Management Series — These tools provide useful and concise information on a variety of human resources technology topics. They serve as solid references to support HRMS managers, professionals, and stakeholders in building and maintaining their relationships within their own organizations and with external resources. They are a practical assembly of recognized success factors from a body of knowledge, which has been created as HRIM and its corresponding ap-

plications have become more widespread across business and public sector enterprises. Pricing: 1 - 49 copies — **US$295**; 50 - 99 copies — **US$235**; 100+ copies — **US$195**. Available in printed version with CD ROM and as PDF.

These publications may be ordered
online at www.ihrim.org or by calling 1.512.453.6363, ext. 110.
Watch for more IHRIM publications throughout 2002.